The Concept of Community

The Concept of Community

READINGS WITH INTERPRETATIONS

EDITED BY DAVID W. MINAR
AND SCOTT GREER

AldineTransaction
A Division of Transaction Publishers
New Brunswick (U.S.A.) and London (U.K.)

First paperback printing 2007

This book is printed on acid-free paper that meets the American National Standard for Permanence of Paper for Printed Library Materials.

Library of Congress Catalog Number: 2007060656
ISBN: 978-0-202-30962-0
Printed in the United States of America

Library of Congress Cataloging-in-Publication Data

The concept of community : readings with interpretations / David W. Minar and Scott Greer, editors.
    p. cm.
Originally published: Chicago : Aldine 1969.
Includes bibliographical references and index.
ISBN 978-0-202-30962-0 (alk. paper)
    1. Communities. I. Minar, David W. II. Greer, Scott A.

HT65.M5   2007
307—dc22   2007060656

Contents

The Concept of Community

The concept of community is a complex, usually unanalyzed, abstraction. It is often a source of confusion for it stands for many things, and when it is used with interchangeable meanings very elementary errors creep into our discourse. This weakness is true of most germinal notions, and the remedy lies in analysis and discrimination.

Frequently we use "community" to refer to a physical concentration of individuals in one place. This is the ecological meaning and accordingly a community is simply whatever happens to exist in a given territory—rabbits and coyotes, businessmen and laborers. It means no more than that. There is another connotation of the word, however, which refers to the social organization among a concentration of individuals. And this latter is the source of still another level of meaning.

For community is both empirically descriptive of a social structure and normatively toned. It refers both to the unit of a society as it is and to the aspects of the unit that are valued if they exist, desired in their absence. Community is indivisible from human actions, purposes, and values. It expresses our vague yearnings for a commonality of desire, a communion with those around us, an extension of the bonds of kin and friend to all those who share a common fate with us. Aldous Huxley remarks that D. H. Lawrence was much more unhappy at the lack of real community than he was at the sexual condition of men: community, in this view, is the precondition for the smaller orders and more idiosyncratic values of individuals.

Looking at this double nature of the term, empirically descriptive and normatively prescriptive, leads us to the basic question: What do we want? We may think of a continuum that begins with the Platonic Republic, in which men are socialized and related to one another so that one wants what he gets and gets what he wants. In such an order that which is good to the individual is right to the group. Self-interest and public interest are different aspects of the same morality.

Nineteenth-century economic liberalism is another effort to reach this end, but by what a different route. Its definition of the proper relation of man as individual and collective emphasized his freedom to do what he wished within very broad limits, ignoring the interests of others in the faith that the "invisible hand" of the market place would allocate values, reward virtue, and punish vices. Individual aggrandizement would result in the greatest good of the collective. This "solution" to the problem of community resulted in encouraging the entrepreneur and the innovator, at considerable cost to the traditional social values and particularly, the weaker social classes. It produced a world valuing change, individuality, heterogeneity, and individual liberty.

Whatever we want, the next question raised by the normative meaning is strictly empirical: Under what conditions is our desired state of affairs possible? Here we look to the social mechanisms that allow and encourage a society like Plato's Republic, or like Nature's Half Acre. Historically, we examine specific social structures, from the Athenian *polis* to Imperial Rome, from the folk society of the Maya to such great world cities as New York, Paris, London. Using sociological concepts, we look at the grounds of community in interdependence, communication, and the ordering of behavior.

Throughout our examination of the concept of community we have found certain recurring antinomies. There is the continual tension between individual interest and the common interest. The Greeks, those idealists of the *polis*, were forever struggling with brilliant individualists who used the freedom of the community to get their way with it: they never solved the empirical problems their ideals posed.

We also find, as Robert MacIver noted before World War I, a continuing tension between the smaller community and the larger, the part and the whole. Localism is a perennial in the organizational system. Rooted in shared fate, isolation, and intense interaction, interdependence, and communication, units based upon localism are always in tension with those based on nationalism. States fly apart for this reason, national policy is slowed, crippled, and distorted for this reason. At the same time the autonomy of the local community is limited, its own values subordinated to those of the larger society, its very reason for being cast in doubt.

And underlying many discussions of community is the antinomy of stability and change. Perhaps the kind of social unit in which we would have identification with the whole and communion with others is simply one that can persist with very slow rates of change over a long period of time. What one expects and what he gets tend to become fitted in such societies; justice occurs. Perhaps the preliterate societies destroyed by nineteenth century expansionism had invented, after their own fashion, a secular version of Plato's Republic. Certainly rapid change has subverted these values.

Change has destroyed the validity of the oldest and in many ways still archetypal form of community, the agricultural village. Created ten thousand years ago during that great creative period we call the Neolithic, it is still the home of most of mankind. But the superior energy sources and power of the urban technological societies everywhere (including nations where a majority still live in the villages), and their expansive tendencies, indicate the obsolescence of the older form.

As this change occurs, another dichotomy is often evoked. From the community of the peasant village to the society of the urban world is a transition from narrow parochialism toward universalism. As the smaller unit becomes integrated into a large-scale society, our ethnocentrism declines (or at least is expanded to embrace a nation) and our freedom to act is increased. We lose the comfort, but also the intellectual sterility, of the smaller scene; we gain broader intellectual horizons but also anxiety, and even vertigo, in the great metropolitan societies.

And finally it is often pointed out that the world based upon the peasant village was ten thousand years in the making; in the most powerful societies, it has been effectively destroyed in the last two centuries. Uncontrolled technological development and economic exploitation were the engines, large-scale and largely urban societies the destination. And now the very liberalism that allowed this world to be created is in a process of decay; the massive interdependencies we call nations simply cannot persist without a greater degree of order than the classical economists prescribed.

In this new crisis there is promise of community, and there is threat. We are now able to solve many problems that forced the Greeks to settle for small communities. Our communications systems make possible a kind of unity over great spaces, our educational systems in our affluence make possible a kind of integration among highly differentiated people never before known. They also make possible a kind of coercion, indoctrination, and control over the behavior of others not possible before. While we may learn from the historical instances available to us, we cannot simply extrapolate from them: we shall have to invent new styles of community.

This book is a circumambient exploration of some of the literature that deals with the varieties and phases of community. It is not definitive nor is it very systematic; it is meant to provide penetrating insights and evoke the kinds of observation and experience that lie behind our unanalyzed abstractions. We have searched in our own experience for those documents which either first introduced us to a new perspective on community or which elicited a shock of recognition because they recreated certain situations that social science deals with. Thus we have used sociology, political science, anthropology, and history, as well as poetry, the novel, polemics, and philosophy to make our points.

There is a heavy emphasis upon the political, particularly in the latter half of the book. This is because, as the discussion above implies, we feel that the two meanings of community—empirically given and normatively prescribed—come together only in the polity. The political community, in this sense, precedes, limits, and to a great degree determines the character and quality of the larger human condition.

PART I

Roots of Community in Social Life Scenes and Kinds of Social Interaction

CHAPTER I

Human Life and Social Interaction

At the roots of the human community lie the brute facts of social life: organization. It has been suggested that life and the potential for life are coterminous with matter. In like manner, it is probably true that some kind of social organization is coterminous with life: society is a universal. And society begins with interaction and the mutual modification of behavior. Such interaction, in turn, becomes patterned by the nature of the activity which calls it into being; it is structured. Certain structures are partly defined by the spatial scene they occur in; through interaction emerge shared perspectives and commitments to the place and its group—that is, the community.

Social interaction is thus an inescapable aspect of human life. It produces organization, and organization in turn structures the interaction. It begins with the interaction of the unborn child and his environment, his mother. It continues through years of dependency, during which the child is taught the shared perspectives of his elders and peers and unwittingly makes his own commitments to place. It continues as he emerges into adult status.

Thus it makes sense to begin our consideration of community by looking at the relationship between interaction and commitment to a given place and its group. In the selection from George Homans' *The Human Group* we have a clear and elegant analysis of certain aspects of observable movement, which he then conceptualizes as action, interaction, and sentiment. His general thesis, argued powerfully in the remainder of his book, is that out of our interdependence and the activity it entails comes interaction, which in turn results in sentiments *of* the individual *for* the interdependent group. Thus the strength of a group, a spatial community, to unite and direct its members' actions will be a result of the degree of interdependence and sentiment generated between members and for the group as a whole.

Homans' discussion is also valuable for its extreme clarity in developing an empirically relevant set of concepts. His insistence that we trace words to observable events is a first commandment in social science; when we deal with words as global as "community" we do well to keep that directive uppermost.

The selection from Golding's novel *Lord of the Flies* indicates the process by which a randomly collected number of children, lost on a desert island, come together. Out of the activities of the first two children emerges a symbol and a social action: the blowing of the conch. Beginning as play, it results in function. The assemblage then begins slowly to structure itself, the interaction part purposeful, part play, part accident. Yet the central tendency, as a statistician would say, is in one direction: toward the generation of interpersonal relationships, sentiment, a community. The treatment of one boy indicates the poignant fact that community-building often finds reinforcement through excluding as well as including the actors in the scene. This is easily documented in everyday life, from the Men's Houses of New Guinea to the Sigma Chi house of any university.

George Homans
Elements of Behavior

EVENTS IN THE SINGLE GROUP

We are going to begin with a description of everyday social events in a society not our own. The world is a stage, and one of its many scenes opens:

The room is low and rectangular. The left wall is filled by a door, closed, and a big stone fireplace, fitted for cooking. Chairs and benches are set around the fireplace. Against the back wall a table stands, and to the right of the table a colored picture hangs over a cabinet containing a small figure. The right wall is taken up by a dresser, full of kitchen gear and crockery, on one side of which is a door and on the other a staircase leading upstairs. Through a window over the table a yard, with a cart in it, is seen in dim light.

A woman opens the door, right, and comes into the room. She goes to the fireplace, rakes together the ashes on the hearth, some of them still alive, puts on new fuel, and rekindles the blaze. Then she fills a kettle with water and hangs it on a hook over the fire. When it boils, she makes tea; meanwhile she lays out dishes, cutlery, bread, and milk on the table, and gets ready to cook eggs.

A middle-aged man and two younger ones enter, exchange a few words with the woman, pull up chairs, sit down at the table, and begin to eat. The woman herself does not sit, but stands by, ready to bring up more food and drink if the men ask for them. When the men have eaten, the older one says to the younger ones, "Well, we'd better be off." They go out.

By this time a girl has joined the woman in the room, but not until the men have left do the two sit down for their meal. Before they have finished, crying is heard outside, right. The woman leaves and later returns carrying a young child in her arms. She fondles and comforts it, then feeds it in its turn.

She turns to the girl, who is already washing the dishes, with a remark about making butter. . . .[1]

We need not go on. This scene or something much like it, has been enacted millions of times in the history of mankind, and it shows, of

From The Human Group by George C. Homans, copyright, 1950, by Harcourt, Brace & World, Inc., and reprinted with their permission.

[1]Adapted from Conrad M. Arensberg and Solon T. Kimball, *Family and Community in Ireland* (Harvard University Press, 1940), p. 35.

course, a farm family beginning a working day. It is not an American farm family, though families of this sort were common not so long ago in America and survive in some places still. It is a countryman's family in the southwest of Ireland. Farm families, differing from this one in some outward appearances, but perhaps not very different in essentials, have for centuries formed the foundations of society in Europe, the Near East, India, China, and much of the Americas. This social unit is characteristic of many of the countries that have the largest populations. Only in recent years and in a few places have we begun to see the appearance of a new kind of family. The old-fashioned farm family—if we may call it that—is still the commonest of human groups.

The scene is familiar. We begin and end with the familiar and are lucky to be able to do so, but the important point at the moment is not the familiarity of the scene. It is rather that a scene like this is part of the raw material of sociology: a description of a series of *events*, in each of which at one particular place and time a person did certain things, in certain physical surroundings, perhaps with certain implements and together with certain other persons. All science begins with process, the flux of things, the passing scene. Generalization must be true to events. We forget their vividness at our peril. And how refreshing they are! "Here," we can say, "is one kind of certainty. No matter how we interpret them, and no matter how far they fall short of telling the whole story, these things, at least these things, *happened*."

There can be little interpretation of, generalization from, single events. We can learn much—and it is good discipline, too—from trying merely to report, that is, from trying to describe human behavior in words altogether flat, simply descriptive, devoid of interpretation. In any strict sense, it cannot be done. Any noun implies some context; even a word like *table* implies something about the use of a physical object. But in the effort to leave out at least the higher levels of meaning, we can discover how much meaning we regularly put into our descriptions. Perhaps we shall see how easy it is to commit ourselves to an interpretation before we know what we are doing.

Our description of the farm family beginning the day is just such a flat description as a playwright might write in setting the opening scene of his play. The meaning unfolds only as the action of the play develops. Thus the older woman is not called the mother of the family, nor the man the father. "Mother" and "father" assume a certain scheme of social relationships, and from the single scene we cannot be sure that we are dealing with that kind of scheme. It is better to begin with distinctions like those between man and woman, youth and age. In the same way, the cabinet is not called a shrine. If we had called it that, we should have been assuming something that the single scene cannot tell us. Nevertheless, there are items in the description that might be remembered, should he run across them again, by anyone anxious to build up a picture of the relationships between the members of the family. For instance, the older man gives orders to the two younger ones or at least gives the signal to go out and begin the day's work. The woman likewise points out to the girl the job—making butter—that the two of them will do in the course of the day. Both women wait for the men to finish eating before they sit down themselves. The older woman comforts and plays with the baby. And so on. An observer builds up his picture of social relationships from repeated events like these.

CUSTOM

The next stage in the analysis of human behavior—and it always implies the first—is reached when we recognize simple recurrences in events, recurrences at different intervals. To go back to our farm family, we note that almost every day the men go out to work in the fields; that every year, at about the same season, they dig potatoes; that in this work the father directs the activities of the sons. The women do the chores around the house but do not work in the fields; so long as there is a youngster in the house, the mother feeds it, goes to it when it cries, comforts and protects it. And so on. The behavior of the members of a group is a symphony, a symphony that may have discords. There are different voices—as the wood winds are a voice in a symphony—each with its themes, which come in at different intervals, sometimes quietly, sometimes loudly, sometimes in the foreground, sometimes in the background. Often there is a conductor who is himself a voice, and there are recurrences in the group of voices, in the movement as a whole. Like lazy listeners, we who are at the symphony never hear all the voices and all their harmonies. We hear only the ones we are interested in hearing.

These recurrences in social behavior, when recognized as recurrences, are called customs. For the moment we are simply going to accept custom as a fact, giving notice at the same time that the fact raises an important question, which will be considered in a later chapter. We mention the question now only to show we are aware of it. Some students of society are inclined to take the recurrences in the behavior of a group for granted. They are interested in the details of particular customs, but not in custom itself as an aspect of group life. Other students go further, as Edmund Burke did years ago, and see custom as useful, even necessary. Men cannot plan for the future without relying on the massive regularities of expected behavior. Yet when everything intelligent has been said about the usefulness of custom, one more profound question remains: What makes custom customary? For the brute fact is that customs do change. In view of the constantly varied forces playing on society, it is amazing that anything can be recognized as persistent. The recurrences are miracles, not commonplaces; and miracles, if they happen often, are just the things we should study most closely. As soon as we do, we find that nothing is more defenseless than a custom, alone. Not single customs, but systems of custom, survive. Anthropologists used to talk about the "tyranny of custom" as if custom were a mold pressing social organization into a shape. This view is misleading. Custom is not something outside of, and apart from, social organization but is implicit in organization. These are large generalizations. We state them now, but only in a much later chapter shall we try to back them up. By that time we hope to have the tools to do the job.

The usual descriptions of groups consist of statements of custom, that is, recurrences in human behavior at different places or at different intervals. "The Irish countrymen live on isolated farms" . . . "The men of a Tikopia village commonly put out to sea together when they go fishing." The books and articles that are our sources, that we must work with, are full of such remarks. But we must never forget, having a lively sense of the shifting sands on which we build, that statements of custom, if they are worth anything, are founded on repeated observations of individual events in single scenes. With this in mind, let us return to the Irish farm family, and now study a description of the relationships between its members, particularly father, mother, and son. The description is a statement of custom: a summary of the recurrences in many single scenes like the one with which this chapter opened.

The growing child ordinarily sees his father as owner and principal worker of the farm. When the whole family group of father, mother, children, and whatever other relatives may be living with them, works in concert, as at the potato planting, the turf cutting, and the haymaking, it is the father who directs the group's activities, himself doing the heavy tasks. . . .

In his earliest childhood, of course, the mother looms larger in the child's consciousness than the father. The child's first duties, as soon as he can speak and walk, are to run on petty errands to neighbors and near-by "friends." Soon he is taking his father's meals to him in the fields or going on errands to the nearest shop. Until he is seven and has gone through First Communion, his place is in the house with the women, and his labor is of very little importance. After First Communion, at six or seven he begins to be thrown more with his elder brothers, and comes to do small chores which bring him more and more into contact with his father and with the other men of the neighborhood . . . But not till he passes Confirmation and leaves school (generally at the same time) does he take on full men's work. Even then, as he becomes adult and takes on more and more of the heavy tasks of the farm work, he never escapes his father's direction, until his father dies or makes over the farm to him at his marriage. . . .

It goes without saying that the father exercises his control over the whole activity of the "boy." It is by no means confined to their work together. Indeed, the father is the court of last resort, which dispenses punishment for deviations from the norm of conduct in all spheres. Within the bounds of custom and law he has full power to exercise discipline. Corporal punishment is not a thing of the past in Ireland, and, especially in the intermediate stages of the child's development, from seven to puberty, it gets full play.

It is during those years that the characteristic relationship between father and son is developed in rural communities. The son has suffered a remove from the previous almost exclusive control of its mother, in which an affective content of sympathy and indulgence was predominant, and is brought into contact for the first time with the father and older men. But the transfer is not completed. There is a hiatus in his development through the years of school when his participation in men's work and his relationship with his father has little chance of developing into an effective partnership. A real union of interests does not take place until after Confirmation and school-leaving, when for the first time his exclusive contacts and his entire day-to-day activity, particularly in farm work, will be with his father and the older men.

This fact colors greatly the relationship of father and son, as far as affective content goes. There is none of the close companionship and intimate sympathy which characterizes, at least ideally, the relationship in other groups. Where such exists, it is a matter for surprised comment to the small farmers. In its place there is developed, necessarily perhaps, a marked respect, expressing itself in the tabooing of many actions, such as smoking, drinking, and physical contact of any sort, which can be readily observed in any small farm family. Coupled with this is the life-long subordination . . . which is never relaxed even in the one sphere in which farmer father and son can develop an intense community of interest—farm work. Nothing prevents the development of great mutual pride, the boy in his experienced and skillful mentor, tutor, and captain in work, and the man in a worthy and skillful successor and fellow workman, but on the other hand everything within the behavior developed in the relationship militates against the growth of close mutual sympathy. As a result, the antagonisms inherent in such a situation often break through very strongly when conflicts arise. . . .

On the other hand, the relationship of mother and son has a very different content. Like that between father and son, it is the product of years of development. It is marked, too, by a similar retention of subordinate status on the part of the son. In farm work the boy is subject to the commands of his mother even when, fully adult, he has passed over exclusively to men's work . . . But within the scope of such a subordination there is a quite different affective history. The relationship is the first and earliest into which a child enters. It is very close, intimate, and all-embracing for the first years of life; only gradually does the experience of the child expand to include brothers, sisters, and last, the older male members of the household.

Until seven, the child of either sex is the constant companion of its mother. If the family is numerous an elder child, usually a sister, may take over much of the mother's role, but the mother is always near-by. As the woman works in the house or fields, the child is kept by her side. In the house it usually sits in a crib by the fire or plays about on the floor, but always within sight and sound. It learns its speech from its mother, amid a flood of constant endearments, admonitions, and encouragements. The woman's work never separates her from the child. Custom imposes no restraints or interruptions in her solicitude. She looks after its comforts, gives it food, dresses it, etc. She constantly exercises restraints and controls over it, teaching it day by day in a thousand situations the elements of prudery, modesty and good conduct.

The controls she exercises are of a different kind from those of the father. She is both guide and companion. Her authority most often makes itself felt through praise, persuasion, and endearment. Only when a grave breach of discipline demands a restraining power greater than hers, or when an appeal to ultimate authority is needed, does the father begin to play his role. Especially in the years before puberty, the farm father enters the child's cognizance as a disciplinary force. The barriers of authority, respect, extra-household interests, and the imperatives of duty rather than of encouragement make it difficult for any intimacy to develop.

Even after Confirmation the child's relationship to his mother is not materially weakened. He becomes confirmed, it is true, in a masculine scorn for feminine interests and pursuits, but he can and must still look for protection to his mother against a too-arbitrary exercise of his father's power. In family disputes the mother takes a diplomatic, conciliatory role. From her intermediary position she can call upon the strongest ties between herself and her sons to restore rifts in parental authority and filial submission.

Throughout the years of the son's full activity in the farm economy under the father's headship, the mother still remains the source of comfort and the preparer of food and is still infinitely solicitous of his welfare. It is only at marriage that the bond is broken. . . . If the child must leave the farm for other walks of life, the closest possible relationship is still maintained. When one goes home, it is to see one's mother. There is always an attempt to carry on a correspondence. In exile, the bond lingers as a profound sentimental nostalgia.[2]

Before we go on to our main purpose, we must get some preliminaries out of the way. This passage describes a relationship between three persons, not the conventional triangle of a love story but the triangle that has father, mother, and son at its corners. The pattern of the relationship is clearly marked—which is a reason why we chose a description of an Irish family and not one of an American family. The latter is more familiar to us but its pattern is not so easily characterized.

[2]Conrad M. Arensberg & Solon T. Kimball, *Family and Community in Ireland*, Cambridge, Mass.: Harvard University Press, Copyright, 1940, '68, by the President and Fellows of Harvard College.

In the Irish family the relationship between mother and son is one of warm affection, the relationship between father and son is one of admiration mixed with respect. Moreover, these relationships are not peculiar to Ireland; it is interesting how often the pattern repeats itself in farm families, and indeed in other families, all over the world. Nor are these relationships inevitable. It is not simply "natural" that a son should love his mother, though we all like to think it is. He loves his mother because the repeated, thousand-times-repeated, events in which the two are brought together are of a certain kind. From earliest childhood she cares for him; but change her behavior and the emotion would change too. In like manner, the son's feeling for the father is colored by the father's control over him in the many-times-repeated events of farm work. Nor, to go a step further, are the two series of events—the events determining these mother-son and father-son relationships—isolated from the rest of the world. Instead they are related to the division of labor and assignment of authority in a going farm enterprise, surviving in an environment.

We shall not be misled by the use of the words "the child," "his mother," and "his father" in the singular. These are shorthand for "children," "mothers," and "fathers." An anthropologist would say that the passages quoted above tell us some of the customs of Irish countrymen, a statistician that they may perhaps express some kind of average in the behavior of a certain number of groups—Irish farm families— over a certain span of time. The statistician might find fault with the passages for not letting him know the relation between the "sample" and the "universe," that is, the relation between the number of groups directly observed and the larger number for whose behavior the average is supposed to hold good. He might also find fault with the passages for giving us no idea of the number of groups—there must be a few— whose behavior deviates in some degree from the average. He might say that the statements are by implication quantitative but that they do not let an outsider make any judgment of their quantitative reliability. His criticisms are good, and they can be answered only by raising new questions: How much more effort, in men, time, and money, would be needed to get the kind of data he wants? Given a limited supply of all three, how far would getting his kind of data interfere with getting a wider, though admittedly less reliable, coverage of group behavior? These are questions not of scientific morality but of strategy, and, in the broad sense, economics: getting the most for one's money. They themselves beg for quantitative answers. And we might finally ask the different and more searching question: How far does the craving to get the kind of data a statistician considers reliable lead social scientists to take up questions for which this kind of data can easily be secured instead of questions that are interesting for other reasons? To which the statistician might reply: If we are not getting what I want, are we getting anything on which we can found a science? We should keep these questions in mind, for much of the material we shall be working with is not of the kind the statistician wants.

DEFINITION OF CONCEPTS

Let us go back over our work so far. We began with a flat description of events within a single group; then we went on to a statement of the customs of an unspecified but limited number of groups: the families of Irish countrymen. The next step is a long one; in fact it will take up the rest of this book. We shall set up some hypotheses—and they will remain hypotheses because we shall only set them up, not prove them —that may sum up a few aspects of social behavior in an unlimited number of groups all over the world. There is no use saying now what these hypotheses are; we shall find out soon enough, and one move in particular we must make before we can formulate any hypotheses of high generalization, such as ours will be. We must define a few of the concepts that come into them. Though we cannot do so by pointing at objects and saying the concept, we can take the next best step. We can examine a passage like the one above, point out certain words in it, ask ourselves whether the aspects of social behavior to which the words refer have anything in common, and then, if they do, give a name to this common element. The name is the concept. We might have written a passage of our own for this purpose, but anyone can solve a problem if he sets it up himself. It is much more convincing to use someone else's passage, as we have done.

ACTIVITY

Let us look, then, at certain words and phrases in this passage, and first, perhaps, at words like these: *potato planting, turf cutting, haymaking, corporal punishment, smoking, drinking, gives food, dresses, looks after, plays, sits, walks, speaks, talks, First Communion, Confirmation.* In the passage we can pick out many more such words, and also some of greater generality, like *work* and *activity.* Let us agree that they have something in common, without committing ourselves on the question whether this something is important. They all refer to things that people do: work on the physical environment, with implements, and with other persons. If we want to be precise, we can say that all these words and phrases refer in the end to movements of the muscles of men, even though the importance of some of the movements, like talk and ceremonies, depends on their symbolic meaning. We shall speak of the characteristic they have in common as an *element* of social behavior, and we shall give it a name, as a mere ticket. It might be called *action*, if *action* had not been given a more general meaning, or *work*, if *work* did not have a special meaning in the physical sciences and may yet have an analogous one in sociology. Instead of either of these, we shall call it *activity*, and use it, in much the same way that it is used in everyday speech, as an analytical concept for the study of social groups.

We call activity an element, not implying that it is some ultimate, indivisible atom of behavior. It is no more than one of the classes into which we choose to divide something that might be divided in other, and less crude, ways. In fact we call it an element just because the vagueness of that word gives us room to move around in. Above all we must realize that activity is not a variable like temperature in physics: it cannot be given a single series of numerical values. Instead, a number of aspects of activity might be measured. We are sometimes able to measure the *output* or rate of production of certain kinds of activity, for instance, factory work, and sometimes the *efficiency* of activity, the relation of input to output. We might even be able to assign an index to the degree of *similarity* of one activity to another. And so on. These are true variables, at least in possibility, though we could not give them numerical values in every piece of research. In later chapters we shall have to make sure, when we speak of activity, which particular variable we have in mind.

INTERACTION

Going back now to the passage we are working with, let us look at expressions like these: the boy is *thrown with* his elder brothers; he comes more and more *into contact with* his father; he never *escapes from* his father's direction; he *participates* in the men's work; he is a *companion* of his mother; he goes to *see* his mother, and so on. The element that these phrases have in common is more or less mixed with other things, for in our language one word seldom states one clear idea. For instance, what does the word *see* mean in the phrase "going to see someone"? Yet there is a common element, and it seems to be some notion of sheer interaction between persons, apart from the particular activities in which they interact. When we refer to the fact that some unit of activity of one man follows, or, if we like the word better, is stimulated by some unit of activity of another, aside from any question of what these units may be, then we are referring to *interaction*. We shall speak of interaction as an element of social behavior and use it as an analytical concept in the chapters that follow.

We may find it hard to think consistently of interaction as separate from the other elements of behavior, but we shall have to do so in this book, and the fact is that in our everyday thinking we often keep it separate without realizing as much. When we say "Tom got in touch with Harry," or "Tom contacted Harry," or "Tom was an associate of Harry's," we are not talking about the particular words they said to one another or the particular activities they both took part in. Instead we are talking about the sheer fact of contact, of association. Perhaps the simplest example of interaction, though we should find it complex enough if we studied it carefully, is two men at opposite ends of a saw, sawing a log. When we say that the two are interacting, we are not referring to the fact that both are sawing: in our language, sawing is an *activity*, but to the fact that the push of one on the saw is followed by the push of the other. In this example, the interaction does not involve words. More often interaction takes place through verbal or other symbolic communication. But when in the armed forces men talk about the chain of command, or in a business ask what officers report to what other ones, they are still talking about channels of communication—the chains of interaction—rather than the communications themselves or the activities that demand communications.

Just as several variables are included under the concept of activity, so several are included under interaction. We can study the *frequency* of interaction: the number of times a day or a year one man interacts with another or the members of a group interact with one another. We can measure the ratio between the amount of time one man is active, for instance, talking, and the *duration* of his interlocutor's activity. Or we can study the *order* of interaction: Who originates action? Where does a chain of interactions start and where does it go? If Tom makes a suggestion to Dick, does Dick pass it on to Harry—[3] Once again, we shall have to make sure from time to time that we are talking about one variable under interaction and not another. Our observations of this element can often be rather precise and definite, which gives them infinite charm for persons of a certain temperament.

When we called the first of our elements *activity*, we may have been using the obvious and appropriate word. But in calling the second element *interaction*, are we not needlessly using a strange word when a familiar one is on hand? Why not speak of *communication* rather than *interaction*? Our answer is: The word *communication* is neither general enough in one sense nor specific enough in another. When people think of communication, they think of communication in words,

---

[3]For a systematic discussion of interaction as an element of social behavior, see E. D. Chapple, with the collaboration of C. M. Arensberg, *Measuring Human Relations* (Genetic Psychology Monographs, Vol. 22 (1940)).

but here we are including under interaction both verbal and nonverbal communication. What is more, the word *communication* is used in several different ways in everyday speech. It may mean the content of the message, signal, or "communication" being transmitted, or the process of transmission itself, as when people speak of "methods of communication," or to the sheer fact, aside from content or process of transmission, that one person has communicated with another. Only to the last of these three do we give the name of interaction, and the unfamiliarity of the word may underline the fact that its meaning is specific. Nevertheless we shall, from time to time, when there is no risk of confusion, use the word *communication* in place of *interaction,* so that our language will not sound hopelessly foreign.

SENTIMENT

Now let us go back to our passage again and consider another set of words and phrases: *sentiments of affection, affective content of sympathy and indulgence, intimate sympathy, respect, pride, antagonism, affective history, scorn, sentimental nostalgia.* To these we shall arbitrarily add others, such as *hunger* and *thirst,* that might easily have come into the passage. What can we say these words have in common? Perhaps the most we can say, and it may not be very much, is that they all refer to internal states of the human body. Laymen and professional psychologists call these states by various names: drives, emotions, feelings, affective states, sentiments, attitudes. Here we shall call them all *sentiments,* largely because that word has been used in a less specialized sense than some of the others, and we shall speak of *sentiment* as an element of social behavior.

Notice the full range of things we propose to call sentiments. They run all the way from fear, hunger, and thirst, to such probably far more complicated psychological states as liking or disliking for individuals, approval or disapproval of their actions. We are lumping together under this word some psychological states that psychologists would certainly keep separate. Our employment of the concept *sentiment* can only be justified by what we do with it, so that at the moment all we can ask is indulgence for our failure in orthodoxy.

We must now consider a question that may not seem important but that has come up again and again, in one form or another, ever since the behaviorists first raised it. We can *see* activities and interactions. But if sentiments are internal states of the body, can we see them in the same way? It is true that a person may say he feels hungry or likes someone, and that in everyday life, if we are dealing with him, we take account of what he has to say about his own feelings. But scientists may be forgiven for believing that subjective judgments are treacherous things to work with. They are not reliable; we cannot tell whether two persons would reach the same judgment under the same circumstances, and reliability is the rock on which science is built. Some scientists even believe that they can reach important generalizations, in psychology and sociology, without paying any attention whatever to subjective judgments; and they would ask us whether there is anything we can point to as sentiment that has not already been included under activity and interaction. Can it be independently observed? Perhaps in some animals the more violent sentiments can be so observed. In a dog or cat, pain, hunger, fear, and rage are marked by measurable changes in the body, particularly in the glands of internal secretion.[4] We assume that this is also true of human beings, but few of the necessary measurements can easily be made. For mild sentiments such as friendliness, and these are the ones we shall be working with most often here, we are not sure how far the bodily changes occur at all. The James-Lange theory that a sentiment and a set of visceral changes are one and the same thing cannot be driven too far. On an occasion that might conceivably have called for emotion, the undamaged human being reacts so as to cut down the amount of visceral change taking place. The body mobilizes for action, if that is appropriate, and reduces the merely emotional changes.

Science is perfectly ready to take leave of common sense, but only for a clear and present gain. Lacking more precise methods for observing sentiments, since the biological methods can only be used in special circumstances, have we anything to gain by giving up everyday practice? Have we not rather a good deal to lose? And what is everyday practice? In deciding what sentiments a person is feeling, we take notice of slight, evanescent tones of his voice, expressions of his face, movements of his hands, ways of carrying his body, and we take notice of these things as parts of a whole in which the context of any one sign is furnished by all the others. The signs may be slight in that the physical change from one whole to another is not great, but they are not slight so long as we have learned to discriminate between wholes and assign them different meanings. And that is what we do. From these wholes we infer the existence of internal states of the human body and call them anger, irritation, sympathy, respect, pride, and so forth. Above all, we infer the existence of sentiments from what men say about what they feel and from the echo that their words find in our own feelings. We can recognize in ourselves what they are talking about. All those who have probed the secrets of the human heart have known how mislead-

[4]See W. B. Cannon, *Bodily Changes in Pain, Hunger, Fear, and Rage.*

ing and ambiguous these indications can sometimes be, how a man can talk love and mean hate, or mean both together, without being aware of what he is doing. Yet we act on our inferences, on our diagnoses of the sentiments of other people, and we do not always act ineffectively. In this book we are trying to learn how the elements of our everyday social experience are related to one another. Leaving out a part of that experience—and sentiment is a part—would be reasonable only if we had a better kind of observation to take its place. Some sciences have something better; ours does not yet.

We may end with a practical argument. This book is, in one of its intentions, an effort to bring out the generalizations implicit in modern field studies of human groups. If the men who made the studies felt that they could infer and give names to such things as sentiments of affection, respect, pride, and antagonism, we shall see what we can do with their inferences, remembering always that a more advanced theory than ours may have to wait for more precise and reliable observations. No theory can be more sophisticated than the facts with which it deals.

Under the element of *sentiment,* several different kinds of studies can and have been made. Perhaps the best-known ones are carried on by the public opinion pollsters and attitude scalers using questionnaires they get people to answer. Especially when they try to find out the *number* of persons that approve or disapprove of, like or dislike, a proposal for action or a candidate for public office, they are studying at least one variable under this element. Often they go further and try to discover not only how many persons approve or disapprove but the *conviction* with which they do so: whether they are sure they are right, feel somewhat less sure, or remain undecided. The pollsters may also try to find out the *intensity* of the sentiments concerned: a man may disapprove of something intellectually and yet not feel strongly about it. His emotions may not have been deeply aroused.

SOCIOMETRY

Especially interesting from our point of view are the methods of studying the likes and dislikes of persons for one another developed by J. L. Moreno and given by him the name of *sociometry.*[5] In the course of his work in the New York Training School for Girls at Hudson, New York, a fairly large community but one in which the girls lived in several small houses rather than under one single institutional roof, Moreno found himself asking this question: How can we choose the membership of a house in such a way that the girls will be congenial

[5]See especially J. L. Moreno, *Who Shall Survive?,* and the journal *Sociometry.*

and that the work of the house, its housekeeping, will be carried on pleasantly and effectively? And he decided to take a very obvious step. He decided to ask the girls whom they would like to live and work with. In particular, he called all the girls in the community together, supplied each one with a pencil and paper, and then gave what he later came to call the *sociometric test*. That is, he asked the girls to answer the following question:

You live now in a certain house with certain other persons according to the directions the administration has given you. The persons who live with you in the same house are not ones chosen by you and you are not one chosen by them. You are now given the opportunity to choose the persons whom you would like to live with in the same house. You can choose without restraint any individuals of this community whether they happen to live in the same house with you or not. Write down whom you would like first best, second best, third best, fourth best, and fifth best. Look around and make up your mind. Remember that the ones you choose will probably be assigned to live with you in the same house.[6]

Moreno asked a question of the same kind about dislikes. In his discussion of the test he argues that its results are apt to be meaningless unless the persons taking the test believe their choices make a difference, and that two conditions must be realized before thay can hold this belief. In the first place, one person does not like another in a vacuum but in a definite setting, and if the setting changes the liking may change too. Therefore, the choice of likes and dislikes must be made according to some definite criterion. At Hudson the girls were asked whom they would, or would not, like to live with. In the second place, the person who administers the test must have the power to put its results into effect; he must be able to do something about it. At Hudson, Moreno had to have the power to assign girls who liked one another to the same house.

The two conditions are seldom realized, so that the sociometric test is not a universal weapon of research and action in sociology. When it can be used, it may be very helpful. The results of the sociometric test were used at Hudson in assigning girls that were fond of one another to the same house, and the administration believed that morale improved. The test, suitably reworded, was also used during the depression in planning resettlement communities. Since then it has been put to work in many different situations.

But we are not immediately interested in the use that can be made of the sociometric test in social action. We are interested in it as a method, available under some circumstances, for mapping out interpersonal sentiments. From one point of view its results are crude, yet

[6]*Who Shall Survive?*, pp 13–14.

they could not otherwise be achieved without direct observation of a group and interviews with its members, carried out over a long period. The test, in short, is economical. It can bring out several main types of relationship between two persons: mutual liking or, as Moreno calls it, mutual attraction; mutual disliking or repulsion; attraction on one side but repulsion on the other; attraction or repulsion on one side but indifference, that is, no choice, on the other; and finally mutual indifference. Using suitable symbols for these relationships, Moreno can diagram various simple types of group structure: the isolated individual, chosen by no one and repelled by many; the isolated pair; the triangle in many forms; the star, or popular girl, liked by many others; and the influential or powerful girl with her followers: she likes and is liked by rather few persons, but they are strategically placed not only in her own house but in others and they themselves are chosen by many persons, so that the original girl is at the center of a complex web of attraction. We shall want to ask why such a person is in fact influential. From these simple structures Moreno goes on to plot out larger emotional networks.[7] Later we shall look at some of the other results of his work. At the moment we must recognize the sociometric test as one simple method of mapping out some of the sentiments that relate members of a group to one another.

Before we take leave of sentiment for the time being, one more point needs to be made. Many studies of sentiments and attitudes are made without any great effort to relate their results to studies of activities and interactions. Some psychologists study attitudes alone. In the future, fruitful results will come increasingly from using several methods in conjunction with one another. If social fact must be analyzed as a mutual dependence of many elements in a whole, then we shall have to investigate social fact with mutually dependent methods.

And now let us go back to our passage for the last time. Of course it includes many words besides the ones we have taken up for scrutiny. In particular there are words like *status, role, direction, control, subordination,* and *authority.* We all use some of these words; we all think we know what they mean, and they all do mean important things. But carefully examined, they seem to refer to complicated combinations of our simpler elements: activity, interaction, sentiment. In Chapter I we have already seen that this is true of *status.* In the same way, a word like *direction* refers not just to the giving of orders by one man to another but to the giving of orders that are obeyed, which is, if we think about it for a minute, a much more complex idea. We shall come back to these things, because they are important in the study of social groups, but we shall avoid real pitfalls if we do not begin with them.

[7]See especially *ibid.,* 53, 89, 90, 115.

William Golding
The Sound of the Shell

"We can use this to call the others. Have a meeting. They'll come when they hear us—"

He beamed at Ralph.

"That was what you meant, didn't you? That's why you got the conch out of the water?"

Ralph pushed back his fair hair.

"How did your friend blow the conch?"

"He kind of spat," said Piggy. "My auntie wouldn't let me blow on account of my asthma. He said you blew from down here." Piggy laid a hand on his jutting abdomen. "You try, Ralph. You'll call the others."

Doubtfully, Ralph laid the small end of the shell against his mouth and blew. There came a rushing sound from its mouth but nothing more. Ralph wiped the salt water off his lips and tried again, but the shell remained silent.

"He kind of spat."

Ralph pursed his lips and squirted air into the shell, which emitted a low, farting noise. This amused both boys so much that Ralph went on squirting for some minutes, between bouts of laughter.

"He blew from down here."

Ralph grasped the idea and hit the shell with air from his diaphragm. Immediately the thing sounded. A deep, harsh note boomed under the palms, spread through the intricacies of the forest and echoed back from the pink granite of the mountain. Clouds of birds rose from the treetops, and something squealed and ran in the undergrowth.

Ralph took the shell away from his lips.

"Gosh!"

His ordinary voice sounded like a whisper after the harsh note of the conch. He laid the conch against his lips, took a deep breath and blew once more. The note boomed again: and then at his firmer pressure, the note, fluking up an octave, became a strident blare more penetrating than before. Piggy was shouting something, his face pleased, his glasses flashing. The birds cried, small animals scuttered. Ralph's breath failed;

the note dropped the octave, became a low wubber, was a rush of air.

The conch was silent, a gleaming tusk; Ralph's face was dark with breathlessness and the air over the island was full of bird-clamor and echoes ringing.

"I bet you can hear that for miles."

Ralph found his breath and blew a series of short blasts.

Piggy exclaimed: "There's one!"

A child had appeared among the palms, about a hundred yards along the beach. He was a boy of perhaps six years, sturdy and fair, his clothes torn, his face covered with a sticky mess of fruit. His trousers had been lowered for an obvious purpose and had only been pulled back half-way. He jumped off the palm terrace into the sand and his trousers fell about his ankles; he stepped out of them and trotted to the platform. Piggy helped him up. Meanwhile Ralph continued to blow till voices shouted in the forest. The small boy squatted in front of Ralph, looking up brightly and vertically. As he received the reassurance of something purposeful being done he began to look satisfied, and his only clean digit, a pink thumb, slid into his mouth.

Piggy leaned down to him.

"What's yer name?"

"Johnny."

Piggy muttered the name to himself and then shouted it to Ralph, who was not interested because he was still blowing. His face was dark with the violent pleasure of making this stupendous noise, and his heart was making the stretched shirt shake. The shouting in the forest was nearer.

Signs of life were visible now on the beach. The sand, trembling beneath the heat haze, concealed many figures in its miles of length; boys were making their way toward the platform through the hot, dumb sand. Three small children, no older than Johnny, appeared from startlingly close at hand where they had been gorging fruit in the forest. A dark little boy, not much younger than Piggy, parted a tangle of undergrowth, walked on to the platform, and smiled cheerfully at everybody. More and more of them came. Taking their cue from the innocent Johnny, they sat down on the fallen palm trunks and waited. Ralph continued to blow short, penetrating blasts. Piggy moved among the crowd, asking names and frowning to remember them. The children gave him the same simple obedience that they had given to the men with megaphones. Some were naked and carrying their clothes; others half-naked, or more or less dressed, in school uniforms, grey, blue, fawn, jacketed or jerseyed. There were badges, mottoes even, stripes of color in stockings and pullovers. Their heads clustered above the trunks in the green shade; heads brown, fair, black, chestnut, sandy, mouse-colored; heads muttering, whispering, heads full of eyes that watched Ralph and speculated. Something was being done.

The children who came along the beach, singly or in twos, leapt into visibility when they crossed the line from heat haze to nearer sand. Here, the eye was first attracted to a black, bat-like creature that danced on the sand, and only later perceived the body above it. The bat was the child's shadow, shrunk by the vertical sun to a patch between the hurrying feet. Even while he blew, Ralph noticed the last pair of bodies that reached the platform above a fluttering patch of black. The two boys, bullet-headed and with hair like tow, flung themselves down and lay grinning and panting at Ralph like dogs. They were twins, and the eye was shocked and incredulous at such cheery duplication. They breathed together, they grinned together, they were chunky and vital. They raised wet lips at Ralph, for they seemed provided with not quite enough skin, so that their profiles were blurred and their mouths pulled open. Piggy bent his flashing glasses to them and could be heard between the blasts, repeating their names.

"Sam, Eric, Sam, Eric."

Then he got muddled; the twins shook their heads and pointed at each other and the crowd laughed.

At last Ralph ceased to blow and sat there, the conch trailing from one hand, his head bowed on his knees. As the echoes died away so did the laughter, and there was silence.

Within the diamond haze of the beach something dark was fumbling along. Ralph saw it first, and watched till the intentness of his gaze drew all eyes that way. Then the creature stepped from mirage on to clear sand, and they saw that the darkness was not all shadows but mostly clothing. The creature was a party of boys, marching approximately in step in two parallel lines and dressed in strangely eccentric clothing. Shorts, shirts, and different garments they carried in their hands; but each boy wore a square black cap with a silver badge on it. Their bodies, from throat to ankle, were hidden by black cloaks which bore a long silver cross on the left breast and each neck was finished off with a hambone frill. The heat of the tropics, the descent, the search for food, and now this sweaty march along the blazing beach had given them the complexions of newly washed plums. The boy who controlled them was dressed in the same way though his cap badge was golden. When his party was about ten yards from the platform he shouted an order and they halted, gasping, sweating, swaying in the fierce light. The boy himself came forward, vaulted on to the platform with his cloak flying, and peered into what to him was almost complete darkness.

"Where's the man with trumpet?"

Ralph, sensing his sun-blindness, answered him.

"There's no man with a trumpet. Only me."

The boy came close and peered down at Ralph, screwing up his face as he did so. What he saw of the fair-haired boy with the creamy shell on his knees did not seem to satisfy him. He turned quickly, his black cloak circling.

"Isn't there a ship, then?"

Inside the floating cloak he was tall, thin, and bony: and his hair was red beneath the black cap. His face was crumpled and freckled, and ugly without silliness. Out of this face stared two light blue eyes, frustrated now, and turning, or ready to turn, to anger.

"Isn't there a man here?"

Ralph spoke to his back.

"No. We're having a meeting. Come and join in."

The group of cloaked boys began to scatter from close line. The tall boy shouted at them.

"Choir! Stand still!"

Wearily obedient, the choir huddled into line and stood there swaying in the sun. None the less, some began to protest faintly.

"But, Merridew. Please, Merridew . . . can't we?"

Then one of the boys flopped on his face in the sand and the line broke up. They heaved the fallen boy to the platform and let him lie. Merridew, his eyes staring, made the best of a bad job.

"All right then. Sit down. Let him alone."

"But Merridew."

"He's always throwing a faint," said Merridew. "He did in Gib.; and Addis; and at matins over the precentor."

This last piece of shop brought sniggers from the choir, who perched like black birds on the criss-cross trunks and examined Ralph with interest. Piggy asked no names. He was intimidated by this uniformed superiority and the offhand authority in Merridew's voice. He shrank to the other side of Ralph and busied himself with his glasses.

Merridew turned to Ralph.

"Aren't there any grownups?"

"No."

Merridew sat down on a trunk and looked round the circle.

"Then we'll have to look after ourselves."

Secure on the other side of Ralph, Piggy spoke timidly.

"That's why Ralph made a meeting. So as we can decide what to do. We've heard names. That's Johnny. Those two—they're twins, Sam 'n Eric. Which is Eric—? You? No—you're Sam—"

"I'm Sam—"

"'n I'm Eric."

"We'd better all have names," said Ralph, "so I'm Ralph."

"We got most names," said Piggy. "Got 'em just now."

"Kids' names," said Merridew. "Why should I be Jack? I'm Merridew."

Ralph turned to him quickly. This was the voice of one who knew his own mind.

"Then," went on Piggy, "that boy—I forget—"

"You're talking too much," said Jack Merridew. "Shut up, Fatty."

Laughter arose.

"He's not Fatty," cried Ralph, "his real name's Piggy!"

"Piggy!"

"Piggy!"

"Oh, Piggy!"

A storm of laughter arose and even the tiniest child joined in. For the moment the boys were a closed circuit of sympathy with Piggy outside: he went very pink, bowed his head and cleaned his glasses again.

Finally the laughter died away and the naming continued. There was Maurice, next in size among the choir boys to Jack, but broad and grinning all the time. There was a slight, furtive boy whom no one knew, who kept to himself with an inner intensity of avoidance and secrecy. He muttered that his name was Roger and was silent again. Bill, Robert, Harold, Henry; the choir boy who had fainted sat up against a palm trunk, smiled pallidly at Ralph and said that his name was Simon.

Jack spoke.

"We've got to decide about being rescued."

There was a buzz. One of the small boys, Henry, said that he wanted to go home.

"Shut up," said Ralph absently. He lifted the conch. "Seems to me we ought to have a chief to decide things."

"A chief! A chief!"

"I ought to be chief," said Jack with simple arrogance, "because I'm chapter chorister and head boy. I can sing C sharp."

Another buzz.

"Well then," said Jack, "I—"

He hesitated. The dark boy, Roger, stirred at last and spoke up.

"Let's have a vote."

"Yes!"

"Vote for chief!"

"Let's vote—"

This toy of voting was almost as pleasing as the conch. Jack started to protest but the clamor changed from the general wish for a chief to an election by acclaim of Ralph himself. None of the boys could have found good reason for this; what intelligence had been shown was traceable to Piggy while the most obvious leader was Jack. But there was a stillness about Ralph as he sat that marked him out; there was his size, and attractive appearance; and most obscurely, yet most powerfully, there was the conch. The being that had blown that, had sat waiting for them on the platform with the delicate thing balanced on his knees, was set apart.

"Him with the shell."

"Ralph! Ralph!"

"Let him be chief with the trumpet-thing."

Ralph raised a hand for silence.

"All right. Who wants Jack for chief?"

With dreary obedience the choir raised their hands.

"Who wants me?"

Every hand outside the choir except Piggy's was raised immediately. Then Piggy, too, raised his hand grudgingly into the air.

Ralph counted.

"I'm chief then."

CHAPTER 2

Culture:
Shared Perspectives

The organization of a human aggregate requires, as we noted earlier, shared perspectives. These, taken together, are called "culture." They are formulated in symbolic terms, usually but not always words; they amount to the agreed-on definitions of what the world is like, what is good and bad about various aspects of it, and what should and should not be done about it. Thus in a sense culture precedes social organization; however, it encodes the existing patterns of behavior, and these in turn may so violate the handed-down prescriptions that eventually the culture has to change.

Ruth Benedict, in the extract from her classic *Patterns of Culture*, calls our attention to the wide range of values a given culture may choose from. Of course such "choice" is rarely self-conscious and planned; instead one emphasizes certain aspects of human life and, since energy and time are limited, thereby excludes others. To choose is to reject. She notes the unity of cultures and their uniqueness through her use of Ramon's metaphor of the "cup of earth," the range among them through her own metaphor of the "arc."

The variability of culture is illustrated by examples of how different societies deal with adolescence, coming of age, and the life cycle. The constraint of culture on human behavior is seen in her discussion of warfare, where she indicates the range from peoples who cannot imagine a state of truce with their neighbors, since they cannot imagine them to be human, to those who cannot imagine warfare. The definition of the "fully human" is a basic aspect of human life: it is translated into racial discrimination on the one hand, "color blindness" on the other; citizenship on the one hand, chattel slavery on the other. To deprive another group of the designation *human* means "everything is permitted" in dealing with them; this we do in war. Contrariwise war, intensifying sentiments of commonality against the excluded enemy, tends to produce the definition of that enemy as "subhuman."

As she emphasizes, most of us are immersed in our own culture and most cultures build in an acceptance of what is as sacred. Anthropology in comparisons of cultures has underlined, however, how little is inescapable in cultural communities—how much is a matter of variation, and how much is the choice made by a given community. This is the distinction between accidents of variation and the essence of human life, convenience and ineluctable need.

Yet people from the most bizarrely diverse cultures can communicate and translate. If this were not so, how could we explain the very work of these same anthropologists? What is the underlying commonality, that which is sometimes called "psychic universality"? Some would lay it to the great primitive inescapables: the long childhood of man when dependence is assured, the protection of the newborn, the social danger of incest. Benedict raises some doubts about these arguments. Others argue that during the millions of years before history, a great unifying culture emerged in the Neolithic era, which provided the base for all that has come since. The question is moot, and probably both arguments hold and can be reconciled.

In any event, the culture which defines "community" varies enormously. In Isaac Bashevis Singer's piece, a chapter from *Satan in Goray*, we are given a picture of the "Old Goray"—a medieval Jewish community in the Polish Pale. Related to its social environment only in narrow and prescribed ways, it is the essence of a spatially defined social group, a community where place, relevant people, important social action, and the resulting sentiments produce a unity. The culture stresses a round of life based upon religion and scholarship, charity and wealth, craft and trade.

These various strands of the culture interweave, as Benedict points out, and one trait gives a distinctive color to another. Thus food in Goray is both secular (and sold to the Gentile peasants) and sacred, a matter of profit and of holiness. Our cities today lack the social-geographical compactness and cultural uniformity of Goray, for much important action straddles a local area and the larger world, and our culture seethes with variations. Yet here too there is the merging of culture traits and the conflict between them. Heavenly City and Earthly City, holiness and profit, continue their wrestling match.

Ruth Benedict
The Diversity of Cultures

1

A chief of the Digger Indians, as the Californians call them, talked
to me a great deal about the ways of his people in the old days. He was
a Christian and a leader among his people in the planting of peaches and
apricots on irrigated land, but when he talked of the shamans who had
transformed themselves into bears before his eyes in the bear dance, his
hands trembled and his voice broke with excitement. It was an in-
comparable thing, the power his people had had in the old days. He
liked best to talk of the desert foods they had eaten. He brought each
uprooted plant lovingly and with an unfailing sense of its importance.
In those days his people had eaten "the health of the desert," he said,
and knew nothing of the insides of tin cans and the things for sale at
butcher shops. It was such innovations that had degraded them in these
latter days.

One day, without transition, Ramon broke in upon his descriptions
of grinding mesquite and preparing acorn soup. "In the beginning," he
said, "God gave to people a cup, a cup of clay, and from this cup
they drank their life." I do not know whether the figure occurred in
some traditional ritual of his people that I never found, or whether it
was his own imagery. It is hard to imagine that he had heard it from
the whites he had known at Banning; they were not given to discussing
the ethos of different peoples. At any rate, in the mind of this humble
Indian the figure of speech was clear and full of meaning. "They all
dipped in the water," he continued, "but their cups were different. Our
cup is broken now. It has passed away."

Our cup is broken. These things that had given significance to the
life of his people, the domestic rituals of eating, the obligations of the
economic system, the succession of ceremonials in the villages, possession in the bear dance, their standards of right and wrong—these were
gone, and with them the shape and meaning of their life. The old
man was still vigorous and a leader in relationships with the whites. He

did not mean that there was any question of the extinction of his people. But he had in mind the loss of something that had value equal to that of life itself, the whole fabric of his people's standards and beliefs. There were other cups of living left, and they held perhaps the same water, but the loss was irreparable. It was no matter of tinkering with an addition here, lopping off something there. The modelling had been fundamental, it was somehow all of a piece. It has been their own.

Ramon had had personal experience of the matter of which he spoke. He straddled two cultures whose values and ways of thought were incommensurable. It is a hard fate. In Western civilization our experiences have been different. We are bred to one cosmopolitan culture, and our social sciences, our psychology, and our theology persistently ignore the truth expressed in Ramon's figure.

The course of life and the pressure of environment, not to speak of the fertility of human imagination, provide an incredible number of possible leads, all of which, it appears, may serve a society to live by. There are the schemes of ownership, with the social hierarchy that may be associated with possessions; there are material things and their elaborate technology; there are all the facets of sex life, parenthood and post-parenthood; there are the guilds or cults which may give structure to the society; there is economic exchange; there are the gods and supernatural sanctions. Each one of these and many more may be followed out with a cultural and ceremonial elaboration which monopolizes the cultural energy and leaves small surplus for the building of other traits. Aspects of life that seem to us more important have been passed over with small regard by peoples whose culture, oriented in another direction, has been far from poor. Or the same trait may be so greatly elaborated that we reckon it as fantastic.

It is in cultural life as it is in speech; selection is the prime necessity. The numbers of sounds that can be produced by our vocal cords and our oral and nasal cavities are practically unlimited. The three or four dozen of the English language are a selection which coincides not even with those of such closely related dialects as German and French. The total that are used in different languages of the world no one has ever dared to estimate. But each language must make its selection and abide by it on pain of not being intelligible at all. A language that used even a few hundreds of the possible—and actually recorded—phonetic elements could not be used for communication. On the other hand a great deal of our misunderstanding of languages unrelated to our own has arisen from our attempts to refer alien phonetic systems back to ours as a point of reference. We recognize only one *k*. If other people have five *k* sounds placed in different positions in the throat and mouth, distinctions of vocabulary and of syntax that depend on these differences are impossible to us until we master them. We have a d and an n. They may have an intermediate sound which, if we fail to identify it, we write now d and now n, introducing distinctions which do not exist. The elementary prerequisite of linguistic analysis is a consciousness of these incredibly numerous available sounds from which each language makes its own selections.

In culture too we must imagine a great arc on which are ranged the possible interests provided either by the human age-cycle or by the environment or by man's various activities. A culture that capitalized even a considerable proportion of these would be as unintelligible as a language that used all the clicks, all the glottal stops, all the labials, dentals, sibilants, and gutturals from voiceless to voiced and from oral to nasal. Its identity as a culture depends upon the selection of some segments of this arc. Every human society everywhere has made such selection in its cultural institutions. Each from the point of view of another ignores fundamentals and exploits irrelevancies. One culture hardly recognizes monetary values; another has made them fundamental in every field of behaviour. In one society technology is unbelievably slighted even in those aspects of life which seem necessary to ensure survival; in another, equally simple, technological achievements are complex and fitted with admirable nicety to the situation. One builds an enormous cultural superstructure upon adolescence, one upon death, one upon after-life.

The case of adolescence is particularly interesting, because it is in the limelight in our own civilization and because we have plentiful information from other cultures. In our own civilization a whole library of psychological studies has emphasized the inevitable unrest of the period of puberty. It is in our tradition a physiological state as definitely characterized by domestic explosions and rebellion as typhoid is marked by fever. There is no question of facts. They are common in America. The question is rather of their inevitability.

The most casual survey of the ways in which different societies have handled adolescence makes one fact inescapable: even in those cultures which have made most of the trait, the age upon which they focus their attention varies over a great range of years. At the outset, therefore, it is clear that the so-called puberty institutions are a misnomer if we continue to think of biological puberty. The puberty they recognize is social, and the ceremonies are a recognition in some fashion or other of the child's new status of adulthood. This investiture with new occupations and obligations is in consequence as various and as culturally conditioned as the occupations and obligations themselves. If the sole honourable duty of manhood is conceived to be deeds of war, the investiture of the warrior is later and of a different sort from that in a society where adulthood gives chiefly the privilege of dancing in a representation of masked gods. In order to understand puberty institutions, we do not most need analyses of the necessary nature of *rites de passage;* we need rather to know what is identified in different cultures with the beginning of adulthood and their methods of admitting to the new status. Not biological puberty, but what adulthood means in that culture conditions the puberty ceremony.

Adulthood in central North America means warfare. Honour in it is the great goal of all men. The constantly recurring theme of the youth's coming-of-age, as also of preparation for the warpath at any age, is a magic ritual for success in war. They torture not one another, but themselves: they cut strips of skin from their arms and legs, they strike off their fingers, they drag heavy weights pinned to their chest or leg muscles. Their reward is enhanced prowess in deeds of warfare.

In Australia, on the other hand, adulthood means participation in an exclusively male cult whose fundamental trait is the exclusion of women. Any woman is put to death if she so much as hears the sound of the bullroarer at the ceremonies, and she must never know of the rites. Puberty ceremonies are elaborate and symbolic repudiations of the bonds with the female sex; the men are symbolically made self-sufficient and the wholly responsible element of the community. To attain this end they use drastic sexual rites and bestow supernatural guaranties.

The clear physiological facts of adolescence, therefore, are first socially interpreted even where they are stressed. But a survey of puberty institutions makes clear a further fact: puberty is physiologically a different matter in the life-cycle of the male and the female. If cultural emphasis followed the physiological emphasis, girls' ceremonies would be more marked than boys'; but it is not so. The ceremonies emphasize a social fact: the adult prerogatives of men are more far-reaching in every culture than women's, and consequently, as in the above instances, it is more common for societies to take note of this period in boys than in girls.

Girls' and boys' puberty, however, may be socially celebrated in the same tribe in identical ways. Where, as in the interior of British Columbia, adolescent rites are a magical training for all occupations, girls are included on the same terms as boys. Boys roll stones down mountains and beat them to the bottom to be swift of foot, or throw gambling-sticks to be lucky in gambling; girls carry water from distant springs, or drop stones down inside their dresses that their children may be born as easily as the pebble drops to the ground.

In such a tribe as the Nandi of the lake region of East Africa, also, girls and boys share an even-handed puberty rite, though, because of the man's dominant role in the culture, his boyhood training period is more stressed than the woman's. Here adolescent rites are an ordeal inflicted by those already admitted to adult status upon those they are now forced to admit. They require of them the most complete stoicism in the face of ingenious tortures associated with circumcision. The rites for the two sexes are separate, but they follow the same pattern. In both the novices wear for the ceremony the clothing of their sweethearts. During the operation their faces are watched for any twinge of pain, and the reward of bravery is given with great rejoicing by the lover, who runs forward to receive back some of his adornments. For both the girl and the boy the rites mark their *entrée* into a new sex status: the boy is now a warrior and may take a sweetheart, the girl is marriageable. The adolescent tests are both a premarital ordeal in which the palm is awarded by their lovers.

Puberty rites may also be built upon the facts of girls' puberty and admit of no extension to boys. One of the most naïve of these is the institution of the fatting-house for girls in Central Africa. In the region where feminine beauty is all but identified with obesity, the girl at puberty is segregated, sometimes for years, fed with sweet and fatty foods, allowed no activity, and her body rubbed assiduously with oils. She is taught during this time her future duties, and her seclusion ends with a parade of her corpulence that is followed by her marriage to her proud bridegroom. It is not regarded as necessary for the man to achieve pulchritude before marriage in a similar fashion.

The usual ideas around which girls' puberty institutions are centred, and which are not readily extended to boys', are those concerned with menstruation. The uncleanness of the menstruating woman is a very widespread idea, and in a few regions first menstruation has been made the focus of all the associated attitudes. Puberty rites in these cases are of a thoroughly different character from any of which we have spoken. Among the Carrier Indians of British Columbia, the fear and horror of a girl's puberty was at its height. Her three or four years of seclusion was called 'the burying alive,' and she lived for all that time alone in the wilderness, in a hut of branches far from all beaten trails. She was a threat to any person who might so much as catch a glimpse of her, and her mere footstep defiled a path or a river. She was covered with a great headdress of tanned skin that shrouded her face and breasts and fell to the ground behind. Her arms and legs were loaded with sinew bands to protect her from the evil spirit with which she was filled. She was herself in danger and she was a source of danger to everybody else.

Girls' puberty ceremonies built upon ideas associated with the menses are readily convertible into what is, from the point of view of the individual concerned, exactly opposite behaviour. There are always two possible aspects to the sacred: it may be a source of peril or it may be a source of blessing. In some tribes the first menses of girls are a potent supernatural blessing. Among the Apaches I have seen the priests themselves pass on their knees before the row of solemn little girls to receive from them the blessing of their touch. All the babies and the old people come also of necessity to have illness removed from them. The adolescent girls are not segregated as sources of danger, but court is paid to them as to direct sources of supernatural blessing. Since the ideas that underlie puberty rites for girls, both among the Carrier and among the Apache, are founded on beliefs concerning menstruation, they are not extended to boys, and boys' puberty is marked instead, and lightly, with simple tests and proofs of manhood.

The adolescent behaviour, therefore, even of girls was not dictated by some physiological characteristic of the period itself, but rather by marital or magic requirements socially connected with it. These beliefs made adolescence in one tribe serenely religious and beneficent, and in another so dangerously unclean that the child had to cry out in warning that others might avoid her in the woods. The adolescence of girls may equally, as we have seen, be a theme which a culture does not institutionalize. Even where, as in most of Australia, boys' adolescence is given elaborate treatment, it may be that the rites are an induction into the status of manhood and male participation in tribal matters, and female adolescence passes without any kind of formal recognition.

These facts, however, still leave the fundamental question unanswered. Do not all cultures have to cope with the natural turbulence of this period, even though it may not be given institutional expression? Dr. Mead has studied this question in Samoa. There the girl's life passes through well-marked periods. Her first years out of babyhood are passed in small neighbourhood gangs of age mates from which the little boys are strictly excluded. The corner of the village to which she belongs is all-important, and the little boys are traditional enemies. She has one duty, that of baby-tending, but she takes the baby with her rather than stays home to mind it, and her play is not seriously hampered. A couple of years before puberty, when she grows strong enough to have more difficult tasks required of her and old enough to learn more skilled techniques, the little girls' play group in which she grew up ceases to exist. She assumes woman's dress and must contribute to the work of the household. It is an uninteresting period of life to her and quite without turmoil. Puberty brings no change at all.

A few years after she has come of age, she will begin the pleasant years of casual and irresponsible love affairs that she will prolong as far as possible into the period when marriage is already considered fitting. Puberty itself is marked by no social recognition, no change of attitude or of expectancy. Her pre-adolescent shyness is supposed to remain unchanged for a couple of years. The girl's life in Samoa is blocked out by other considerations than those of physiological sex maturity, and puberty falls in a particularly unstressed and peaceful period during which no adolescent conflicts manifest themselves. Adolescence, therefore, may not only be culturally passed over without ceremonial; it may also be without importance in the emotional life of the child and in the attitude of the village toward her.

Warfare is another social theme that may or may not be used in any culture. Where war is made much of, it may be with contrasting objectives, with contrasting organization in relation to the state, and with contrasting sanctions. War may be, as it was among the Aztecs, a way of getting captives for the religious sacrifices. Since the Spaniards fought to kill, according to Aztec standards they broke the rules of the game. The Aztecs fell back in dismay and Cortez walked as victor into the capital.

There are even quainter notions, from our standpoint, associated with warfare in different parts of the world. For our purposes it is sufficient to notice those regions where organized resort to mutual slaughter never occurs between social groups. Only our familiarity with war makes it intelligible that a state of warfare should alternate with a state of peace in one tribe's dealings with another. The idea is quite common over the world, of course. But on the one hand it is impossible for certain peoples to conceive the possibility of a state of peace, which in their notion would be equivalent to admitting enemy tribes to the category of human beings, which by definition they are not even though the excluded tribe may be of their own race and culture.

On the other hand, it may be just as impossible for a people to conceive of the possibility of a state of war. Rasmussen tells of the blankness with which the Eskimo met his exposition of our custom. Eskimos very well understand the act of killing a man. If he is in your way, you cast up your estimate of your own strength, and if you are ready to take it upon yourself, you kill him. If you are strong, there is no social retribution. But the idea of an Eskimo village going out against another Eskimo village in battle array or a tribe against tribe, or even of another village being fair game in ambush warfare, is alien to them. All killing comes under one head, and is not separated, as ours is, into categories, the one meritorious, the other a capital offense.

I myself tried to talk of warfare to the Mission Indians of California, but it was impossible. Their misunderstanding of warfare was abysmal. They did not have the basis in their own culture upon which the idea could exist, and their attempts to reason it out reduced the great wars to which we are able to dedicate ourselves with moral fervour to the level of alley brawls. They did not happen to have a cultural pattern that distinguished between them.

War is, we have been forced to admit even in the face of its huge place in our own civilization, an asocial trait. In the chaos following the World War all the wartime arguments that expounded its fostering of courage, of altruism, of spiritual values, gave out a false and offensive ring. War in our own civilization is as good an illustration as one can take of the destructive lengths to which the development of a culturally selected trait may go. If we justify war, it is because all peoples always justify the traits of which they find themselves possessed, not because war will bear an objective examination of its merits.

Warfare is not an isolated case. From every part of the world and from all levels of cultural complexity it is possible to illustrate the overweening and finally often the asocial elaboration of a cultural trait. Those cases are clearest where, as in dietary or mating regulations, for example, traditional usage runs counter to biological drives. Social organization, in anthropology, has a quite specialized meaning owing to the unanimity of all human societies in stressing relationship groups within which marriage is forbidden. No known people regard all women as possible mates. This is not in an effort, as is so often supposed, to prevent inbreeding in our sense, for over great parts of the world it is an own cousin, often the daughter of one's mother's brother, who is the predestined spouse. The relatives to whom the prohibition refers differ utterly among different peoples, but all human societies are alike in placing a restriction. No human idea has received more constant and complex elaboration in culture than this of incest. The incest groups are often the most important functioning units of the tribe, and the duties of every individual in relation to any other are defined by their relative positions in these groups. These groups function as units in religious ceremonials and in cycles of economic exchange, and it is impossible to exaggerate the importance of the role they have played in social history.

Some areas handle the incest tabu with moderation. In spite of the restrictions there may be a considerable number of women available for a man to marry. In others the group that is tabu has been extended by a social fiction to include vast numbers of individuals who have no traceable ancestors in common, and choice of a mate is in consequence excessively limited. This social fiction receives unequivocal expression in the terms of relationship which are used. Instead of distinguishing lineal from collateral kin as we do in the distinction between father and uncle, brother and cousin, one term means literally 'man of my father's group (relationship, locality, etc.) of his generation,' not distinguishing between direct and collateral lines, but making other distinctions that are foreign to us. Certain tribes of eastern Australia use an extreme form of this so-called classificatory kinship system. Those whom they call brothers and sisters are all those of their generation with whom they recognize any relationship. There is no cousin category or anything that corresponds to it; all relatives of one's own generation are one's brothers and sisters.

This manner of reckoning relationship is not uncommon in the world, but Australia has in addition an unparalleled horror of sister marriage and an unparalleled development of exogamous restrictions. So the Kurnai, with their extreme classificatory relationship system, feel the Australian horror of sex relationship with all their "sisters," that is, women of their own generation who are in any way related to them. Besides this, the Kurnai have strict locality rules in the choice of a mate. Sometimes two localities, out of the fifteen or sixteen of which the tribe is composed, must exchange women, and can have no mates in any other group. Sometimes there is a group of two or three localities that may exchange with two or three others. Still further, as in all Australia, the old men are a privileged group, and their prerogatives extend to marrying the young and attractive girls. The consequence of these rules is, of course, that in all the local group which must by absolute prescription furnish a young man with his wife, there is no girl who is not touched by one of these tabus. Either she is one of those who through relationship with his mother is his "sister," or she is already bargained for by an old man, or for some lesser reason she is forbidden to him.

That does not bring the Kurnai to reformulate their exogamous rules. They insist upon them with every show of violence. Therefore, the only way they are usually able to marry is by flying violently in the face of the regulations. They elope. As soon as the village knows that an elopement has occurred, it sets out in pursuit, and if the couple are caught the two are killed. It does not matter that possibly all the pursuers were married by elopement in the same fashion. Moral indignation runs high. There is, however, an island traditionally recognized as a safe haven, and if the couple can reach it and remain away till the birth of a child, they are received again with blows, it is true, but they may defend themselves. After they have run the gauntlet and been given their drubbing, they take up the status of married people in the tribe.

The Kurnai meet their cultural dilemma typically enough. They have extended and complicated a particular aspect of behaviour until it is a social liability. They must either modify it, or get by with a subterfuge. And they use the subterfuge. They avoid extinction, and they maintain their ethics without acknowledged revision. This manner of dealing with the *mores* has lost nothing in the progress of civilization. The older generation of our own civilization similarly maintained monogamy and supported prostitution, and the panegyrics of monogamy were never so fervent as in the great days of the red-light districts. Societies have always justified favourite traditional forms. When these traits get out of hand and some form of supplementary behaviour is called in, lip service is given as readily to the traditional form as if the supplementary behaviour did not exist.

Such a bird's-eye survey of human cultural forms makes clear several common misconceptions. In the first place, the institutions that human cultures build up upon the hints presented by the environment or by man's physical necessities do not keep as close to the original impulse as we easily imagine. These hints are, in reality, mere rough sketches, a list of bare facts. They are pin-point potentialities, and the elaboration that takes place around them is dictated by many alien considerations. Warfare is not the expression of the instinct of pugnacity. Man's pugnacity is so small a hint in the human equipment that it may not be given any expression in inter-tribal relations. When it is institutionalized, the form it takes follows other grooves of thought than those implied in the original impulse. Pugnacity is no more than the touch to the ball of custom, a touch also that may be withheld.

Such a view of cultural processes calls for a recasting of many of our current arguments upholding our traditional institutions. These arguments are usually based on the impossibility of man's functioning without these particular traditional forms. Even very special traits come in for this kind of validation, such as the particular form of economic drive that arises under our particular system of property ownership. This is a remarkably special motivation and there are evidences that even in our generation it is being strongly modified. At any rate, we do not have to confuse the issue by discussing it as if it were a matter of biological survival values. Self-support is a motive our civilization has capitalized. If our economic structure changes so that this motive is no longer so potent a drive as it was in the era of the great frontier and expanding industrialism, there are many other motives that would be appropriate to a changed economic organization, Every culture, every era, exploits some few out of a great number of possibilities. Changes may be very disquieting, and involve great losses, but this is due to the difficulty of change itself, not to the fact that our age and country has hit upon the one possible motivation under which human life can be conducted. Change, we must remember, with all its difficulties, is inescapable. Our fears over even very minor shifts in custom are usually quite beside the point. Civilizations might change far more radically than any human authority has ever had the will or the imagination to change them, and still be completely workable. The minor changes that occasion so much denunciation today, such as the increase of divorce, the growing secularization in our cities, the prevalence of the petting party, and many more, could be taken up quite readily into a slightly different pattern of culture. Becoming traditional, they would be given the same richness of content, the same importance and value, that the older patterns had in other generations.

The truth of the matter is rather that the possible human institutions and motives are legion, on every plane of cultural simplicity or complexity, and that wisdom consists in a greatly increased tolerance toward their divergencies. No man can thoroughly participate in any culture unless he has been brought up and has lived according to its forms, but he can grant to other cultures the same significance to their participants which he recognizes in his own.

2

The diversity of culture results not only from the ease with which societies elaborate or reject possible aspects of existence. It is due even more to a complex interweaving of cultural traits. The final form of any traditional institution, as we have just said, goes far beyond the original human impulse. In great measure this final form depends upon the way in which the trait has merged with other traits from different fields of experience.

A widespread trait may be saturated with religious beliefs among one people and function as an important aspect of their religion. In another area it may be wholly a matter of economic transfer and be therefore an aspect of their monetary arrangements. The possibilities are endless and the adjustments are often bizarre. The nature of the trait will be quite different in the different areas according to the elements with which it has combined.

It is important to make this process clear to ourselves because otherwise we fall easily into the temptation to generalize into a sociological law the results of a local merging of traits, or we assume their union to be a universal phenomenon. The great period of European plastic art was religiously motivated. Art pictured and made common property the religious scenes and dogmas which were fundamental in the outlook of that period. Modern European aesthetics would have been quite different if mediaeval art had been purely decorative and had not made common cause with religion.

As a matter of history great developments in art have often been remarkably separate from religious motivation and use. Art may be kept definitely apart from religion even where both are highly developed. In the Pueblos of the Southwest of the United States, art forms in pottery and textiles command the respect of the artist in any culture, but their sacred bowls carried by the priests or set out on the altars are shoddy and the decorations crude and unstylized. Museums have been known to throw out Southwest religious objects because they were so far below the traditional standard of workmanship. 'We have to put a frog there,' the Zuni Indians say, meaning that the religious exigencies eliminate any need of artistry. This separation between art and religion is not a unique trait of the Pueblos. Tribes of South America and of Siberia make the same distinction, though they motivate it in various ways. They do not use their artistic skill in the service of religion. Instead, therefore, of finding the sources of art in a locally important subject matter, religion, as older critics of art have sometimes done, we need rather to explore the extent to which these two can mutually interpenetrate, and the consequences of such merging for both art and religion.

The interpenetration of different fields of experience, and the consequent modification of both of them, can be shown from all phases of existence: economics, sex relations, folklore, material culture, and religion. The process can be illustrated in one of the widespread religious traits of the North American Indians. Up and down the continent, in every culture area except that of the Pueblos of the Southwest, supernatural power was obtained in a dream or vision. Success in life, according to their beliefs, was due to personal contact with the supernatural. Each man's vision gave him power for his lifetime, and in some tribes he was constantly renewing his personal relationship with the spirits by seeking further visions. Whatever he saw, an animal or a star, a plant or a supernatural being, adopted him as a personal protege, and he could call upon him in need. He had duties to perform for his visionary patron, gifts to give him and obligations of all kinds. In return the spirit gave him the specific powers he promised him in his vision.

In every great region of North America this guardian spirit complex took different form according to the other traits of the culture with which it was most closely associated. In the plateaus of British Columbia it merged with the adolescent ceremonies we have just spoken of. Both boys and girls, among these tribes, went out into the mountains at adolescence for a magic training. Puberty ceremonies have a wide distribution up and down the Pacific Coast, and over most of this region they are quite distinct from the guardian spirit practices. But in British Columbia they were merged. The climax of the magic adolescent training for boys was the acquisition of a guardian spirit who by its gifts dictated the lifetime profession of the young man. He became a warrior, a shaman, a hunter, or a gambler according to the supernatural visitant. Girls also received guardian spirits representing their domestic duties. So strongly is the guardian spirit experience among these peoples moulded by its association with the ceremonial of adolescence that anthropologists who know this region have argued that the entire vision complex of the American Indians had its origin in puberty rites. But the two are not genetically connected. They are locally merged, and in the merging both traits have taken special and characteristic forms.

In other parts of the continent, the guardian spirit is not sought at puberty, nor by all the youths of the tribe. Consequently the complex has in these cultures no kind of relationship with puberty rites even when any such exist. On the southern plains it is adult men who must acquire mystic sanctions. The vision complex merged with a trait very different from puberty rites. The Osage are organized in kinship groups in which descent is traced through the father and disregards the mother's line. These clan groups have a common inheritance of supernatural blessing. The legend of each clan tells how its ancestor sought a vision, and was blessed by the animal whose name the clan has inherited. The ancestor of the mussel clan sought seven times, with the tears running down his face, a supernatural blessing. At last he met the mussel and spoke to it, saying:

O grandfather,
The little ones have nothing of which to make their bodies.
Thereupon the mussel answered him:
You say the little ones have nothing of which to make their bodies.
Let the little ones make of me their bodies.
When the little ones make of me their bodies,
They shall always live to see old age.
Behold the wrinkles upon my skin [shell]
Which I have made to be the means of reaching old age.
When the little ones make of me their bodies
They shall always live to see the signs of old age upon their skins
The seven bends of the river [of life]
I pass successfully.
And in my travels the gods themselves have not the power to see the
    trail that I make.
When the little ones make of me their bodies
No one, not even the gods, shall be able to see the trail they make.

Among these people all the familiar elements of the vision quest are present, but it was attained by a first ancestor of the clan, and its blessings are inherited by a blood-relationship group.

This situation among the Osage presents one of the fullest pictures in the world of totemism, that close mingling of social organization and of religious veneration for the ancestor. Totemism is described from all parts of the world, and anthropologists have argued that the clan totem originated in the "personal totem," or guardian spirit. But the situation is exactly analogous to that of the plateaus of British Columbia where the vision quest merged with the adolescent rites, only that here it has merged with hereditary privileges of the clan. So strong has this new association become that a vision is no longer thought to give a man power automatically. The blessings of the vision are attained only by inheritance, and among the Osage long chants have grown up describing the ancestor's encounters, and detailing the blessings which his descendants may claim in consequence.

In both these cases it is not only the vision complex which receives a different character in different regions as it merges with puberty rites or clan organization. The adolescence ceremonies and the social organization are equally coloured by the interweaving of the vision quest. The interaction is mutual. The vision complex, the puberty rites, the clan organization, and many other traits that enter also into close relationship with the vision, are strands which are braided in many combinations. The consequences of the different combinations that result from this intermingling of traits cannot be exaggerated. In both the regions of which we have just spoken, both where the religious experience was merged with puberty rites and where it was merged with clan organization, as a natural corollary of the associated practices all individuals of the tribe could receive power from the vision for success in any undertaking. Achievement in any occupation was credited to the individual's claim upon a vision experience. A successful gambler or a successful hunter drew his power from it just as a successful shaman did. According to their dogma all avenues of advancement were closed to those who had failed to obtain a supernatural patron.

In California, however, the vision was the professional warrant of the shaman. It marked him as a person apart. It was just in this region, therefore, that the most aberrant aspects of this experience were developed. The vision was no longer a slight hallucination for which the stage could be set by fasting and torture and isolation. It was a trance experience which overtook the exceptionally unstable members of the community and especially the women. Among the Shasta it was the convention that only women were so blessed. The required experience was definitely cataleptic and came upon the novice after a preliminary dreaming had prepared the way. She fell senseless and rigid to the ground. When she came to herself, blood oozed from her mouth. All the ceremonies by which for years after she validated her call to be a shaman were further demonstrations of her liability to cataleptic seizures and were regarded as the cure by which her life was saved. In tribes like the Shasta not only the vision experience had changed its character to a violent seizure which differentiated religious practitioners from all others, but the character of the shamans was equally modified by the nature of the trance experience. They were definitely the unstable members of the community. In this region contests between shamans took the form of dancing each other down, that is, of seeing which one could withstand longest in a dance the cataleptic seizure which would inevitably overtake them. Both the vision experience and shamanism had been profoundly affected by the close relationship into which they had entered. The merging of the two traits, no less than the merging of the vision experience and puberty rites or clan organization, had drastically modified both fields of behaviour.

In the same way in our own civilization the separateness of the church and of the marriage sanction is historically clear, yet the religious sacrament of wedlock for centuries dictated developments both in sex behaviour and in the church. The peculiar character of marriage during those centuries was due to the merging of two essentially unrelated cultural traits. On the other hand, marriage has often been the means by which wealth was traditionally transferred. In cultures where this is true, the close association of marriage with economic transfer may quite obliterate the fact that marriage is fundamentally a matter of sexual and child-rearing adjustments. Marriage in each case must be understood in relation to other traits to which it has become assimilated, and we should not run into the mistake of thinking that "marriage" can be understood in the two cases by the same set of ideas. We must allow for the different components which have been built up into the resulting trait.

We greatly need the ability to analyze traits of our own cultural heritage into their several parts. Our discussions of the social order would gain in clarity if we learned to understand in this way the complexity of even our simplest behaviour. Racial differences and prestige prerogatives have so merged among Anglo-Saxon peoples that we fail to separate biological racial matters from our most socially conditioned prejudices. Even among nations as nearly related to the Anglo-Saxons as the Latin peoples, such prejudices take different forms, so that, in Spanish-colonized countries and in British colonies racial differences have not the same social significance. Christianity and the position of women, similarly, are historically interrelated traits, and they have at different times interacted very differently. The present high position of women in Christian countries is no more a "result" of Christianity than was Origen's coupling of woman with the deadly temptations. These interpenetrations of traits occur and disappear, and the history of culture is in considerable degree a history of their nature and fates and associations. But the genetic connection we so easily see in a complex trait and our horror at any disturbance of its interrelationships is largely illusory. The diversity of the possible combinations is endless, and adequate social orders can be built indiscriminately upon a great variety of these foundations.

Isaac Bashevis Singer
The Old Goray and the New

Goray was unquiet. A runner who had left for a distant village a day after the Feast of Tabernacles had not returned, and it was said that for his thirty-odd groschen the peasants had murdered him. Only by a miracle had a youth who traveled from farm to farm buying up produce escaped disaster. Spending the night in the silo of a peasant he had been wakened by the sound of his host murderously sharpening a hatchet. The feeble wasted away, and one by one they died. Each death brought Grunam the Beadle running through town in the early morning. Hurriedly, he would rap twice on each shutter with his wooden mallet, as a sign that the water was to be poured out of the house's water-run to thwart evil spirits (that no evil spirits might be mirrored there) and the household was to prepare for a funeral.

Rabbi Benish labored to be with the poor in their hour of need. He issued a decree that the wealthy must share a tithe of their bread and grits, yellow peas and beans, linseed oil, and cords of wood. Tuesdays, two public-spirited citizens made the rounds of the town with a bag for the tithe; but the high cost of things had made people mean, and they hid their food. There should have been no lack of meat, since calves were cheap. But the old slaughterer had been killed, and no new one had settled in Goray. Anyone who wanted to slaughter a beast had to drive it to a slaughterhouse miles away.

The old Jewish town of Goray was unrecognizable. Once upon a time everything had proceeded in an orderly fashion. Masters had labored alongside their apprentices, and merchants had traded; fathers-in-law had provided board and lodging, and sons-in-law had studied the holy teachings; boys had gone off to school, and school mistresses had visited the girls at home. Reb Eleazar Babad and the seven town elders had kept a sharp watch on all town affairs. Those who sinned were brought to court; those who did not obey the court's ruling were flogged, or pilloried in the prayer-house anteroom. On Thursdays and Fridays the needy went from house to house carrying beggars' bags, collecting food for the Sabbath; on the Sabbath itself the good women

Reprinted from *Satan in Goray* by Isaac Bashevis Singer with the permission of Farrar, Straus & Giroux, Inc. Copyright 1955 by Isaac Bashevis Singer.

of the town collected white bread and meat, fish and fruit for the needy. If a poor man had a daughter over fifteen years old who was still unwed, the community contrived to arrange a trousseau, and give her in marriage to an orphan youth or an elderly widower. The money that the groom received at the wedding sufficed to support them for months. After that, the man worked at something or other, or went about the countryside with a writ from the community certifying that he was a pauper. Of course, all sorts of misfortunes occurred. At times man and wife fell to quarreling, and they would have to journey to Yanov for a divorce—for the Goray stream had two names, and no one knew which was the proper one to use in locating Goray in the bill of divorcement according to the strict letter of the law. (*"The town of Goray, on the banks of the River thus-and-thus."*) Sometimes a man would go off, leaving his wife behind him, or be drowned somewhere in some body of endless waters whence his corpse might never be recovered. In such a case the widow could not marry again. Every year before Passover there would be a great furor in Goray over the paschal wheat, which the community would give as a concession to some man of influence—who would eventually always be accused of mixing the meal with chaff before selling it. As a rule, he would be roundly cursed and would not live out the year. Nevertheless, the next year another man was always found to profit from the Passover wheat. Every year on the day of the Rejoicing of the Law, there would be a fight in the tailor's prayer house concerning who was to have the honor of being the first to carry the Torah scroll around the lectern. Afterward the burial society would get drunk at the feast and break dishes. Several times a year there would be an epidemic, and Mendel the Gravedigger would end up with a few extra guilders. But such, after all, is the way of the world. The Jews of Goray dwelled in peace with the village Christians; in the town itself there lived only a few gentiles: a Sabbath gentile, to do the necessary work forbidden Jews on the Sabbath, a bath attendant, and a few others who lived in side streets, their houses surrounded by high picket fences so as not to flaunt their presence.

Before the Christian holidays, when large numbers of gentiles passed through Goray on the way to a shrine, young boys were everywhere industriously selling the pilgrims barrelsful of sweetened water. The Goray fairs were famous throughout the countryside. Peasants from all the nearby villages would come riding for the fair. Horses neighed, cows mooed, goats bleated. Horse traders—powerful Jews dressed in heavy jackets and sheepskin hats summer and winter—leaped to grab kicking stallions. They shouted as coarsely as any of the peasants. Bloody-handed butchers, with sharp knives thrust in their belts, would drag by the horn bound oxen who were no longer fit for the plow. In those days the grain merchants' bins were always full, and fat, white-bellied mice dined there; country whiskey at the taverns was mixed with whole buckets of water. All during the fair the children of Ham rejoiced in their own way. They danced with their women, pounding the floor with their feet, whistling and singing coarse songs. The women screamed and shook their hips, the men fought, swinging mighty fists. And what merchandise did Jews not sell! They sold women's flower-patterned shawls and headkerchiefs, egg rolls and long, twisted white breads; children's shoes and wading-boots; spices and nuts; iron yokes and nails; gilded bridal gifts and ready-made dresses; noisemakers for night watchmen, and Christmas Eve masks. True, often enough Rabbi Benish had interdicted Jews' dealing in Christian images. Nevertheless, secretly sales continued of missals with gilded covers and pages, wax candles and even holy pictures of saints with halos round their heads. In some out-of-the-way corner of the fair stood the few Goray gentiles, selling beet-brown salamis and white hog fat. Once a fastidious young man passed by them and conspicuously held his nose, as though something smelled afterward, he remarked peevishly, "The goy certainly eats well . . . you can smell it for a mile!"

In the evening the sober peasants would ride off. Drunks would be thrown out of the taverns into the mud, and their angry women would pull them home by the ears. The dark circle of the fair grounds would be covered with dung, and from it would rise the rustic smell of manure. In Jewish homes oil lamps, candles, and pieces of kindling would be lit. Women wearing enormous deep-pocketed aprons would spit on their palms to ward off the evil eye, and feverishly count the copper money they transferred to pots; in houses where there was no counting of money, it was deemed that the blessing of good fortune would be more apt to enter. Goray Jews had great needs. They needed board and lodging for sons-in-law and gifts for bridegrooms; satin dresses and velvet coats for brides and fur hats and silk coats for the men. For the holidays they needed: citrus fruit for the Feast of Tabernacles, the white un-leavened bread for Passover, and olive oil for the Feast of Lights. Jews needed money to lend to wicked lords and to silence possible slanderers. More than once it was necessary to send an intercessor to Lublin. And then there were community needs: The town of Goray maintained a rabbi and his assistant, beadles and school teachers, one ritual slaughterer and ten charity scholars, as well as attendants for the bathhouse, one for the men and one for the women, besides the poor and sick in the infirmary. And how many times did not Goray, this town at the end of the world, have to send money to other communities that had been despoiled or burned down!

CHAPTER 3

Community as Place

By customary usage, community often means place. Thus "What is your community?" is usually answered by reference to a town or neighborhood. We have come to think of community as the physical space where people live.

These sections of the book are in part designed to displace this notion with a broader view of community as a set of social identifications and interactions, and sections that follow reveal the various kinds of settings in which community may flourish. Nonetheless, place is important to community for certainly most of the social systems to which we would apply the concept are geographic entities of one sort or another. The human contacts on which feelings of commitment and identity are built are most likely to occur among people sharing the same piece of ground. The mere fact that they live together gives rise to common problems that push them toward common perspectives and induce them to develop organizational vehicles for joint action. The geography of the local living and working situations, in other words, remains important.

As we shall see in later sections of the book, modern life has raised some havoc with men's ability to identify themselves with the locality, to create a community in it. The technology and life style of the modern urban man pulls much of his attention and activity into broader spheres, into the larger world of the corporation, the profession, the labor union, and the like. The automobile has erased local boundaries, so that they no longer confine his occupational life, and often not his leisure, his shopping, or his friendships.

This tendency raises interesting questions about the relationship of community and geographic place. It makes urgent the question of whether community can exist for man in meaningful ways without the locality as a nexus of loyalties. Must community, in other words, be place-oriented? This is a way of asking if urban life is workable.

The relationship between place and community is one of the theoretical questions ultimately involved in moves to decentralize the governments of American cities, to devise new "federal" forms of metropolitan re-organization, and the like.

The selections from Robert Redfield's *Folk Culture of the Yucatan* and Thomas Wolfe's *Look Homeward, Angel* illustrate some of the powers of attachment to the local place. For Redfield's tribal group and Wolfe's fictitious small-town dwellers, relationship with the local environment defined and delimited social interactions. In the isolated village of the Yucatan, place is the basis of culture and community life; the sociopolitical structure flows from mutual dependence on the local environment. The symbols, rituals, ceremonial aspects of the community are closely tied to its characteristics and the demands they make. The short passage from Wolfe illustrates how a town is the site of attachment, opportunity, and despair for the people who live in it. We see land as community and land as property.

Robert Redfield
The Villager's View of Life

Four chief terms define the terrestrial world within which man moves: the bush, the cenote, the village, and the milpa. The first two are of nature, that is to say, of the gods, while the village and the milpa are what man has made out of nature with the permission and protection of the gods. The bush covers almost everything; it is the background within which lie all other special features of earth's surface. It is never reduced permanently to man's use; the milpas are but temporary claims made by men upon the good will of the deities who animate and inhabit the bush; after a few years each planted field returns to its wild state and becomes again an undifferentiated part of the forest. Therefore, each new invasion of the tall bush must be accomplished with prudent and respectful attention to the gods of the bush, the *kuilob-kaaxob*. For the same reason—that is only when the gods grant to man the use of a piece of bush that is then wild, that is theirs—a man makes the ceremony of recompense ("dinner of the milpa") and makes the offering of first fruits only in respect to the first crop grown on land he has cleared.

The milpero marks off only so much bush for felling as will correspond with the future milpa. Thus an understanding is reached between the kuilob-kaaxob and the milpero: the milpero respects the bush, making use of only so much as he needs and wasting none; in return the gods of the bush will refrain from deflecting the swung ax against the milpero's foot. All relations with the gods have this character of a contract or, rather, of mutual expressions of good faith. The ceremonies that attend the fields and the beehives are essentially renewed pledges of pious respect and temporary discharges of a persisting obligation that is reciprocal between gods and men. Whenever a man takes from the fields or from the hives their yield, it is felt that he owes an appropriate return to the deities for what they have granted him. The first-fruit ceremonies and the rituals called "dinner of the milpa" and "dinner of the hives" formally return to the gods what they have granted. If the return is not at once made, the agriculturalist

Reprinted from *The Folk Culture of Yucatan* by Robert Redfield by permission of The University of Chicago Press. Copyright 1941 by The University of Chicago.

recognizes the existence of a debt that must be discharged. For each yield a certain return is due. Thus a large fowl and a small one should be offered for each springtime yield of honey. But the return need not be made at once; the debt may accumulate. But, when at last the appropriate ceremony is performed, the fowls sacrificed equal in number and kind the amount of the total obligation. So man keeps an account with the gods. Yet it is not simply a matter of arithmetical accounting. Good will must be present too. A man who scrimps against the deities is "haggling"; his health will suffer and his crops will fail. So one does not too long accumulate a debt to the deities. As another year passes without the performance of the proper ceremony, as the harmonious adjustment between man and the gods is by that much more disturbed, so increases the danger of sickness and crop failure, misfortunes by means of which the gods punish.

The obligation not to fell more bush than one needs is a part of the more general obligation never to take from the gods all the yield that is available. When the honey is taken from the hives, a little is left. When the ripe corn is taken from the field, some ears must be offered to the gods before man eats of them. When a deer is slain, certain parts must first be given to the spiritual protectors of the deer before the hunter eats his venison. For all the yield of bush and field is the gods', because the bush and the animals therein belong to the gods. These offerings return in part and in symbol what is essentially the property of the gods and which is by them ceded to men of pious conduct.

The bush is, then, the principal lodging-place of the supernatural beings. All aspects of nature have their spiritual aspect; each tree or knoll or cave may hold an invisible being and should therefore be approached with circumspection and without irreverence; and some natural features are more particularly associated with supernatural beings. The silk-cotton tree is the haunt of the x-tabai, the being in woman's form who may entice men to their death. The mounds of red earth made by the leaf-cutter ant are the abiding-place of the devil and are therefore likewise to be avoided. And throughout the bush and especially along the roads may pass the balamob, the invisible protectors of the cornfield and of the village. In certain places the bush is taller; there grow wine palms, and there the milpero finds mounds built by the ancients. Here especially lurk the *aluxob,* little mischievous beings, who are not the owners of wood or field, as are the gods, but who must on some occasions be propitiated. The bush teems with unseen inhabitants. Especially at night does the native hear a multitude of rustlings, murmurings, and whistlings that make known the presence of the many beings who people the bush. And each of these is disposed, well or ill, toward man, and of them man must take account.

Of all natural features, that attended by the most important considerations is the cenote—the natural well perforated by erosion through
the limestone upon which grows the bush. The bush, even in the
rainy season, is tough and thorny and after months without rainfall is
a sere and dusty tangle of brittle branches and vines. But the cenote,
a shaft down to the distant water, is ringed with fresh verdure. From
its mouth emerges air, moist and cool; swallows twitter about its sides.
The plants about the cenote are green and soft and luxuriant; they
are, therefore, the plants used in the ceremonies to the rain-gods. Similarly the frogs, toads, and tortoises that are found near the cenotes
are the animals of the rain-gods. The cenotes are the places of the
rain-gods, the chaacs. These, residing behind a doorway in the eastern
sky, come to earth and are also thought of as dwellers in these natural
wells. The land is known largely by the cenotes; they are the points by
which are located other features of the bush. In the prayers uttered by
the shaman-priest in the agricultural ceremonies all the cenotes in the
region in which the native moves and makes his milpas are mentioned
by name; thus the priest calls, one by one, upon the chaacs associated
with the cenotes. For the chaacs have within their power the granting
or the withholding of the rain upon which the maize and, therefore, the
life of the people depends. Of all the gods of nature, the chaacs come
first in importance.

The chaacob, the balamob, and the kuilob-kaaxob are guardians,
respectively, of the rain, the village and the milpa, and the bush. Lesser
features of nature have also their protectors. The deer are watched over
by spiritual beings called "zip," who have the form of deer; and the
cattle have their guardian who is himself in form a great steer. Certain
birds who frequent the milpa but appear not to eat the grain are the
alakob of the balamob, as the frogs are the alakob of the rain-gods. The
principal wild animals are the domestic animals of their protectors;
they are yielded to man only under appropriate conditions, as crops are
yielded and the honey which the bees make. The bees, too, are under
the tutelage of special deities. All these wild animals are, therefore, referred to in prayers as alakob, "domestic animals"; and, when man
makes an offering to the gods, he offers his own alakob, hens or turkeys.

All these supernatural beings are not of the substance of which this
world is made. They are, the native says, "of wind." The wind that
blows suggests these beings and may, in fact, be them. The wind that
blows from the cenotes, or from dry caves, comes from the sea to which
all winds return. The winds, as they blow to refresh the land or to fan
the flames at burning time, are beneficent; but there abound innumerable winds, often not felt at all—winds only in the sense of incorporeal
spirits—that are evil, actually or potentially. These winds may go about

of themselves, but also they attend all supernatural beings and all critical, dangerous, or morally wrong situations and human beings involved in such situations. Together the gods of bush, milpa, rain, and village are "the Lords," the yuntzilob. Wherever the yuntzilob go, the winds go too. So the gods are a source of danger to men; their sacred quality involves a peril. Also the Lords may send the evil winds to punish the impious or those careless of their obligations to the deities. So the ceremonies, besides propitiating the deities, ward off the evil winds or, in certain cases, clear from the bodies of the afflicted the evil winds that have attacked them.

The cenotes are particularly the sources of the winds. As the water makes its cycle, carried by the rain-gods from the cenotes up into the sky to fall as fertilizing rain upon the milpa, so the winds have their sources in the sea and pass up through the cenotes. Therefore, in certain ceremonies offerings are thrown into the cenotes to propitiate the winds. The cenotes are also the openings to the underworld; the suicide, worst of sinners, hurls himself into the cenote to pass directly into hell.

Except for rainfall, the cenotes are the only source of water. They determine the position of human settlements. Each cluster of milpas that has any permanency of settlement, each established village, centers about a cenote. The cenotes in the uninhabited bush retain more of their sacred quality; some, indeed, may not be approached by women and are visited by men only when water of that high degree of sacredness is to be fetched for use in the most important ceremony. But the cenote of the village becomes a part of the mundane and human life. To it the women and girls come for water; there they exchange gossip and talk, and there the cattle are driven to water.

The village, like the world itself, is a square with its corners in the four cardinal directions. The cenote is its center. So five crosses should be set up in each village: one at each corner and one at the cenote. Each village has its five (some say four) protecting balamob. Four hover above the four entrances to pounce upon noxious beast or evil wind that might attempt to enter. The fifth stations himself above the center point. The milpa also is square, and similarly oriented, and provided with its five balamob. Five rain-gods occupy, respectively, the cardinal points of the sky and the center of the heavens. In all these sets of five the smallest of the five occupies the position either at the east or at the center. Though he is the smallest, he is the most powerful. The word for him (thup) suggests to the native the smallest and the most powerful of a series; by the same adjective is known the kind of corn that produces small ears early in the season; for this corn, because of its special virtue in ripening before other corn, a special ceremony must be made.

Of the four cardinal directions, the east is dominant. From the east blow the principal winds, out of the east arise sun, moon, and planets; and from the east, in springtime, the first clouds and rains, carried by the chaacs, emerge. In the dense forests to the east dwell the bee-gods and a number of lesser supernatural beings; and inconceivably far, somewhere to the east, lies Jerusalem, where Jesus Christ lived. When a man prays, therefore, he faces east; and every altar, from the little table of poles set up by a milpero in his field, when he makes an offering at the time of sowing, to the altar elaborately laid out by the shaman-priest for the rain ceremony, is oriented to the points of the compass and so arranged that the worshiper kneels before it to face the east. At the rain ceremony the rain-gods of the cardinal directions are impersonated by men placed at the four corners of the altar, and four boys, impersonating frogs, alakob of the rain-gods, sit at the four supports of the altar.

The milpa, also, is thought of as square, and its four corners are protected by four balamob; a fifth, the thup, is sometimes conceived as occupying the central point. When the agriculturalist makes an offering in the milpa, he sets one bowl of cornmeal-in-water in each corner of the milpa and may add a fifth in the center. In the center of the field he builds his granary, and here he leaves his corn for months, it may be, coming there after the harvest only from time to time to supply the needs of his household. There the maize is safe, for who would take it from under the eyes of the unseen gods who have set a watch upon it? The milpa is, indeed, not only a work place but a place of worship. It is a place that must not be sullied. One works, eats, talks, and prays in a milpa. But one should not act boisterously in a milpa. Though one may take one's wife to a milpa, one should not have sexual intercourse under the sky out in a milpa but only within a house of shelter.

That the milpa, like the cenote and the bush, is set aside from the ordinary life of the village is indicated when the native says that the milpa is *zuhuy*. Everything that is protected from or is not exposed to the contamination of the ordinary, the earthly, the profane, is zuhuy. What is held from contaminating experiences is zuhuy: a girl who does not go about with other people, especially with men; a fowl penned by itself to make it ready for offering to the gods; a tablecloth that has never been used; water in a cenote to which women have not had access. What is appropriate to or associated with the gods is zuhuy: balche, the bark beer offered to the gods at the rain ceremony; the piece of ground upon which the ceremony has just been held; a milpa. The maize is zuhuy, especially as long as it is growing in the milpa. One does not rudely grasp a growing maize plant; one does not wantonly throw kernels of maize on the ground or crack them between the teeth. The Virgin herself is one of the guardians of the maize; by such a term she is addressed in the prayers used in agricultural ceremonies. So long as the maize is in the milpa it is not referred to by the word used for maize as it is prepared for eating or as it is sold in the market (*ixim*) but by the same word (*gracia*) used to denote the spiritual essence of offerings made to the gods.

Not only have the gods their special functions and their special positions in the quadrilaterals of village, milpa, earth, and sky but they have also their positions in a hierarchy of power and authority. When the offerings are laid out on the altar of the agricultural ceremonies, this relative order of power and importance is expressed in the placing of the offerings: the largest breads are committed to the highest beings and are closest to the candle that marks the central point of the eastern side of the table altar, while the smaller breads, for the lesser gods, are placed farther away from the candle. There are, the native recognizes, two hierarchies, but the two interlock, and there is one supreme head to them both. This is the *Hahal Dios,* the Great God, who sits in a place, called Glory, very remote, beyond the sky. Nothing happens but that he has it so; yet he is too remote to deal directly with men. The great saints sit high, but below him, and below them are the lesser saints and the souls of the virtuous and baptized dead. Some of the saints are protectors of the animals of the forest and are to be propitiated along with the windlike supernatural deer who watch their corporeal kinds. The saints have their embodiment in their effigies, but these are also saints, with personalities and powers in their own right, especially those of miraculous origin. Each family may have a saint of this sort, but every village must have one. This saint is the protector of the entire community and the intermediary between the people and the Hahal Dios, as the balamob of the village protect it from terrestrial invasion by evil winds and marauding animals. One of the great saints, St. Michael, is chief of the chaacs. Through him the Hahal Dios controls the rain. Captain of the chaacs when they ride across the sky is the *Kun-ku-Chaac,* the great rain-god. Under orders from St. Michael, he leads the other rain-gods, who are subordinated to him down to the least chaac, the thup, who, being the least, has special powers to produce rain in torrents.

As it is with the gods, so it is the proper condition of men that they respect their proper order of duty and responsibility. One must be chief and father, expecting and receiving respect and obedience, while he gives protection and dispenses justice. So it is with the family, where the father is head; so with the village where the comisario (chosen by the people more frequently than was the old batab who held his office for life) leads his people, composes their disputes, and determines punishments; and so it is with the state, where the governor has this role. Under each such leader come others who are next in authority. Everyone in a post of authority has supporters—his *noox*. When one stick is set up to support another, it is a noox. So the comisario has his *suplente*, and so the *cargador*, who is in principal charge of the annual festival of the patron saint, has his *nakulob* to help him. The municipal officers are a hierarchy, and so are the men composing the organization that maintains the festival of the patron; in each case there is one head and a distribution of authority and responsibility downward. In the case of the organization maintaining the festival this hierarchy is expressed in the ritual wherein certain festal foods are solemnly and publicly transferred from the outgoing cargador to his successor and are then distributed among the supporters of the new cargador, first to the three next responsible, and then among the lesser followers and votaries.

In the natural order of authority men are above women, and the old above the young. So, when a married couple leave the church, the bride walks ahead of her husband to show that he is to command; and so they walk afterward on the trail. A woman's activities center around the hearth; her usual path is from the house to the cenote. The path of men leads to the milpa and to the town; men and not women are concerned with public affairs. At all gatherings for the discussion of affairs outside the large family only men are present, or, if women are present they do not take part. When the ceremony of *hetzmek* is performed to assure that an infant will develop as it should, the objects placed in its hand to symbolize its future capacities include a needle if it be a girl, an ax if a boy.

Among one's kinsmen one occupies, at every age, a well understood position in an order of respect, authority, and responsibility. To one's father one owes the greatest obedience and also respect; while he cares for you, his commands are to be obeyed. To one's father's or mother's brothers, but especially to the former, respect and obedience, but less, are due. One's older brother is distinguished from one younger than one's self by a different term which implies the obedience due him. If the father dies, the oldest brother will take his place at the head of the family. To an older brother (*zucuun*) one may go for help and advice as one would to a father or an uncle. But these kinsmen by blood are not the only members of this constellation of duty and obligation. By baptism and by hetzmek ceremony the parents provide *padrinos* for the child, older persons who stand ready to aid, to advise, and, if necessary, to chide their godchild. To these persons one shows the greatest respect, and this respect is expressed, throughout life, in gestures of greeting

and in the making of gifts. Upon marriage one's parents-in-law become
still another pair of these older persons to whom respect is due. So the
younger person is inclosed, so to speak, within pairs of older persons.
And the older persons, linked with one another through the sponsor-
ship involved in baptism or hetzmek, and in the marrying of their respective offspring, are linked with one another in bonds of mutual respect and trust. After one marries and has children, one arranges, for
each, the padrinos of the baptism and of the hetzmek and later sees to
it that one's son finds a wife. And each of these undertakings to complete the social position of that child for whom one is responsible creates a new tie between one's self and one's wife and the person or the
couple chosen to sponsor one's child or with the parents of the child's
spouse. Or, at the least, it solemnizes and sanctifies a relation of intimacy and trust that has already come into existence through kinship or
friendship.

Each of these relationships is created in ritual and sanctioned by
tradition; some are renewed or later recognized in other rituals. When
parents come to ask a couple to sponsor their child at baptism, they
express their solemn petition through formal speech expressed through
an intermediary, and the unbreakable relation established is signalized
by the offering and acceptance of certain traditional foods and by eating
and drinking together. The petitioner kisses the hand of the man he
seeks as compadre, for, though the respect is to be mutual, the gratitude
moves from the child's parents to the godparents. This gratitude later
receives formal recognition in a special ceremony when the parents
kneel before their compadres and wash their hands and in which the
tie between the child and his godparents is expressed by placing the
child in the godparents' arms. The responsibility assumed by the godparents of the baptism is paralleled by that assumed by the person
who "makes hetzmek" with the child, first placing it astride the hip,
where it will therefore be carried until it learns to walk; and a short
domestic ceremony expresses this relationship and the assurance which
performance of the ritual gives of the future sound development of the
child. The relationships established by marriage are likewise signalized
in procedures that are formal, solemn, traditional, and appropriate.
Marriage is not only an arrangement for the adult condition of two
young people; it is also the forging of a new relationship between two
groups of kindred. As men take the leadership, so the parents of the
boy come to the parents of the girl to ask for the girl's hand. As formal
matters should be expressed through third persons, it is well to engage
one specializing in the negotiation of marriages to express the petition
and prosecute the negotiations. As every petitioner brings a gift, those
coming with the petition bring rum, chocolate, cigarettes, and bread.

And as the matter under consideration is important and concerns relatives on both sides, as well as the boy and girl, four visits are made and negotiations are extended. In the determination of the amount and nature of the gift to be made to the girl by the boy's parents and in the settlement of the details of the marriage arrangements, grandparents and perhaps godparents have an appropriate place, as well, it may be, as have uncles on both sides or elder brothers. If the old-style marriage is followed, a ceremony will be held in which the boy's parents are hosts. In this, by an order of kneeling and of offering rum, by the formal speeches made by the sponsor of the marriage, and finally by the offering of cooked turkeys by the boy's father to the girl's father and by the boy's father to the sponsor of the marriage, all the new relationships of obligation and respect are expressed and appropriately sealed.

So each new tie in the web of social relationships is fastened with rituals meaningful of the character and importance of the relationships. As ties are broken by death, new ones are formed. The new ties bring in new individuals, but they merely repeat the old patterns so that the design in the texture is always the same.

Thomas Wolfe
from *Look Homeward, Angel*

Eliza saw Altamont not as so many hills, buildings, people: she saw it in the pattern of a gigantic blueprint. She knew the history of every piece of valuable property—who bought it, who sold it, who owned it in 1893, and what it was now worth. She watched the tides of traffic cannily; she knew by what corners the largest number of people passed in a day or an hour; she was sensitive to every growing-pain of the young town, gauging from year to year its growth in any direction, and deducing the probable direction of its future expansion. She judged distances critically, saw at once where the beaten route to an important centre was stupidly circuitous, and looking in a straight line through houses and lots, she said:

"There'll be a street through here some day."

Her vision of land and population was clear, crude, focal—there was nothing technical about it: it was extraordinary for its direct intensity. Her instinct was to buy cheaply where people would come; to keep out of pockets and *culs de sac,* to buy on a street that moved toward a centre, and that could be given extension.

Thus, she began to think of Dixieland. It was situated five minutes from the public square, on a pleasant sloping middleclass street of small homes and boarding-houses. Dixieland was a big cheaply constructed frame house of eighteen or twenty drafty high-ceilinged rooms: it had a rambling, unplanned, gabular appearance, and was painted a dirty yellow. It had a pleasant green front yard, not deep but wide, bordered by a row of young deep-bodied maples: there was a sloping depth of one hundred and ninety feet, a frontage of one hundred and twenty. And Eliza, looking toward the town, said: "They'll put a street behind there some day."

In winter, the wind blew howling blasts under the skirts of Dixieland: its back end was built high off the ground on wet columns of rotting brick. Its big rooms were heated by a small furnace which sent up, when charged with fire, a hot dry enervation to the rooms of the first floor, and a gaseous but chill radiation those upstairs.

The place was for sale. Its owner was a middle-aged horse-faced gentleman whose name was the Reverend Wellington Hodge: he had begun life favorably in Altamont as a Methodist minister, but had run foul of trouble when he began to do double service to the Lord God of Hosts and John Barleycorn—his evangelical career came to an abrupt ending one winter's night when the streets were dumb with falling snow. Wellington, clad only in his winter heavies, made a wild sortie from Dixieland at two in the morning, announcing the kingdom of God and the banishment of the devil, in a mad marathon through the streets that landed him panting but victorious in front of the Post Office. Since then with the assistance of his wife, he had eked out a hard living at the boarding-house. Now, he was spent, disgraced, and weary of the town.

Besides, the sheltering walls of Dixieland inspired him with horror—he felt that the malign influence of the house had governed his own disintegration. He was a sensitive man, and his promenades about his estate were checked by inhibited places: the cornice of the long girdling porch where a lodger had hanged himself one day at dawn, the spot in the hall where the consumptive had collapsed in a hemorrhage, the room where the old man cut his throat. He wanted to return to his home, a land of fast horses, wind-bent grass, and good whisky—Kentucky. He was ready to sell Dixieland.

Eliza pursed her lips more and more thoughtfully, went to town by way of Spring Street more and more often.

"That's going to be a good piece of property some day," she said to Gant.

CHAPTER 4

The Bonds of Community: Commitment and Loyalty

What finally binds a community together is a state of mind on the part of its members, a sense of interdependence and loyalty. In earlier sections we have seen that communities are characterized by people's engagement in activities that demand interrelationship of efforts, they give rise to shared culture, and they are often sited in a specified geographic locale. Out of these conditions grow attachments to the social group, and these attachments form the basis on which people respond to its collective demands. Most of these responses are doubtless the product of habit, the indirect result of early socialization to community ways; some grow out of the individual's conscious calculation about his own needs. They form the cement that makes it possible for the group to hold together on a more or less permanent basis.

The following selections illustrate this dimension of community from two perspectives, the analytic and the descriptive. Scott Greer in *Social Organization* discusses the creative effects on social groups of functional interdependence, a source from which commitment and loyalty may grow. In his contrast of rural and urban life settings, he suggests that differences in condition may affect the capacities of populations to create such bonds. As urbanization brings about changes in the objective relationship of man to organization the quality of the subjective relationship is altered.

The other selections in this chapter deal with what is ordinarily thought to be the Western world's most highly developed community, the Greek *polis*. H. D. F. Kitto's description of the *polis* emphasizes its psychological content, its basis in the overriding dedication of its citizens. As Kitto interprets it, the mark of the *polis* ultimately lay in loyalty and commitment; recall that Socrates took the hemlock out of love for a community whose specific and immediate condition he decried. It should be noted from Kitto's commentary that the Greek *polis* was a relatively small place where community could be based on primary interactions among people. Whether larger societies can also be communities is a question that has bothered students of society from the time of ancient Athens down to the present day. Can the Athens so movingly eulogized by Pericles in his funeral oration provide any model at all for a nation of two hundred million people?

In modern times critical questions about the relationship of man and community have been raised by the predominant liberal-individualist tradition of Western social thought. Perhaps three questions will suggest the trend of this critique: (1) How much loyalty is required for community to exist? (2) How much loyalty to the community is too much? (3) What are the consequences for the individual of the community's demand for loyalty? These remain among the central questions of political science and political practice.

Scott Greer
Major Types of Human Groups

Historically man's social life seems to have originated in small roving groups or local bands which hunted and grazed over delimited areas. Some of them still exist in Malaya (the Semang), in Brazil (the Caingang), and a few others in out-of-the-way places. Such groups constitute the entire society of their individual members. Encompassing all of their social relations, they are necessarily multifunctional. They are therefore of dominating importance for the individual's need-economy. The members are few in number and close together physically; there is relatively little status differentiation (chiefly age and sex), and the subgroups tend to interact constantly and intensely. These conditions result in a powerful primary dimension, limiting and reinforcing the secondary level. In such a local group there is only one social frame of reference in the individual's life, the concrete group that is all of society for him. This inclusive group has a tremendous predictive power for the individual's behavior, since all major functions are served by the same aggregate.

However, when man invented agriculture and settled into villages, the resulting division of labor and specialization of individual roles resulted in a much more complex social system. The surplus created by agriculture allowed for wider variations in wealth; the sedentary life led to wider integration of groups (the extended group growing in importance); and the multiplication of villages in many parts of the world stimulated the rise of urban cultures.

The village in its traditional form, however, whether among primitives or peasants, also has a powerful controlling effect upon the behavior of individual persons. It is usually a social group, not just an aggregate. The famous "peasant mentality," cursed by revolutionary theorists, for example, Karl Marx, and revered by sophisticated primitivists such as Tolstoi, is stamped with the power of the peasant village as a group. The reasons, once more, can be found in the functional interdependence of the villagers. Each person is dependent upon the village for his status, his access to production, his share of the surplus, his social and personal security, his place in the world. Such villages tend to be largely self-sufficient, and the inhabitants are consequently dependent upon the village world. As with the local band, so many functions are served by the same group in isolation from outsiders that a rich and complete symbolic flow occurs, and a corresponding wealth of primary relations characterizes the social order.

When a territorially defined group, like the village, is a true functional group for all of its members and when it manifests a powerful primary dimension, we call it a *community*. However, even a community does not order all the behavior of its members. It is one set of limits only. Within these limits there still exist other structures, such as the extended family, age groups, conjugal families—and any or all of these structures may contradict, modify, or destroy the controlling power of the community in specific instances. Yet by and large community controls are powerful enough to create highly uniform behavior on the part of the villagers, so much so that the cultural anthropologists are usually justified in taking a few informants as representative samples of the whole homogeneous world of village behavior.

Village communities have formed the economic and demographic base for the majority of the world's population since the Neolithic era, and the great majority of human beings have been peasant villagers since that time. Spatially defined groups have been, in the past, communities.

But the high points of history have occurred in the city. The "urbs," the people of cities, are the ones who have made history. (Even Christ found it necessary to finish his mission in Jerusalem, as a moving passage testifies, and His followers were for many centuries chiefly the free and slave proletariat of the Roman ports and world cities.)

What is a city? A city is a concentration of population in a space so small that it cannot produce its own necessities; instead, the city exports certain goods (military power, manufactures, credit, administrative order) and imports its food and raw materials from the open country, or hinterland. Such concentrations can, therefore, occur only when there are many agricultural villages, since it is upon the surplus production of the peasants that the urban population is supported.[1]

The occupational differentiation of the population which has some importance in the peasant village increases spectacularly in the city. The city can live only through a wide division of labor. Thus, in the city the professions grow up; the priesthood, soldiery, governmental staff, merchants, and so forth have recognizably similar ways of life in all urban cultures. The ordinary population is also specialized, with trade and industry and service work absorbing the majority. Occupa-

[1]For a discussion of the dependence of urban centers upon village economy, see Ralph Turner: *The Great Cultural Traditions*, New York, McGraw-Hill Book Co., Inc., 1941, especially Vol. II, Chap. XX.

tional differentiation is reinforced by cultural variation through the continual migration of foreigners and countrymen into the city.

The city population is not only highly differentiated but also physically and, to some extent, socially mobile. Even in the cities of classical societies the population moved about within the city far more than peasant villagers moved from one village to another. Urban mobility is conducive to social insulation, for through movement the individual may escape local "public opinion." Such escape is not easy for the peasant villager, whose village group is apt to be the only human society he knows.

What are the consequences of these urban characteristics for the territorially inclusive group? Three tendencies can be briefly summarized:

1. The individual's functional interdependence in the city is typically based upon many social groups. One group may provide income, another recreation, another religious communion, and so on. The kin group, rather than being a carrier of all or most of these functions, may have a separate status and may become relatively unimportant in social life.

2. Functional interdependence creates new, specialized groups, but such groups are not geographically inclusive. Thus the corporation and the factory draw persons from anywhere within ten or fifteen miles of the workplace; at the same time, many of the individual's most important social relations take place far from his home and neighborhood.

3. The lessening of the local group's functional importance (for religion, recreation, and work) results in a weakening of the social process which is a necessary basis for the primary dimension. Hence, the decline of the urban neighborhood. One's true neighbors in the city are apt to be work associates, not "nigh-dwellers."

In short, the city typically develops a multiplicity of subgroups which are functional for the society and have a controlling influence over their members. The citizen who was, in the classical city state, a member of a privileged minority (a ruling class) was a member of a definite social group, but the citizen in democratic America is a member of his city only in a very vestigial fashion. One can predict little of his behavior through knowing he is a citizen of New York or Duluth. Perhaps his behavior is as limited by group membership as that of the Athenian, but the controlling groups are not identical with the territorially defined city. Except for the payment of taxes and fines and the observance of some of its laws, the citizen is part of a social group only on certain sporadic occasions when the normal division of labor breaks down. The latter situation is the phenomenon of a transitory group.

H. D. F. Kitto
The Polis

"Polis" is the Greek word which we translate "city-state." It is a bad translation, because the normal polis was not much like a city, and was very much more than a state. But translation, like politics, is the art of the possible; since we have not got the thing which the Greeks called "the polis," we do not possess an equivalent word. From now on, we will avoid the misleading term "city-state," and use the Greek word instead. In this chapter we will first inquire how this political system arose, then we will try to reconstitute the word "polis" and recover its real meaning by watching it in action. It may be a long task, but all the time we shall be improving our acquaintance with the Greeks. Without a clear conception what the polis was, and what it meant to the Greeks, it is quite impossible to understand properly Greek history, the Greek mind, or the Greek achievement.

First then, what was the polis? In the *Iliad* we discern a political structure that seems not unfamiliar—a structure that can be called an advanced or a degenerate form of tribalism, according to taste. There are kings, like Achilles, who rule their people, and there is the great king, Agamemnon, King of Men, who is something like a feudal over-lord. He is under obligation, whether of right or of custom to consult the other kings or chieftains in matters of common interest. They form a regular council, and in its debates the sceptre, symbol of authority, is held by the speaker for the time being. This is recognizably European, not Oriental; Agamemnon is no despot, ruling with the unquestioned authority of a god. There are also signs of a shadowy Assembly of the People, to be consulted on important occasions: though Homer, a courtly poet, and in any case not a constitutional historian, says little about it.

Such, in outline, is the tradition about pre-conquest Greece. When the curtain goes up again after the Dark Age we see a very different picture. No longer is there a "wide-ruling Agamemnon" lording it in Mycenae. In Crete, where Idomeneus had been ruling as sole king, we find over fifty quite independent poleis, fifty small "states" in the place

of one. It is a small matter that the kings have disappeared; the important thing is that the kingdoms have gone too. What is true of Crete is
true of Greece in general, or at least of those parts which play any
considerable part in Greek history—Ionia, the islands, the Pelopon-
nesus except Arcadia, Central Greece except the western parts, and
South Italy and Sicily when they became Greek. All these were divided
into an enormous number of quite independent and autonomous political units.

It is important to realize their size. The modern reader picks up a
translation of Plato's *Republic* or Aristotle's *Politics*; He finds Plato
ordaining that his ideal city shall have 5,000 citizens, and Aristotle
that each citizen should be able to know all the others by sight; and he
smiles, perhaps, at such philosophic fantasies. But Plato and Aristotle
are not fantasts. Plato is imagining a polis on the normal Hellenic scale;
indeed he implies that many existing Greek poleis are too small—for
many had less than 5,000 citizens. Aristotle says, in his amusing way
—Aristotle sometimes sounds very like a don—that a polis of ten
citizens would be impossible, because it could not be self-sufficient, and
that a polis of a hundred thousand would be absurd, because it could
not govern itself properly. And we are not to think of these "citizens"
as a "master-class" owning and dominating thousands of slaves. The
ordinary Greek in these early centuries was a farmer, and if he owned a
slave he was doing pretty well. Aristotle speaks of a hundred thousand
citizens; if we allow each to have a wife and four children, and then
add a liberal number of slaves and resident aliens, we shall arrive at
something like a million—the population of Birmingham; and to
Aristotle an independent "state" as populous as Birmingham is a lecture-
room joke. Or we may turn from the philosophers to a practical man,
Hippodamas, who laid out the Piraeus in the most up-to-date American
style; he said that the ideal number of citizens was ten thousand, which
would imply a total population of about 100,000.

In fact, only three poleis had more than 20,000 citizens—Syracuse and
Acragas (Girgenti) in Sicily, and Athens. At the outbreak of the
Peloponnesian War the population of Attica was probably about 350,-
000, half Athenian (men, women and children), about a tenth resident
aliens, and the rest slaves. Sparta, or Lacedaemon, had a much smaller
citizenbody, though it was larger in area. The Spartans had conquered
and annexed Messenia, and possessed 3,200 square miles of territory.
By Greek standards this was an enormous area: it would take a good
walker two days to cross it. The important commercial city of Corinth
had a territory of 330 square miles—about the size of Huntingdonshire.
The island of Ceos, which is about as big as Bute, was divided into four
poleis. It had therefore four armies, four governments, possibly four

different calendars, and, it may be, four different currencies and systems of measures—though this is less likely. Mycenae was in historical times a shrunken relic of Agamemnon's capital, but still independent. She sent an army to help the Greek cause against Persia at the battle of Plataea; the army consisted of eighty men. Even by Greek standards this was small, but we do not hear that any jokes were made about an Army sharing a cab.

To think on this scale is difficult for us, who regard a state of ten million as small, and are accustomed to states which, like the U.S.A. and the U.S.S.R., are so big that they have to be referred to by their initials; but when the adjustable reader has become accustomed to the scale, he will not commit the vulgar error of confusing size with significance. The modern writer is sometimes heard to speak with splendid scorn of "those petty Greek states, with their interminable quarrels." Quite so; Plataea, Sicyon, Aegina and the rest are petty, compared with modern states. The Earth itself is petty, compared with Jupiter—but then, the atmosphere of Jupiter is mainly ammonia, and that makes a difference. We do not like breathing ammonia—and the Greeks would not much have liked breathing the atmosphere of the vast modern State. They knew of one such, the Persian Empire—and thought it very suitable, for barbarians. Difference of scale, when it is great enough, amounts to difference of kind.

But before we deal with the nature of the polis, the reader might like to know how it happened that the relatively spacious pattern of pre-Dorian Greece became such a mosaic of small fragments. The Classical scholar too would like to know; there are no records, so that all we can do is to suggest plausible reasons. There are historical, geographical and economic reasons; and when these have been duly set forth, we may conclude perhaps that the most important reason of all is simply that this is the way in which the Greeks preferred to live.

The coming of the Dorians was not an attack made by one organized nation upon another. The invaded indeed had their organization, loose though it was; some of the invaders—the main body that conquered Lacedaemon—must have been a coherent force; but others must have been small groups of raiders, profiting from the general turmoil and seizing good land where they could find it. A sign of this is that we find members of the same clan in different states. Pindar for example, was a citizen of Thebes and a member of the ancient family of the Aegidae. But there were Aegidae too in Aegina and Sparta, quite independent poleis, and Pindar addresses them as kinsmen. This particular clan therefore was split up in the invasions. In a country like Greece this would be very natural.

In a period so unsettled the inhabitants of any valley or island

might at a moment's notice be compelled to fight for their fields. Therefore a local strong-point was necessary, normally a defensible hill-top
somewhere in the plain. This, the "acropolis" ("high-town"), would
be fortified, and here would be the residence of the king. It would also
be the natural place of assembly, and the religious centre.

This is the beginning of the town. What we have to do is to give
reasons why the town grew, and why such a small pocket of people remained an independent political unit. The former task is simple. To
begin with, natural economic growth made a central market necessary.
We saw that the economic system implied by Hesiod and Homer was
"close household economy"; the estate, large or small, produced nearly
everything that it needed, and what it could not produce it did without.
As things became more stable a rather more specialized economy became possible: more goods were produced for sale. Hence the growth of
a market.

At this point we may invoke the very sociable habits of the Greeks,
ancient or modern. The English farmer likes to build his house on his
land, and to come into town when he has to. What little leisure he
has he likes to spend on the very satisfying occupation of looking over a
gate. The Greek prefers to live in the town or village, to walk out to
his work, and to spend his rather ampler leisure talking in the town or
village square. Therefore the market becomes a market-town, naturally
beneath the Acropolis. This became the centre of the communal life of
the people—and we shall see presently how important that was.

But why did not such towns form larger units? This is the important
question.

There is an economic point. The physical barriers which Greece has
so abundantly made the transport of goods difficult, except by sea, and
the sea was not yet used with any confidence. Moreover, the variety of
which we spoke earlier enabled quite a small area to be reasonably self-
sufficient for a people who made such small material demands on life as
the Greek. Both of these facts tend in the same direction; there was in
Greece no great economic interdependence, no reciprocal pull between
the different parts of the country, strong enough to counteract the desire
of the Greek to live in small communities.

There is a geographical point. It is sometimes asserted that this
system of independent poleis was imposed on Greece by the physical
character of the country. The theory is attractive, especially to those
who like to have one majestic explanation of any phenomenon, but it
does not seem to be true. It is of course obvious that the physical subdivision of the country helped; the system could not have existed, for
example, in Egypt, a country which depends entirely on the proper
management of the Nile flood, and therefore must have a central gov-

ernment. But there are countries cut up quite as much as Greece—Scotland, for instance—which have never developed the polis-system; and conversely there were in Greece many neighbouring poleis, such as Corinth and Sicyon, which remained independent of each other although between them there was no physical barrier that would seriously incommode a modern cyclist. Moreover, it was precisely the most mountainous parts of Greece that never developed poleis, or not until later days—Arcadia and Aetolia, for example, which had something like a canton-system. The polis flourished in those parts where communications were relatively easy. So that we are still looking for our explanation.

Economics and geography helped, but the real explanation is the character of the Greeks—which those determinists may explain who have the necessary faith in their omniscience. As it will take some time to deal with this, we may first clear out of the way an important historical point. How did it come about that so preposterous a system was able to last for more than twenty minutes?

The ironies of history are many and bitter, but at least this must be put to the credit of the gods, that they arranged for the Greeks to have the Eastern Mediterranean almost to themselves long enough to work out what was almost a laboratory-experiment to test how far, and in what conditions, human nature is capable of creating and sustaining a civilization. In Asia, the Hittite Empire had collapsed, the Lydian Kingdom was not aggressive, and the Persian power, which eventually overthrew Lydia, was still embryonic in the mountainous recesses of the continent; Egypt was in decay; Macedon, destined to make nonsense of the polis-system, was and long remained in a state of ineffective semi-barbarism; Rome had not yet been heard of, nor any other power in Italy. There were indeed the Phoenicians, and their western colony, Carthage, but these were traders first and last. Therefore this lively and intelligent Greek people was for some centuries allowed to live under the apparently absurd system which suited and developed its genius instead of becoming absorbed in the dull mass of a large empire, which would have smothered its spiritual growth, and made it what it afterwards became, a race of brilliant individuals and opportunists. Obviously some day somebody would create a strong centralized power in the Eastern Mediterranean—a successor to the ancient sea-power of King Minos. Would it be Greek, Oriental, or something else? This question must be the theme of a later chapter, but no history of Greece can be intelligible until one has understood what the polis meant to the Greek; and when we have understood that, we shall also understand why the Greeks developed it, and so obstinately tried to maintain it. Let us then examine the word in action.

It meant at first that which was later called the Acropolis, the stronghold of the whole community and the centre of its public life. The town which nearly always grew up around this was designated by another word, "asty." But "polis" very soon meant either the citadel or the whole people which, as it were, "used" this citadel. So we read in Thucydides, "Epidamnus is a polis on the right as you sail into the Ionian gulf." This is not like saying "Bristol is a city on the right as you sail up the Bristol Channel," for Bristol is not an independent state which might be at war with Gloucester, but only an urban area with a purely local administration. Thucydides' words imply that there is a town—though possibly a very small one—called Epidamnus, which is the political centre of the Epidamnians, who live in the territory of which the town is the centre—not the "capital"—and are Epidamnians whether they live in the town or in one of the villages in this territory.

Sometimes the territory and the town have different names. Thus, Attica is the territory occupied by the Athenian people; it comprised Athens—the "polis" in the narrower sense—the Piraeus, and many villages; but the people collectively were Athenians, not Attics, and a citizen was an Athenian in whatever part of Attica he might live.

In this sense "polis" is our "state." In Sophocles' *Antigone* Creon comes forward to make his first proclamation as king. He begins, "Gentlemen, as for the polis, the gods have brought it safely through the storm, on even keel." It is the familiar image of the Ship of State, and we think we know where we are. But later in the play he says what we should naturally translate, "Public proclamation has been made . . ." He says in fact, "It has been proclaimed to the polis . . ."—not to the "state," but to the "people." Later in the play he quarrels violently with his son; "What?" he cries, "is anyone but me to rule in this land?" Haemon answers, "It is no polis that is ruled by one man only." The answer brings out another important part of the whole conception of a polis, namely that it is a community, and that its affairs are the affairs of all. The actual business of governing might be entrusted to a monarch, acting in the name of all according to traditional usages, or to the heads of certain noble families, or to a council of citizens owning so much property, or to all the citizens. All these, and many modifications of them, were natural forms of "polity"; all were sharply distinguished by the Greek from Oriental monarchy, in which the monarch is irresponsible, not holding his powers in trust by the grace of god, but being himself a god. If there was irresponsible government there was no polis. Haemon is accusing his father of talking like a "tyrannos"[1] and thereby destroying the polis—but not "the state."

[1] I prefer to use the Greek form of this (apparently) Oriental word. It is the Greek equivalent of "dictator," but does not necessarily have the colour of our word "tyrant."

To continue our exposition of the word. The chorus in Aristophanes' *Acharnians,* admiring the conduct of the hero, turns to the audience with an appeal which I render literally, "Dost thou see, O whole polis?" The last words are sometimes translated "thou thronging city," which sounds better, but obscures an essential point, namely that the size of the polis made it possible for a member to appeal to all his fellow-citizens in person, and this he naturally did if he thought that another member of the polis had injured him. It was the common assumption of the Greeks that the polis took its origin in the desire for Justice. Individuals are lawless, but the polis will see to it that wrongs are redressed. But not by an elaborate machinery of state-justice, for such a machine could not be operated except by individuals, who may be as unjust as the original wrongdoer. The injured party will be sure of obtaining justice only if he can declare his wrongs to the whole polis. The word therefore now means "people" in actual distinction from "state."

Iocasta, the tragic Queen in the *Oedipus,* will show us a little more of the range of the word. It becomes a question if Oedipus her husband is not after all the accursed man who had killed the previous king Laius. "No, no," cries Iocasta, "it cannot be! The slave said it was 'brigands' who had attacked them, not 'a brigand.' He cannot go back on his word now. The polis heard him, not I alone." Here the word is used without any "political" association at all; it is, as it were, off duty, and signifies "the whole people." This is a shade of meaning which is not always so prominent, but is never entirely absent.

Then Demosthenes the orator talks of a man who, literally, "avoids the city"—a translation which might lead the unwary to suppose that he lived in something corresponding to the Lake District, or Purley. But the phrase "avoids the polis" tells us nothing about his domicile; it means that he took no part in public life—and was therefore something of an oddity. The affairs of the community did not interest him.

We have now learned enough about the word polis to realize that there is no possible English rendering of such a common phrase as, "It is everyone's duty to help the polis." We cannot say "help the state," for that arouses no enthusiasm; it is "the state" that takes half our incomes from us. Not "the community," for with us "the community" is too big and too various to be grasped except theoretically. One's village, one's trade union, one's class, are entities that mean something to us at once, but "work for the community," though an admirable sentiment, is to most of us vague and flabby. In the years before the war, what did most parts of Great Britain know about the depressed areas? How much do bankers, miners and farm-workers understand each other? But the "polis" every Greek knew; there it was, complete, before his eyes. He could see the fields which gave it its sustenance—or did not, if the crops failed; he could see how agriculture, trade and industry dovetailed into one another; he knew the frontiers, where they were strong and where weak; if any malcontents were planning a *coup*, it was difficult for them to conceal the fact. The entire life of the polis, and the relation between its parts, were much easier to grasp, because of the small scale of things. Therefore to say "It is everyone's duty to help the polis" was not to express a fine sentiment but to speak the plainest and most urgent common sense.[2] Public affairs had an immediacy and a concreteness which they cannot possibly have for us.

One specific example will help. The Athenian democracy taxed the rich with as much disinterest enthusiasm as the British, but this could be done in a much more gracious way, simply because the State was so small and intimate. Among us, the payer of super-tax (presumably) pays much as the income-tax payer does: he writes his cheque and thinks, "There! *That's* gone down the drain!" In Athens, the man whose wealth exceeded a certain sum had, in a yearly rota, to perform certain "liturgies"—literally, "folk-works." He had to keep a warship in commission for one year (with the privilege of commanding it, if he chose), or finance the production of plays at the Festival, or equip a religious procession. It was heavy burden, and no doubt unwelcome, but at least some fun could be got out of it and some pride taken in it. There was satisfaction and honour to be gained from producing a trilogy worthily before one's fellow-citizens. So, in countless other ways, the size of the polis made vivid and immediate, things which to us are only abstractions or wearisome duties. Naturally this cut both ways. For example, an incompetent or unlucky commander was the object not of a diffused and harmless popular indignation, but of direct accusation; he might be tried for his life before an Assembly, many of whose past members he had led to death.

Pericles' Funeral Speech, recorded or recreated by Thucydides, will illustrate this immediacy, and will also take our conception of the polis a little further. Each year, Thucydides tells us, if citizens had died in war—and they had, more often than not—a funeral oration was delivered by "a man chosen by the polis." Today, that would be someone nominated by the Prime Minister, or the British Academy, or the B.B.C. In Athens it meant that someone was chosen by the Assembly who had often spoken to that Assembly; and on this occasion Pericles spoke from a specially high platform, that his voice might reach as many as possible. Let us consider two phrases that Pericles used in that speech.

He is comparing the Athenian polis with the Spartan, and makes the point that the Spartans admit foreign visitors only grudgingly, and from

---

[2] It did not, of course, follow that the Greek obeyed common sense any oftener than we do.

time to time expel all strangers, "while we make our polis common to all." "Polis" here is not the political unit; there is no question of naturalizing foreigners—which the Greeks did rarely, simply because the polis was so intimate a union. Pericles means here: "We throw open to all our common cultural life," as is shown by the words that follow, difficult though they are to translate: "nor do we deny them any instruction or spectacle"—words that are almost meaningless until we realize that the drama, tragic and comic, the performance of choral hymns, public recitals of Homer, games, were all necessary and normal parts of "political" life. This is the sort of thing Pericles has in mind when he speaks of "instruction and spectacle," and of "making the polis open to all."

But we must go further than this. A perusal of the speech will show that in praising the Athenian polis Pericles is praising more than a state, a nation, or a people; he is praising a way of life; he means no less when, a little later, he calls Athens the "school of Hellas." And what of that? Do not we praise "the English way of life"? The difference is this; we expect our State to be quite indifferent to "the English way of life"—indeed, the idea that the State should actively try to promote it would fill most of us with alarm. The Greeks thought of the polis as an active, formative thing, training the minds and characters of the citizens; we think of it as a piece of machinery for the production of safety and convenience. The training in virtue, which the medieval state left to the Church, and the polis made its own concern, the modern state leaves to God knows what.

"Polis," then, originally "citadel," may mean as much as "the whole communal life of the people, political, cultural, moral"—even "economic," for how else are we to understand another phrase in this same speech, "the produce of the whole world comes to us, because of the magnitude of our polis"? This must mean "our national wealth."

Religion too was bound up with the polis—though not every form of religion.[3] The Olympian gods were indeed worshipped by Greeks everywhere, but each polis had, if not its own gods, at least its own particular cults of these gods. Thus, Athena of the Brazen House was worshipped at Sparta, but to the Spartans Athena was never what she was to the Athenians, "Athena Polias," Athena guardian of the City. So Hera, in Athens, was a goddess worshipped particularly by women, as the goddess of hearth and home, but in Argos "Argive Hera" was the supreme deity of the people. We have in these gods tribal deities, like Jehovah, who exist as it were on two levels at once, as gods of the individual polis, and gods of the whole Greek race. But beyond these

[3]Not the mystery-religions.

Olympians, each polis had its minor local deities, "heroes" and nymphs, each worshipped with his immemorial rite, and scarcely imagined to exist outside the particular locality where the rite was performed. So that in spite of the panhellenic Olympian system, and in spite of the philosophic spirit which made merely tribal gods impossible for the Greek, there is a sense in which it is true to say that the polis is an independent religious, as well as political, unit. The tragic poets at least could make use of the old belief that the gods desert a city which is about to be captured. The Gods are the unseen partners in the city's welfare.

How intimately religious and "political" thinking were connected we can best see from the *Oresteia* of Aeschylus. This trilogy is built around the idea of Justice. It moves from chaos to order, from conflict to reconciliation; and it moves on two planes at once, the human and the divine. In the *Agamemnon* we see one of the moral Laws of the universe, that punishment must follow crime, fulfilled in the crudest possible way; one crime evokes another crime to avenge it, in apparently endless succession—but always with the sanction of Zeus. In the *Choephori* this series of crimes reaches its climax when Orestes avenges his father by killing his mother. He does this with repugnance, but he is commanded to do it by Apollo, the son and the mouthpiece of Zeus —Why? Because in murdering Agamemnon the King and her husband, Clytemnestra has committed a crime which, unpunished, would shatter the very fabric of society. It is the concern of the Olympian gods to defend Order; they are particularly the gods of the Polis. But Orestes' matricide outrages the deepest human instincts; he is therefore implacably pursued by other deities, the Furies. The Furies have no interest in social order, but they cannot permit this outrage on the sacredness of the blood-tie, which it is their office to protect. In the *Eumenides* there is a terrific conflict between the ancient Furies and the younger Olympians over the unhappy Orestes. The solution is that Athena comes with a new dispensation from Zeus. A jury of Athenian citizens is empanelled to try Orestes on the Acropolis where he has fled for protection—this being the first meeting of the Council of the Areopagus. The votes on either side are equal; therefore, as an act of mercy, Orestes is acquitted. The Furies, cheated of their legitimate prey, threaten Attica with destruction, but Athena persuades them to make their home in Athens, with their ancient office not abrogated (as at first they think) but enhanced, since henceforth they will punish violence within the polis, not only within the family.

So, to Aeschylus, the mature polis becomes the means by which the Law is satisfied without producing chaos, since public justice supersedes private vengeance; and the claims of authority are reconciled with the instincts of humanity. The trilogy ends with an impressive piece of pageantry. The awful Furies exchange their black robes for red ones, no longer Furies, but "Kindly Ones" (Eumenides) ; no longer enemies of Zeus, but his willing and honoured agents, defenders of his now perfected social order against intestine violence. Before the eyes of the Athenian citizens assembled in the theatre just under the Acropolis—and indeed guided by citizen-marshals—they pass out of the theatre to their new home on the other side of the Acropolis. Some of the most acute of man's moral and social problems have been solved, and the means of the reconciliation is the Polis.

A few minutes later, on that early spring day of 458 B.C., the citizens too would leave the theatre, and by the same exits as the Eumenides. In what mood? Surely no audience has had such an experience since. At the time, the Athenian polis was confidently riding the crest of the wave. In this trilogy there was exaltation, for they had seen their polis emerge as the pattern of Justice, or Order, of what the Greeks called Cosmos; the polis, they saw, was—or could be—the very crown and summit of things. They had seen their goddess herself acting as President of the first judicial tribunal—a steadying and sobering thought. But there was more than this. The rising democracy had recently curtailed the powers of the ancient Court of the Areopagus, and the reforming statesman had been assassinated by his political enemies. What of the Eumenides, the awful inhabitants of the land, the transformed Furies, whose function it was to avenge the shedding of a kinsman's blood? There was warning here, as well as exaltation, in the thought that the polis had its divine as well as its human members. There was Athena, one of those Olympians who had presided over the formation of ordered society, and there were the more primitive deities who had been persuaded by Athena to accept this pattern of civilized life, and were swift to punish any who, by violence from within, threatened its stability.

To such an extent was the religious thought of Aeschylus intertwined with the idea of the polis; and not of Aeschylus alone, but of many other Greek thinkers too—notably of Socrates, Plato, and Aristotle. Aristotle made a remark which we most inadequately translate "Man is a political animal." What Aristotle really said is "Man is a creature who lives in a polis"; and what he goes on to demonstrate, in his *Politics,* is that the polis is the only framework within which man can fully realize his spiritual, moral and intellectual capacities.

Such are some of the implications of this word: we shall meet more later, for I have deliberately said little about its purely "political" side —to emphasize the fact that it is so much more than a form of political organization. The polis was a living community, based on kinship, real or assumed—a kind of extended family, turning as much as possible of life into family life, and of course having its family quarrels, which were the more bitter because they were family quarrels.

This it is that explains not only the polis but also much of what the Greek made and thought, that he was essentially social. In the winning of his livelihood he was essentially individualist: in the filling of his life he was essentially "communist." Religion, art, games, the discussion of things—all these were needs of life that could be fully satisfied only through the polis—not, as with us, through voluntary associations of like-minded people, or through *entrepreneurs* appealing to individuals. (This partly explains the difference between Greek drama and the modern cinema.) Moreover, he wanted to play his own part in running the affairs of the community. When we realize how many of the necessary, interesting and exciting activities of life the Greek enjoyed through the polis, all of them in the open air, within sight of the same acropolis, with the same ring of mountains or of sea visibly enclosing the life of every member of the state—then it becomes possible to understand Greek history, to understand that in spite of the promptings of common sense the Greek could not bring himself to sacrifice the polis, with its vivid and comprehensive life, to a wider but less interesting unity. We may perhaps record an Imaginary Conversation between an Ancient Greek and a member of the Athenaeum. The member regrets the lack of political sense shown by the Greeks. The Greek replies, "How many clubs are there in London?" The member, at a guess, says about five hundred. The Greek then says, "Now, if all these combined, what splendid premises they could build. They could have a club-house as big as Hyde Park." "But," says the member, "that would no longer be a club." "Precisely," says the Greek, "and a polis as big as yours is no longer a polis."

After all, modern Europe, in spite of its common culture, common interests, and ease of communication, finds it difficult to accept the idea of limiting national sovereignty, though this would increase the security of life without notably adding to its dullness; the Greek had possibly more to gain by watering down the polis—but how much more to lose. It was not common sense that made Achilles great, but certain other qualities.

Thucydides
Pericles' Funeral Oration

Most of my predecessors in this place have commended him who made this speech part of the law, telling us that it is well that it should be delivered at the burial of those who fall in battle. For myself, I should have thought that the worth which had displayed itself in deeds, would be sufficiently rewarded by honours also shown by deeds; such as you now see in this funeral prepared at the people's cost. And I could have wished that the reputations of many brave men were not to be imperilled in the mouth of a single individual, to stand or fall according as he spoke well or ill. For it is hard to speak properly upon a subject where it is even difficult to convince your hearers that you are speaking the truth. On the one hand, the friend who is familiar with every fact of the story, may think that some point has not been set forth with that fullness which he wishes and knows it to deserve; on the other, he who is a stranger to the matter may be led by envy to suspect exaggeration if he hears anything above his own nature. For men can endure to hear others praised only so long as they can severally persuade themselves of their own ability to equal the actions recounted: when this point is passed, envy comes in and with it incredulity. However, since our ancestors have stamped this custom with their approval, it becomes my duty to obey the law and to try to satisfy your several wishes and opinions as best I may.

I shall begin with our ancestors: it is both just and proper that they should have the honour of the first mention on an occasion like the present. They dwelt in the country without break in the succession from generation to generation, and handed it down free to the present time by their valour. And if our more remote ancestors deserve praise, much more do our own fathers, who added to their inheritance the empire which we now possess, and spared no pains to be able to leave their acquisitions to us of the present generation. Lastly, there are few parts of our dominions that have not been augmented by those of us here, who are still more or less in the vigour of life; while the mother

From *The History of the Peloponnesian War* by Thucydides. Translated by Richard Crawley, Everyman's Library Edition. Reprinted by permission of E. P. Dutton & Co., Inc.

country has been furnished by us with everything that can enable her
to depend on her own resources whether for war or for peace. That part
of our history which tells of the military achievements which gave us
our several possessions, or of the ready valour with which either we or
our fathers stemmed the tide of Hellenic or foreign aggression, is a
theme too familiar to my hearers for me to dilate on, and I shall therefore pass it by. But what was the road by which we reached our position, what the form of government under which our greatness grew,
what the national habits out of which it sprang; these are questions
which I may try to solve before I proceed to my panegyric upon these
men; since I think this to be a subject upon which on the present
occasion a speaker may properly dwell, and to which the whole assemblage, whether citizens or foreigners, may listen with advantage.

Our constitution does not copy the laws of neighbouring states; we
are rather a pattern to others than imitators ourselves. Its administration favours the many instead of the few; this is why it is called a
democracy. If we look to the laws, they afford equal justice to all in
their private differences; if no social standing, advancement in public
life falls to reputation for capacity, class considerations not being allowed to interfere with merit; nor again does poverty bar the way, if a
man is able to serve the state, he is not hindered by the obscurity of
his condition. The freedom which we enjoy in our government extends
also to our ordinary life. There, far from exercising a jealous surveillance over each other, we do not feel called upon to be angry with
our neighbour for doing what he likes, or even to indulge in those
injurious looks which cannot fail to be offensive, although they inflict
no positive penalty. But all this ease in our private relations does not
make us lawless as citizens. Against this fear is our chief safeguard,
teaching us to obey the magistrates and the laws, particularly such as
regard the protection of the injured, whether they are actually on the
statute book, or belong to that code which, although unwritten, yet
cannot be broken without acknowledged disgrace.

Further, we provide plenty of means for the mind to refresh itself
from business. We celebrate games and sacrifices all the year round, and
the elegance of our private establishments forms a daily source of
pleasure and helps to banish the spleen; while the magnitude of our
city draws the produce of the world into our harbour, so that to the
Athenian the fruits of other countries are as familiar a luxury as those
of his own.

If we turn to our military policy, there also we differ from our
antagonists. We throw open our city to the world, and never by alien
acts exclude foreigners from any opportunity of learning or observing,
although the eyes of an enemy may occasionally profit by our liberality;
trusting less in system and policy than to the native spirit of our citizens;

while in education, where our rivals from their very cradles by a painful discipline seek after manliness, at Athens we live exactly as we please, and yet are just as ready to encounter every legitimate danger. In proof of this it may be noticed that the Lacedæmonians do not invade our country alone, but bring with them all their confederates; while we Athenians advance unsupported into the territory of a neighbour, and fighting upon a foreign soil usually vanquish with ease men who are defending their homes. Our united force was never yet encountered by any enemy, because we have at once to attend to our marine and to dispatch our citizens by land upon a hundred different services; so that, wherever they engage with some such fraction of our strength, a success against a detachment is magnified into a victory over the nation, and a defeat into a reverse suffered at the hands of our entire people. And yet if the habits not of labour but of ease, and courage not of art but of nature, we are still willing to encounter danger, we have the double advantage of escaping the experience of hardships in anticipation and of facing them in the hour of need as fearlessly as those who are never free from them.

Nor are these the only points in which our city is worthy of admiration. We cultivate refinement without extravagance and knowledge without effeminacy; wealth we employ more for use than for show, and place the real disgrace of poverty not in owning to the fact but in declining the struggle against it. Our public men have, besides politics, their private affairs to attend to, and our ordinary citizens, though occupied with the pursuits of industry, are still fair judges of public matters; for, unlike any other nation, regarding him who takes no part in these duties not as unambitious but as useless, we Athenians are able to judge at all events if we cannot originate, and instead of looking on discussion as a stumbling-block in the way of action, we think it an indispensable preliminary to any wise action at all. Again, in our enterprises we present the singular spectacle of daring and deliberation, each carried to its highest point, and both united in the same persons; although usually decision is the fruit of ignorance, hesitation of reflection. But the palm of courage will surely be adjudged most justly to those, who best know the difference between hardship and pleasure and yet are never tempted to shrink from danger. In generosity we are equally singular, acquiring our friends by conferring, not by receiving, favours. Yet, of course, the doer of the favour is the firmer friend of the two, in order by continued kindness to keep the recipient in his debt; while the debtor feels less keenly from the very consciousness that the return he makes will be a payment, not a free gift. And it is only the Athenians who, fearless of consequences, confer their benefits not from calculations of expediency, but in the confidence of liberality.

In short, I say that as a city we are the school of Hellas; while I doubt if the world can produce a man, who where he has only himself to depend upon, is equal to so many emergencies, and graced by so happy a versatility, as the Athenian. And that this is no mere boast thrown out for the occasion, but plain matter of fact, the power of the state acquired by these habits proves. For Athens alone of her contemporaries is found when tested to be greater than her reputation, and alone gives no occasion to her assailants to blush at the antagonist by whom they have been worsted, or to her subjects to question her title by merit to rule. Rather, the admiration of the present and succeeding ages will be ours, since we have not left our power without witness, but have shown it by might proofs; and far from needing a Homer for your panegyrist, or other of his craft whose verses might charm for the moment only for the impression which they gave to melt at the touch of fact, we have forced every sea and land to be the highway of our daring, and everywhere, whether for evil or for good, have left imperishable monuments behind us. Such is the Athens for which these men, in the assertion of their resolve not to lose her, nobly fought and died; and well may every one of their survivors be ready to suffer in her cause.

Indeed if I have dwelt at some length upon the character of our country, it has been to show that our stake in the struggle is not the same as theirs who have no such blessings to lose, and also that the panegyric of the men over whom I am now speaking might be by definite proofs established. That panegyric is now in a great measure complete; for the Athens that I have celebrated is only what the heroism of these and their like have made her, men whose fame, unlike that of most Hellenes, will be found to be only commensurate with their deserts. And if a test of worth be wanted, it is to be found in their closing scene, and this not only in the cases in which it set the final seal upon their merit, but also in those in which it gave the first intimation of their having any. For there is justice in the claim that steadfastness in his country's battles should be as a cloak to cover a man's other imperfections; since the good action has blotted out the bad, and his merit as a citizen more than outweighed his demerits as an individual. But none of these allowed either wealth with its prospect of future enjoyment to unnerve his spirit, or poverty with its hope of a day of freedom and riches to tempt him to shrink from danger. No, holding that vengeance upon their enemies was more to be desired than any personal blessings, and reckoning this to be the most glorious of hazards, they joyfully determined to accept the risk, to make sure of their vengeance and to let their wishes wait; and while committing to hope the uncertainty of final success, in the business before them they thought fit to act boldly and trust in themselves. Thus choosing to die resisting, rather than to live submitting, they fled only from dishonour, but met danger face to face, and after one brief moment, while at the summit of their fortune, escaped, not from their fear, but from their glory.

So died these men as became Athenians. You, their survivors, must determine to have as unfaltering a resolution in the field, though you may pray that it may have a happier issue. And not contented with ideas derived only from words of the advantages which are bound up with the defence of your country, though these would furnish a valuable text to a speaker even before an audience so alive to them as the present, you must yourselves realize the power of Athens, and feed your eyes upon her from day to day, till love of her fills your hearts; and then when all her greatness shall break upon you, you must reflect that it was by courage, sense of duty, and a keen feeling of honour in action that men were enabled to win all this, and that no personal failure in an enterprise could make them consent to deprive their country of their valour, but they laid it at her feet as the most glorious contribution that they could offer. For this offering of their lives made in common by them all they each of them individually received that renown which never grows old, and for a sepulchre, not so much that in which their bones have been deposited, but that noblest of shrines wherein their glory is laid up to be eternally remembered upon every occasion on which deed or story shall call for its commemoration. For heroes have the whole earth for their tomb; and in lands far from their own, where the column with its epitaph declares it, there is enshrined in every breast a record unwritten with no tablet to preserve it, except that of the heart. These take as your model, and judging happiness to be the fruit of freedom and freedom of valour, never decline the dangers of war. For it is not the miserable that would most justly be unsparing of their lives; these have nothing to hope for: it is rather they to whom continued life may bring reverses as yet unknown, and to whom a fall, if it came, would be most tremendous in its consequences. And surely, to a man of spirit, the degradation of cowardice must be immeasurably more grievous than the unfelt death which strikes him in the midst of his strength and patriotism!

Comfort, therefore, not condolence, is what I have to offer to the parents of the dead who may be here. Numberless are the chances to which, as they know, the life of a man is subject; but fortunate indeed are they who draw for their lot a death so glorious as that which has caused your mourning, and to whom life has been so exactly measured as to terminate in the happiness in which it has been passed. Still I know that this is a hard saying, especially when those in question of whom you will constantly be reminded by seeing in the homes of others of which once you also boasted: for grief is felt not so much for the want of what we have never known, as for the loss of that to which we have been long accustomed. Yet you who are still of an age to beget children must bear up in the hope of having others in their stead; not only will they help you to forget those whom you have lost, but will be to the state at once a reinforcement and a security; for never can a fair or just policy be expected of the citizen who does not, like his fellows, bring to the decision the interests and apprehensions of a father. While those of you who have passed your prime must congratulate yourselves with the thought that the best part of your life was fortunate, and that the brief span that remains will be cheered by the fame of the departed. For it is only the love of honour that never grows old; and honour it is, not gain, as some would have it, that rejoices the heart of age and helplessness.

Turning to the sons or brothers of the dead, I see an arduous struggle before you. When a man is gone, all are wont to praise him, and should your merit be ever so transcendent, you will still find it difficult not merely to overtake, but even to approach their renown. The living have envy to contend with, while those who are no longer in our path are honoured with a goodwill into which rivalry does not enter. On the other hand, if I must say anything on the subject of female excellence to those of you who will now be in widowhood, it will be all comprised in this brief exhortation. Great will be your glory in not falling short of your natural character; and greatest will be hers who is least talked of among the men whether for good or for bad.

My task is now finished. I have performed it to the best of my ability, and in word, at least, the requirements of the law are now satisfied. If deeds be in question, those who are here interred have received part of their honours already, and for the rest, their children will be brought up till manhood at the public expense: the state thus offers a valuable prize, as the garland of victory in this race of valour, for the reward both of those who have fallen and their survivors. And where the rewards for merit are greatest, there are found the best citizens.

And now that you have brought to a close your lamentations for your relatives, you may depart.

PART II

Kinds of Communities

CHAPTER 5

Town and Village

Through most of the recorded life of mankind most men have lived in villages, small settlements of peasants and farmers. We have seen one such settlement described in Singer's "Old Goray"; it differed markedly from the norm, however, in being dominated by craft and trade. More typical is Van Wyck Brooks' picture of an American village in the early nineteenth century. It is a community almost as isolated as Goray, and almost as self sufficient. It too has developed a strong and binding culture, resting upon the commitment of its members to this particular town.

In such a situation *place* becomes sacred. In the United States the view of land as place was widespread and important during the period before the Civil War. The value of land as place was reinforced by the nature of the economy, for after all most of the residents drew their livelihood directly from this soil, and few of them had seen any other place that differed much from theirs. Then, too, government in that period was usually local, and representation at higher levels was by locality. No wonder politics ranked first as a subject for discussion; religion, important as it was, was of a lesser order. One might say that politics was the formal religion of place in early America, a local patriotism we now find hard to imagine.

For the pastoral village Van Wyck Brooks describes is dead. Like most dead things it is mythologized, and in his picture there is more than a little pious nostalgia. The harsh long hours of physical labor, the narrow outlooks, the rigid limitations of that world, would strike most of us as oppressive; the coercive religion and the pressure of gossip and public opinion on the deviant would seem tyrannous. It is easy to imagine oneself spending most of one's time in jail.

Thorstein Veblen cannot be accused of glamorizing the country town of his day. To be sure, he is writing of a later period in history, one which, he thinks, began after the Civil War and reached its peak around the turn of the century. It is a period in which land as *place* was rapidly transformed into land as *property*. Speculation and salesmanship were the order of the day. With malicious glee Veblen traces all that follows from commitment to "self help and cupidity," noting its ramifications for religion, manners, and morals.

Even as he described his archetypal "country town," however, it was in process of losing its dominance over American society. He notes the reasons—technological change and the growing network of a national society, which destroyed the monopoly of Main Street and set it into competition with larger cities and enterprises. In his opinion, however, the thinking and the mores of Main Street live on, translated into the behavior of "Big Business." And it must be admitted that even in our wealthy and massive metropolitan areas today, the commitment to land as property continually frustrates our efforts to treat it as place, as sacred symbol and resource for community.

These two versions of small-town America are not without overlap, though much has happened from the time of Brooks' town to Veblen's. In both we still see limitation of interaction, imposed by the cost of travel and communication—that is, the friction of space. In both the basic source of wealth is the soil. In both there is a high degree of cultural uniformity. The differences are great, however, and they are probably magnified by the authors' differing styles of thought and language. Brooks's idyllic picture of bucolic early America reflects his fondness for the period; Veblen's mordant irony reflects his basic commitment to craft and labor and his contempt for the businessman's ethos, which he saw as dominating and corrupting the total society. Then, too, Brooks was a literary historian, a teller of tales; Veblen was an economist, an analyst of interests and the allocation of scarce resources.

The small town has been glorified and reviled. As a symbol of that perfect community we have never known, it attracts; as a symbol of constraint and parochialism, limiting the universality which we believe a good culture should embody, it repels. Revolt from the village and return to the village are continuing themes in human thought.

Van Wyck Brooks
The Coast and the Hinterland

The mansion people formed an invisible chain, stretching across the country, through which the currents of the great world passed. Outside, the village life continued in its primal innocence. Even the rural aristocracy, touched as it was by foreign influences, retained its strong indigenous character. America was the only land it knew, or that its forebears had known for seven generations. In towns near the seaboard, one found a loyalist family here and there. A few old ladies lingered on who spoke of themselves as "eating the King's bread," because their father had fought on the Tory side and they still received a British pension. Miss Debby Barker of Hingham, a town that was much like "Cranford"—as everyone saw at once when the book came out— went into mourning, donned a purple dress, at the death of George the Fourth. There were many Miss Debby Barkers in Boston and Newport, but most of the country aristocracy had always opposed the crown. The village folk in general, mainly of the purest English stock, carried on their ancient village ways, not in a spirit of Anglophobia, but rather as if England had never existed.[1] They formed a self-sufficing Yankee world, separated by a pathless ocean from the ways of the mother-country. They were farmers almost to a man, aside from a few mechanics. Most of the ministers tilled their own soil. Each village had its Indian population, a cluster of huts on the outskirts, a few negroes who had once been slaves, sometimes two or three Irishmen and one or two beggars and paupers. The larger towns had public reading-rooms, possibly a Franklin Institute, where a few odd volumes of Shakespeare, Hume and Milton, Young's *Night Thoughts,* Thomson's *Seasons,* Rollin's *Ancient*

[1]Anglomania, in all its forms, social or poetic, was confined to the fashionable urban classes. The British, from the rural point of view, were as foreign as any other foreigners, and most of the country-people, high and low, deprecated intermarriage with them. Miss Fortune, in *The Wide, Wide World,* undoubtedly expressed their attitude: "I wish Morgan could have had the gumption to marry in his own country; but he must go running after a Scotchwoman! A Yankee would have brought up his child to be worth something. Give me Yankees!"

History, filled the shelves with old books of sermons, Owen on Sin or *An Arrow Against Profane and Promiscuous Dancing.*

Every village had its squire and parson, a Deacon Hart, living on the turnpike, where he raised the golden squashes, the full-orbed pumpkins, the rustling Indian corn and the crimson currants that straggled by the painted picket fence. Further on, dwelt some Abihu Peters. An Ebenezer Camp contrived the shoes. A Patience Mosely made the village bonnets, hard by Comfort Scran's general store. There were always two or three hired men, a handy-andy, usually a fiddler, who had made his violin from the bole of a maple and strung his bow from the tail of the family horse. Now and then one found a village drunkard, who might have been a poet, perhaps some scalawag of a Stephen Burroughs, the worst boy in the town, who was often kept in chains in the county jail. There were a few Yankees of the swindling kind who found their proper sphere in the peddling business. Sometimes they were caught as counterfeiters. The Yankee mind was quick and sharp, but mainly it was singularly honest—as honest as the men of Maine a hundred years later. Everyone who travelled through the country marvelled that the New England farmers' doors were seldom locked or barred, even at night; and, while the land flowed with rum, and even overflowed,[2] the great popular drink was homely cider. The cider-barrel was never empty at weddings and ordinations, on training-days, at huskings, at Thanksgiving, when the sounds of chopping and pounding and baking and brewing rose from the smoke-browned walls of the farmhouse kitchen. Those who grew up in these inland regions, looking back on the old village life, saw it in the light of Goldsmith's Auburn, abounding in mild virtues, faithful swains, rural virgins, peace and innocence. The goodman's daughters made his shirts and stockings; his garments were provided by his flocks and herds. So were those of the women-folk, who, as they spun and knitted, discussed the weekly sermon.

For religion filled the horizon of the village people, all that was left by politics and law. On Sunday morning, in the church, one heard the Psalms repeated, in Sternhold and Hopkins's version, which some of the old women believed were the very strains King David had sung to his harp,—"The Lord will come, and he will not," and, after a pause, another line, which most of the children thought was another idea, "Keep silence, but speak out." The old-fashioned polemical sermon followed, fortified with texts and garnished with quotations in Greek and Hebrew, for most of the clergy were still learned men. Perhaps only the week before, the minister had driven in his one-horse

[2]When the Reverend John Pierpont made his pilgrimage to the Holy Land, the first object he saw, on the wharf at Beirut, was a hogshead of New England rum.

chaise twenty or thirty miles across the country to meet some reverend brother and settle some nice point in theology on which he was writing a treatise: he could not agree with Dr. Stern that God had created sin deliberately, and he wished to lay his case before his flock. Many of the village ministers, whose cocked hats and gold-headed canes were symbols of their unquestioned authority, as shepherds and judges of the people devoted their lives to writing these treatises. The farmers discussed them over their ploughs, and the farm-wives over their spinningwheels. For religion was their romance. They named their children after the Biblical heroes, and the Bible places, Chimmin and the Isles, Dan and Beersheba, Kedar and Tarshish were stations on the map of their El Dorado. The congregations followed the web of the sermons with a keen and anxious watchfulness, eager to learn the terms of their damnation. And they talked about fate and freedom and how evil came, and what death is, and the life to come, as familiarly as they talked of their crops and the weather.

All New England seethed with these discussions. One heard about "potential presence" and "representative presence" and "representative identity," and Dr. Bancroft's sermon on the fourth commandment. Blacksmiths and farriers, youths and maidens argued about free will and predestination, about "natural ability" and "moral ability" and "God's efficiency" and "man's agency." Sometimes it was a morbid interest, when the children sat on "anxious seats" and wept over their wicked little hearts. The conscience of New England was precocious. Even Cotton Mather had observed that "splenetic maladies" throve among the people, maladies that were scarcely allayed by some of the more emotional preachers. One heard of "sweating" sermons and "fainting" sermons, followed by "convulsion-fit" sermons, in the best tradition of Whitefield.[3] Sometimes, in the frontier settlements, on the borders of the wilderness, in the forests of New Hampshire and Vermont, where men almost forgot that they had voices, and only the axe and the hammer broke the silence, where, on the frozen slopes, the snow fell for days together, strange and terrible thoughts rose in the mind. A Green Mountain boy with an axe in his hand might sing his happy songs in the busy summer, rejoicing in the Alpine air, scented with fir and hemlock, for the Green Mountain boys had their mountain freedom. But when the snow began to fall, and he sat brooding beside the stove, over his calfskin Bible, in the close, foul air of the farmhouse kitchen, digesting food that was never meant for man, then, as he conned the mystical Revelations and the savage mythology of the ancient Jews, visions of blood-atonement swept his brain. Among the

[3]See the Reverend Mr. Stoker, in Holmes's *The Guardian Angel.*

native ballads of the Vermonters, bloodshed was an omnipresent theme. They felt the presence of the God of Vengeance. They heard voices that were not benign. From them was to spring, a few years hence, the cult of Joseph Smith and Brigham Young,[4] where flourished now, as foretastes of the Mormons, the quiet murder and the loud revival.

[4]Both born in Vermont.

Thorstein Veblen
The Case of America:
The Country Town

The country town of the great American farming region is the perfect flower of self-help and cupidity standardised on the American plan. Its name may be Spoon River or Gopher Prairie, or it may be Emporia or Centralia or Columbia. The pattern is substantially the same, and is repeated several thousand times with a faithful perfection which argues that there is no help for it, that it is worked out by uniform circumstances over which there is no control, and that it wholly falls in with the spirit of things and answers to the enduring aspirations of the community. The country town is one of the great American institutions; perhaps the greatest, in the sense that it has had and continues to have a greater part than any other in shaping public sentiment and giving character to American culture.

The location of any given town has commonly been determined by collusion between "interested parties" with a view to speculation in real estate, and it continues through its life-history (hitherto) to be managed as a real estate "proposition." Its municipal affairs, its civic pride, its community interest, converge upon its real-estate values, which are invariably of a speculative character, and which all its loyal citizens are intent on "booming" and "boosting"—that is to say, lifting still farther off the level of actual ground-values as measured by the uses to which the ground is turned. Seldom do the current (speculative) values of the town's real estate exceed the use-value of it by less than 100 per cent; and never do they exceed the actual values by less than 200 per cent, as shown by the estimates of the tax assessor; nor do the loyal citizens ever cease their endeavours to lift the speculative values to something still farther out of touch with the material facts. A country town which does not answer to these specifications is "a dead one," one that has failed to "make good," and need not be counted with, except as a warning to the unwary "boomer."[1] Real estate is the

From *The Portable Veblen* edited by Max Lerner. Copyright 1923 by B. W. Huebsch, 1951 by Ann B. Sims. Reprinted by permission of The Viking Press, Inc.
[1]"The great American game," they say, is Poker. Just why Real Estate should not come in for honourable mention in that way is not to be explained off hand. And

one community interest that binds the townsmen with a common bond;
and it is highly significant—perhaps it is pathetic, perhaps admirable—
that those inhabitants of the town who have no holdings of real estate
and who never hope to have any will commonly also do their little
best to inflate the speculative values by adding the clamour of their
unpaid chorus to the paid clamour of the professional publicity-agents,
at the cost of so adding a little something to their own cost of living in
the enhanced rentals and prices out of which the expenses of publicity
are to be met.

Real estate is an enterprise in "futures," designed to get something
for nothing from the unwary, of whom it is believed by experienced
persons that "there is one born every minute." So, farmers and townsmen together throughout the great farming region are pilgrims of hope
looking forward to the time when the community's advancing needs
will enable them to realise on the inflated values of their real estate,
or looking more immediately to the chance that one or another of those
who are "born every minute" may be so ill advised as to take them at
their word and become their debtors in the amount which they say
their real estate is worth. The purpose of country-town real estate, as of
farm real estate in a less extreme degree, is to realise on it. This is
the common bond of community interest which binds and animates the
business community of the country town. In this enterprise there is con-
certed action and a spirit of solidarity, as well as a running business of
mutual manoeuvring to get the better of one another. For eternal vigi-
lance is the price of country-town real estate, being an enterprise in
salesmanship.

Aside from this common interest in the town's inflated real estate,
the townsmen are engaged in a vigilant rivalry, being competitors in
the traffic carried on with the farm population. The town is a retail
trading-station, where farm produce is bought and farm supplies are
sold, and there are always more traders than are necessary to take care
of this retail trade. So that they are each and several looking to increase
their own share in this trade at the expense of their neighbours in the
same line. There is always more or less active competition, often under-
hand. But this does not hinder collusion between the competitors with
a view to maintain and augment their collective hold on the trade with
their farm population.

From an early point in the life-history of such a town collusion

---

an extended exposition of the reasons why would be tedious and perhaps distasteful,
besides calling for such expert discrimination as quite exceeds the powers of a
layman in these premises. But even persons who are laymen on both heads will
recognise the same family traits in both.

habitually becomes the rule, and there is commonly a well recognised ethical code of collusion governing the style and limits of competitive manoeuvres which any reputable trader may allow himself. In effect, the competition among business concerns engaged in any given line of traffic is kept well in hand by a common understanding, and the traders as a body direct their collective efforts to getting what can be got out of the underlying farm population. It is on this farm trade also, and on the volume and increase of it, past and prospective, that the real-estate values of the town rest. As one consequence, the volume and profit of the farm trade is commonly over-stated, with a view to enhancing the town's real-estate values.

Quite as a matter of course the business of the town arranges itself under such regulations and usages that it foots up to a competition, not between the business concerns, but between town and country, between traders and customers. And quite as a matter of course, too, the number of concerns doing business in any one town greatly exceeds what is necessary to carry on the traffic; with the result that while the total profits of the business in any given town are inordinately large for the work done, the profits of any given concern are likely to be modest enough. The more successful ones among them commonly do very well and come in for large returns on their outlay, but the average returns per concern or per man are quite modest, and the less successful ones are habitually doing business within speaking-distance of bankruptcy. The number of failures is large, but they are habitually replaced by others who still have something to lose. The conscientiously habitual overstatements of the real-estate interests continually draw new traders into the town, for the retail trade of the town also gets its quota of such persons as are born every minute, who then transiently become super-numerary retail traders. Many fortunes are made in the country towns, often fortunes of very respectable proportions, but many smaller for-tunes are also lost.

Neither the causes nor the effects of this state of things have been expounded by the economists, nor has it found a place in the many formulations of theory that have to do with the retail trade; presum-ably because it is all, under the circumstances, so altogether "natural" and unavoidable. Exposition of the obvious is a tedious employment, and a recital of commonplaces does not hold the interest of readers or audience. Yet, for completeness of the argument, it seems necessary here to go a little farther into the details and add something on the reasons for this arrangement. However obvious and natural it may be it is after all serious enough to merit the attention of anyone who is interested in the economic situation as it stands, or in finding a way out of this situation; which is just now (1923) quite perplexing, as the futile endeavours of the statesmen will abundantly demonstrate.

However natural and legitimate it all undoubtedly may be, the arrangement as it runs today imposes on the country's farm industry an annual overhead charge which runs into ten or twelve figures, and all to the benefit of no one. This overhead charge of billions, due to duplication of work, personnel, equipment, and traffic, in the country towns is, after all, simple and obvious waste. Which is perhaps to be deprecated, although one may well hesitate to find fault with it all, inasmuch as it is all a simple and obvious outcome of those democratic principles of self-help and cupidity on which the commonwealth is founded. These principles are fundamentally and eternally right and good—so long as popular sentiment runs to that effect—and they are to be accepted gratefully, with the defects of their qualities. The whole arrangement is doubtless all right and worth its cost; indeed it is avowed to be the chief care and most righteous solicitude of the constituted authorities to maintain and cherish it all.

To an understanding of the country town and its place in the economy of American farming it should be noted that in the great farming regions any given town has a virtual monopoly of the trade within the territory tributary to it. This monopoly is neither complete nor indisputable; it does not cover all lines of traffic equally nor is outside competition completely excluded in any line. But the broad statement is quite sound, that within its domain any given country town in the farming country has a virtual monopoly of trade in those main lines of business in which the townsmen are chiefly engaged. And the townsmen are vigilant in taking due precautions that this virtual monopoly shall not be broken in upon. It may be remarked by the way that this characterisation applies to the country towns of the great farming country, and only in a less degree to the towns of the industrial and outlying sections.

Under such a (virtual) monopoly the charge collected on the traffic adjusts itself, quite as a matter of course, to what the traffic will bear. It has no other relation to the costs or the use-value of the service rendered. But what the traffic will bear is something to be determined by experience and is subject to continued readjustment and revision, with the effect of unremittingly keeping the charge close up to the practicable maximum. Indeed, there is reason to believe that the townsmen are habitually driven by a conscientious cupidity and a sense of equity to push the level of charges somewhat over the maximum; that is to say, over the rate which would yield them the largest net return. Since there are too many of them they are so placed as habitually to feel that they come in for something short of their just deserts, and their endeavour to remedy this state of things is likely to lead to overcharging rather than the reverse.

What the traffic will bear in this retail trade is what the farm population will put up with, without breaking away and finding their necessary supplies and disposing of their marketable products elsewhere, in some other town, through itinerant dealers, by recourse to brokers at a distance, through the mail-order concerns, and the like. The two dangerous outside channels of trade appear to be the rival country towns and the mail-order houses, and of these the mail-order houses are apparently the more real menace as well as the more dreaded. Indeed they are quite cordially detested by right-minded country-town dealers. The rival country towns are no really grave menace to the usurious charges of any community of country-town business men, since they are all and several in the same position, and none of them fails to charge all comers all that the traffic will bear.

There is also another limiting condition to be considered in determing what the traffic will bear in this retail trade, though it is less, or at least less visibly, operative; namely, the point beyond which the charges can not enduringly be advanced without discouraging the farm population unduly; that is to say, the point beyond which the livelihood of the farm population will be cut into so severely by the overcharging of the retail trade that they begin to decide that they have nothing more to lose, and so give up and move out. This critical point appears not commonly to be reached in the ordinary retail trade—as, e.g., groceries, clothing, hardware—possibly because there still remains, practicable in an extremity, the recourse to outside dealers of one sort of another. In the business of country-town banking, however, and similar money-lending by other persons than the banks, the critical point is not infrequently reached and passed. Here the local monopoly is fairly complete and rigorous, which brings on an insistent provocation to over-reach.

And then, too, the banker deals in money-values, and money-values are forever liable to fluctuate; at the same time that the fortunes of the banker's farm clients are subject to the vicissitudes of the seasons and of the markets; and competition drives both banker and client to base their habitual rates, not on a conservative anticipation of what is likely to happen but on the lucky chance of what may come to pass barring accidents and the acts of God. And the banker is under the necessity—"inner necessity," as the Hegelians would say—of getting all he can and securing himself against all risk, at the cost of any whom it may concern, by such charges and stipulations as will insure his net gain in any event.

It is the business of the country-town business community, one with another, to charge what the traffic will bear; and the traffic will bear charges that are inordinately high as counted on the necessary cost or the use-value of the work to be done. It follows, under the common-sense logic of self-help, cupidity, and business-as-usual, that men eager to do business on a good margin will continue to drift in and out into the traffic until the number of concerns among whom the gains are to be divided is so large that each one's share is no more than will cover costs and leave a "reasonable" margin of net gain. So that while the underlying farm population continues to yield inordinately high rates on the traffic, the business concerns engaged, one with another, come in for no more than what will induce them to go on; the reason being that in the retail trade as conducted on this plan of self-help and equal opportunity the stocks, equipment and man-power employed will unavoidably exceed what is required for the work, by some 200 to 1000 per cent—those lines of the trade being the more densely over-populated which enjoy the nearest approach to a local monopoly, as, e.g., groceries, or banking.[2]

It is perhaps not impertinent to call to mind that the retail trade throughout, always and everywhere, runs on very much the same plan of inordinately high charges and consequently extravagant multiplication of stocks, equipment, work, personnel, publicity, credits, and costs. It runs to the same effect in city, town and country. And in city, town or country town it is in all of these several respects the country's largest business enterprise in the aggregate; and always something like three-fourths to nine-tenths of it is idle waste, to be cancelled out of the community's working efficiency as lag, leak and friction. When the statesmen and the newspapers—and other publicity-agencies—speak for the security and the meritorious work of the country's business men, it is something of this sort they are talking about. The bulk of the

---

[2]The round numbers named above are safe and conservative, particularly so long as the question concerns the staple country towns of the great farming regions. As has already been remarked, they are only less securely applicable in the case of similar towns in the industrial and outlying parts of the country. To some they may seem large and loose. They are based on a fairly exhaustive study of statistical materials gathered by special inquiry in the spring of 1918 for the Statistical Division of the Food Administration, but not published hitherto.

There has been little detailed or concrete discussion of the topic. See, however, a very brief paper by Isador Lubin on "The Economic Costs of Retail Distribution," published in the Twenty-second Report of the Michigan Academy of Science, which runs in great part of the same material.

It is, or should be, unnecessary to add that the retail trade of the country towns is neither a unique nor an extravagant development of business-as-usual. It is in fact very much the sort of thing that is to be met with in the retail trade everywhere, in America and elsewhere.

country's business is the retail trade, and in an eminent sense the retail trade is business-as-usual.

The retail trade, and therefore in its degree the country town, have been the home ground of American culture and the actuating center of public affairs and public sentiment throughout the nineteenth century, ever more securely and unequivocally as the century advanced and drew toward its close. In American parlance "The Public," so far as it can be defined, has meant those persons who are engaged in and about the business of the retail trade, together with such of the kept classes as draw their keep from this traffic. The road to success has run into and through the country town, or its retail-trade equivalent in the cities, and the habits of thought engendered by the preoccupations of the retail trade have shaped popular sentiment and popular morals and have dominated public policy in what was to be done and what was to be left undone, locally and at large, in political, civil, social, ecclesiastical, and educational concerns. The country's public men and official spokesmen have come up through and out of the country-town community, on passing the test of fitness according to retail-trade standards, and have carried with them into official responsibility the habits of thought induced by these interests and these habits of life.

This is also what is meant by democracy in American parlance, and it was for this country-town pattern of democracy that the Defender of the American Faith once aspired to make the world safe. Meantime democracy, at least in America, has moved forward and upward to a higher business level, where larger vested interests dominate and bulkier margins of net gain are in the hazard. It has come to be recognised that the country-town situation of the nineteenth century is now by way of being left behind; and so it is now recognised, or at least acted on, that the salvation of twentieth-century democracy is best to be worked out by making the world safe for Big Business and then let Big Business take care of the interests of the retail trade and the country town, together with much else. But it should not be overlooked that in and through all this it is the soul of the country town that goes marching on.

Toward the close of the century, and increasingly since the turn of the century, the trading community of the country towns has been losing its initiative as a maker of charges and has by degrees become tributary to the great vested interests that move in the background of the market. In a way the country towns have in an appreciable degree fallen into the position of toll-gate keepers for the distribution of goods and collection of customs for the large absentee owners of the business. Grocers, hardware dealers, meat-markets, druggists, shoe-shops, are more and more extensively falling into the position of local distributors for jobbing houses and manufacturers. They increasingly handle "package goods" bearing the brand of some (ostensible) maker, whose chief connection with the goods is that of advertiser of the copyright brand which appears on the label. Prices, and margins, are made for the retailers, which they can take or leave. But leaving, in this connection, will commonly mean leaving the business—which is not included in the premises. The bankers work by affiliation with and under surveillance of their correspondents in the sub-centers of credit, who are similarly tied in under the credit routine of the associated banking houses in the great centers. And the clothiers duly sell garments under the brand of "Cost-Plus," or some such apocryphal token of merit.

All this reduction of the retailers to simpler terms has by no means lowered the overhead charges of the retail trade as they bear upon the underlying farm population; rather the reverse. Nor has it hitherto lessened the duplication of stocks, equipment, personnel and work, that goes into the retail trade; rather the reverse, indeed, whatever may yet happen in that connection. Nor has it abated the ancient spirit of self-help and cupidity that has always animated the retail trade and the country town; rather the reverse; inasmuch as their principals back in the jungle of Big Business cut into the initiative and the margins of the retailers with "package goods," brands, advertising, and agency contracts; which irritates the retailers and provokes them to retaliate and recoup where they see an opening, that is at the cost of the underlying farm population. It is true, the added overcharge which so can effectually be brought to rest on the farm population may be a negligible quantity; there never was much slack to be taken up on that side.

The best days of the retail trade and the country town are past. The retail trader is passing under the hand of Big Business and so is ceasing to be a masterless man ready to follow the line of his own initiative and help to rule his corner of the land in collusion with his fellow townsmen. Circumstances are prescribing for him. The decisive circumstances that hedge him about have been changing in such a way as to leave him no longer fit to do business on his own, even in collusion with his fellow townsmen. The retail trade and the country town are an enterprise in salesmanship, of course, and salesmanship is a matter of buying cheap and selling dear; all of which is simple and obvious to any retailer, and holds true all around the circle from grocer to banker and back again. During the period while the country town has flourished and grown into the texture of the economic situation, the salesmanship which made the outcome was a matter of personal qualities, knack and skill that gave the dealer an advantage in meeting his customers man to man, largely a matter of tact, patience and effrontery; those qualities, in short, which have qualified the rustic horse-trader and have cast a glamour of adventurous enterprise over American country life. In this connection it is worth recalling that the personnel engaged in the retail trade of the country towns has in the main been drawn by self-selection from the farm population, prevailingly from the older-settled sections where this traditional animus of the horse-trader is of older growth and more untroubled.

All this was well enough, at least, during the period of what may be called the masterless country town, before Big Business began to come into its own in these premises. But this situation has been changing, becoming obsolete, slowly, by insensible degrees. The factors of change have been such as: increased facilities of transport and communication; increasing use of advertising, largely made possible by facilities of transport and communication; increased size and combination of the business concerns engaged in the wholesale trade, as packers, jobbers, ware-house-concerns handling farm products; increased resort to package-goods, brands, and trademarks, advertised on a liberal plan which runs over the heads of the retailers; increased employment of chain-store methods and agencies; increased dependence of local bankers on the greater credit establishments of the financial centres. It will be seen, of course, that this new growth finally runs back to and rests upon changes of a material sort, in the industrial arts, and more immediately on changes in the means of transport and communication.

In effect, salesmanship, too, has been shifting to the wholesale scale and plane, and the country-town retailer is not in a position to make use of the resulting wholesale methods of publicity and control. The conditioning circumstances have outgrown him. Should he make the shift to the wholesale plan of salesmanship he will cease to be a country-town retailer and take on the character of a chain-store concern, a line-yard lumber syndicate, a mail-order house, a Chicago packer instead of a meat market, a Reserve Bank instead of a county-seat banker, and the like; all of which is not contained in the premises of the country-town retail trade.

The country town, of course, still has its uses, and its use so far as bears on the daily life of the underlying farm population is much the same as ever; but for the retail trade and for those accessory persons and classes who draw their keep from its net gains the country town is no longer what it once was. It has been falling into the position of a way-station in the distributive system, instead of a local habitation where a man of initiative and principle might reasonably hope to come in for a "competence"—that is a capitalised free livelihood—and bear his share in the control of affairs without being accountable to any master-concern "higher-up" in the hierarchy of business. The country town and the townsmen are by way of becoming ways and means in the hands of Big Business. Barring accidents, Bolshevism, and the acts of God or of the United States Congress, such would appear to be the drift of things in the calculable future; that is to say, in the absence of disturbing causes.

This does not mean that the country town is on the decline in point of population or the volume of its traffic; but only that the once master-less retailer is coming in for a master, that the retail trade is being standardised and reparcelled by and in behalf of those massive vested interests that move obscurely in the background, and that these vested interests in the background now have the first call on the "income stream" that flows from the farms through the country town. Nor does it imply that that spirit of self-help and collusive cupidity that made and animated the country town at its best has faded out of the mental-ity of this people. It has only moved upward and onward to higher duties and wider horizons. Even if it should appear that the self-acting collusive store-keeper and banker of the nineteenth-century country town "lies a-moldering in his grave," yet "his soul goes marching on." It is only that the same stock of men with the same traditions and ideals are doing Big Business on the same general plan on which the country town was built. And these men who know the country town "from the ground up" now find it ready to their hand, ready to be turned to account according to the methods and principles bred in their own bone. And the habit of mind induced by and conducive to business-as-usual is much the same whether the balance sheet runs in four figures or in eight.

It is an unhappy circumstance that all this plain speaking about the country town, its traffic, its animating spirit, and its standards of merit, unavoidably has an air of finding fault. But even slight reflection will show that this appearance is unavoidable even where there is no in-clination to disparage. It lies in the nature of the case, unfortunately. No unprejudiced inquiry into the facts can content itself with anything short of plain speech, and in this connection plain speech has an air of disparagement because it has been the unbroken usage to avoid plain speech touching these things, these motives, aims, principles, ways and means and achievements, of these substantial citizens and their business and fortunes. But for all that, all these substantial citizens and their folks, fortunes, works, and opinions are no less substantial and meri-torious, in fact. Indeed one can scarcely appreciate the full measure of their stature, substance and achievements, and more particularly the moral costs of their great work in developing the country and taking over its resources, without putting it all in plain terms, instead of the salesmanlike parables that have to be employed in the make-believe of trade and politics.

The country town and the business of its substantial citizens are and have ever been an enterprise in salesmanship; and the beginning of wisdom in salesmanship is equivocation. There is a decent measure of equivocation which runs its course on the hither side of prevarication or duplicity, and an honest salesman—such "an honest man as will bear watching"—will endeavour to confine his best efforts to this highly moral zone where stands the upright man who is not under oath to tell the whole truth. But "self-preservation knows no moral law"; and it is not to be overlooked that there habitually enter into the retail trade of the country towns many competitors who do not falter at prevarication and who even do not hesitate at outright duplicity; and it will not do for an honest man to let the rogues get away with the best—or any—of the trade, at the risk of too narrow a margin of profit on his own business—that is to say a narrower margin than might be had in the absence of scruple. And then there is always the base-line of what the law allows; and what the law allows can not be far wrong. Indeed, the sane presumption will be that whoever lives within the law has no need to quarrel with his conscience. And a sound principle will be to improve the hour today and, if worse comes to worst, let the courts determine tomorrow, under protest, just what the law allows, and there-fore what the moral code exacts. And then, too, it is believed and credible that the courts will be wise enough to see that the law is not allowed to apply with such effect as to impede the volume or narrow the margins of business-as-usual.

"He either fears his fate too much, Or his deserts are small, Who dare not put it to the touch" and take a chance with the legalities and the moralities for once in a way, when there is easy money in sight and no one is looking, particularly in case his own solvency—that is his life as a business concern—should be in the balance. Solvency is always a meritorious work, however it may be achieved or maintained; and so long as one is quite sound on this main count one is sound on the whole, and can afford to forget peccadillos, within reason. The country-town code of morality at large as well as its code of business ethics, is quite sharp, meticulous; but solvency always has a sedative value in these premises, at large and in personal detail. And then, too, solvency not only puts a man in the way of acquiring merit, but it makes him over into a substantial citizen whose opinions and preferences have weight and who is therefore enabled to do much good for his fellow citizens—that is to say, shape them somewhat to his own pattern. To create mankind in one's own image is a work that partakes of the divine, and it is a high privilege which the substantial citizen commonly makes the most of. Evidently this salesmanlike pursuit of the net gain has a high cultural value at the same time that it is invaluable as a means to a competence.

The country-town pattern of moral agent and the code of morals and proprieties, manners and customs, which come up out of this life of salesmanship is such as this unremitting habituation is fit to produce. The scheme of conduct for the business man and for "his sisters and his cousins and his aunts" is a scheme of salesmanship, seven days in the week. And the rule of life of country-town salesmanship is summed up in what the older logicians have called *suppressio veri* and *suggestio falsi*. The dominant note of this life is circumspection.[3] One must avoid offense, cultivate good-will, at any reasonable cost, and continue unfailing in taking advantage of it; and, as a corollary to this axiom, one should be ready to recognise and recount the possible short-comings of one's neighbours, for neighbours are (or may be) rivals in the trade, and in trade one man's loss is another's gain, and a rival's disabilities count in among one's assets and should not be allowed to go to waste.

One must be circumspect, acquire merit, and avoid offense. So one must eschew opinions, or information, which are not acceptable to the common run of those whose good-will has or may conceivably come to have any commercial value. The country-town system of knowledge and belief can admit nothing that would annoy the prejudices of any appreciable number of the respectable townsfolk. So it becomes a system of intellectual, institutional, and religious holdovers. The country town is conservative; aggressively and truculently so, since any assertion or denial that runs counter to any appreciable set of respectable prejudices would come in for some degree of disfavour, and any degree of disfavour is intolerable to men whose business would presumably suffer from it. Whereas there is no (business) harm done in assenting to, and so in time coming to believe in, any or all of the commonplaces of the day before yesterday. In this sense the country town is conservative, in that it is by force of business expediency intolerant of anything but holdovers. Intellectually, institutionally, and religiously, the country towns of the great farming country are "standing pat" on the ground taken somewhere about the period of the Civil War; or according to the wider chronology, somewhere about Mid-Victorian times. And the men of affairs and responsibility in public life, who have passed the test of country-town fitness, as they must, are men who have come through and made good according to the canons of faith and conduct imposed by this system of holdovers.

Again it seems necessary to enter the caution that in so speaking of this system of country-town holdovers and circumspection there need be no hint of disparagement. The colloquial speech of our time, outside of the country-town hives of expedient respectability, carries a note

[3]It might also be called salesmanlike pusillanimity.

of disallowance and disclaimer in all that it has to say of holdovers; which is an unfortunate but inherent defect of the language, and which it is necessary to discount and make one's peace with. It is only that outside of the country towns, where human intelligence has not yet gone into abeyance and where human speech accordingly is in continued process of remaking, sentiment and opinion run to the unhappy effect which this implicit disparagement of these holdovers discloses.

Indeed, there is much, or at least something, to be said to the credit of this country-town system of holdovers, with its canons of salesmanship and circumspection. It has to its credit many deeds of Christian charity and Christian faith. It may be—as how should it not?—that many of these deeds of faith and charity are done in the businesslike hope that they will have some salutary effect on the doer's balance sheet; but the opaque fact remains that these business men do these things, and it is to be presumed that they would rather not discuss the ulterior motives.

It is a notorious commonplace among those who get their living by promoting enterprises of charity and good deeds in general that no large enterprise of this description can be carried through to a successful and lucrative issue without due appeal to the country towns and due support by the businesslike townsmen and their associates and their associates and accessory folks. And it is likewise notorious that the country-town community of business men and substantial households will endorse and contribute to virtually any enterprise of the sort, and ask few questions. The effectual interest which prompts to endorsement of and visible contribution to these enterprises is a salesmanlike interest in the "prestige value" that comes to those persons who endorse and visibly contribute; and perhaps even more insistently there is the loss of "prestige value" that would come to anyone who should dare to omit due endorsement and contribution to any ostensibly public spirited enterprise of this kind that has caught the vogue and does not violate the system of prescriptive holdovers.

Other interest there may well be, as, e.g., human charity or Christian charity—that is to say solicitude for the salvation of one's soul—but without due appeal to salesmanlike respectability the clamour of any certified solicitor of these good deeds will be but as sounding brass and a tinkling cymbal. One need only try to picture what would be the fate, e.g., of the campaigns and campaigners for Red Cross, famine relief, Liberty Bonds, foreign missions, Inter-Church fund, and the like, in the absence of such appeal and of the due response. It may well be, of course, that the salesmanlike townsman endorses with the majority and pays his contribution as a mulct, under compunction of expediency, as a choice between evils, for fear of losing good-will. But the main fact remains. It may perhaps all foot up to this with the common run, that no man who values his salesmanlike well-being will dare follow his own untoward propensity in dealing with these certified enterprises in good deeds, and speak his profane mind to the certified campaigners. But it all comes to the same in the upshot. The substantial townsman is shrewd perhaps, or at least he aims to be, and it may well be that with a shrewd man's logic he argues that two birds in the bush are worth more than one in the hand; and so pays his due peace-offering to the certified solicitor of good deeds somewhat in the spirit of those addicts of the faith who once upon a time brought Papal indulgences. But when all is said, it works; and that it does so, and that these many adventures and adventurers in certified mercy and humanity are so enabled to subsist in any degree of prosperity and comfort is to be credited, for the major part, to the salesmanlike tact of the substantial citizens of the country towns.

One hesitates to imagine what would be the fate of the foreign missions, e.g., in the absence of this salesmanlike solicitude for the main chance in the country towns. And there is perhaps less comfort in reflecting on what would be the terms of liquidation for those many churches and churchmen that now adorn the land, if they were driven to rest their fortunes on unconstrained gifts from *de facto* worshippers moved by the first-hand fear of God, in the absence of that more bounteous subvention that so comes in from the quasi-consecrated respectable townsmen who are so constrained by their salesmanlike fear of a possible decline in their prestige.

Any person who is seriously addicted to devout observances and who takes his ecclesiastical verities at their face might be moved to deprecate this dependence of the good cause on these mixed motives. But there is no need of entertaining doubts here as to the ulterior goodness of these businesslike incentives. Seen in perspective from the outside—as any economist must view these matters—it should seem to be the part of wisdom, for the faithful and for their businesslike benefactors alike, to look steadfastly to the good end and leave ulterior questions of motive on one side. There is also some reason to believe that such a view of the whole matter is not infrequently acted upon. And when all is said and allowed for, the main fact remains, that in the absence of this spirit of what may without offense be called salesmanlike pusillanimity in the country towns, both the glory of God and the good of man would be less bountifully served, on all these issues that engage the certified solicitors of good deeds.

This system of innocuous holdovers, then, makes up what may be called the country-town profession of faith, spiritual and secular. And so it comes to pass that the same general system of holdovers imposes its bias on the reputable organs of expression throughout the community—pulpit, public press, courts, schools—and dominates the conduct of public affairs; inasmuch as the constituency of the country town, in the main and in the everyday run, shapes the course of reputable sentiment and conviction for the American community at large. Not because of any widely prevalent aggressive preference for that sort of thing, perhaps, but rather because it would scarcely be a "sound business proposition" to run counter to the known interests of the ruling class; that is to say, the substantial citizens and their folks. But the effect is much the same and will scarcely be denied.

It will be seen that in substantial effect this country-town system of holdovers is of what would be called a "salutary" character; that is to say, it is somewhat intolerantly conservative. It is a system of professions and avowals, which may perhaps run to no deeper ground than a salesmanlike pusillanimity, but the effect is much the same. In the country-town community and its outlying ramifications, as in any community of men, the professions made and insisted on will unavoidably shape the effectual scheme of knowledge and belief. Such is the known force of inveterate habit. To the young generation the prescriptive holdovers are handed down as self-evident and immutable principles of reality, and the (reputable) schools can allow themselves no latitude and no question. And what is more to the point, men and women come to believe in the truths which they profess, on whatever ground, provided only that they continue stubbornly to profess them. Their professions may have come out of expedient make-believe, but, all the same, they serve as premises in all the projects, reflections, and reveries of these folks who profess them. And it will be only on provocation of harsh and protracted exposure to material facts running unbroken to the contrary that the current of their sentiments and convictions can be brought to range outside of the lines drawn for them by these professed articles of truth.

The case is illustrated, e.g., by the various and widely-varying systems of religious verities current among the outlying peoples, the peoples of the lower cultures, each and several of which are indubitably and immutably truthful to their respective believers, throughout all the bizarre web of their incredible conceits and grotesqueries, none of which will bear the light of alien scrutiny.[4] Having come in for these profes-

---

[4] There is, of course, no call in this Christian land to throw up a doubt or question touching any of the highly remarkable verities of the Christian confession at large. While it will be freely admitted on all hands that many of the observances and beliefs current among the "non-Christian tribes" are grotesque and palpable errors of mortal mind; it must at the same time, and indeed by the same

sions of archaic make-believe, and continuing stubbornly to profess
implicit faith in these things as a hopeful sedative of the wrath to come,
these things come to hedge about the scheme of knowledge and belief
as well as the scheme of what is to be done or left undone. In much the
same way the country-town system of prescriptive holdovers has gone
into action as the safe and sane body of American common sense; until
it is now self-evident to American public sentiment that any derange-
ment of these holdovers would bring the affairs of the human race to a
disastrous collapse. And all the while the material conditions are pro-
gressively drawing together into such shape that this plain country-
town common sense will no longer work.

---

token, be equally plain to any person of cultivated tastes in religious superstition,
and with a sound bias, that the corresponding convolutions of unreason in the
Christian faith are in the nature of a divine coagulum of the true, the beautiful,
and the good, as it was in the beginning, is now, and ever shall be: World without
end. But all the while it is evident that all these "beastly devices of the heathen,"
just referred to, are true, beautiful and good to their benighted apprehension
only because their apprehension has been benighted by their stubborn profession
of these articles of misguided make-believe, through the generations; which is the
point of the argument.

CHAPTER 6

The City as Community

We may be nostalgic for whatever degree of community once obtained, in peasant village, Greek *Polis*, feudal manor, or New England town, but our present is overwhelmingly urban and growing more so every minute. Our problem is to abstract the values of community from the historical patterns that have nurtured it, then translate those patterns into the structure of our expanding, metropolitan world.

Perhaps this is impossible. Still, the medieval city analyzed by Pirenne is often termed a "commune." It was a profoundly religious and traditional society, but it was revolutionary despite itself. Pirenne outlines the ways in which the medieval city expanded the scope of individual rights and duties—first freeing itself in large degree from the feudality through alliance with the monarch, then gaining freedom from the latter through its access to that commodity rare in an agrarian society, liquid capital. And, as he notes, the expanding network of urban centers affected the countrymen in between, changing cultures and social structures as it grew.

But this medieval city was still an island of urbanity in a sea of peasantry and nobility. Its walls symbolized its independence of the country and its political autonomy. In this way it was in feudal society, but not completely of it. Its economy rested upon the production of the peasants; indeed it was a possibility only because they produced a surplus beyond their needs, but peasantry and citizenry were quite different social categories.

Those categories broke down only as the urban network came to dominate the society. This change occurred when men discovered how to use nonhuman energy through those elaborate tools, machines, as substitute and improvement over the human musculature. These consequences are, at least in the short run, inimical to the close, culturally integrated community of the medieval city; they are conducive to individual liberties (outside the labor market at least) and to increasing wealth for all. That spread of wealth was not, of course, the aim of those whose actions, with little specific purpose to do so, destroyed a world and created another. Within the ideology of Manchester *laisser faire,* using the new technologies to maximize profit, they created the vast brick warrens described by Dickens in the excerpt from *Hard Times.* It was (and in many places still is) a world stripped to the minimum, based on buying cheap and selling dear, a world that has lost an older tradition and not yet created a new one instead. This comic view of utilitarianism and liberalism in action and results is no exaggeration; the industrial revolution everywhere substitutes machine for man, slum for cottage, brick for earth, and property for place.

One of the actors instrumental in the design and creation of American urban forms is visible in Sinclair Lewis' comic portrait of Babbitt. Here we see a man who is almost caricature, yet it is truthfully drawn: men like Babbitt are as much a programmed part of the free market in land as the latter is their creation. Indeed, Babbitt's major rationalization is simply "If I don't do it somebody else will." He is quite correct in thinking so, for the conditions of trade, the nature of land use, result in a form of Gresham's law. Profitable "deals" drive out of business the less profitable business of creating a viable public scene for a responsible community.

Indeed, until the social community can be created the physical layout of the city will continue to emerge from the actions of Babbitt.

Henri Pirenne
Cities and European Civilization

The birth of cities marked the beginning of a new era in the internal history of Western Europe. Until then, society had recognized only two active orders: the clergy and the nobility. In taking its place beside them, the middle class rounded the social order out or, rather, gave the finishing touch thereto. Thenceforth its composition was not to change; it had all its constituent elements, and the modifications which it was to undergo in the course of centuries were, strictly speaking, nothing more than different combinations in the alloy.

Like the clergy and like the nobility, the middle class was itself a privileged order. It formed a distinct legal group and the special law it enjoyed isolated it from the mass of the rural inhabitants which continued to make up the immense majority of the population. Indeed, as has already been seen, it was obliged to preserve intact its exceptional status and to reserve to itself the benefits arising therefrom. Freedom, as the middle class conceived it, was a monopoly. Nothing was less liberal than the caste idea which was the cause of its strength until it became, at the end of the Middle Ages, a cause of weakness. Nevertheless to that middle class was reserved the mission spreading the idea of liberty far and wide and of becoming, without having consciously desired to be, the means of the gradual enfranchisement of the rural classes. The sole fact of its existence was due, indeed, to have an immediate effect upon these latter and, little by little, to attenuate the contrast which at the start separated them from it. In vain it strove to keep them under its influence, to refuse them a share in its privileges, to exclude them from engaging in trade and industry. It had not the power to arrest an evolution of which it was the cause and which it could not suppress save by itself vanishing.

For the formation of the city groups disturbed at once the economic organization of the country districts. Production, as it was there carried on, had served until then merely to support the life of the peasant and supply the prestations due to his seigneur. Upon the suspension of commerce, nothing impelled him to ask of the soil a surplus which it would have been impossible for him to get rid of, since he no longer had outside markets to call upon. He was content to provide for his daily bread, certain of the morrow and longing for no amelioration of his lot, since he could not conceive the possibility of it. The small markets of the towns and the burgs were too insignificant and their demand was too regular to rouse him enough to get out of his rut and intensify his labor. But suddenly these markets sprang into new life. The number of buyers was multiplied, and all at once he had the assurance of being able to sell the produce he brought to them. It was only natural for him to have profited from an opportunity as favorable as this. It depended on himself alone to sell, if he produced enough, and forthwith he began to till the lands which hitherto he had let lie fallow. His work took on a new significance; it brought him profits, the chance of thrift and of an existence which became more comfortable as it became more active. The situation was still more favorable in that the surplus revenues from the soil belonged to him in his own right. The claims of the seigneur were fixed by demesnial custom at an immutable rate, so that the increase in the income from the land benefited only the tenant.

But the seigneur himself had a chance to profit from the new situation wherein the development of the cities placed the country districts. He had enormous reserves of uncultivated land, woods, heaths, marshes and fens. Nothing could be simpler than to put them under cultivation and through them to profit from these new outlets which were becoming more and more exigent and remunerative as the towns grew in size and multiplied in number. The increase in population would furnish the necessary hands for the work of clearing and draining. It was enough to call for men; they would not fail to show up.

By the end of the eleventh century the movement was already manifest in its full force. Monasteries and local princes thenceforth were busy transforming the idle parts of their demesnes into revenue-producing land. The area of cultivated ground which, since the end of the Roman Empire, had not been increased, kept growing continually greater. Forests were cleared. The Cistercian Order, founded in 1098, followed this new path from its very origin. Instead of adopting for its lands the old demesnial organization, it intelligently adapted itself to the new order of things. It adopted the principle of farming on a big scale and, depending upon the region, gave itself over to the most remunerative form of production. In Flanders, where the needs of the towns were greater since they themselves were richer, it engaged in raising cattle. In England, it devoted itself particularly to the sale of wool, which the same cities of Flanders consumed in greater and greater quantity.

Meanwhile, on all sides, the seigneurs, both lay and ecclesiastic, were founding "new" towns. So was called a village established on virgin soil, the occupants of which received plots of land in return for an annual rental. But these new towns, the number of which continued to grow in the course of the twelfth century, were at the same time *free* towns. For in order to attract the farmers the seigneur promised them exemption from the taxes which bore down upon the serfs. In general, he reserved to himself only jurisdiction over them; he abolished in their favor the old claims which still existed in the demesnial organization. The charter of Lorris (1155) in the Gatinais, that of Beaumont in Champagne (1182), that of Priches in the Hainault (1158) present particularly interesting types of charters of the new towns, which were also to be found everywhere in neighboring countries. That of Breteuil in Normandy, which was taken over in the course of the twelfth century by a number of localities in England, Wales, and even Ireland, was of the same nature.

Thus a new type of peasant appeared, quite different from the old. The latter had serfdom as a characteristic; the former enjoyed freedom. And this freedom, the cause of which was the economic disturbance communicated by the towns to the organization of the country districts, was itself copied after that of the cities. The inhabitants of the new towns were, strictly speaking, rural burghers. They even bore, in a good number of charters, the name of *burgenses*. They received a legal constitution and a local autonomy which was manifestly borrowed from city institutions, so much so that it may be said that the latter went beyond the circumference of their walls in order to reach the country districts and acquaint them with liberty.

And this new freedom, as it progressed, was not long in making headway even in the old demesnes, whose archaic constitution could not be maintained in the midst of a reorganized social order. Either by voluntary emancipation, or by prescription or usurpation, the seigneurs permitted it to be gradually substituted for the serfdom which had so long been the normal condition of their tenants. The form of government of the people was there changed at the same time as the form of government of the land, since both were consequences of an economic situation on the way to disappear. Commerce now supplied all the necessaries which the demesnes had hitherto been obliged to obtain by their own efforts. It was no longer essential for each of them to produce all the commodities for which it had use. It sufficed to go get·them at some nearby city. The abbeys of the Netherlands, which had been endowed by their benefactors with vineyards situated either in France or on the banks of the Rhine and the Moselle where they produced the wine needed for their consumption, began, at about the start of the thirteenth century, to sell these properties which had now become use-less and whose working and upkeep henceforth cost more than they brought in.

No example better illustrates the inevitable disappearance of the old demesnial system in an era transformed by commerce and the new city economy. Trade, which was becoming more and more active, necessarily favored agricultural production, broke down the limits which had hith-erto bounded it, drew it towards the towns, modernized it, and at the same time set it free. Man was therefore detached from the soil to which he had so long been enthralled, and free labor was substituted more and more generally for serf labor. It was only in regions remote from commercial highways that there was still perpetuated in its primitive rigor the old personal serfdom and therewith the old forms of demesnial property. Everywhere else it disappeared, the more rapidly especially where towns were more numerous. In Flanders, for example, it hardly existed at all after the beginning of the thirteenth century, although, to be sure, a few traces were still preserved. Up to the end of the old order there were still to be found, here and there, men bound by the law of mortemain or subject to forced labor, and lands encumbered by various seignorial rights. But these survivals of the past were almost al-ways simple taxes and he who paid them had, for all that, full personal liberty.

The emancipation of the rural classes was only one of the conse-quences provoked by the economic revival of which the towns were both the result and the instrument. It coincided with the increasing importance of liquid capital. During the demesnial era of the Middle Ages, there was no other form of wealth than that which lay in real estate. It ensured to the holder both personal liberty and social prestige. It was the guaranty of the privileged status of the clergy and the nobility. Exclusive holders of the land, they lived by the labor of their tenants whom they protected and whom they ruled. The serfdom of the masses was the necessary consequence of such a social organization. There was no alternative save to own the land and be a lord, or to till it for another and be a serf.

But with the origin of the middle class there took its place in the sun a class of men whose existence was in flagrant contradiction to this traditional order of things. The land upon which they settled they not only did not cultivate but did not even own. They demonstrated and made increasingly clear the possibility of living and growing rich by the sole act of selling, or producing exchange values.

Landed capital had been everything, and now by the side of it was made plain the power of liquid capital. Heretofore money had been sterile. The great lay or ecclesiastic proprietors in whose hands was concentrated the very scant stock of currency in circulation, by means of either the land taxes which they levied upon their tenants or the alms which the congregations brought to the churches, normally had no way of making it bear fruit. To be sure, it was often the case that monasteries, in time of famine, would agree to usurious loans to nobles in distress who would offer their lands as security. But these transactions, forbidden otherwise by canonical law, were only temporary expedients. As a general rule cash was hoarded by its possessors and most often changed into vessels or ornaments for the Church, which might be melted down in case of need. Trade, naturally, released this captive money and restored its proper function. Thanks to this, it became again the instrument of exchange and the measure of values, and since the towns were the centers of trade it necessarily flowed towards them. In circulating, its power was multiplied by the number of transactions in which it served. Its use, at the same time, became more general; payments in kind gave way more and more to payments in money.

A new notion of wealth made its appearance: that of mercantile wealth, consisting no longer in land but in money or commodities of trade measurable in money. During the course of the eleventh century, true capitalists already existed in a number of cities; several examples have been cited above, to which it is unnecessary to refer again here. These city capitalists soon formed the habit of putting a part of their profits into land. The best means of consolidating their fortune and their credit was, in fact, the buying up of land. They devoted a part of their gains to the purchase of real estate, first of all in the same town where they dwelt and later in the country. But they changed themselves, especially, into money-lenders. The economic crisis provoked by the irruption of trade into the life of society had caused the ruin of, or at least trouble to, the landed proprietors who had not been able to adapt themselves to it. For in speeding up the circulation of money a natural result was the decreasing of its value and by that very fact the raising of all prices. The period contemporary with the formation of the cities was a period of high cost of living, as favorable to the business men and artisans of the middle class as it was painful to the holders of the land who did not succeed in increasing their revenues. By the end of the eleventh century many of them were obliged to have recourse to the capital of the merchants in order to keep going. In 1127 the charter of St. Omer mentioned, as a current practice, the loans contracted among the burghers of the town by the knights of the neighborhood.

But more important operations were already current at this era. There was no lack of merchants rich enough to agree to loans of considerable amount. About 1082 some merchants of Liége lent money to the abbot of St. Hubert to permit him to buy the territory of Chavigny, and a few years later advanced to Bishop Otbert the sums necessary to acquire from Duke Godfrey, on the point of departing for the Crusades, his château of Bouillon. The kings themselves had recourse, in the course of the twelfth century, to the good services of the city financiers. William Cade was the money-lender to the King of England. In Flanders, at the beginning of the reign of Philip Augustus, Arras had become pre-eminently a city of bankers. William the Breton describes it as full of riches, avid of lucre and glutted with usurers:

Atrabatum . . . potens urbs . . . plena
Divitiis, inhians lucris et foenore gaudens.

The cities of Lombardy and, following their example, those of Tuscany and Provence, went much further in carrying on that commerce which the Church vainly sought to oppose. By the beginning of the thirteenth century, Italian bankers had already extended their operations north of the Alps and their progress there was so rapid that a half century later, thanks to the abundance of their capital and the more advanced technique of their procedure, they had everywhere taken the place of the local lenders.

The power of liquid capital, concentrated in the cities, not only gave them an economic ascendancy but contributed also towards making them take part in political life. For as long as society had known no other power than that which derived from the possession of the land, the clergy and the nobility alone had had a share in the government. The feudal hierarchy was made up entirely on the basis of landed property. The fief, in reality, was only a tenure and the relations which it created between the vassal and his liege lord were only a particular modality of the relations which existed between a propietor and a tenant. The only difference was that the services due from the first to the second, in place of being of an economic nature, were of a military and political nature. Just as each local prince required the help and counsel of his vassals so, being himself a vassal of the king, was he held on his part to similar obligations. Thus only those who held land entered into the direction of public affairs. They entered into them, moreover, only in paying through their own person; that is to say, using the appropriate expression, *consilio et auxilio*—by their counsel and help. Of a pecuniary contribution towards the needs of their sovereign there could be no question at an epoch when capital, in the form of real estate alone, served merely for the maintenance of its possessors. Perhaps the most striking character of the feudal State was its almost absolute lack of finances. In it, money played no rôle. The demesnial revenues of the prince replenished only his privy purse. It was impossible for him to increase his resources by taxes, and his financial indigence prevented him from taking into his service revocable and salaried agents. Instead of functionaries, he had only hereditary vassals, and his authority over them was limited to the oath of fidelity they gave him.

But as soon as the economic revival enabled him to augment his revenues, and cash, thanks to it, began to flow to his coffers, he took immediate advantage of circumstances. The appearance of bailiffs, in the course of the thirteenth century, was the first symptom of the political progress which was going to make it possible for a prince to develop a true public administration and to change his suzerainty little by little into sovereignty. For the bailiff was, in every sense of the term, a functionary. With these revocable officeholders, remunerated not by grants of land but by stewardships, there was evinced a new type of government. The bailiff, indeed, had a place outside the feudal hierarchy. His nature was quite different from that of the old justices, mayors, or castellans who carried on their functions under an hereditary title. Between them and him there was the same difference that there was between the old serfholds and the new freeholds. Identical economic causes had changed simultaneously the organization of the land and the governing of the people. Just as they enabled the peasants to free themselves, and the proprietors to substitute the quit-rent for the demesnial *mansus,* so they enabled the princes, thanks to their salaried agents, to lay hold of the direct government of their territories. This political innovation, like the social innovations with which it was contemporary, implied the diffusion of ready cash and the circulation of money. This is quite clearly shown to be the case by the fact that Flanders, where commercial life and city life were developed sooner than in the other regions of the Netherlands, knew considerably in advance of these latter the institution of bailiffs.

The connections which were necessarily established between the princes and the burghers also had political consequences of the greatest import. It was necessary to take heed of those cities whose increasing wealth gave them a steadily increasing importance, and which could put on the field, in case of need, thousands of well equipped men. The feudal conservatives had at first only contempt for the presumption of the city militia. Otto of Freisingen was indignant when he saw the communes of Lombardy wearing the helmet and cuirass and permitting themselves to cope with the noble knights of Frederick Barbarossa. But the outstanding victory won by these clodhoppers at Legnano (1176) over the troops of the emperor soon demonstrated what they were capable of. In France, the kings did not neglect to have recourse to their services and to ally them to their own interests. They set themselves up as the protectors of the communes, as the guardians of their liberties, and made the cause of the Crown seem to them to be solidary with the city franchises. Philip Augustus must have garnered the fruits of such a skilful policy. The Battle of Bouvines (1214), which definitely established the sway of the monarchy in the interior of France and caused its prestige to radiate over all Europe, was due in great part to military contingents from the cities.

The influence of the cities was not less important in England at the same era, although it was manifest in a quite different way. Here, instead of supporting the monarchy, they rose against it by the side of the barons. They helped, likewise, in the creation of parliamentary government, the distant origins of which may be dated back to the Magna Carta (1215).

It was not only in England, furthermore, that the cities claimed and obtained a more or less large share in the government. Their natural tendency led them to become municipal republics. There is but little doubt but that, if they had had the power, they would have everywhere become States within the State. But they did not succeed in realizing this ideal save where the power of the State was impotent to counterbalance their efforts.

This was the case with Italy, in the twelfth century, and later, after the definite decline of the imperial power, with Germany. Everywhere else they had not succeeded in throwing off the superior authority of the princes, whether, as in Germany and France, the monarchy was too powerful to have to capitulate before them, or whether, as in the Netherlands, their particularism kept them from combining their efforts in order to attain an independence which immediately put them at grips with one another. They remained as a general rule, then, subject to the territorial government.

But this latter did not treat them as mere subjects. It had too much need of them not to have regard for their interests. Its finances rested in great part upon them, and to the extent that they augmented the power of the State and therewith its expenses, it felt more and more frequently the need of going to the pocketbooks of the burghers. It has already been stated that in the twelfth century it borrowed their money. And this money the cities did not grant without security. They well knew that they ran great risks of never being reimbursed, and they exacted new franchises in return for the sums which they consented to loan. Feudal law permitted the suzerain to exact of his vassals only certain well defined dues which were restricted to particular cases always identical in character. It was therefore impossible for him to subject them arbitrarily to a poll-tax and to extort from them supplies, however badly needed. In this respect the charters of the cities granted them the most solemn guaranties. It was, then, imperative to come to terms with them. Little by little the princes formed the habit of calling the burghers into the councils of prelates and nobles with whom they conferred upon their affairs. The instances of such convocations were still rare in the twelfth century; they multiplied in the thirteenth; and in the fourteenth century the custom was definitely legalized by the institution of the Estates in which the cities obtained, after the clergy and the nobility, a place which soon became, although the third in dignity, the first in importance.

Although the middle classes, as we have just seen, had an influence of very vast import upon the social, economic and political changes which were manifest in Western Europe in the course of the twelfth century, it does not seem at first glance that they played much of a role in the intellectual movement. It was not, in fact, until the fourteenth century that a literature and an art was brought forth from the bosom of the middle classes, animated with their spirit. Until then, learning remained the exclusive monopoly of the clergy and employed no other tongue than the Latin. What literature was written in the vernacular had to do solely with the nobility, or at least expressed only the ideas and the sentiments which pertained to the nobility as a class. Architecture and sculpture produced their masterpieces only in the construction and ornamentation of the churches. The markets and belfries, of which the oldest specimens date back to the beginning of the thirteenth century—as for example the admirable Cloth Hall of Ypres, destroyed during the Great War—remained still faithful to the architectural style of the great religious edifices.

Upon closer inspection, however, it does not take long to discover that city life really did make its own contribution to the moral capital of the Middle Ages. To be sure, its intellectual culture was dominated by practical considerations which, before the period of the Renaissance, kept it from putting forth any independent effort. But from the very first it showed that characteristic of being an exclusively lay culture. By the middle of the twelfth century the municipal councils were busy founding schools for the children of the burghers, which were the first lay schools since the end of antiquity. By means of them, instruction ceased to be furnished exclusively for the benefit of the novices of the monasteries and the future parish priests. Knowledge of reading and writing, being indispensable to the practice of commerce, ceased to be reserved for the members of the clergy alone. The burgher was initiated into them long before the noble, because what was for the noble only an intellectual luxury was for him a daily need. Naturally, the Church immediately claimed supervision over the municipal schools, which gave rise to a number of conflicts between it and the city authorities. The question of religion was naturally completely foreign to these debates. They had no other cause than the desire of the cities to control the schools created by them and the direction of which they themselves intended to keep.

However, the teaching in these communal schools was limited, until the period of the Renaissance, to elementary instruction. All who wished to have more were obliged to turn to the clerical establishments. It was from these latter that came the "clerks" who, starting at the end of the twelfth century, were charged with the correspondence and the accounts of the city, as well as the publication of the manifold Acts necessitated by commercial life. All these "clerks" were, furthermore, laymen, the cities having never taken into their service, in contradistinction to the princes, members of the clergy who by virtue of the privileges they enjoyed would have escaped their jurisdiction.

The language which the municipal scribes employed was naturally, at first, Latin. But after the first years of the thirteenth century they adopted more and more generally the use of national idioms. It was by the cities that the vulgar tongue was introduced for the first time into administrative usage. Thereby they showed an initiative which corresponded perfectly to that lay spirit of which they were the preeminent representatives in the civilization of the Middle Ages.

This lay spirit, moreover, was allied with the most intense religious fervor. If the burghers were very frequently in conflict with the ecclesiastic authorities, if the bishops thundered fulsomely against them with sentences of excommunication, and if, by way of counterattack, they sometimes gave way to decidedly pronounced anti-clerical tendencies, they were, for all of that, none the less animated by a profound and ardent faith. For proof of this is needed only the innumerable religious foundations with which the cities abounded, the pious and charitable confraternities which were so numerous there. Their piety showed itself with a naïveté, a sincerity and a fearlessness which easily led it beyond the bounds of strict orthodoxy. At all times, they were distinguished above everything else by the exuberance of their mysticism. It was this which, in the eleventh century, led them to side passionately with the religious reformers who were fighting simony and the marriage of priests; which, in the twelfth century, spread the contemplative asceticism of the Beguines and the Beghards; which, in the thirteenth century, explained the enthusiastic reception which the Franciscans and the Dominicans received. But it was this also which assured the success of all the novelties, all the exaggerations and all the deformations of religious thought. After the twelfth century no heresy cropped out which did not immediately find some followers. It is enough to recall here the rapidity and the energy with which the sect of the Albigenses spread.

Both lay and mystic at the same time, the burghers of the Middle Ages were thus singularly well prepared for the role which they were to play in the two great future movements of ideas: the Renaissance, the child of the lay mind, and the Reformation, towards which religious mysticism was leading.

Charles Dickens
The Keynote

Coketown, to which Messrs. Bounderby and Gradgrind now walked, was a triumph of fact; it had no greater taint of fancy in it than Mrs. Gradgrind herself. Let us strike the keynote, Coketown, before pursuing our tune.

It was a town of red brick, or of brick that would have been red if the smoke and ashes had allowed it; but as matters stood it was a town of unnatural red and black like the painted face of a savage. It was a town of machinery and tall chimneys, out of which interminable serpents of smoke trailed themselves forever and ever, and never got uncoiled. It had a black canal in it, and a river that ran purple with ill-smelling dye, and vast piles of building full of windows where there was a rattling and a trembling all day long, and where the piston of the steam-engine worked monotonously up and down like the head of an elephant in a state of melancholy madness. It contained several large streets all very like one another, and many small streets still more like one another, inhabited by people equally like one another, who all went in and out at the same hours, with the same sound upon the same pavements, to do the same work, and to whom every day was the same as yesterday and tomorrow, and every year the counterpart of the last and the next.

These attributes of Coketown were in the main inseparable from the work by which it was sustained; against them were to be set off comforts of life which found their way all over the world, and elegancies of life which made, we will not ask how much of the fine lady, who could scarcely bear to hear the place mentioned. The rest of its features were voluntary, and they were these.

You saw nothing in Coketown but what was severely workful. If the members of a religious persuasion built a chapel there—as the members of eighteen religious persuasions had done—they made it a pious warehouse of red brick, with sometimes (but this is only in highly ornamental examples) a bell in a bird-cage on the top of it. The solitary exception was the New Church; a stuccoed edifice with a square steeple over the door, terminating in four short pinnacles like florid wooden

From *Hard Times*, 1854.

legs. All the public inscriptions in the town were painted alike, in severe characters of black and white. The jail might have been the infirmary, the infirmary might have been the jail, the town-hall might have been either, or both, or anything else, for anything that appeared to the contrary in the graces of their construction. Fact, fact, fact, everywhere in the material aspect of the town; fact, fact, fact, everywhere in the immaterial. The McChoakumchild school was all fact, and the school of design was all fact, and the relations between master and man were all fact, and everything was fact between the lying-in hospital and the cemetery, and what you couldn't state in figures, or show to be purchaseable in the cheapest market and saleable in the dearest, was not, and never should be, world without end, Amen.

A town so sacred to fact, and so triumphant in its assertion, of course got on well? Why no, not quite well. No? Dear me!

No. Coketown did not come out of its own furnaces in all respects like gold that had stood the fire. First, the perplexing mystery of the place was, Who belonged to the eighteen denominations? Because, whoever did, the labouring people did not. It was very strange to walk through the streets on a Sunday morning and note how few of *them* the barbarous jangling of bells that was driving the sick and nervous mad called away from their own quarter, from their own close rooms, from the corners of their own streets, where they lounged listlessly, gazing at all the church- and chapel-going, as at a thing with which they had no manner of concern. Nor was it merely the stranger who noticed this, because there was a native organization in Coketown itself whose members were to be heard of in the House of Commons every session, indignantly petitioning for acts of Parliament that should make these people religious by main force. Then came the Teetotal Society, who complained that these same people *would* get drunk, and showed in tabular statements that they did get drunk, and proved at tea parties that no inducement, human or divine (except a medal), would induce them to forgo their custom of getting drunk. Then came the chemist and druggist, with other tabular statements, showing that when they didn't get drunk they took opium. Then came the experienced chaplain of the jail, with more tabular statements, outdoing all the previous tabular statements, and showing that the same people *would* resort to low haunts, hidden from the public eye, where they heard low singing and saw low dancing, and mayhap joined in it; and where A.B., aged twenty-four next birthday, and committed for eighteen months' solitary, had himself said—not that he had ever shown himself particularly worthy of belief—his ruin began, as he was perfectly sure and confident that otherwise he would have been a tip-top moral specimen. Then came Mr. Gradgrind and Mr. Bounderby, the two gentlemen at this present moment walking through Coketown, and both eminently practical, who could, on occasion, furnish more tabular statements derived from their own personal experience, and illustrated by cases they had known and seen, from which it clearly appeared—in short, it was the only clear thing in the case—that these same people were a bad lot altogether, gentlemen; that do what you would for them they were never thankful for it, gentlemen; that they were restless, gentlemen; that they never knew what they wanted; that they lived upon the best, and bought fresh butter, and insisted on Mocha coffee, and rejected all but prime parts of meat, and yet were eternally dissatisfied and unmanageable. In short, it was the moral of the old nursery fable:

> There was an old woman, and what do you think?
> She lived upon nothing but victuals and drink;
> Victuals and drink were the whole of her diet,
> And yet this old woman would *never* be quiet.

Is it possible, I wonder, that there was any analogy between the case of the Coketown population and the case of the little Gradgrinds? Surely none of us in our sober senses and acquainted with figures are to be told at this time of day that one of the foremost elements in the existence of the Coketown working-people had been for scores of years deliberately set at nought? That there was any Fancy in them demanding to be brought into healthy existence instead of struggling on in convulsions? That exactly in the ratio as they worked long and monotonously, the craving grew within them for some physical relief—some relaxation, encouraging good humour and good spirits, and giving them a vent—some recognized holiday, though it were but for an honest dance to a stirring band of music—some occasional light pie in which even McChoakumchild had no finger—which craving must and would be satisfied aright, or must and would inevitably go wrong, until the laws of the Creation were repealed?

Sinclair Lewis
from *Babbitt*

Babbitt's virtues as a real-estate broker—as the servant of society in the department of finding homes for families and shops for distributors of food—were steadiness and diligence. He was conventionally honest, he kept his records of buyers and sellers complete, he had experience with leases and titles and an excellent memory for prices. His shoulders were broad enough, his voice deep enough, his relish of hearty humor strong enough, to establish him as one of the ruling caste of Good Fellows. Yet his eventual importance to mankind was perhaps lessened by his large and complacent ignorance of all architecture save the types of houses turned out by speculative builders; all landscape gardening save the use of curving roads, grass, and six ordinary shrubs; and all the commonest axioms of economics. He serenely believed that the one purpose of the real-estate business was to make money for George F. Babbitt. True, it was a good advertisement at Boosters' Club lunches, and all the varieties of Annual Banquets to which Good Fellows were invited, to speak sonorously of Unselfish Public Service, the Broker's Obligation to Keep Inviolate the Trust of His Clients, and a thing called Ethics, whose nature was confusing but if you had it you were a High-class Realtor and if you hadn't you were a shyster, a piker, and a fly-by-night. These virtues awakened Confidence, and enabled you to handle Bigger Propositions. But they didn't imply that you were to be impractical and refuse to take twice the value of a house if a buyer was such an idiot that he didn't jew you down on the asking-price.

Babbitt spoke well—and often—at these orgies of commercial righteousness about the "realtor's function as a seer of the future development of the community, and as a prophetic engineer clearing the pathway for inevitable changes"—which meant that a real-estate broker could make money by guessing which way the town would grow. This guessing he called Vision.

In an address at the Boosters' Club he had admitted, "It is at once the duty and the privilege of the realtor to know everything about his own city and its environs. Where a surgeon is a specialist on every vein and mysterious cell of the human body, and the engineer upon electricity in all its phases, or every bolt of some great bridge majestically arching o'er a mighty flood, the realtor must know his city, inch by inch, and all its faults and virtues."

Though he did know the market-price, inch by inch, of certain districts of Zenith, he did not know whether the police force was too large or too small, or whether it was in alliance with gambling and prostitution. He knew the means of fire-proofing buildings and the relation of insurance-rates to fire-proofing, but he did not know how many firemen there were in the city, how they were trained and paid, or how complete their apparatus. He sang eloquently the advantages of proximity of school-buildings to rentable homes, but he did not know —he did not know that it was worth while to know—whether the city schoolrooms were properly heated, lighted, ventilated, furnished; he did not know how the teachers were chosen; and though he chanted "One of the boasts of Zenith is that we pay our teachers adequately," that was because he had read the statement in the *Advocate-Times*. Himself, he could not have given the average salary of teachers in Zenith or anywhere else.

He had heard it said that "conditions" in the County Jail and the Zenith City Prison were not very "scientific"; he had, with indignation at the criticism of Zenith, skimmed through a report in which the notorious pessimist Seneca Doane, the radical lawyer, asserted that to throw boys and young girls into a bull-pen crammed with men suffering from syphilis, delirium tremens, and insanity was not the perfect way of educating them. He had controverted the report by growling, "Folks that think a jail ought to be a bloomin' Hotel Thornleigh make me sick. If people don't like a jail, let 'em behave 'emselves and keep out of it. Besides, these reform cranks always exaggerate." That was the beginning and quite completely the end of his investigations into Zenith's charities and corrections; and as to the "vice districts" he brightly expressed it, "Those are things that no decent man monkeys with. Besides, smatter fact, I'll tell you confidentially: it's a protection to our daughters and to decent women to have a district where tough nuts can raise cain. Keeps 'em from our own homes."

As to industrial conditions, however, Babbitt had thought a great deal, and his opinions may be coordinated as follows:

"A good labor union is of value because it keeps out radical unions, which would destroy property. No one ought to be forced to belong to a union, however. All labor agitators who try to force men to join a union should be hanged. In fact, just between ourselves, there oughtn't to be any unions allowed at all; and as it's the best way of fighting the unions, every business man ought to belong to an employers'-

association and to the Chamber of Commerce. In union there is strength. So any selfish hog who doesn't join the Chamber of Commerce ought to be forced to."

In nothing—as the expert on whose advice families moved to new neighborhoods to live there for a generation—was Babbitt more splendidly innocent than in the science of sanitation. He did not know a malaria-bearing mosquito from a bat; he knew nothing about tests of drinking water; and in the matters of plumbing and sewage he was as unlearned as he was voluble. He often referred to the excellence of the bathrooms in the houses he sold. He was fond of explaining why it was that no European ever bathed. Someone had told him, when he was twenty-two, that all cesspools were unhealthy, and he still denounced them. If a client impertinently wanted him to sell a house which had a cesspool, Babbitt always spoke about it—before accepting the house and selling it.

When he laid out the Glen Oriole acreage development, when he ironed woodland and dipping meadow into a glenless, orioleless, sunburnt flat prickly with small boards displaying the names of imaginary streets, he righteously put in a complete sewage-system. It made him feel superior; it enabled him to sneer privily at the Martin Lumsen development, Avonlea, which had a cesspool; and it provided a chorus for the full-page advertisements in which he announced the beauty, convenience, cheapness, and supererogatory healthfulness of Glen Oriole. The only flaw was that the Glen Oriole sewers had insufficient outlet, so that waste remained in them, not very agreeably, while the Avonlea cesspool was a Waring septic tank.

The whole of the Glen Oriole project was a suggestion that Babbitt, though he really did hate men recognized as swindlers, was not too unreasonably honest. Operators and buyers prefer that brokers should not be in competition with them as operators and buyers themselves, but attend to their clients' interests only. It was supposed that the Babbitt-Thompson Company were merely agents for Glen Oriole, serving the real owner, Jake Offutt, but the fact was that Babbitt and Thompson owned sixty-two per cent of the Glen, the president and purchasing agent of the Zenith Street Traction Company owned twenty-eight per cent, and Jake Offutt (a gang-politician, a small manufacturer, a tobacco-chewing old farceur who enjoyed dirty politics, business diplomacy, and cheating at poker) had only ten per cent, which Babbitt and the Traction officials had given to him for "fixing" health inspectors and fire inspectors and a member of the State Transportation Commission.

But Babbitt was virtuous. He advocated, though he did not practise, the prohibition of alcohol; he praised, though he did not obey, the laws against motor-speeding; he paid his debts; he contributed to the church, the Red Cross, and the Y.M.C.A.; he followed the custom of his clan and cheated only as it was sanctified by precedent; and he never descended to trickery—though, as he explained to Paul Riesling:

"Course I don't mean to say that every ad I write is literally true or that I always believe everything I say when I give some buyer a good strong selling-spiel. You see—you see it's like this: In the first place, maybe the owner of the property exaggerated when he put it into my hands, and it certainly isn't my place to go proving my principal a liar! And then most folks are so darn crooked themselves that they expect a fellow to do a little lying, so if I was fool enough to never whoop the ante I'd get the credit for lying anyway! In self-defense I got to toot my own horn, like a lawyer defending a client—his bounden duty, ain't it, to bring out the poor dub's good points? Why, the Judge himself would bawl out a lawyer that didn't, even if they both knew the guy was guilty! But even so, I don't pad out the truth like Cecil Rountree or Thayer or the rest of these realtors. Fact, I think a fellow that's willing to deliberately up and profit by lying ought to be shot!"

CHAPTER 7

National Community

Among the more difficult questions of our age are several having to do with the kind of community comprised by the nation state. We may wonder, for example, whether a large agglomeration of people like that in the contemporary nation can truly create a community; we may wonder about the circumstances under which they are most likely to do so, and the internal and external consequences that will follow if they do. We may also ask what the chances are of the development of a larger community bridging the nation states in our world. Answers to these questions have much to do with the possibilities of maintaining civic order and international comity.

The nation state is essentially a modern invention that began to take shape during the Renaissance. From that point forward the Western world was dominated by the growth of large aggregations of power, both economic and military, that are the familiar and fundamental-seeming units of political organization today. To most people, a world made up of separate "sovereign" nations is an entirely natural sort of phenomenon.

Nations, however, had to be "built," and indeed they are still abuilding. Machiavelli's *The Prince,* one of the great early works of modern Western thought, is probably most usefully understood as advice about how to create a nation. Among the elements of nationhood is a sense of community (or something very much like it) : a feeling of identity, shared fate, common loyalty. The modern notions of nationalism and patriotism have much in common with the concept of community as it is projected on the nation-state scale. Wars, revolutions, and repressions, especially those of the nineteenth and twentieth centuries, have often erupted out of the search for or establishment of national community. Part of the problem has rested in the effort to generate a sense of oneness in the large nation as a basis for common political action; part has a measure of national unity has been attained.

Three aspects of community have received much attention in recent decades. One is the matter of creating a satisfactory basis in community for the political and economic development of the "new nations" of the non-Western areas of the world, a process often referred to as "national integration." A second is the effort to create regional community among nations, notably among those of Western Europe, as, for example, through the Common Market. A third is the entire problem of attempting to promote world community as a basis for international cooperation and peace. These are touched upon in other sections of the book; all may be analyzed through their relationship to the concept of community.

The short selection from David Minar's *Ideas and Politics* proposes two points about the development of national community in America. One is that the Western tradition of liberal individualism is in major ways anticommunity in bias. The other is that the creation of a sense of community was a part of the growth process in the United States from Revolutionary times, despite the ideological resistance of liberalism and the heterogeneity of the social and cultural base on which the country was built. In the passage quoted from *Common Sense* Thomas Paine urged the creation in America of a spirit of nationhood.

We see very similar feelings, expressed in contemporary language, in the "Foreword" to *The Democratic Revolution in the West Indies* by Vernon Arnett. Mr. Arnett, a distinguished public leader in the new nation of Jamaica, should be read in two ways. First, he presents a penetrating analysis of the interaction among the pre-existing community of Jamaicans, the spirit of nationalism resulting from the fight for independence from Great Britain, and the results of nationalism for that community. As in the United States some two hundred years ago, the creation of a nation state pulled together diverse Jamaicans into a new and different community.

At the same time Mr. Arnett is a passionate protagonist for the new nations. His is a polemic in favor of a radical change in the "terms of trade" between new nations and old. He is the "thing itself."

David W. Minar
Political Change

English liberalism and in good part the liberalism of the French enlightenment tended to be anticommunity in bias. That is to say, they viewed the individual as the integral element in social life and the more inclusive units as his artificial creations. Thus, community was not a thing in itself but an aggregate without independent existence and will, at best an instrument to individual welfare. Rousseau, borrowing in this sense the classical position, saw community as something organic, morally prior to the individual, and having its own will. Perhaps in the labeling of political theories, Rousseau's may best be called "communitarian" as contrasted with "individualist." Its standards for judging political acts (or policy or regime) are framed in terms of needs or goods of "the community," not those of individuals.

The *Declaration* [*of Independence*] seems to imply shadings of the organic interpretation of community, though they are only shadings and faint ones at that. The first sentence speaks of the necessity of "one people" to dissolve political bonds and to "assume among the powers of the earth" a "separate and equal station." These glimmerings are easily lost in the rationalist—individualist tone of most of the document, and, to be sure, the *Declaration* declares the independence of sovereign *states*. Significance does not lie, however, with quibbles about the "real" meaning of its words, but with what they suggest about a sense of community incipient in revolutionary society. This may, taking some liberty, be described as a seed of American nationalism, a nationalism destined to grow by fits and starts into a major political force three-quarters of a century later. It did not, of course, take that long to assume recognizable embryonic form.

Nationalism is thought by many analysts of the current scene to be one of the principal characteristics and motive forces of present-day political activities and arrangements. The nation-state had well taken form by the time of the American Revolution, though its more extreme symbols developed later. But the point is that while the American Revolution can scarcely be interpreted as a nationalistic revolution, it did

From David W. Minar, *Ideas and Politics, The American Experience* (Homewood, Ill.: The Dorsey Press, 1964), pp. 81–82. Reprinted by permission.

have nationalistic overtones that bind it, however tenuously in ideology, to the modern revolutions, from the French one forward, in which nationalism has been a central appeal. The American Revolution is a part of this slowly developing modern political outlook; it is not an antiquarian relic or a thing in itself, entirely detached from the nationalistic, community-centered demands of later periods.

Thomas Paine
Of the Present Ability of America

The infant state of the Colonies, as it is called, so far from being against, is an argument in favor of independence. We are sufficiently numerous, and were we more so, we might be less united. It is a matter worthy of observation, that the more a country is peopled, the smaller their armies are. In military numbers, the ancients far exceeded the moderns: and the reason is evident, for trade being the consequence of population, men become too much absorbed thereby to attend to any thing else. Commerce diminishes the spirit, both of patriotism and military defence. And history sufficiently informs us, that the bravest achievements were always accomplished in the non-age of a nation. With the increase of commerce, England hath lost its spirit. The city of London, notwithstanding its numbers, submits to continued insults with the patience of a coward. The more men have to lose, the less willing are they to venture. The rich are in general slaves to fear, and submit to courtly power with trembling duplicity of a Spaniel.

Youth is the seed time of good habits, as well in nations as in individuals. It might be difficult, if not impossible, to form the Continent into one government half a century hence. The vast variety of interests, occasioned by an increase of trade and population, would create confusion. Colony would be against colony. Each being able might scorn each other's assistance; and while the proud and foolish gloried in their little distinctions, the wise would lament, that the union had not been formed before. Wherefore, the *present time* is the *true time* for establishing it. The intimacy which is contracted in infancy, and the friendship which is formed in misfortune, are, of all others, the most lasting and unalterable. Our present union is marked with both these characters: we are young, and we have been distressed; but our concord hath withstood our troubles, and fixes a memorable era for posterity to glory in.

From *Common Sense*, 1776.

Vernon L. Arnett
from *The Democratic Revolution in the West Indies*

I am a Citizen of Jamaica. This formula may be multiplied seventy times with a mere change of nation to mark the sealing of the constitutional instruments which has in the past few years removed the colonial patchwork from the map of the world. A few scattered protected territories are today the embarrassing residue of the pride of empire. The proconsuls have packed their bags and handed over the keys. Keys to a brave, new world?

The future of all the peoples of the world depends on the answer to this question. With the transfer from colonial rule to independence, national equality has been achieved in the United Nations Assembly for peoples in Africa, Asia and the West Indies who were formerly the subjects of one or other of the metropolitan powers. These were the have-nots who could clearly be identified as colonial. They have now joined the other have-nots who won their citizenship from the revolutionary 18th century on or whose subjugation has never been politically formalized. In the community of nations today, therefore, the haves and the have-nots face each other across the vast gap which marks the division between the many nations of the greater part of the world and the handful of nations who have achieved hegemony at their expense. Can this gap be bridged and, if so, what are the new relationships that will make this possible? And, if there can be no meeting, what happens to all the world?

.   .   .   .

The climacteric of independence was seen by Nehru. Inaugurating the Asian Conference in New Delhi in 1947, he said, "standing on this watershed which divides two epochs of human history and endeavour, we can look back on our long past and look forward to the future that is taking shape before our eyes." Nehru saw more than a billion people living in new independence in a world of technological advance and shrinking distances, farming and exploring the wealth of soil, of sea and all the universe. If nuclear research and achievement have so far

Reprinted by permission from Wendell Bell, ed., *The Democratic Revolution in the West Indies*, copyright 1967 Schenkman Publishing Company.

done no more than lead the world into a dead end, overshadowed by clouds of destruction, then those who are fresh on the march and with still a great distance to go must take the lead out of the dead end.

.   .   .   .

The new nations have taken with them into independence a great backlog of problems. They are economically under-developed and many labour under a sense of inferiority. But even with the will—where are the tools? Or how are they come by? How must the effort go? There is the double task of bringing everyday life closer to the standards of advanced societies which have given us their laws and culture but not their lathe and plough. Then there is the task of re-claiming and rehabilitating a mass of the population, already beyond school age and worn down by adversity, while trying to cope with the care and education of the newcomers. In Jamaica, for example, with 100,000 children for whom there are no school places, there are 50,000 children now annually reaching the age of five years. With un-employment at over 16% of the work force, the vast majority of the idle are in the 15–19 age group with only 15% in that age group pur-suing full time studies. The temptation is very great to choose a new father in different clothes and for the new image (if ever clearly seen) to be blurred by the shadows of the old.

It would be wrong to conclude, however, that the achievement of political independence has created a new situation, fraught with diffi-culty and risk, as well as promise, for the have-nots alone. Much public attention has been drawn to the obstacles which they face in achieving economic viability for their societies and higher standards of living for their peoples. Aid by way of finance and technical services is stressed and advertised as essential from the more advanced countries. It has become fashionable, now that colonialism is not in vogue, to revert to the motif of the "white man's burden" because of a protective and bene-ficial relationship to the advantage of the protected and at the expense of the protector. Foreign aid may therefore be represented as a con-tinuation of these idealistic policies but might equally be represented either as a form of recompense for past exploitation or as a means of preserving and extending economic control since aid is tied not only to goods but also to behaviour. The fact that former overlords are also at risk in the new situation should not be over-looked; and it is a risk which looms for their economies as a whole just as directly as it is a risk for those of their nationals who have come to own, in many in-stances, the greater part of the productive and trading enterprises of the former colonial and semi-colonial territories. . . .

The few great of the earth, therefore, appear to have a tremendous material stake in the maintenance of a system in which there are many poor. There is the compulsion of maintaining an economic relationship and of trying to contain the impact of new, lusty nationalism on the social and cultural pattern which made economic exploitation an accepted feature of society. Nationalism and independence clearly present a threat to this. Landownership is concentrated in a few hands, there is foreign ownership and exploitation of resources, the economy is based mainly on export agriculture and the import of consumer goods. Against this, there are poverty and unemployment at one end and conspicuous consumption at the other. Opportunities are severely limited and status is denied to the majority. This complex can be the base for revolutionary action. There may be confiscation because of the choice between paying (some say twice) for wealth that has been created and providing the means of development. There may be drastic changes in economic power and in the direction of the economy towards more food, houses and education and away from the maintenance of vested interests.

Nationalism can therefore be an explosive force primed by discontent and the desire for change. For those whose interests lie in the preservation of the status quo, there has been a weapon close to hand in the attachment of the tag of Communism to the nationalist movement with international consequences. The smear has become the war cry against the move for self-determination and the natural desire to use political power, backed by universal suffrage, to achieve economic independence. Intervention, aid or embargo, and the skills of diplomacy are the manoeuvres on the battlefield and strange bearers carry the banners of freedom.

In the result, capital and technical aid, Peace Corps and food for peace can become suspect as part of the plot to keep things as they are. Are science and technology, the establishment of international agencies, the efforts of the United Nations, the enlargement of trade and exchange facilities—all so urgently needed—to be under the aegis of economic domination and continued exploitation? Are these things to make the gap wider between haves and have-nots, fueling the anger? Is there no way out of parcelling the world willy-nilly between two camps?

Consequently, the new nations in seeking change for themselves cannot confine the effects to their own societies. The changes they must make and the new things they must do will have a profound effect on the greater nations. The struggle of the haves and the have-nots is more than the internal conflict within each nation—new or old. The conflict is now international. Accommodations between Washington and Moscow will not solve the issue as between those who now have political power and seek to use it to take economic control over their societies from those who will have to learn to live without it. Can a new relationship be established or will economic imperialism, divested of political power, intensify the threat to world peace in the effort to hold what they have?

There has been no period in world history in which there have not been wars for the control of territory, resources, trade routes, goods and people. These wars have always been fought in the name of freedom. Wars in the past could be localised according to spheres of influence and power. It was not until this century that two world wars came. Today the border conflicts or the conflicts between racial or cultural groups cannot be as easily confined. The world position has been sharpened to the edge by the right of the new nations, acting in political independence, to bring off internal coups or to hold peaceful elections as the case may be, and these may result in realignments. A war is escalated in Vietnam, a match sputters in the Dominican Republic, the Congo may flare or India and Pakistan or Malaysia and Indonesia may cause the explosion. The new nations have come to independence dependent on some great power or other economically and militarily. A new nation may occupy no more than a strategic position such as Cyprus. It is the new nations who are first in danger. When a nuclear conflict comes it will be over their dead bodies. If they seek to achieve equality within their own boundaries, it may set the match to the powder keg. The cynic holds that it is best to live with the parcelling of the world between the two powers who hold the nuclear aces. How far can the new nations go? At least, they must put the matter to the test and do so better collectively rather than as single spies. Can equality be achieved in an unequal world and can the new nations find sufficient strength among themselves to make their impact in the creation of a new world order? Each nation must try for itself and with others. Their effort will be the test of democracy and the validity of freedom. But no new nation can do the job of freeing itself until it first frees its own people.

The political independence of the new nations, therefore, can be seen as setting the stage for two revolts: the revolt of the new nations against the dominance of the powerful nations who have up to now had the power to arrange world affairs between themselves and, failing agreement, to come to blows and, secondly, the revolt of oppressed classes within these new nations themselves. The significance of the latter revolt lies in the fact that, like their counterparts in the industrial countries, they must now make their demands and press their struggle against their own national leaders instead of combining with those leaders, as in the nationalist movement in a colonial country, to wrest the right of political self-determination from an imperialist master.

In their introduction to *The Democratic Revolution in the West Indies,* Professors Bell and Oxaal say that the six studies in general deal with "the spread and development of the democratic revolution through time and space from the eighteenth-century Atlantic community to the twentieth-century global society." The word "revolution" is accepted in this study, they say, in the meaning attached to it by R. R. Palmer as a conflict between incompatible images of the future and opposing views of what the community ought to be, because it includes serious political protest and a series of rapid changes resulting in the reconstitution of government and society. Bell and Oxaal say,

> We take as our underlying hypothesis the proposition that much of the political, economic, and social change that is going on in the world today, and has gone on in the recent past, can be understood as a continuation of the democratic revolution—especially as an extension of the drive toward equality —to which the Europe and America of the latter part of the eighteenth century gave birth as a realizable human aspiration in this world.

The fundamental question must be asked: Can or will the new nations, now having the right to change, follow the path of the old? The development of the parliamentary system as a means of breaching the privilege of feudalist classes was accompanied by the industrial revolution, and new social and economic organisation partnered political democratisation. In the new nations, universal adult suffrage and elected governments have succeeded foreign bureaucratic rule but the use of political power for social and economic reorganisation does not necessarily flow as the natural consequence since to a great extent the means are in the hands of the former political masters and caught up in the external trading and financial mechanisms. The will to change, even if not for social and cultural reasons, is conditioned accordingly.

Bell, for example, quotes R. R. Palmer as seeing the democratic revolution aimed against feudalism, aristocracy and privilege and he includes colonialism. This power may be broken constitutionally within the country where the persons who hold this power, in whatever form, are an elite within the community. In the case where political and economic power are in foreign hands, the democratic revolution must be in two stages: the power of choice (political) and the use of this power for social and economic change. Without exception, the new nations of the 20th century must face not only vested class interest within the community but the vested interest also of those without the community who enjoy the backing of the greatest and richest countries of the world. The difficulties are that much greater, some say immeasurably greater, but the new nations still have their future to make for themselves. They must have an image of the future and they must have the will and the endurance and the capacity for sacrifice to work towards it. If they lack the will, then the keys they have been handed open only into a cave of dead sea fruit.

If this, broadly stated, is the core of the problem, the role of the social scientist and the studies of the sort encompassed herein must be of profound interest insofar as the motivations of leaders and people may be interpreted at a point in history when profound changes are inevitable. The past has left its mark and scored significant patterns for great and small and poor and rich. Existing modes of production and a social organisation which have developed out of the needs of the past cannot be rationalised and made the means in a future in which the new men of the new nations have in their grasp the effective power to decide what they wish to do and how they choose to do it. The industrial revolution of the 19th century and all its consequences, including the sowing of the seeds of equality, can evolve today into what Bell describes as the spread of the democratic revolution throughout the world. But whether democratic or not (or peaceful or not), revolution is inevitable since the wine of independence is heady and cannot be contained in old skins. It has come in the West Indies to a society which on the surface had adopted the culture of the former rulers: their religion, concept of rule of law, parliamentary system, social stratification and concept of property rights, and worship of the Western gods of creative activity. But there is a great mass of the population for whom these concepts have little more significance than the appurtenances of a privileged class to be enjoyed or not as the opportunity may arise. It is largely this section of the population for whom the existing society has brought no benefits, and since they see no real opportunity of improving their lot they can hardly be expected to have absorbed reverence for a culture in the same way as those for whom it has given status, security and hope of advancement. This is the natural consequence of colonialism which could not have achieved even the limited ends it set itself without dividing the population and creating its fifth column suitably inspired with a "well nurtured sense of inferiority."

Imperialist exploitation of the West Indies was not a tip-and-run affair necessitating at the most the control of a port as a trading centre. Jamaica and the other West Indian islands were ideally suited to the cultivation of sugar cane and Britain joined with France and Spain in this exploitation, embarking on the essential and profitable sideline of transporting captured or purchased Africans to be entered in the estate books as pieces of equipment, necessary capital to be written off as obsolescent or added to as the case might be. There was other machinery to be protected and gradually a large investment in sugar, later expanding into coffee, chocolate and cattle rearing. Stability was necessary for this investment (and still is) and stability could not indefinitely be assured by arms or even by expatriate owners and overseers. Progress towards a stable middle class, satisfactorily acculturated to the needs of the imperialist power, was hastened by formal and informal alliances between white and black producing a coloured middle class who understandably sought by all means at hand to advance themselves as rapidly as possible away from an African mother to a father from the master race. There was the plantocracy—the upper ruling class and at the other end a mass of enslaved Africans who were to be left to their own devices at emancipation while their owners received cash for the value lost. In between, there grew up a skilled, professional and trading middle class advancing into a local capitalism, subservient to the needs of imperialism, counting all their blessings of status, wealth, conspicuous consumption and opportunity as flowing from a foreign domination and culture.

.   .   .   .

Jamaica and the West Indies, like every other new nation, are now free to decide. To what extent the decisions they make will be influenced by the legacy of the past will significantly determine the future of these peoples. An effort of will is needed to take hold of the future and, where necessary, make the clean break with the past. Leaders and people will have to combine in an effort to secure united identification as one people. If the present divisions are to be abolished, it can only be as a result of a policy for equality and full participation in the social and economic structure of the society. It is essential as a first step for the leaders to divest themselves of the "inferiority complex" of colonialism. In my new country, they must seek to hold up an image of Jamaica for the Jamaican people and not strain after an artificial image for the powerful financial centre of the world. They must be prepared to go a Jamaican way, hew it out if need be, rather than stick to a way merely because a more powerful nation might be willing to go that way with them. There is a limited time in which to make these decisions. The revolution is inevitable. If it can come about as the result of a national choice and be dynamised by a national effort then it can be the democratic revolution.

The leaders of the new nations owe it to their own peoples and to all the peoples of the world not to try to contain the desire for change but to channel it into the national movement. While there is much to be done and while the tools for the job are often inadequate and, in some cases, lacking, the revolution of rising expectations will find the men, and the men will find the means. The new world of science and ideas which has accompanied the political liberation of the last decade has opened up for those who have had so little and have so much to gain. What is needed is the will and the endurance. I am confident that the new world has these qualities and it is because of this that the new nations have an essential role to play in creating a world in which man, and not the bomb, is master.

CHAPTER 8

The Community of Function

At various points in the preceding pages we have suggested that urban society has brought about specialization and functional interdependence. Whereas formerly men carried on highly similar occupational lives, with urbanization their work has become differentiated, some doing one kind of job, others doing another. Tasks have also been specialized by organization for the performance of services and the production of goods the society wants. The organizations thus developed threaten in one way or another the relationships that have traditionally revolved around the localities where people live.

The threat to the local community is double-edged; functional specialization pulls men out of an important part of their interaction with their neighbors, and bodies of specialized men themselves become communities, but communities independent of place. They develop within themselves the loyalties, senses of identification, values, and other marks of the cohesive subculture. Thus the factory, the trade union, the corporation structure, the profession become communities bound together by shared function rather than shared space. Some argue that these are more "real" communities, *i.e.*, communities with greater effects on men's lives, than their towns and neighborhoods.

The readings offered in this section speak to several sides of this phenomenon. Each deals with a functional community based on a different social-economic grouping: Cottrell with that of the working railroader, Goode with the professional, Long with the corporate employee, and Snow with the faculty of an English college. Cottrell's article shows how the constraints of a function, in this case the compulsion of time on the railroad man, throw him into relation with his occupational community and out of joint with his residential neighbors. It is hard to imagine the social effects of a job described more graphically than they are here. Goode provides a valuable conceptual analysis of community and discusses its relevance to the professions. He treats the professional community from two standpoints: the reasons for and ways it creates community among its members through socialization and control; and its relation with what he calls the "containing" society, the larger social grouping of which it is a part. Long is also concerned with the internal character of a functional group, the modern corporation, but his emphasis falls on its external consequences, more particularly on the destructive effects of the corporate economy on the local polity. The problem again lies with the compulsions and distractions of the organizational role. Snow in the epilogue to his novel *The Masters* describes the evolution of two complementary functional organizations, the college and the university, and their relations to the developing nation and the "scientific community."

The importance of functional communities to modern life is obviously far-reaching. They make the town, the city, and the nation more complicated and probably more difficult places to govern. They create multiple and sometimes conflicting loyalties. They often carry more power than the supposedly "sovereign" jurisdictions of the political state. The entire relationship of functional group and polity is one of the most puzzling for contemporary society.

Though we have been concerned here almost exclusively with communities that grow out of occupational or economic identification, similar problems may arise from other subgroupings in society. Communities of leisure activity, of religion, of ethnicity, for example, while not comparable in all ways to those of function, are common in today's city, and their consequences for the city as a community are similarly great.

W. F. Cottrell
Of Time and the Railroader

The fourth dimension has been a subject for everything from highly abstract and critical thinking to fantastic imagination. It has served to modify fixed points in an established science and to support time worn religions. Likewise, calculations in which time is taken as an aspect of all other measurements have imposed new restrictions on human behavior.

That the centuries have witnessed a modification in the concept of time, Sorokin[1] has adequately demonstrated. There is no need for us to raise the question as to whether in the long run the present conception of time may be altered, for, in the moment that we are considering, the use of the Newtonian system of mechanics for the creation of our technology binds us to the use of a mechanical conception of time. We may argue long and bitterly about the nature of time, but we know that if we want to catch a train, see a kick-off, or hear a radio program, our frame of reference forces us to consult an accurate clock.

The vast subdivision of labor which characterizes our technology requires coordination in time and space—neither axis alone is adequate. The backbone of industrialism is the railroad. Split-second timing of industrial operations reflects back along the line of transportation and imposes constantly new and closer limits upon those who operate trains.

Time is an important factor in any social pattern. Social interaction requires time coordination, and to the degree that occupation determines time distribution, time limits all forms of social participation. As technology controls time for the railroader, it also determines the tempo and the interval of other social relationships and sets a pattern for the personality.

After consulting Gulliver on the function of his watch, the Lilli-

Reprinted from the *American Sociological Review*, April 1939, pp. 190–198 by permission of The American Sociological Association and the author.

[1]Pitirim Sorokin *et. al.*, *Social and Cultural Dynamics*, Vol. 2, 413–428, New York, 1937. A further development of the concept of "Social Time," Pitirim A. Sorokin and Robert K. Merton, *Amer. J. Sociol.*, March, 1937, 615–629 indicates that the current concept of time is merely an attribute of our "sensate culture." An interesting rejoinder and reply to the rejoinder reveal another point of view. *Amer. J. Sociol.*, May, 1938, 667–670.

putians came to the conclusion that it was his God. Observing the money spent and the care lavished on his watch, a Martian might conclude the same thing of the railroader. All those who have direct responsibility for the actual operations of trains must carry a fine timepiece which will gain or lose not more than forty seconds in two weeks and which must be cleaned and regulated twice a year by a railroad watch inspector. A delay of thirty seconds in leaving a terminal calls for explanation, five minutes' delay means investigation, and a half hour gives apoplexy to every official from the superintendent to the lowest foreman. On single track roads where trains meet at passing tracks, thirty seconds' delay means that one of the trains will be almost a half mile from a passing track when the other reaches it, and that means delay of a second train, with possible misunderstanding and resultant disaster.

Delays at crossovers may mean a reversal in the order in which trains use the intersection, possible increased delay while clearance is secured, and a whole series of new orders to care for trains that otherwise would be met as a matter of course by other trains over which they have the right of way. The timetable is not only a convenience for the fidgeting tourist who uses it to chart his progress and occupy himself; it is a habit-system, or a "subconscious mind," for the railway "organism." Trainmen meet all scheduled trains in accordance with this table and plan to take sidings or make stops with a margin of time great enough to clear automatic signals for superior trains. The timetable makes all these coordinations as automatic as a conditioned reflex as far as the operating brain in the dispatcher's office is concerned. Delays mean that a new situation must be faced; operative intelligence is required for too many things at once and operating efficiency falls. The fatigued brain of the trick dispatcher is much more likely to err when it is called upon to take a load additional to that involved in planning only for extra trains. The technique of railroading itself makes it necessary to operate thousands of tons, moving at extremely high speeds with an accuracy greater than that maintained on many a factory assembly line.

This operating technique, determined by the nature of *things*, if disaster is to be avoided, is intensified by the interest and insurance calculus of capitalist civilization. To the African, time is like air, a free good, and therefore has no exchange value. To the American business man, who uses it as frequently as any other unit in determining price and exchange value, time becomes a cost factor of no little significance. Passenger trains were first to feel the impact of this factor. The plainsman planning to rejoin his fur-trapping "pardner" was content to rejoin him "after the snow melts" or "when the grass turns green," or more accurately "in April" or "six moons from now." Wagon trains made planning of trips calculable within a matter of weeks, stage coaches were due on a certain day, but no efficiency expert computed the value of a half-hour's delay for five hundred people, nor calculated the insurance rate on the whole outfit. Nowadays, business executives accustomed to making decisions involving millions after an interview lasting a few hours or even minutes, demand accurate coordination so that these precious minutes may be calculated far in advance, and even salesmen of less importance schedule their day in minutes. Interdependence with schedules of competing roads and other means of transportation led to increased emphasis on *time,* until the five- or ten-second error permitted on passenger trains became a commonplace.

Then luxury goods began to require the same sort of accuracy. Silk trains, valued in millions, speeding from Pacific Coast ports to silk centers the width of a continent away, were heavily insured. The insurance was high and calculated not in days but hours; the road which could promise accurate delivery could save in insurance sums large enough to make special schedules for silk a paying proposition.

Vitamin research and the necessity for stimulating the jaded palate of America with fresh fruits and vegetables next laid their toll on the railroader. For instance, lettuce can be picked only during two or three hours of the day if it is to remain fresh and firm, and a delay of an hour or two in delivery to a commission house means that the morning auctions are over, buyers surfeited and huge losses must be sustained. The radio and telegraphic reports on the market give sellers and buyers instantaneous information on which they may act, but the goods put in transit on that information must reach their destination within the range of a few hours if they are to meet the market for which they are intended. Railroads bidding for the milk business must guarantee schedules as accurate as those of passenger trains if losses due to spoilage are not to eat up profits. Even though beef can be refrigerated and kept indefinitely, its delivery to meet a certain day's market, or to keep the production line of a packing house going, means that cattle trains have to be put on penalty schedule if a competing road is not to get the business.

All this is as nothing compared to the demand imposed by new mass production industry and the cost accountants of our new business firms. Assemblage of an automobile on the Pacific Coast from parts manufactured at a half hundred or more widely scattered plants all over the United States makes the railroad *part of the assembly line.* When branch plants were first set up, management expected to carry overhead in the form of inventory great enough to permit some flexibility in delivery by the railroads, but cost accountancy quickly revealed a saving for "up and coming" firms, and now many a plant manager boasts that he closes each day without a single item of inventory and opens the next morning with the expectancy that all items brought from all over the United States will be found waiting on his siding. Perhaps the tremendous impetus given to this movement for increased speed can best be shown if we consider something of the history of train speed in America. *The Railroad Gazette,* and its successor, *The Railway Age,* has published an interesting series of tables showing fast and unusual runs all over the world.[2] Study of them is particularly enlightening. In 1905, a Pennsylvania train reached the speed of 127.2 miles an hour, and until very recent times that remained the record for railroad performance in the United States. In fact, in 1928 the conclusion reached by the editor was, "The improvement which has been made in locomotive service since 1895 is shown not so much in higher speed per se as in the heavier trains now hauled without diminution of speed and at sustained speeds for long distances." Another comparison might also show the nature of changes. In 1906, there were only two trains, traveling a total of 114 miles scheduled at sixty miles an hour or more; in 1928 the same two trains, now covering 135 miles, were the only trains scheduled to do more than sixty miles an hour. The next highest train speed in 1928 was the 48 m.p.h. average maintained between New York and Chicago by extra fare trains, and adding two other runs scheduled at more than forty-five miles per hour brought the total mileage schedule at that speed or better to a little less than 2500 miles all told. That these limitations were not technical in character will be observed when we see what was done with the same equipment when the depression forced railroad management to make adjustments.

In two significant articles, Steffee[3] shows the dramatic increase in scheduled train speeds. In 1936, there were six hundred and forty-four different runs scheduled at sixty miles or more an hour including stops from start to finish of the run. They cover a distance of 40,205 miles of which 29,301 are scheduled daily. The fastest long run scheduled in that year was the Santa Fe's *Superchief* which covered 202 miles of its eastbound trip at a cool 84 miles per hour. On one ten-mile stretch, it was *scheduled* to do 108 miles an hour. It is interesting to note that of the 40,000 mile-a-minute miles, 14,000 are made by steam

---

[2]*Railroad Gazette,* June 11, 1897, 415; Jan. 11, 1901, 24; Dec. 15, 565–566; Nov. 12, 1906, 394–395; *Railway Age,* July 7, 1928, 20–21; April 4, 1936, 583–586; see letter to editor, April 25, 1936, 700–701. See also letter in *The Railway Gazette* (British), Feb. 4, 1938, 210–214.

[3]Donald M. Steffee, "North America's Mile-A-Minute Runs," *Railroad Stories,* Oct. 1936, 20–27; same author and title, *Railroad Magazine,* April 1938, 7–20.

locomotives, in many cases the same engines in use in 1928. That the trend established between 1928 and 1936 is still accelerating can be seen when we look at the figures showing increases during 1937. During that year, the number of runs at a mile or more a minute jumped to 781, the total mileage of these runs jumped to 46,242 miles and the daily mileage increased by more than a third—from 28,301 to 38,523 miles of mile-a-minute trains. This was accompanied by some read-justments in the extreme scheduled time between certain points. There was a general increase in the speed of trains so that forty-five miles an hour becomes commonplace and Steffee[4] states that there is a "whole army" of trains operating at more than 55 miles an hour. Another significant trend is seen in that an increasing proportion of the fast runs are made by steam trains. For us, this means that the check on this rapid movement for speed which would naturally have resulted if new Diesel or electrics were required does not exist. Standard equip-ment already in existence is being used in increasing amounts. Of the 38,000 miles run daily, 20,000 miles of mile-a-minute runs are pulled by steam engines.

While comparable figures are not available to show increased freight speeds, some summaries are available which show a like trend. For example, the *Monthly Labor Review*, July, 1937, 45:78–101, cites aver-age freight train speed in 1926 at 11.9 miles per hour; 1933, 15.7; 1934, 15.9; and 1935, 16.1. The American Railway Association adver-tises an increase in speed of 43 percent in five years, 1932 to 1937, and many freight time cards show scheduled speeds of more than forty miles an hour.

The complete interdependence of mass production industries is re-vealed by such events as the strikes of 1937 in which the absence of single items such as an induction coil or brakeshoe brought the whole automobile industry to a halt. The result is, of course, that the penalties imposed for a few hours' delay in delivering any one of hundreds of items may be fantastic.

Time penalties come to figure highly in the minds of business man-agers; therefore, railroads have made seemingly impossible promises of delivery because they must bid for regular accounts from shippers who, by Interstate Commerce regulation and antirebate laws, are denied the price cutting and special discounts by which other industries secure contracts. These impossibilities are then turned into realities through pressure on the railroader. The traffic department which has secured a "juicy bit" of business gets apoplectic when a delay threatens to lose it; therefore, down the line, from general manager to car inspector, goes out the edict, "Delay *this* train at peril of your job." Supervisors are bombarded with messages, "Meet this train"; "No explanation for delay of this train will be accepted"; "From this date, train operates on such and such a schedule, no delay can be permitted." In the meantime, under the same pressure from "efficiency experts," men are fired or laid off, trains increased in length, the number of service-stops cut, and less money is spent on repairs and maintenance. The second hand of his watch becomes a sword of Damocles to the railroader.

The twenty-four hour day and the three hundred and sixty-five day year are as necessary to the railroad as to the calendar. There are no holidays. Christmas day in Chicago is two days before Christmas in Los Angeles, if you are moving east, and two days after Christmas if you move west. No break in service at one point would correspond with delivery date at another except where short distances are involved. So the pressure is incessant. For the railroader, split-second timing never ceases; he is always on call. The plant is never shut down. A wreck, a washout, a split switch, a sudden increased demand for power, an engine failure, frozen steam pipes, clogged toilet facilities, failure of air conditioning, a broken train line—any one of a thousand incidents may threaten to cause delay or to inconvenience patrons, so the railroader must be available even though his shift is over and he is supposedly a "free man." He is a slave to the clock; intense time-consciousness marks the railroader in all his social relationships.

This time-emphasis is, of course, an aspect of the lives of all moderns. They catch the timed trains, eat by the clock, quit by the clock and are clocked in their amusement: "The next feature will begin at 8:12"; "Twenty-five cents for the first three minutes, five cents for each additional minute"; "The kickoff will be at 2:30"; and so on, *ad infinitum.*

Coordination in time takes its toll from all of us but probably among few other classes is it so complete and coercive as among railroaders. It becomes a marked irritant in his relationship with other less time-conscious groups. "Dinner at eight" means *eight, not* eight-ten or eight-twenty; "I'll meet you at seven," means *seven, not* seven-thirty or the debutante's eight-thirty. The casualness with which people in other walks of life take delays irritates the railroader and in turn his irritation produces counterirritation among his fellows. A railroad worker expects to lay down his tools with the whistle, or a little before. To the railroader, the callousness with which a building contractor, storekeeper, or other employer, exacts an additional five minutes' work is unforgiveable.

The "sixteen hour law" under which the Federal Government regulates the working hours of trainmen and enginemen is absolute. If a hapless crew "lets the monkey get them" or, in other words, finds itself on the road at the expiration of sixteen hours from their terminal of departure, they must stop all active operations. When they sense the approach of the limit, the crew takes to a siding, notifies the dispatcher of their situation and waits for a relief crew to be sent to bring them in. Even delays occasioned by landslide, washout, the derailment of another train, or other accident, do not serve as excuse. If the crew has been on duty during the waiting time, they cannot move the train under penalty of heavy fine on the employing road. If an accident holds the train on the main line while the sixteen hour limit elapses, its crew may not even move the train to clear traffic for others. Protecting it from collision with track "torpedoes" and "fusees" (flares), they must wait until a crew with legal rest arrives to take charge of it.

Eight hours' rest is required out of every twenty-four in which sixteen hours are worked. A crew may not be called to take a train out before that rest has elapsed, but if another crew *is* called and takes their place and it is later shown that the legal rest of the first crew was up before the train departed, a "run around," or pay for the trip, is given the crew so deprived of their proper "turn". Time is certainly the essence of this contract.

The obverse of this occupational dependence on the clock is the almost complete denial of the opportunity to "time-plan" other relationships. Shopmen working on general repairs, or those on a three-shift basis, such as dispatchers, car and engine inspectors, can normally expect to work one shift and be through, but men on the extra-board, or trainmen and enginemen working on a "chain gang," in which crews take their turns on whatever business is handled, car repairers who may be called out to handle repairs or service extra trains, and many others, find that the demands of occupation make all other plans conditional. Like other aspects of railroading, this is more typical of trainmen than it is of workers in the other crafts.

"We can't plan to have Johnny in the Christmas play because his father may be 'in' right then and we want him to be home." "Mary can't promise to come at that time because her father may want his dinner and he likes to have the children at meals." "I can't join the bridge club because I want to be with John when he is home and I might have to miss too many times." "We did want to have Sunday dinner with the Browns but Will is going to be 'out' and we have to have our dinner Saturday night instead." "We'll go to the benefit if John is 'in' and has his rest, but I can't buy a ticket because he may want to sleep." "We don't want to sign up for that series because you never know whether you can go or not." "The boys were *so* disappointed. They planned to go fishing with their Dad on the Fourth but there was an excursion and he had to take it 'out'." "I had the nicest Easter outfit and then we couldn't go to church because Henry was 'called' at nine o'clock." These are typical of the irritations which

beset the life of the railroader and his family when he is still on un-
scheduled freight or the extra-board, which usually occurs while his
family, if he has one, is young, and when the demarcation which this
sort of life serves to make between the railroader and others, and between various railroaders, is most important. Meals may be required
at any hour; sometimes two or three series of meals in a day must be
prepared depending upon school schedules and those of men on various
shifts. Car inspectors, for example, eat their lunch when they can get
it. The noon meal may come any time between eleven and three,
depending on the arrival of nonscheduled extra trains, or the amount
of "running repairs" that have to be done. The rest of the community—its schools, its churches, lodges, bridge clubs, official meetings
of boards of trustees, town councilmen, benefits, socials, theaters (except
movies)—also run on a time schedule, but it is not so rigid as that of
the railroad, although it is much more definite and therefore will
permit more time-planning than is possible for those railroaders who
operate trains.

Membership in any organization with regular meetings is difficult to
maintain and the socializing effect of such contacts is lost. Forms of
recreation that depend upon no collaboration with others must be
indulged in. In cities, there are continuous shows, night clubs and
restaurants, taxi dancehalls, and other individualized amusements; in
rural areas, fishing and hunting, pool parlors, or saloons are offered;
in both, the ubiquitous crapgame and other forms of gambling.

Civic participation is rendered difficult. No membership in governing
boards is feasible, promised aid in community service may be impossible when the "layover" between runs comes at the other end of the
line or a "bump" may put one on another run. Indifference created by
occupationally induced mobility is heightened by this time-factor, and
the other members of the community resent the refusal of this group,
usually the most financially able, to take any responsibility in community affairs.

Family life is greatly affected. If the wife and mother attempts to
make her family an integrated part of the community, she must con-
form to its timing. Meals must be ready for the children so that they
can attend school and Sunday School. Promises as to their participation
in athletics, school government, and extracurricular activities must be
kept. If this be done, it may mean that the husband and father will see
the children only rarely. He can expect that at least half the time his
rest will come during the time they are sleeping; their whole day is
normally taken at school; if his meals cannot be made to coincide with
theirs (and frequently, if he is to get any sleep, they cannot), he may
not see his children at all, unless they give up all plans of their own.

The wife labors under a double difficulty. In the absence of the father of her children, she has the whole problem of discipline. She cannot even threaten "when your father comes home tonight" for that may be at three o'clock in the morning. She must be prepared to have meals ready whenever he comes in, which means constant preparation for the unexpected; she seldom knows in which particular meal her husband will share. She cannot plan with any degree of certainty her own recreation or community participation. If she joins club, church, guild, or lodge, and takes office, she may incur the displeasure of a husband deprived of what he regards as his right to her time and attention when he is 'in.' If she does not join, she is likely to be deprived of almost all recreation since she is denied the equivalent of the forms of recreation her husband may have, and if she chooses to go to public dances or any other public place where couples are expected, she is immediately suspected by all the "good" people of the community. Small wonder that family life during this period is frequently so distasteful and disorganized as to rob later years, when a satisfactory "run" has been earned, of most of its satisfactions. Yet the very situations that make family life difficult also serve to increase the significance of the family in the life of the railroader. In many cases, it is the only group in which he functions, and an idealized attitude toward children frequently results, making for a romantic indulgence of their whims.

Other classes of employees in continuous service, particularly telegraphers and "agents" in small stations, with no relief operator, are made even more dependent upon the clock. Interrupted rest periods are a commonplace. Though the station be officially closed, emergencies may make their presence at the "key" necessary, and many of these men have slept for years with a telegraph repeater in the room, paying no attention to its continuous clatter until the call letters of their own station shock them into instant wakefulness. The newer dependence upon the "dispatcher's" telephone with a selector that rings only the operator for whom it is intended has somewhat reduced this tension, but no operator, whether on or off duty, ever gets out of hearing of his "call bell" without a sense of guilt. To wives anxious to escape the confines of a lonely station, this marriage to a telegraph key is frequently an almost unbearable form of polygamy.

"Agents" in small stations work all trains, the clock around, meeting passengers, selling tickets, arranging for the loading and unloading of freight; securing a doctor to treat the train-sick old lady from Dubuque and a nurse to hold the hand of a homeward bound conventionite who has imbibed not wisely but too much; checking on the whoops of a child about to board the train to discover whether he will become liable for permitting a person with contagious disease to cross a state line; ordering a California-bound farmer's wife with preserves packed in straw to substitute paper in order to avoid another penalty; all under the continuous pressure of time, and with the knowledge that error in transmitting or receiving a "train order" may mean disaster and death.

The higher the railroader climbs on the supervisory ladder, the less he is able to plan his own life. The foreman is expected to supervise even those employees who work night shifts, to meet trains when necessary regardless of the hour, and to be in continuous presence during the day when the regular shifts of "dead workers," "rip track" men, section men, janitors, etc., are working. If he reaches the rarefied atmosphere of the office of "trainmaster," "roadmaster," or "master mechanic," he is expected to maintain an office in regular contact both with superiors and foremen and to be physically present at numerous points scattered over as much as a thousand miles. Getting up in the middle of the night to catch trains, getting meals when he can, and in emergency, neither getting nor expecting sleep, is the lot of the supervisor as well as his underlings. Is it any wonder that these "real railroaders" look with envious contempt at the comfortable "plush polishers" in the central offices, who live in a world of the eight-hour day, forty-hour week, and who take all legal holidays?

As "time marches on," its rhythm is set, not by organic impulse, but by the clacking of wheels on rail joints, the clatter of a telegraph key, and the distant whistle of a train departing "on time."

William J. Goode
Community Within a Community:
The Professions

This paper is concerned with a little explored area of social theory: the structural strains and supports between a contained community and the larger society of which it is a part and on which it is dependent. Presumably, the body of theory used for analyzing a community must be translated, qualified, or changed when that community exists within a larger society. Examples of such communities are fraternal orders such as the Masons, secret or extreme political parties, ethnic islands whether rural or urban, organized political or economic interest groups, or a specific profession such as medicine.[1]

From a broad inquiry into such structural relations between the contained community and the larger one, it may later be possible to derive important hypotheses about the forces that maintain both of them. The community studied is the professional community, which is different in important respects from the other examples.[2] Only two sets of links have been chosen for exploration: (1) socialization and social control, and (2) client choice or evaluation of the professional.

Characteristic of each of the established professions, and a goal of each aspiring occupation, is the "community of profession." Each pro-

Reprinted from *American Sociological Review*, Vol. XXII (April 1957), pp. 194-200 by permission of The American Sociological Association, and the author.

[1]See, for example, Georg Simmel, "The Secret and the Secret Society," in *The Sociology of Georg Simmel*, translated by Kurt Wolff, New York: The Free Press of Glencoe, 1950, pp. 307-379; William F. Whyte, *Street Corner Society*, Chicago, University of Chicago Press, 1943; Louis Kriesberg, "National Security and Conduct in the Steel Gray Market," *Social Forces*, 34 (March 1956), pp. 268-277, and "Customer *versus* Colleague Ties Among Retail Furriers," *Journal of Retailing*, 29-30 (Winter 1954-5, pp. 173-176; *The Executive Life*, ed. *Fortune*, Garden City: Doubleday, 1956; Allan W. Eister, "The Oxford Group Movement", *Sociology and Social Research*, 34 (November 1949); David Riesman, "Some Informal Notes on American Churches and Sects," *Confluence*, 4 (July 1955), pp. 127-159; Paula Brown, "Bureaucracy in a Government Laboratory," Institute of Industrial Relations Reprint No. 36, Los Angeles: University of California, 1954; etc.

[2]Other areas are analyzed in William J. Goode, Robert K. Merton, and Mary Jean Huntington, *The Professions in Modern Society*, New York: Russell Sage Foundation, 1957.

fession is a community without physical locus and, like other communities with heavy in-migration, one of whose founding fathers are linked only rarely by blood with the present generation. It may nevertheless be called a community by virtue of these characteristics: (1) Its members are bound by a sense of identity. (2) Once in it, few leave, so that it is a terminal or continuing status for the most part.[3] (3) Its members share values in common. (4) Its role definitions *vis-à-vis* both members and non-members are agreed upon and are the same for all members. (5) Within the areas of communal action there is a common language, which is understood only partially by outsiders. (6) The community has power over its members. (7) Its limits are reasonably clear, though they are not physical and geographical, but social. (8) Though it does not produce the next generation biologically, it does so socially through its control over the selection of professional trainees, and through its training processes it sends these recruits through an adult socialization process. Of course, professions vary in the degree to which they are communities, and it is not novel to view them as such.[4]

The elite of any profession are usually conscious of a communal identity. Indeed, the elite of an occupation aspiring to professional status may prematurely lay claim to belonging to a community.[5] Both the correct and the incorrect claims deserve sociological attention. First, it is likely that in speeches of the arrived or of the aspiring profession, no themes are so common as the ideal of service and the community of profession. Second, when such ideals are asserted as injunctions, goals, or descriptions of fact, they become justifications for many policies and subsidiary goals. Third, if indeed there is a positive response of the supposed community to such ideals, that response becomes at once an index of the power of the community and a means for furthering the goals of the community.

Consequently, it is likely that as the profession comes into being, or

[3]But we see the qualifications stated by Albert J. Reiss, "Occupational Mobility of Professional Workers," *American Sociological Review*, 20 (December 1955), pp. 693–700.

[4]See the extended discussion of "Discipline," p. 394 ff. in A.M. Carr-Saunders and P. A. Wilson, *The Professions*, Oxford: Clarendon, 1933; Morris L. Cogan, "Toward a Definition of Profession," *Harvard Educational Review*, 23 (Winter 1953), p. 35; Roscoe Pound, *The Lawyer from Antiquity to Modern Times*, St. Paul: West, 1953, pp. 4–10; Abraham Flexner, "Is Social Work a Profession?" *School and Society*, 1, (1915), pp. 901–911; Louis D. Brandeis, *Business—A Profession*, Boston: Small, Maynard, 1914, p. 2; Robert D. Leigh, *The Public Library in the United States*, New York: Columbia University Press, 1950, pp. 186–189.

[5]See, for example, the self-analysis in the professional journals of nursing, social work, librarianship, vocational counseling, school teaching, administration, business management, etc.

as an occupation begins to approach the pole of professionalism, it begins to take on the traits of a community. If a containing society becomes industrialized, it depends increasingly upon professional skills. The United States is probably typical of industrialized societies, in that its occupational life is coming to be characterized by professionalism, whose essence is the "community of occupation." To select only two facts which reflect this change: There is a higher number of professionals per 100,000 population (859 in 1870 to 3,310 in 1950, with little change in the older professions), and a growing number of occupations that aspire to professional status.[6]

Many of the traits that make the professions sociologically interesting grow from the dimensions of community. Typically a profession, through its association and its members, controls admission to training and requires far more education from its trainees than the containing community demands. Although the occupational behavior of members is regulated by law, the professional community exacts a higher standard of behavior than does the law. Both of the foregoing characteristics allow the professions to enjoy more prestige from the containing community than can other occupations. Thus, professionals stand at the apex of prestige in the occupational system.[7] Because of the controls over entrance and over professional behavior, and the possession of a monopoly of particular skills, the professional communities obtain incomes higher than those of other occupations.[8] Moreover, since each professional community has a monopoly over its skills, it must be consulted by the containing community and thus the professions generally hold a disproportionate share of seats in state and national legislative houses, on boards of directors, on advisory and technical commissions, and so on.[9] Little legislation relating to any profession is

---

[6]Alba M. Edwards, *Comparative Occupation Statistics for the United States, 1870–1940*, Washington, D. C.: U.S.G.P.O., 1943 pp. 91, 11, 178–179; *U. S. Census of Population*: 1950, Vol. II, *Characteristics of Population*, Part 1, p. 3, and p. 261. See also Edwards' discussion of "Comparability."

[7]*National Opinions on Occupations*, NORC, University of Denver, 1947, pp. 15–17. Interestingly, most professionals feel that their prestige is not high.

[8]Milton Friedman and Simon Kuznets, *Income from Independent Professional Practice*, New York: National Bureau of Economic Research, 1945, Ch. 3; George J. Stigler, *Employment and Compensation in Education*, New York; National Bureau of Economic Research, Occasional Paper No. 33, 1950, Tables 34, 36.

[9]P. A. Sorokin, "Leaders of Labor and Radical Movements in the United States and Foreign Countries," *American Journal of Sociology*, 33 (November 1927), p. 339; see also *inter alia* Hans D. Mauksch, *The Social and Political Background of the Members of the Seventy-sixth United States Congress*, M. A. thesis, University of Chicago, 1951, pp. 102–103; John Brown Mason, "Lawyers in the 71st to 75th Congress: Their Legal Education and Experience," *Rocky Mountain Law Review*, 10 (December, 1944, p. 44; etc. See also Jack N. Lott and Robert H. Coray, *Law in Medical and*

passed without being largely shaped by that profession. (In this society, at least, one cannot speak of the powerless professions.)

"Community" alone would not give so much power, of course, but each community of practitioners also demands high education of its members. This education is evaluated by the larger society as crucial in both individual and societal matters: disease and death, liberty and property, the problem of evil, construction and production, war, and so on. It is this last factor, the values of the larger society, in interaction with the prior two, which gives rise to the power of the professional community. No such power would be given, however, if there were not a professional community to demand it and be responsible for its use. As a consequence of the rewards given by the larger society, the community of profession can also demand higher talent in its recruits and require that they go through a considerable adult socialization process.

The advantages enjoyed by professionals thus rest on evaluations made by the larger society, for the professional community could not grant these advantages to itself. That is, they represent structured relations between the larger society and the professional community.

SOCIALIZATION AND SOCIAL CONTROL

Socialization and social control in the professions are made important by the peculiarly exploitative opportunities the professions enjoy. The problems brought to the professional are usually those the client cannot solve, and only the professional can solve. The client does not usually choose his professional by a measurable criterion of competence, and after the work is done, the client is not usually competent to judge if it was properly done.[10] In the face of these opportunities to exploit the larger society, the professional community is nevertheless given considerable discretion and power.

Dental Practice, Chicago: Foundation Press, 1942, Ch. VI. A common career pattern of the successful professional is to become increasingly involved in administrative and advisory affairs.

[10] As to adequacy of performance, each profession has its version of "copping a lesser plea," by which the professional convinces his client and, perhaps, himself that the professional work was well done, even if the result is not satisfactory. Cf. Oswald C. Hering, "The Architect and His Clients," *The American Architect,* 96 (October 13, 1909), pp. 141, 143; Joseph Hudnut, "Confessions of an Architect," *Journal of American Institute of Architecture,* 14 (August 1950), p. 109; Lee R. Steiner, *Where do People Take Their Troubles,* Boston: Houghton, Mifflin, 1945; Oswald Hall, *The Informal Organization of Medical Practice in an American City,* unpublished Ph.D. dissertation, University of Chicago, 1944, pp. 114–115; and Josephine J. Williams, "Patients and Prejudice: Lay Attitudes Toward Women Physicians," *American Journal of Sociology,* 51 (January 1946), p. 285.

Indeed, the very great prestige of the professions is a response of the society to their apparent self-denial, i.e., they can, but typically do not, exploit. This is not to say that professionals are nobler than lay citizens. Instead, the professional community holds that exploitation would inevitably lower the prestige of the professional community and subject it to stricter lay controls. It is at least clear that if individual clients believed that their practitioners were seeking to exploit them, they would not trust them so far as they do. More fundamentally, as in any other community, the highest rewards of prestige and money are most likely to be granted to the practitioners who actually live up to the professional role obligations. The practitioner who tries to live by the doctrine of *caveat emptor* might, unlike the business man, find himself expelled from his community, either informally or formally.

These larger forces operating on the two communities are implemented by the specific role definitions of the professional *vis-à-vis* his client. This means, in turn, that to the extent that community of profession is strong, its members face real temptations, and its behavioral demands are different from the demands of the lay world—to that extent it must put its recruits through a set of adult socialization processes and maintain procedures for continuing social controls over the practicing professional. Three professions—the clergy, the military, and medicine —almost isolate their recruits from important lay contacts for several years, furnish new ego ideals and reference groups, impress upon the recruits his absolute social dependence upon the profession for his further advancement, and punish him for inappropriate attitudes or behavior.[11] This socialization cannot be so complete as that of the child in the lay world, but that is not necessary, for the values of the professional community do not differ drastically from those of the larger society.

Social controls buttress the effects of socialization, and here again the larger society and the professional community interact in a complex way. There is probably a correlation between the degree of community of the profession and the extent of difference between the values of the practitioners and those of the larger society or of clients. However, in

---

[11]For various aspects of this adult socialization process, see Lawrence S. Kubie, "Some Unsolved Problems of the Scientific Career," Part II, *American Scientist*, (January 1954), pp. 105–106, 112; William Osler, "The Master-Word in Medicine," *Aequanimitas*, Philadelphia: Blakiston, 1926, p. 379; Mary Jean Huntington, "The Development of a Professional Self-Image Among Medical Students," in *The Student Physician*, edited by Robert K. Merton, forthcoming; and Howard S. Becker and James W. Carper, "The Development of Identification with an Occupation," *American Journal of Sociology*, 61 (January 1956), pp. 291–292.

its bid for respect from the larger society, the professional community must justify each provision in its code of ethics or etiquette by invoking ethical notions that are also accepted by the larger society, even when certain provisions seem to the lay eye at least potentially exploitative. As an additional complexity, the client may be only partially aware of the provisions that guard him, and is himself not bound to do much in order to be protected by them. It is the professional who must abide by them.

Corresponding to these potential strains, the "working codes" of ethics—written or unwritten—largely define appropriate professional behavior with respect to four categories of people: the larger community, fellow practitioners, unauthorized practitioners, and clients. The lawyer must control his own client in court. The physician must not refer a patient to an unauthorized practitioner, and the professional community puts pressure on the lay society to enforce legislation against the unauthorized. Obviously, codes can demand conformity from only one of these, professional colleagues. On the other hand, colleagues control each other's behavior with respect to the other categories.

In turn *each* of the four categories of persons possesses some measures of social control: the larger community through the legal agencies of the state; the client through his choice or rejection of the professional; the professional community, or colleagues, through their control over prestige and career advancement, as well as over the legal agencies of the state, such as licensing boards; and unauthorized practitioners by offering services to clients who are not satisfied with the professions.

But professions vary in the degree to which they rely upon one of these controls rather than another. None seems to rely greatly upon state control agencies, which in any event are largely staffed by professionals. The professional community exercises less control itself, when *client* economic controls are based on criteria that are accepted by the profession. Indeed, the professional group requires its control over its own members precisely *because* its judgments do not coincide generally with those of clients. As a consequence, its members *need* the protection of the professional community and will submit to its demands. A negative case is engineering, where the client is usually experienced, has mainly a contractual relationship with his engineer, and demands from the engineer what the profession itself would demand. As a result, compared with other professions, the engineering community has relatively less control over individual members. At the other extreme are professions dealing in human relations, such as the clergy or medicine, where the client is thought to be a poor judge of the professional product. Consequently, his choices would not reflect the judgment of the professional community, and the latter·exercises strong moral control over the practitioner. The unauthorized practitioner is most successful where the profession has poor technical control over a given problem.

Bureaucracy opens a further range of structural relationships. The professional who is also a bureaucrat becomes less *directly* dependent on the professional community for his career advancement, so that the ordinary sanctions of that community may have less impact. Nevertheless, the bureaucracy usually hires, fires, or advances him upon the advice of peer or superior professionals, who in turn may feel themselves to be part of the professional community. Correlatively, the bureaucracy makes and enforces rules for the professional, and thus becomes—like the professional community from which it derived most of those rules—a responsible control agent for the larger society. In turn, of course, the professional community is responsible to the bureaucracy for proper staffing.

By way of compensation, the professional community offers two main kinds of protection to its members. It protects the professional against client or lay community charges that it considers inappropriate or irrelevant. For example, as Hughes has noted, it takes a statistical view of professional errors of judgment.[12] It also offers advantages to those who are part of this community, by structuring professional practice so that the insiders will generally fare better than outsiders, in spite of erroneous judgments, that clients tend to make about professionals.[13] Thus, in exchange for protection against the larger lay society, the professional accepts the social control of the professional community.

As a consequence, the larger society has obtained an *indirect* social control by yielding *direct* social control to the professional community, which thus can make judgments according to its own norms. As a corollary, the normative structure of the professional community is reinforced, while this community can avoid the loss of prestige that nonpunishment of offenders would eventually cause. Professionals assert this relationship in their literature, and claim that their community is judged in lay society by their worst members. Moreover, they frequently argue that the most effective technique for avoiding lay control over the professional community is to maintain strong control over its members. Thus it is that the social control of the professional community

---

[12]Everett C. Hughes, "Mistakes at Work," *Canadian Journal of Economics and Political Science*, 17 (August 1951), pp. 320-327.

[13]An excellent analysis of this pattern in a well-controlled profession is that of Oswald Hall. See *op. cit.* and his "The Informal Organization of the Medical Profession," *Canadian Journal of Economic and Political Science*, 12 (February 1946) pp. 30-44, and "The Stages of a Medical Career," *American Journal of Sociology*, 53 (March 1948), pp. 327-336.

over its members may be seen as a response to the threat of the larger lay society to control it. Failure to discipline would mean both a loss of prestige in the society, and a loss of community autonomy.

CLIENT CHOICE AND PUBLIC RANKINGS

Client choices are a form of social control. They determine the survival of a profession or a specialty, as well as the career success of particular professionals. In turn, these choices determine the kind of professional help the society gets.

Almost no client *willingly* goes to an unethical or incompetent practitioner, and clients almost always claim that their own professionals are excellent. Yet, both informally and in their literature, professionals express a generally poor opinion of these choices. But, if these are *not* wise decisions, and the professional community is the only body that is competent to judge correctly, it would seem to be a violation of the professional ideal of service not to inform the larger society of its judgments. That is, if the larger society were to gain the benefit of professional knowledge, the professional community would publish evaluations of its members. Thereby, the larger society would benefit from better professional help, and the professional community might make individual practitioners more dependent on its approval.

Of course, professions are accustomed to ratings. In numerous professional schools, students are ranked. Examinations for entrance into the professions yield rankings that are sometimes made known. There are prizes for outstanding work. Professional associations place their honored members on boards and commissions. There are continuous professional judgments of high or low achievement. To the extent that any community exists, it evaluates the behavior of its members. Professional life is so fundamentally based on achievement, that such judgments of rank are made constantly. Indeed, rankings within the profession are a mode of social control.

However, such data are not generally available to the public, and are not widely known, even when not secret. The professional community will not rank its members for the larger society; and the latter cannot do so. In fact, the existing intra-professional evaluations create hostilities within the community, and the limitless challenge of professional life, for instance in the sciences, creates strong anxieties. The most successful practitioner, loaded with honors, worries about his failures and ineptness. The protective walls of the professional community keep those hostilities and anxieties within bounds by defining, for a given level of age, experience, training, and type of practice, what is a *passable* competence and achievement; and by forbidding the expression of such hostilities before the larger society. The guild asserts essentially that all, or nearly all, are colleagues, and that if reasonable allowances are made, they are wiser in their craft than outsiders can be.[14] As a corollary, these definitions protect the individual practitioner against impossible demands of the larger society, e.g., that he not make any errors in judgment, that he know all the latest discoveries and techniques, etc. Thus, colleague criticism is rarely permitted before laymen, and the professions justify the rule by asserting that such criticism would lower the standard of the profession in the larger society. A closely related sociological proposition is also offered as a justification—that such criticism, and presumably public rankings, would weaken the ties of the professional community, while it is the strength of these ties that makes possible *any* achievements of this community. That is, it cannot achieve its other, more important, goals if it ceases to be a community.

Structurally, to evaluate *colleagues* publicly is different from evaluating *trainees*. The latter are not yet community members. That is, the very process of evaluation denies or questions status inside the community, even if the ultimate judgment is favorable. Moreover, such evaluations would have to be made continuously, so that no practitioner could be certain of his membership—yet, it is this certainty of a shared identity, a common career, that is the central element in any community. An empirical approximation of this interaction occurs when the standards for entrance are raised substantially. This is, in effect, an announcement to the public that certain older members of the professional community have not been adequately trained. However, allegiance to the professional collectivity outweighs the service obligation to the public, and "grandfather clauses" lessen the severity of that indictment.

Two further corollaries must be noted. Although public rankings might seem to increase the power of the community, in fact they would give over social controls to the larger society. For, even if the rankings were broken down into classes of practitioners, by specialization, rural-urban location, or experience, the economic effect on those toward the bottom of *any* list would be catastrophic. The result, then, would be that the utilization of such evaluations could be in the hands of the clients or lay public—and this would be a denial of the primacy of the professional community in affairs of social control. Rankings would then have little independent potency within the community.

A final structural corollary is that each professional community would then have to make exorbitant demands on the containing society for

---

[14]Note that the academic puts great stress on achievement, but insists on "equality of the colleague" even when the colleague has a lower rank.

talented recruits and increased training facilities. For if a substantial proportion of the existing practitioners are given little client support because of such rankings, then other and better professionals must be trained. If all professions were to attempt this simultaneously, competing as they do for public support and the available supply of talent, the total demands could not be met.

These structural factors in the interaction between the professional community and the larger society suggest that the evaluations, which are the daily experience of all professionals, cannot and will not be formalized and made public. On the other hand, to leave the client— whether a bureaucracy or an individual—without any guidance is to put the professional community entirely at the mercy of the untutored client. Consequently, there are community patterns and processes that give at least indirect guidance to the larger society. Among these are: (1) institutional advertising, (2) professional referrals, (3) various types of reference plans, such as the Legal Reference Plan, or the emergency medical referral system,[15] (4) the informal association of specialists within physically contiguous offices, (5) formal lists and directories,[16] (6) positions in bureaucracies, (7) awards and prizes, etc.

These are but rough and indirect guides, but they do serve to reduce the randomness of the choices made by the larger society without weakening the essential bonds within each professional community. It does not seem likely, on the other hand, that each professional community has found, unaided, the sociologically correct point of optimum balance between these two.

SUMMARY

The complex structural relations presented here cannot be summarized briefly. We have first noted how important a characteristic of the profession is that of "community." Second, we have pointed out that it is like many other types of communities in that it exists within and is dependent on a larger society. Thus, theoretical notions derived from this nexus may have wider applications. Third, we have analyzed two specific sets of such relations, (1) socialization and social control, and

[15]Charles O. Porter, *Lawyer Reference Plans: A Manual for Local Bar Associations,* Boston: Poole Bros. for Survey of Legal Profession, 1949; and Edgar A. Schuler, Robert J. Mowitz, and Albert J. Mayer, *Medical Public Relations,* Detroit: Edwards, 1952, pp. 14ff.

[16]See the range of data in *American Architects Directory,* edited by George S. Koyl, New York: Bowker, 1955; Martindale-Hubbell Law Directory, 1956; *Medical Directory of New York State,* Vol. 46, New York: Medical Society of the State of New York, 1955; etc.

(2) client choice and evaluation of the professional, noting the structural strains and supports of the community and the society. It is suggested here that these relations between and within the contained community and the larger society form an important, but hitherto little explored, area.

Norton Long
The Corporation, its Satellites, and the Local Community

The corporation has made possible in many cases what before has been possible only in the rare and exceptional case: the amassing of large aggregates of enterprise under a single centralized direction. While the occasional great family—Ford, Rockefeller, Carnegie, or Harriman—might amass this power and create a personally owned economic empire, in the nature of the case this had to be exceptional. Without the corporation the bulk of enterprise would probably have remained locally owned and locally managed. With it, at least in major segments of the economy, enterprise becomes increasingly characterized by the branch plant and the headquarters office. Major parts of the local community's economy become not just members of a regional or national market but field offices of a far-flung bureaucracy with a new structure of roles, loyalties, and goals.

The large corporation takes its place along with the church and the armed services as an organization that transcends the local territory and cuts across political boundaries, at times even those of the nation and state.

For some of the members at least, the corporation represents a value-laden institution that outranks the local community as a focus of loyalty and a medium for self-realization. It would scarcely be saying too much and perhaps is tritely apparent that people may be more citizens of the corporations for whom they work than of the local communities in which they reside. Those whom Lloyd Fisher and Clark Kerr have dubbed "the plant sociologists," writers such as Elton Mayo, see the corporation as a means to harmonize the conflicting drives of modern man and achieve a happy union of the putative psychological blessings of medieval society with the material blessings of modernity.[1]

Philip Selznik, in his recent book on executive leadership, calls for a

Reprinted by permission of the publishers from Edward S. Mason, ed., *The Corporation in Modern Society* (Cambridge, Mass.: Harvard University Press). Copyright, 1959, by the President and Fellows of Harvard College.

[1]Clark Kerr, Lloyd Fisher, "Plant Sociology: The Elite and the Aborigines," Reprint no. 107, Institute of Industrial Relations (Berkeley, 1958).

kind of Aristotelian statesmanship on the part of top corporate management.[2] The highest duty of the executive he finds to consist in infusing the organization with value and preserving the value so infused—the spirit of the corporate policy—against stasis and decay. Carl Kaysen, writing not so long ago on monopoly, sees the goals of the large corporation as growth and survival rather than profit in the classical sense.[3] These conceptions are more conventionally appropriate to the calculations of statesmen than businessmen. If they are actually those that substantially control the thinking of large-scale corporate managements, they indicate the obsolescence of conventional economics for their description and the increasing relevance of politics. The corporation becomes more like a college, a church, or a state than an economic instrument valued almost solely as a source of income. The famous Hawthorne experiment brought tardy recognition to what socialists like De Man had long contended, that the process of the organization was valued by many as much or more than its product. The corporation provides a complex habitation for managers and men. As greater and greater effort is made to bind its members with a more-than-pecuniary loyalty, it aspires to the status of a social institution competing with church, family, and territorial community for the allegiance of men.

The corporation has profoundly changed the role structure of the local community. Increasingly, it replaces the old families as owner and operator of the most profitable local business. In all except the largest communities, a growing number of enterprises are branch plants run by bureaucratic birds of passage with career lines stretching onward and upward to the magic haven of the head office. The libraries, hospitals, and museums that bear the names of leading local families stand out as monuments of a civic past. The charities of the leading local citizen have been replaced by the corporation's committee on solicitations, whose federal-tax-induced beneficence has replaced the older order. In the lesser communities, the officers charged with the duty of corporate almoner are frequently limited to Community Chest and Red Cross, requiring higher approval for any departures from defined head-office policies on company benefactions.

Branch plant managers in their proconsular role are worlds apart from the leading citizen-owners of the past. As Schulze has pointed out in his study of Ypsilanti, their role as economic dominants does not give them the grip on local social institutions possessed by their pre-

[2]Philip Selznik, *Leadership in Administration, A Sociological Interpretation* (White Plains, New York, 1957).

[3]Carl Kaysen, "The Social Significance of the Modern Corporation," *The American Economic Review*, 23: 311 (May 1957).

decessors.[4] A recent study of a smaller southern community supports the view that branch plant managers are too sensitive to home-office approval to risk rocking the public-relations boat by decisive action. The phenomenon of absentee ownership, on which Veblen lavished his irony, has developed into the practice of absentee management by nonowners. That this lack of ownership interest has made absentee management by corporate headquarters staffs any less responsible, from the point of view of the local community, is doubtful. In fact the professionalization of corporate managements and their public visibility and newspaper accountability seems to have given them a thinness of skin quite uncharacteristic of the earlier race of absentee owners.

While the local catastrophe pictured by John Bartlow Martin in the mine disaster of Centralia Number 5 is a phenomenon of absentee management as well as absentee ownership, it is likely that absentee corporate managers were far more sensitive to newspaper criticism and public opinion then absentee owners.[5] This criticism flowing along the wires of the press services from the local community, can come to haunt them at their distant executive suites and jar their security and cloud their careers. The mine disaster of Centralia, with its tragedy of well-nigh classic Greek proportions of foredestined doom for the men in the pits, appealing to remote political, business, and union hierarchs to save their lives, dramatizes the general problem of remote control over vital decisions in the local community. In this case absentee corporate control of the mine was paralleled by, and even largely determined, absentee political and union control of decisions that could have saved miners' lives. In the Centralia case there was almost the ideal type of the local community so eviscerated of vital decision-making power that it lacked even the elemental capacity of self-preservation.

Yet absentee corporate control is far different from market control, and, while corporate centralization may not be quite the grave-digger of capitalism that Schumpeter warned us it was, it seems inexorably to socialize a kind of responsibility that approaches the political. The management decision made in New York to close a mill in the Piedmont of North Carolina may provoke repercussions in Washington, labor troubles elsewhere, and an unfavorable piece of publicity in the St. Louis *Post Dispatch*. The size of the giant corporation, which at first sight seems to give self-evident verification to the ascriptions of managerial omnipotence given currency in Marxian, Veblenite, and the C.

[4]Robert O. Schulze, "The Role of Economic Dominants in Community Power Structure," *American Sociological Review*, vol. 23 (February 1958).

[5]John Bartlow Martin, "The Blast in Centralia No. 5, A Mine Disaster No One Stopped," *Harpers Magazine*, 196: 193-220 (March 1948).

Wright Mills schools of thought, creates a vulnerability both to external pressure and to internal political weakness. As John Gunther in his *Inside U.S.A.* remarked of the automotive titans of Detroit, they resemble Japanese wrestlers, enormous but flabby, easily set quivering by a public-relations panic. A Harvard professor of government in the troubled days of the thirties was asked by a leading public-relations impressario what to do about a client's employees who had welded shut the doors of the plant in the course of a sit-down strike. The professor somewhat callously suggested the use of an acetylene torch. The gentleman from Madison Avenue, in horrified tones, said that this would never do, it would violate the God-the-Father governmental image.

In a short thirty years we have passed from a corporate order whose managerial style derived from the so-called "robber barons," the divine-right Bayers, and the public-be-damned Vanderbilts, to the business-school-trained, public-relations-conscious professional of the highly specialized complex corporate bureaucracy of today. While the latter-day manager may not be as other-directed as Riesman and William H. Whyte, Jr., suggest as a nonowner and a professional manager, he has a concern for harmony and the avoidance of trouble that sets him apart from his predecessors. His attitude toward striking employees can never quite have the same sense of outraged feudal lordship confronted with a servile revolt that envenoms the Kohler strike. Nor as a nonowner can he have quite the same view of the corporation as his property to do with as he pleased, by God, as seemed so right and fitting to the self-made Calvinists of American industry's heroic stage.

The company town had an attraction for the older industrialist of the past. The names Lowell, Lawrence, Hershey, Pullman, Kohler sound like so many industrial duchies. The conflict in Marquand's *Sincerely, Willis Wade* illustrates the familiar owner with sentimental and patriarchal concern for employees and local community and the business-school managerialist. A Harcourt finds it hard to close the Harcourt Mills. For Willis Wade it is but a business transaction, albeit one to be treated with finesse, a degree of humanity, and a great deal of public-relations concern. All over the country, the paternalistic company town with mill-supported public service is giving way to a new philosophy that shuns the responsibility and the doubtful glory of conspicuous community dominance. Few corporations today regard it as desirable to have a major portion of the local labor force dependent on their payroll. When business decisions have too visible an effect, management must weigh public relations in the scales with economics, frequently to the disadvantage of the latter. Birch in his study of Glossop, the seat of the Dukes of Norfolk, points out how the Dukes built a branch railroad for the local community, a benefaction it could never expect from the corporations of the present.[6] The modern corporation has found the price of community dominance an inconvenient conspicuousness, that in a day when distant publics are potent, seriously limits corporate freedom of action.

If the corporation no longer views the company town with favor, the same cannot be said of its feelings toward the suburban satellite that enjoys access to a central city labor force but immunity from central city taxes and welfare problems. The literature of corporate location policy, at least latterly, pays homage to the principle of paying the corporate way for its employees' schools and other services. However, the suburb with nothing but the plant and lots zoned for five acres produces a congenial neighborly environment that has its temptations. The move from high-rise, narrow-bay structures to the single story wide-bay modern plant and the tremendous demand for parking space have played a dominant part in the suburbanization of industry. River Rouge, Aliquippa, and other industry suburbs antedate this more recent technologically induced development. Reputedly, the explanation of them resides in company desire to control the local police, avoid central city taxes, and escape responsibility for the relief of their periodically unemployed hands. In one case, anxiety over company control of suburban police is given as a major reason for one of the early failures to secure metropolitan government in the Pittsburgh area.

The strikes that ushered in the great labor-organizing drive of the thirties strained and tested the allegiance of all segments of the local community. The Mohawk Valley Formula, as described by R.R.R. Brooks, successfully pursued, lined up all respectable elements in the community on the side of law and order and against the strikers.[7] Almost as crucial in determining the outcome of the strike as the role of police and militia was the shutting off of credit by the local merchants. In case of a showdown between strikers and mill, whatever their private sentiments, sooner or later the stores and the landlords were bound to side with management.

Perhaps the most important change in the local scene is the growing evidence that this one-sided line-up has shown a dramatic shift. Peter Rossi's studies of Zanesville, Ohio, and Gary, Indiana, show that not only do the local merchants continue to give credit to the strikers, but the whole community, including the police, tends to side with them.[8] While this phenomenon may not be wholly chargeable to the develop-

[6]Anthony Harold Birch, *Small Town Politics: A Study of Political Life in Glossop* (New York, 1959).

[7]R.R.R. Brooks, *When Labor Organizes* (New Haven, 1937).

[8]Peter Rossi, "The Impact of Party Organization in an Industrial Setting," to be published in a forthcoming volume entitled *Community Political Systems*, edited by M. Janowitz and H. Eulau, Chicago.

ment of absentee corporate control and branch plant management, it seems vitally related to it.

Rossi's data and evidence from other sources point to the effect of the branch plant system on local susceptibilities. Economic dominants who are not, and do not become, part of the local social structure may be as foreign within local communities in the United States as the United Fruit Company in Latin America. The upward-mobile branch plant executive and his associated corporate birds of passage may be as alien as the white plantation manager in the tropics. The phenomenon of colonial nationalism is not irrelevant to the politics and attitudes of local communities in the United States. Southern resentment against "Yankee imperialism" is an old story, but the development of absentee corporate control has given a visibility to alien power in the local community that the impersonality of the market tended to hide. The passing of the regime of the old families has created a gap between positions in the economic and social tables of organization.

A further indication of a new order of local power and prestige is the gradual but increasing local recognition of labor leaders in the Community Chest and the Red Cross. These middle-class-minded organizations have been rather reluctant to admit labor leaders to effective participation in their decision-making process. Inability of corporate executives to insure worker contributions has forced recognition of the changed facts of power.

The corporation, by merging the individual plants in separate local communities, has created the tangential relationship from which the large and industrial union has sprung. It is part of the folklore of the labor movement that a highly centralized industry was far easier to organize than one characterized by a host of small firms. Certainly this was the experience with textiles in New England. No opponent of unionization was quite so bitter as the small marginal owner-operator. The large company with its bureaucratic management was far easier to crack.

The case of union centralization in the United Mine workers that eviscerated local union decision-making in the Centralia disaster is on the extreme end of the labor continuum. Local union discretion in the generality of communities is probably much higher than that of local management. Furthermore, continuity in positions of power in the union and lengthy local residence gives the local union hierarchy more identity with the local social structure than is likely to be the case for the more mobile members of a large corporate career structure.

In a curious sense the corporation is more absorbing for the latter-day nonowning managers than for the older generation of owners. Clearly, branch managers have the public opinion of the central office to consider as well as any local opinion. Careers are made in the company rather than the community. Concentration on business and avoiding any involvement in local controversy is the counsel of wisdom. The stakes of local community action for the branch plant manager are unknown but quite possibly they are serious penalties if he gets in trouble, dubious and uncertain rewards if he succeeds. The ritual activities of Community Chest and Red Cross, the noncontroversial symbolic activities, are helpful if they don't take too much time from the business, but controversy is poison.

The galloping succession of assistant secretaries in the Department of Defense and other Washington agencies under the Eisenhower Administration indicates not just the unwillingness of corporation executives to put up with the lower monetary rewards and the harassments of public life, but a genuine fear that the world—their corporate world—will pass them by if they absent themselves too long from the stage of their primary careers. Others will replace them if they stay away too long. William H. Whyte, Jr., has reported how reluctant executives are to take even a month off. The business must go on; someone will be messing in one's personal files. One might be found out. The apparent solidity of the corporation conceals an internal political weakness. *Executive Suite* may be overdrawn, but the rivalries, insecurities, and anxieties beyond the middle management of the corporate hierarchy are real.[9]

When a president of the largest bank in a community says, "We are all hired hands here," of himself and other local corporation executives, he is not echoing the proud humility of *servus servorum Dei*. Rather he expresses the felt limitation of the paid professional manager who doesn't own the business. Berle's and Means's *Modern Corporation and Private Property* documented a position of management via the proxy mechanism that seemed to render it as potent as any owners of the earlier period. Indeed, the doings of the holding-company era supported such a view. But present managerial behaviors give rise to doubt as to unrestrained managerial power. How management is surrounded by a network of constraints and fears is as yet an unwritten chapter in industrial sociology. Certainly bureaucratic specialization and division of labor in the management team has given rise to internal checks within the corporation that amount to vested interest in specialized skills and lores. The office of the general counsel of the corporation threatens erring colleagues with the vague menaces of the law—must threaten them, too, if the prestige of the shop is to be maintained. The public-relations vice-president or public-relations consultant must mag-

[9]Cameron Hawley, *Executive Suite* (Boston, 1952).

nify the dangers and importance of the irrational demonic force of public opinion as well as the capacity of his skill group to sell or charm the public Caliban. The personnel department has a vested interest in union perversities and its needed capacity to deal with them. The lobbyist and political fixer, corporate hierarch or consultant, has a like interest in his special capacity to deal with the distant underworld of politics. Each corporate specialty has the same amiable adversary affinity to its subject as the cancer fund to its disease.

The modern large corporation executive likes to think of himself as a professional. Ideally, if not typically, he is the product of a business school. The business schools, *Business Week, Fortune, The Wall Street Journal,* and other media have appointed themselves the task of turning business managers into unimpassioned bureaucrats who worship along with the city manager at the altar of administrative science. In practice this has meant that corporate executives are rather vulnerable to the intellectual fashions that sweep the business schools and the media from which they derive their ideas as to what is currently modish in top-drawer management thinking. This is especially the case with respect to those matters that are remote from the segment of reality that comes under their corporate competence. A St. Louis insurance executive will inveigh against the jurisdictional mess of his metropolitan area in a staff-ghosted speech that repeats uncomprehendingly the clichés of current municipal reform. This activity is good corporate citizenship, the more so as the executive hasn't the foggiest idea as to how the changes he advocates will help his company, though doubtless in all honesty he thinks they will. It is difficult for the corporation executive to avoid a kind of ritualistic do-gooding when he embarks on the unfamiliar role of city father.

Where issues hit home to the corporate profit and loss account, there is a reasonably realistic calculus of appropriate action. At least the executive confronted with choices as to taxes, off-street parking, highways, and other governmental activities that seem to affect his business directly has a basis for rational action. This action may be as short-sighted, as when downtown stores seek to route an expressway through their basements, but at least the calculus is in principle rational rather than magical.

Top positions in the large corporation form a major segment of the prestige structure of the local community. Occupants of these positions are a natural target for the pressgangs seeking to man the local civic-committee structures. The executive finds the civic committee both a burden and an opportunity. Some activities, such as the Community Chest and the Red Cross, are built into company work loads and are even expected parts of a man's job. Moving up in them is part of man's career. Good marks in them are functional to a man's favorable evaluation by his superiors. A smashing success in a fund drive may be a more visible mark of personal achievement than any company activity makes possible. In many quarters good corporate citizenship is regarded as a major public-relations value. Top management must personify, if not, as Maitland quipped of the British monarch, parsonify the institution. A president of a lesser corporation will candidly avow that his board of directors thought it not a bad thing for him to serve on a committee that might yield first-name acquaintance with the president of a large insurance company.

Such committees are usually safe vehicles for mixing with the prestigious members of the business community and securing pleasant and even useful publicity as a public-spirited leading citizen who represents the kind of corporation that has a "soul." Corporate executives discussing their roles in publicized civic committees point out that their service impresses and pleases their employees.

There is, however, a modicum of danger in the civic committee or even the assignment to a usually merely honorific post on a public board. Top-level civic committees are in the ordinary run merely required to lend their names to ceremonial occasions, the civic luncheon with its press release, the legitimatizing of some civic staff proposal, or, in the more arduous case, joining a plane-load of their peers in a flight to Washington or New York to plead the cause of the Chamber of Commerce in the wooing of a building. The unpleasant side of this otherwise merely time-consuming and occasionally profitable involvement is the frustration and loss of face when the publicized civic ceremonial fails. Usually failure is hidden from view by a change in the newspaper spotlight or obscurity as to just what the ritual is supposed to accomplish in particular. However from time to time newspapers, politicians, and public turn on the corporate elite as the savages beat their idols when they fail to bring rain. The expectation that the top corporate hierarchy should display some kind of effective leadership is fitful but real. The places of the leading families have to be filled or a kind of lubberland emerges. For a variety of reasons, the politicians cannot in the main attain the prestige of members of the corporate hierarchy. Where, however, the corporate elite fails to replace the old families in the top positions of the social structure, a situation results in which the rest of the local society is inclined to regard the management of the corporation as an alien force—almost, as was stated before, as the colonial representative of a foreign imperialism.

The process of suburbanization has placed many corporate managers, in even quite large head-office cities, in positions not unlike those of branch plant managers in smaller communities. The executive tends to be neither an active citizen in his suburban dormitory, nor more than a chamber-of-commerce ceremonial citizen of the central city where his office lies. The suburban politico and small businessman is likely to look on him as a resident alien and a spokesman for the big-town chamber of commerce, rather than for the local interests. In the central city, lack of residence and vote has a crippling effect on a more than ceremonial or checkwriting role. Beyond these disabilities a major, and often neglected, one is that of the corporate executive's preoccupation with his business. Amazingly enough he is busy, and this simple fact accounts for a good deal of his difficulty in competing with others of lesser status who are full-time professionals. The tired and overworked executive is wheedled and wheeled into place by civic and other staffs to provide the needed trappings of legitimacy to their own activities. The very scarcity value of prestige insures that a small group of top executives must stumble from one civic committee to another, without time for preparation and with exhausting demands on the limited time they can rob from their business, their families, and the daily toll of commuting.

Since prestige can only inhere in a few at the top—to spread the load would pack the "House of Lords" and fatally cheapen the titles—the few must pay the penalty of being both overworked and used. Their ceremonial roles are too numerous to be self-directed. Their conspicuousness, the fatal result of corporate status, makes them vulnerable to public demands for their services. These services they can only refuse at the cost of seeming callously aloof from the folk belief in their duties as work givers and civic problem solvers. They must touch for the king's evil whether they will or no. At best they can avoid being had by the numerous band of public and private courtiers who seek to further their own ends through the manipulation of their prestige.

The alienation of the corporate hierarchy from other segments of the local community is the progressive result of the trend toward corporate centralization and the branch plant. Even when top management resides in the headquarters city there is a tendency for it to regard its responsibilities as so national in character as to inhibit conspicuous local citizenship activities. Uncharitably viewed, this might appear a mere rationalization to escape a burdensome chore. However, in many cases the dilemma is sincere enough and Rousseau's caustic remark about the philosophers, that they loved the world in general in order to escape having to love anyone in particular, does not apply. The contrast between top managers whose status is derived from family and inherited wealth—the Rockefellers, the Fords, and the Mellons—and the nonfamilied is striking. For the man of family and inherited position, conspicuous local leadership has an appearance of legitimacy and appropriateness of role that seems lacking in the other case. In a real sense, a Rockefeller twice removed from the robber baron may be as much an acceptable gentry image as an earlier gentry several times removed from its robber-baron predecessors. The security with which some familied men of wealth have been able to appeal for the suffrages of the public at large is in marked contrast to the anxiety and almost wallflower-like withdrawal of their associates in the corporate hierarchy from a dance whose steps are beyond them and whose necessary contacts repel them.

In an earlier day the utilities, requiring public franchises and deeply dependent on municipal politics, were in the thick of it. The relationships described by Lincoln Steffens were close and the major figures in the companies were in intimate and sometimes sordid contact with the world of politics. The satiation of businesses with the fruits of successful political activity led to a withdrawal from overt and intense participation in the field of local politics. The activity of tending the local political fences became a specialized department in the corporate hierarchy and was no longer a main concern of top management. The position in the hierarchy of the man responsible for taking care of the corporation's local political problems became downgraded and with the intensified disesteem of politics and politicians, especially at the local level, his post suffered from the bad odor of its clientele. The courts and a successful lobby with the state legislature permitted a growing neglect if not contempt for local politics. Suburbanization meant a physical unconcern for all but company-related local services, and the politics of top management's suburban residence represents scarcely anything more momentous than the politics of the country club. Thus the replacement of robber baron, resident owners, and leading families by a withdrawn managerial elite has left vacant positions in the local structure.

The managerial elite has been neither willing nor able to fill these positions except in a ritualistic fashion that seems transparently the product of company public relations rather than a personal community commitment and identification. The socially perceived public responsibilities of the manager's positions in the local economic hierarchy have differed increasingly from their own perception of their role as representatives of the company in the local banana plantation (apologies to Keynes). While their economic position has made the managers seem to be the appropriate and duty-bound incumbent of top local civic statuses, their lack of family legitimacy and enduring local residence identification in the community makes them more the representatives of a foreign power than the rightful chiefs of the local tribe. This alien allegiance on the part of the corporate segment of the local structure is productive of public disaffection from the corporation and a sense of anxiety and alienation in the corporate hierarchy.

A recent statement of General Electric on relocation policy, in which the corporation expresses its alarmed concern with conditions in New England and New York, is illustrative of the type of anxious sense of alienation from the local community expressed in many corporate statements. A paragraph from the General Electric release published in the September-October, 1955, issue of *Industrial Development* is worth quoting at length. Under the title "Community Loyalty," the paragraph proceeds as follows:

> We watch to see if the thought leaders and other representatives in the community speak well of the *deserving* employers there or consider them whipping posts. Spokesmen for unions and other organizations, as well as individuals among clergymen, teachers, politicians and publishers can all have a very material effect for good or bad on the *cost of producing goods* and on the *amount and regularity* of the *sale* of those goods. A little noted fact is that public criticism of an employer—to the extent it is believed—tends to cut down jobs for employees. Likewise—understanding, approval and warranted public praise of an employer tend to cut his costs and increase his sales—*and jobs.*

In the earlier portions of this extraordinary statement the corporation is represented as being ready to pick up its dolls and go elsewhere if local public opinion and action prove too unsympathetic. This, be it noted, the company is prepared to do at the cost of millions of dollars of investment that would be wiped out by the move. How oddly the voice of C. Wright Mills' *Power Elite* [10] and Hunter's *Community Power Structure* [11] sounds in this rather querulous appeal for affection and understanding from the local natives who, in the company eyes, seem ready to kill, or at least drive away, the goose that lays the golden eggs.

Company attitude and local attitude are startlingly like that of a Middle East or South American oil company and the native inhabitants in the throes of colonial nationalism and the threats of withdrawal and shutdown on the one hand and expropriation on the other. It is interesting to note that in both cases the company is reduced to the threat of emigration.

Why doesn't the corporation's management have enough acceptance in the local social structure to be able to fight back? With a case as strong as that presented by General Electric management should be able to secure allies enough to win the fight rather than run away.

[10] C. Wright Mills, *The Power Elite* (New York, 1956).
[11] Floyd Hunter, *Community Power Structure; A Study of Decision Makers* (Chapel Hill, 1953).

Andrew Hacker, in a short study, *Politics and the Corporation,* gives an important part of the answer.[12] Hacker finds that the growing class of "middle-middle class"—executives below the policy level, increasingly in demand by the large corporation—are typically transients and propertyless. Without roots in the local community and without the security property would afford, they have become spectators of politics. Such interests as they have are so vague and general that they perceive no ready way for their achievement. This new corporate middle class is inert and apathetic. To use a union phrase, it is a free loader on the body politic. Hacker's concern is with the depth of commitment to democratic values. Corporation executives are more concerned with the depth of its commitment to the Republican Party and the political activity they believe necessary to preserve and protect the "enterprise system."

Shocked at the Republican weakness at the polls, corporations such as General Electric have gone out to educate their middle and lower managements for political action. The revelation of corporate weakness in the local communities has been startling. The reaction, however, has seemed more like an attempt to buy a political patent medicine or some educational nostrum to vitalize Republican precinct workers, actual or potential, than a realistic assessment of the situation. Long ago Machiavelli warned the Prince that if he wanted to rule a captured province he had better live there. This is a lesson the corporation would do well to heed if it wants to avoid the ugly effects of colonial nationalism as local populations turn against even beneficent alien rule.

The reintegration of economic dominants into the local social structure is one of the main problems of our local civic life. This is a problem not only for the corporation and its alien caste of career bureaucrats; it is also to an acute degree a problem of labor. The president of a large corporation in a relaxed moment will admit that heads of a national union aren't such bad fellows; they too abominate wildcat strikes. But that Mulligan who leads the local wildcat strike, he's trying to prove something: his local power to the national union. Local autonomy in capital and labor is difficult to reconcile with effective centralized control. And local territorial loyalties provide a fertile field for those who would stir up resistance to the remote control of outsiders with no local legitimization for their power.

Clearly there are wide ranges of corporations and communities with differences ranging from the twenty-thousand-acre corporate ranch with Mexican peons, through the automobile company with a tough union facing a tough management, to the multi-million-dollar insurance com-

---

[12] Andrew Hacker, "Politics and the Corporation," Occasional Paper, Fund for the Republic, New York, 1958.

pany with its docile world of secretaries and file clerks headed by the million-a-year salesmen.

What the corporation is doing to the local community is an abstraction as dangerous as any Weberian ideal type of construction. Yet as an intuitive impression from a broad but scattered collection of data, there seems reason to suspect that the conflict between the corporation as an institutionalized center of loyalties and the local territorial community is real and important. It seems clear also that the vacuum created in the local social structure by the decline of the old owning families and resident economic dominants has upset the informal structure of political power. Whether the public-relations and educational onslaught on the problem of corporate political decline will succeed seems dubious. Re-establishing a valued legitimate elite structure in the local community is a major and possibly insoluble task. In the divided loyalty between corporation and local community, can one or other be more than synthetic? It would be reassuring to be able to say that a system of centralized corporations and unions is compatible with the reality of vigorous local self-government.

C. P. Snow

Reflections on the College Past

The community was usually a very small one. This college of ours was founded, by taking over a simple boarding-house, towards the end of the fourteenth century. It was given rents of a few manors in order to maintain a Master (usually a youngish teacher, a master of arts who lectured in the schools), eight fellow-scholars, who had passed their first degree and were studying for higher ones (they were normally youths of about twenty) and thirty-six scholars, who were boys coming up for the courses in the schools. These were the college; and it was in that sense that we still used the arrogant phrase "the college," meaning the Master and fellows. "The governing body" was a modern and self-conscious term, which betrayed a recognition of hundreds of young men, who liked to think that they too were the college. The eight fellow-scholars elected their own Master; the number stayed eight until the college received a large benefaction in the 1640's.

This was the college when it began. It was poor, unpretentious, attempted little save to keep its scholars out of mischief, counted for very little. It had the same first court as now, a Master, some of the same titles. In everything else it was unrecognisably different.

Then three things happened, as in all Oxford and Cambridge colleges of that time. Two were obvious and in the nature of things. The third, and the most important, is mysterious to this day. The first thing was that the Master and the young fellow-scholars took to looking over the young boys' studies. They heard their exercises, heard them speak Latin, coached them in disputing. Instead of staying a simple boarding-house, the college became a coaching establishment also. Before long, the college teaching was as important as the lectures in the schools. The university still consisted of those who lectured in the schools, conducted examinations, gave degrees; but, apart from the formal examination, the colleges took over much that the university used to do.

That was bound to happen. It happened in much the same fashion in the great mother university of Paris, the university of the Archpoet, Gerson, William of Ockham, and Villon, and in Bologna, Siena, Orleans, the universities all over Europe.

Reprinted from *The Masters*, pp. 336–374, by C. P. Snow with the permission of Charles Scribner's Sons. Copyright 1951 C. P. Snow.

It was also natural that the colleges should begin to admit not only scholars to whom grants were paid, but also boys and young men who paid their own way—the "pensioners." These young men were allowed into the colleges on sufferance, but soon swamped the rest in numbers. They added to the power and influence of the colleges, and considerably to their income—though the endowments were always enough, from the foundation down to the time of Brown and Chrystal, for the fellows to survive without any undergraduates at all.

That raises the question of the third process which gave Oxford and Cambridge their strange character and which is, as I said, still unexplained. For some reason or by some chance, the colleges flourished from the beginning. They attracted considerable benefactions in their first hundred years; this college of ours, which started smaller than the average, was enriched under the Tudors and drew in two very large benefactions in the seventeenth century (it then became a moderately prosperous college of almost exactly the middle size). The colleges became well-to-do as early as the Elizabethan period; old members gave their farms and manors, complete outsiders threw in a lease of land or a piece of plate. Astonishingly quickly for such a process, the colleges became wealthy, comfortable, in effect autonomous, far more important than the university. And the process once properly started, it went on like the growth of a snowball; the colleges could attract the university teachers to be Masters or fellows, because they could pay them more. The university was poor; no one left it money, it was too impersonal for that, men kept their affection and loyalty and nostalgia for the house where they had lived in their young manhood; the university had just enough to pay its few professorships, to keep up the buildings of the schools, where the relics of the old lectures still went on; the university still had the right to examine and confer degrees. Everything else had passed to the colleges. Quite early, before the end of the sixteenth century, they did all the serious teaching; they had the popular teachers, the power, the prestige, the glamour, and the riches. As the years passed, they got steadily richer.

And so there developed the peculiar dualism of Oxford and Cambridge. Nowhere else was there this odd relation between the university and the colleges—a relation so odd and intricate, so knotted with historical accidents, that it has always seemed incomprehensible to anyone outside.

It remains a mystery why this relation only grew up in England. Why was it only at the two English universities—quite independently—that the colleges became rich, powerful, self-sufficient, indestructible? At Paris, Bologna and all the medieval universities, boarding-houses were transformed into colleges, just as in England; at Paris, for example, they were endowed, given much the same start in property, and almost exactly the same statutes and constitution. Yet by 1550, when the Cambridge colleges were already dwarfing the university, those in Paris were dead.

At any rate, I thought, this college was, except in detail, typical of all the middle-sized English ones, and had gone through all their changes. By the sixteenth century it had long ceased to be a boarding-house, and become instead a cross between a public school and a small self-contained university. The boys up to seventeen and eighteen were birched in the college hall (which would have been unthinkable in less organised, less prosperous, freer days). The young men went out, some to country livings, some to the new service of administrative jobs required by Tudor England. The Masters were usually married even now, the Lodge was enlarged, the great bedroom came into use; the fellows were predominantly, as they remained till 1880, unmarried young clerics, who took livings as their turn came round. Their interests were, however, very close to the social conflicts of the day: the active and unrebellious, men like Jago and Chrystal and Brown, were drawn into the Elizabethan bureaucracy: the discussions at high table, though put into religious words, must often have been on topics we should call 'political', and many of the idealistic young threw themselves into Calvinism, were deprived of their fellowships by the government, and in exile led their congregations to wonder about the wilderness across the Atlantic sea.

The seventeenth century saw, really for the first time, some fellows busy with scholarship and research. The times were restless and dangerous: trade was on the move, organised science took its place in the world. A few gifted men stayed all their lives in the college, and did solid work in botany and chemistry. Some of my contemporaries, I sometimes thought, would have fitted into the college then, more easily than into any time before our own.

The country quietened into the eighteenth century peace, there was a lull before the technological revolution. For the first time since its foundation, the college, like all others, declined. In 1540 the college had been admitting 30 undergraduates a year, in 1640 the number had gone up to 50 (larger than at any time until after the 1914–18 war). In 1740 the number was down to 8. No one seemed very much to mind. The dividends stayed unaffected (about £100 a year for the ordinary fellow), the college livings did pretty well out of their tithes; it just remained for one of them to come along. The college had for the time being contrived to get cut off from the world: from the intellectual world of the London coffee-houses, from the rough-and-ready experiments of the agricultural revolution, from any part in politics except to beg patronage from the great oligarchs. The college had stopped being a boarding-house, a school; had almost stopped being in any sense a place of education; it became instead a sort of club. Most people think affectionately now of an eighteenth century Cambridge college; it was a very unexacting place. Most people have a picture of it—of middle-aged or elderly men, trained exclusively in the classics, stupefying themselves on port. The picture is only wrong in that the men in fact were not middle-aged or elderly, but very young: they were trained first and foremost, not in classics, but in mathematics; and they drank no more than most of their successors. Roy Calvert would have joined one of their harder sessions, and gone off without blinking to give a lecture in German on early Soghdian. But they had the custom of drinking their port twice a day—once after dinner, which began about two o'clock, and again after supper at seven. They must have been sleepy and bored, sitting for a couple of hours on a damp, hot Cambridge afternoon, drinking their wine very slowly, making bets on how soon a living would fall vacant, and how long before the last lucky man to take a living got married or had a child.

By the nineteenth century, the deep revolution (threatened faintly by seventeenth century science: acted on, in the nineteenth century factories) was visible everywhere. There had never been such a change so quickly as between the England of 1770 and the England of 1850: and the college felt it too. Something was happening: men wanted to know more. The country needed scientists. It needed every kind of expert knowledge. It needed somewhere to educate the commercial and industrial middle class that had suddenly grown up. Between 1830 and 1880 the college, like all Cambridge, modernised itself as fast as Japan later in the century. In 1830 the young clergymen still sat over their port each afternoon; in the '80's the college had taken on its present shape. Nine English traditions out of ten, old Eustace Pilbrow used to say, date from the latter half of the nineteenth century.

The university courses were revolutionised. The old rigid training, which made each honours student begin with a degree in mathematics, was thrown away. It became possible for a man, if he were so adventurous, to start his course in classics. In 1860 it even became possible to study natural science; and the Cavendish, the most famous of scientific laboratories, was built in 1874. Experimental science was taught; and the new university laboratories drew students as the old schools had drawn them in the middle ages; here no college could compete, and university teaching, after hundreds of years, was coming back to pre-eminence again.

The college kept up with the transformation. It made some changes itself, in others had to follow the Royal Commissions. Fellows need not be in orders; were allowed to marry; were no longer elected for life. At a step the college became a secular, adult, settled society. For five hundred years it had been a place which fellows went from when they could: at a stroke, it became a place they stayed in. By 1890 the combination room was inhabited by bearded fathers of families. The average age of the fellows mounted. Their subjects were diverse: there were scientists, oriental linguists, historians—and M. H. L. Gay, one of the younger fellows, had already published two books on the historical basis of the Icelandic sagas. The scholarly work of the college became greater out of all knowledge.

The college suddenly became a place of mature men. They were as frail as other men, but they won respect because of their job, and they had great self-respect. They were men of the same make as Winslow, Brown, Chrystal, Crawford, Jago and Francis Getliffe; and Gay and Pilbrow had lived through from those days to these. From those days to now, the college had been truly the same place.

Gay and Pilbrow, as young fellows, had seen the college, the whole of Cambridge, settle into the form which, to Luke for example, seemed eternal. Organised games, bumping races, matches with Oxford, college clubs, May week, competitive scholarships, club blazers and ties, the Council of the Senate, most Cambridge slang, were all nineteenth century inventions. Gay had been elected at a time when some of his colleagues were chafing for the 1880 statutes to become law, so that they could marry. He had been through four elections to the Mastership. They were all elections dominated by the middle-aged, like this one about to come. He had seen the college move to the height of its prosperity and self-confidence. And now, his memory flickering, he sat with us and heard of another election, the last that would come his way.

There was one irony about it all. Just as the college reached its full mature prosperity, it seemed that the causes which brought it there would in the end change it again, and this time diminish it. For the nineteenth century revolution caused both the teaching of experimental science and the college as we knew it, rich, proud, full of successful middle-aged men, so comfortably off that the Master no longer lived in a separate society. The teaching of experimental science had meant the revival of the powers and influence of the university; for no college, however rich, not even Trinity, could finance physics and engineering laboratories on a modern scale. To cope with this need, the university had to receive contributions from the colleges and also a grant from the state. This meant as profound a change as that by which the colleges cut out the university as the prime source of teaching. It meant inevitably that the reverse must now happen. The university's income began to climb into £1,000,000 a year: it needed that to provide for twentieth century teaching and research: no college's endowment brought in more than a tenth the sum. By the 1920's the university was in charge of all laboratories, and all formal teaching: it was only left to colleges to supplement this by coaching, as they had done in their less exalted days. There were, by the way, great conveniences for the fellows in this resurrection of the university; nearly all of them had university posts as well as college ones, and so were paid twice. It was this double source of pay that made the income of Jago, Chrystal, Brown and the others so large; everyone between thirty and seventy in the college, except for Nightingale, was earning over £1,000 a year. But it meant beyond any doubt whatever that the colleges, having just known their mature and comfortable greatness, would be struggling now to keep their place. It sometimes seemed that the time must come when they became boarding-houses again, though most superior ones.

I regretted it. They had their faults, but they had also great humanity.

However, that change was in the future. It did not trouble the fellows as I knew them. Of all men, they had the least doubts about their social value. They could be as fond of good works as Pilbrow, as modest as Brown, but still they were kept buoyed up by the greatest confidence and self-respect in their job. By the 'thirties, the conscience of the comfortable classes was sick: the sensitive rich, among my friends, asked themselves what use they were: but that was not a question one would have heard in the college. For everyone, inside and out, took it for granted that the academic life was a valuable one to live; scientists such as Crawford, Francis Getliffe, and Luke had become admired like no other professional men, and the rest of us, with a shade of envy, took a little admiration for ourselves. In England, the country with the subtlest social divisions (Pilbrow said the most snobbish of countries), Oxford and Cambridge had had an unchallenged social cachet for a long time; even Lady Muriel, though she did not feel her husband's colleagues were her equals, did not consider them untouchable; and so a man like Francis Getliffe, when asked what was his job, answered with a double confidence, knowing that it was valued by serious people and also had its own curious place among the smart. Many able men entered the academic life in those years because, with a maximum of comfort, it settled their consciences and let them feel that their lives were not utterly without a use.

For many it was a profound comfort to be one of a society completely sure of itself, completely certain of its values, completely without misgivings about whether it was living a good life. In the college there were men varied enough to delight anyone with a taste in human things: but none of them, except Roy Calvert in one of his fits of melancholy, ever doubted that it was a good thing to be a fellow. They took it for granted, felt they were envied, felt it was right they should be envied: enjoyed the jokes about dons, which to some, such as Chrystal, Brown and Francis Getliffe, as they thought of their busy efficient lives, seemed peculiarly absurd: wanted to grow old in the college, and spend their last years as Gay and Pilbrow were doing now.

When I arrived in the college, I had already moved about a good deal among the layers of society; and I had not come to the end of my journey yet. I had the luck to live intimately among half-a-dozen different vocations. Of all those I had the chance to see, the college was the place where men lived the least anxious, the most comforting, the freest lives.

PART III

Politics and Community

CHAPTER 9

The Nature of
Political Culture

Politics and community are neither identical nor separable; that is the implication of much of the material of this book. At this point we face directly the character of the relationship between these two aspects of social life, first considering political culture, then the integrative and destructive effects of politics on community.

Though the term political culture has not been in use very long, the idea is familiar and rather obvious. Culture in general means established usages, customs, ideas, attitudes, and the like, as they are shared among members of a social group and passed along from generation to generation. Political culture embraces those aspects with political reference. Thus the political culture is the way of life and thought of a society as it has organized itself for the activities of government.

Culture and community are concepts that have much in common. We have used the term community to refer to a group, united in space, function, or other interest, and sharing perspectives that bind them together for some degree of common action. Culture is the more inclusive term, for it does not necessarily unite, but a community both develops a culture and draws from it.

In politics, the culture is "the way things are done," the norms of behavior in a given system. A political culture, for example, might proscribe any form of violence as a means of influence but it might condone bribery. Or, to illustrate further, the mutual expectations of people might be that they should all show interest in politics and participate in certain of its activities, or they may encourage apathy toward politics. The American Constitution, seen not simply as a written document but as that document plus its elaboration in law and custom, is a sort of codification of the nation's political culture. It establishes institutions (that is, regularized modes of behavior) and sets limits to the substance and processes of the political system.

The selections presented in this chapter offer both analysis and examples of the nature of political culture. Aristotle in the passage quoted from the *Politics* sets out his most fundamental notions about the role of politics in the human community; his theory argues that the political community (*polis*) is a "natural" sort of creature required by the interdependence of men. Carefully read, the quotation emphasizes the basic character of the political culture in human association, for it points out the role of shared language and common perceptions of justice and goodness, in the life of the polity: "it is association in (a common perception of) these things which makes a family and a polis." It is not to be supposed that Aristotle meant to suggest that all political communities have the same specific characteristics. Elsewhere he emphasized the differences among them, noting that each develops a set of ways of its own, and that the mission of the political system is to nurture the life manifested in these cultural features of the civic group.

The selection presented from Theodore White's *The Making of the President, 1960* describes the cleavages that divide the American culture into subcultures along ethnic and religious lines. The varying experiences of these groups create in each of them distinctive reactions to political stimuli. The differences in political form from one to another illustrate the importance of cultural characteristics to the development of political action. The material on the Negro and politics would probably be written differently today; the pace of cultural change among Black Americans has rendered this account obsolete in a very few years.

William Brammer in *The Gay Place* and William Riordon in *Plunkitt of Tammany Hall* illustrate the form of political activity in two American subcultural settings, the former in Texas in recent times, the latter in early twentieth-century New York. Brammer's book is a novel of political life, Riordon's an account of machine politics based on his discussions with a Tammany district leader.

Aristotle
from *Politics, Book I*

If, accordingly, we begin at the beginning, and consider things in the process of their growth, we shall best be able, in this as in other fields, to attain scientific conclusions by the method we employ. First of all, there must necessarily be a union or pairing of those who cannot exist without one another. Male and female must unite for the reproduction of the species—not from deliberate intention, but from the natural impulse, which exists in animals generally as it also exists in plants, to leave behind them something of the same nature as themselves. Next, there must necessarily be a union of the naturally ruling element with the element which is naturally ruled, for the preservation of both. The element which is able, by virtue of its intelligence, to exercise fore-thought, is naturally a ruling and master element; the element which is able, by virtue of its bodily power, to do what the other element plans, is a ruled element, which is naturally in a state of slavery; and master and slave have accordingly (as they thus complete one another) a common interest. . . . The female and the slave (we may pause to note) are naturally distinguished from one another. Nature makes nothing in a spirit of stint, as smiths do when they make the Delphic knife to serve a number of purposes: she makes each separate thing for a separate end; and she does so because each instrument has the finest finish when it serves a single purpose and not a variety of purposes. Among the barbarians, however (contrary to the order of nature), the female and the slave occupy the same position—the reason being that no naturally ruling element exists among them, and conjugal union thus comes to be a union of a female who is a slave with a male who is also a slave. This is why our poets have said,

Meet it is that barbarous people should be governed by the Greeks

—the assumption being that barbarian and slave are by nature one and the same. . . .

The first result of these two elementary associations (of male and

From *The Politics of Aristotle,* edited and translated by Sir Ernest Barker. Oxford University Press, 1946. Reprinted by permission.

female, and of master and slave) is the household or family. Hesiod spoke truly in the verse,

> First house, and wife, and ox to draw the plough

for oxen serve the poor in lieu of household slaves. The first form of association naturally instituted for the satisfaction of daily recurrent needs is thus the family; and the members of the family are accordingly termed by Charondas "associates of the breadchest," as they are also termed by Epimenides the Cretan "associates of the manger." The next form of association—which is also the *first* to be formed from more households than one, and for the satisfaction of something more than daily recurrent needs—is the village. The most natural form of the village appears to be that of a colony or offshoot from a family; and some have thus called the members of the village by the name of "sucklings of the same milk," or, again, of "sons and the sons of sons . . ." This, it may be noted, is the reason why each Greek polis was originally ruled—as the peoples of the barbarian world still are—by kings. They were formed of persons who were already monarchically governed (i.e., they were formed from households and villages, and) households are always monarchically governed by the eldest of the kin, just as villages, when they are offshoots from the household, are similarly governed in virtue of the kinship between their members. This primitive kinship is what Homer describes (in speaking of the Cyclopes) :

> Each of them ruleth
> Over his children and wives,

a passage which shows that they lived in scattered groups, as indeed men generally did in ancient times. The fact that men generally were governed by kings in ancient times, and that some still continue to be governed in that way, is the reason that leads us all to assert that the gods are also governed by a king. We make the lives of the gods in the likeness of our own—as we also make their shapes . . .

When we come to the final and perfect association, formed from a number of villages, we have already reached the polis—an association which may be said to have reached the height of full self-sufficiency; or rather (to speak more exactly) we may say that while it *grows* for the sake of mere life (and is so far, and at that stage, still short of full self-sufficiency) , it *exists* (when once it is fully grown) for the sake of a good life (and is therefore fully self-sufficient).

Because it is the completion of associations existing by nature, every polis exists by nature, having itself the same quality as the earlier associations from which it grew. It is the end or consummation to which those associations move, and the 'nature' of things consists in their end or consummation; for what each thing is when its growth is completed we call the nature of that thing, whether it be a man or a horse or a family. Again (and this is a second reason for regarding the state as natural) the end, or final cause, is the best. Now self-sufficiency (which it is the object of the state to bring about) is the end, and so the best; (and on this it follows that the state brings about the best, and is therefore natural, since nature always aims at bringing about the best).

From these considerations it is evident that the polis belongs to the class of things that exist by nature, and that man is by nature an animal intended to live in a polis. He who is without a polis, by reason of his own nature and not of some accident, is either a poor sort of being, or a being higher than man: he is like the man of whom Homer wrote in denunciation: "Clanless and lawless and hearthless is he." The man who is such by nature (i.e., unable to join in the society of a polis) at once plunges into a passion for war; he is in the position of a solitary advanced piece in a game of draughts.

The reason why man is a being meant for political association, in a higher degree than bees or other gregarious animals can ever associate, is evident. Nature, according to our theory, makes nothing in vain; and man alone of the animals is furnished with the faculty of language. The mere making of sounds serves to indicate pleasure and pain, and is thus a faculty that belongs to animals in general: their nature enables them to attain the point at which they have perceptions of pleasure and pain, and can signify those perceptions to one another. But language serves to declare what is advantageous and what is the reverse, and it therefore serves to declare what is just and what is unjust. It is the peculiarity of man, in comparison with the rest of the animal world, that he alone possesses a perception of good and evil, of the just and the unjust, and of other similar qualities; and it is association in (a common perception of) these things which makes a family and a polis.

We may now proceed to add that (though the individual and the family are prior in the order of time) the polis is prior in the order of nature to the family and the individual. The reason for this is that the whole is necessarily prior (in nature) to the part. If the whole body be destroyed, there will not be a foot or a hand, except in that ambiguous sense in which one uses the same word to indicate a different thing, as when one speaks of a "hand" made of stone; for a hand, when destroyed (by the destruction of the whole body), will be no better than a stone "hand." All things derive their essential character from their function and their capacity; and it follows that if they are no longer fit to discharge their function, we ought not to say that they are still the same things, but only that, by an ambiguity, they still have the same names.

We thus see that the polis exists by nature and that it is prior to the individual. (The proof of both propositions is the fact that the polis is a whole, and that individuals are simply its parts.) Not being self-sufficient when they are isolated, all individuals are so many parts all equally depending on the whole (which alone can bring about self-sufficiency). The man who is isolated—who is unable to share in the benefits of political association, or has no need to share because he is already self-sufficient—is no part of the polis, and must therefore be either a beast or a god. (Man is thus intended by nature to be a part of a political whole, and) there is therefore an immanent impulse in all men towards an association of this order. But the man who first *constructed* such an association was none the less the greatest of benefactors. Man, when perfected, is the best of animals; but if he be isolated from law and justice he is the worst of all. Injustice is all the graver when it is armed injustice; and man is furnished from birth with arms (such as, for instance, language) which are intended to serve the purposes of moral prudence and virtue, but which may be used in preference for opposite ends. That is why, if he be without virtue, he is a most unholy and savage being, and worse than all others in the indulgence of lust and gluttony. Justice (which is his salvation) belongs to the polis; for justice, which is the determination of what is just, is an ordering of the political association.

Theodore H. White
Retrospect on Yesterday's Future

It is this impossibility of exactitude that makes American politics such an art. How many Americans are so tied to their past that they cannot be summoned to face the American future? To how many of each group must a politician give insurance policies of protection and respect? How many of each group will be offended by a coarse appeal to their tribal origin that divides them from all other Americans? All, all, are Americans, for the harmony of America's origins is what gives America its symphonic vitality. Yet the politician, roughly cherishing this knowledge, also knows for sure that he cannot ignore the strength of kinship politics.

Thus the politician's map of America differs from the geographical map. For the political campaigners, the South, the border states, the farm states reaching up through the Dakotas (as well as patches of upper New England and upper New York) are areas of British stock, parent-stock country. Buffalo, Detroit, Chicago and some of the upper Midwest farm country bring to mind the Polish vote. Wisconsin, Minnesota, Montana, Washington suggest the Scandinavian vote. The Jewish vote registers on the politician's mind with overwhelming impact in New York City and its suburbs, and then again in Chicago, Philadelphia, Boston, Los Angeles and Miami. The voters of German stock are so broadly spread across the country that except in Wisconsin they cannot be treated separately. The Italian voters make themselves felt as a bloc with particular vigor in New York City, Connecticut, Rhode Island, northern New Jersey, Pittsburgh, and Ohio.

The Irish are a special case. For the Irish, as the earliest of the great migrant communities, have had the longest stretch of American experience, and the operation of the many influences of American culture has produced in them the greatest political diversity of any of the immigrant stocks except for the parent colonial stock. Until 1870 they were the largest foreign-born nationality group in America, to be replaced thereafter by the Germans. But their role as political pioneers for the other late-coming arrivals persisted long after they were outnumbered in the immigration tallies by other nationalities; and it is this role of pioneer that explains how that stock figure of jest, the "Irish politician" came to be born.

The "Irish politician" is worth pausing over in American political history; for whether he is described as a figure of honor or vilification, his role was absolutely essential in the shaping of modern American political life. On the urban frontier he was the builder and architect of a political system that lasted for almost sixty years.

His role is easy to explain. As the millions of European immigrants came off their boats in New York, Boston and Philadelphia, they found themselves, all of them, tongueless, hungry and despised in this strange land of their hope. They brought no understanding of the workings of democracy from the autocracies of old Europe, nor even the faintest concept of the working of Anglo-Saxon jurisprudence. They could all vote, just as soon as they had learned to read and write primitive English. But what they were voting for, or how the system of government that enfranchised them within five years of arrival worked, they did not know.

Among all these immigrant groups who shared the slums and tenements, who looked at the police with fear and trembling, who offered their untaught skills for whatever wages industry chose to offer, there stood out only one that could speak the tongue of the land: the Irish. Such words as "sheriff," "surrogate," "mayor," "alderman" were familiar in all the counties of Erin. The Irish, alone at first and for generations almost unchallenged by other immigrants, understood the instrumentation of government set up by the settlers of British tradition. Government to the immigrants was important: government was the policeman who could pinch or release a peddler, the judge who could jail or pardon a first offender, the school that could be pried open or remain barred to children. And so, in their need for government and in their alien tongueless wonder, the other groups accepted the Irish among them as leaders because the Irish understood, at once, the English language, the immigrant needs and the American government.

What political power the Irish won in the big cities of the North in the closing decades of the nineteenth century they hung on to with tenacity for years and years afterward in the command machinery of the Democratic Party.

It was only in the 1930s that two events shook the grip of the Irish Democratic leadership in the big cities. One was, of course, the New Deal in Washington, whose generosity in relief and jobs dwarfed anything the local Irish machines could provide for their clients. The New Deal freed the slum clients of the machines from utter dependence on the machine's sporadic generosity and favor. The second event, slower maturing, was simply the growth in education and dignity of the sons and grandsons of later immigrants who had arrived a generation or two after the Irish. English-speaking now, American-trained, American by instinct, they began to shove and push the Irish for leadership in American city life. Some groups made a lateral penetration, as did the Jews, through the professions or via Washington. Others, like the Italians, fought a jungle war of claw and fang with Irish leadership for their place in the sun. (It is noteworthy that in New York City, where the Italians constitute the largest single ethnic group of the population, it was not until 1932 that the Irish-led Tammany Hall permitted a single Italian district leader to sit in its councils—and that seat was won not by gentle persistence but in a bare-knuckled, head-cracking East Side fight.)

There are still, to be sure, many small-time politicians of Irish extraction in the big-city machines—but they are indistinguishable from their Italian, Jewish, Polish, Negro colleagues; they win no city or statewide leadership by right of inheritance or because there are no others to challenge them. There is, I believe, only one "Irish politician" left in the country who exercises anything like the old-fashioned backroom control over a statewide coalition of races. Where Irish names stand out in political leadership today, they stand out in the open— Daley of Chicago, Lawrence of Pennsylvania, Green of Philadelphia, Shelley of San Francisco are men who run openly for Congress, mayoralty, or governorship. Their political wars are conducted in the open and their victories are claimed at the polls, not in the back rooms. And beyond such men there is yet the third political wave of Irish descent— the young men and women of the fourth and fifth generation, educated at the great universities, who find their homes alike in the Democratic and Republican Parties, staffing the Stevensonians and the reformists, the Nixon and the Rockefeller organizations, with no sense of parochialism, entirely merged in the common American attitude to life.

Every national election takes account of these facts. Both National Committees analyze and reanalyze the ethnic groups every four years, knowing that the old colonial stock splits North and South into Republican and Democrat, that German and Scandinavian stock will split heavily for the Republicans, that Jews, Poles and Italians will break heavily for the Democrats, that the Irish are now unpredictable—and that a coalition must be made of all of them, so that the victorious candidate, when President, can claim the full loyalty of every group and, with this confidence, can summon them to their tasks and duties as Americans at home and abroad.

In the election of 1960, however, two other cleavages were to acquire an importance in electoral strategy greater than ever before in American political history.

These were the cleavages, first between white Americans and Negro Americans; and next between Protestant Americans and Catholic Americans. Here the weight of the past had the heaviest impact on the campaign.

The mingling of white and Negro Americans has been the most terrible problem of American politics since the Constitution makers first became embrangled in a hopeless search for its solution; out of their inability to find a humane solution came the Civil War; this mingling of white and Negro remains today, along with peace-and-war and the proper conduct of the economy, one of the three cardinal problems of American life.

It is not so much color that divides Negro and white Americans as the way the past has created different conditions of life and thus different social habits and mores.

The past begins with the abomination of slavery. Some historians believe that in the discovery and colonial eras more black than white persons were brought to the new hemisphere; estimates of the African transshipment run from a low of 6,000,000 to an unbelievable 15,000,-000. Trapped in Africa (by their own kind), then manacled and sold to the white traders (who commerced in them), Negroes were exported as animal energy to the New World. The estimate of those Africans who were brought to what is now America runs from a generally accepted figure of 350,000 to 400,000 up to a million. So merciless were the conditions of life under which they were penned, however, that, by the time of America's own revolution a century and a half after the first Negroes arrived only an estimated 500,000 could be counted alive as slaves; and as slaves then, for another eighty-five years, they were worked, bred and beaten, like nonhumans, in one of those sins of mankind for which there can never be expiation. Divorced from all culture and refinements; denied, except rarely, the rights and sacraments of marriage; forbidden the opportunity of hope or education, they were freed in 1865 and cast hopelessly adrift in a Southern society that still used them on farm and field more as animals than as people. Until 1870, 80 per cent of all Negroes in America could neither read nor write. And until only twenty years, ago, the Negro was an *object* of American political discussion—not a participant.

What has happened in the past decade is that Negro Americans insist on discussing their own fate with white Americans; in the campaign of 1960, this insistence, and the recognition of it by American politics, became an overriding consideration of both candidates.

The rise of this insistence, the power to enforce this insistence, comes from the greatest geographic migration in American life since the settlers took their covered wagons west—the movement of the Negro from the South to the North and West, and (in both South and North) from farm to city. There is little to be seen or photographed of this vast continuing migrant movement. One can stand any evening at midnight in the 63rd Street Station on Chicago's South Side as the Illinois Central Railroad brings its gleaming orange-and-brown special, "The City of New Orleans," up from its all-day run out of the lower Mississippi valley. There are usually no more than twenty, fifty, sometimes eighty Southern Negroes who step off the train, blinking in the station lights, some dressed in their best go-to-meeting clothes, others dressed in tattered work clothes, with all their possessions wrapped in a cloth sack. Relatives greet them and they disappear inconspicuously in the night. They are similarly inconspicuous as they climb out of the weather-beaten, flat-spring trucks that unload platoons of migrant labor each summer to work on the farms of New Jersey and New York; the trucks return south each fall, but they carry fewer Negroes back than they brought north. The Negro trickle is as unnoticed on arrival as was the daily but incessant trickle of white people that arrived at Castle Gardens in New York seventy years ago from Europe. Negroes, like other immigrants, become visible only when they clot in the big cities; only then is their migration measurable.

There is no specific count made of any group of Americans as they move about the country; in some years it is estimated the Negro migration from the South may be as low as 100,000, in other years as high as 200,000. Only in retrospect can the United States census measure what has happened. In 1910, 90 per cent of all American Negroes lived in the states of the Old South, left to the mercies of Southern custom, excluded totally from all American politics, working in the field. By the 1960 census it was revealed that only 52 per cent of American Negroes still lived in the old Confederacy—almost half now lived in the North and West, and these Negroes gathered preponderantly in the great metropolitan centers of the North.[1]

The change, both North and South, has been dramatic. In the South no state any longer counts a majority of Negroes (as did Mississippi and South Carolina before the war). In the decade of the 1940s alone, the net migration from Mississippi of Negroes was nearly 260,000—approximately one fourth the total Negro population of the state in 1940; and the Negroes who left were the youngest and most vigorous—nearly

---

[1] Nationally, the census of 1960 recorded the number of Negroes at 18,871,000, or 10.5 per cent of the total American population. In 1950 it had been 15,048,000, or 10.0 per cent.

one half of all Mississippi Negroes who reached the age of thirty in the 1940s fled that state.

In the North the result of the migration has not only been dramatic—but just short of explosive. In 1960 the city of Washington, D.C., the nation's capital, became the first major city of the world to count a Negro majority of population (54 per cent in 1960 as against 35 per cent in 1950). New York City has seen the number of its Negroes grow from 775,000 in 1950 (9.8 per cent of the total) to 1,087,000 in 1960 (14 per cent of the total). (In the Borough of Manhattan, with a population of 1,900,000, three quarters of all children in the public elementary schools are either Negro or Puerto Rican.) Philadelphia's population is set at 26 per cent Negro today and Detroit's at 29 per cent; the Negro population of Newark, New Jersey, has almost doubled in the past decade—going from 75,000 (or 17 per cent) in 1950 to 138,000 (or 35 per cent) in 1960. In 1940, Newark counted only 10 per cent Negroes. All the major cities of the Northeast have lost population in the past decade, says the census. The population they have lost has been white population; the population that has replaced them has been Negro. (New York has lost over 450,000 white people in this decade; its Negro population has grown by more than 300,000; Newark has lost 100,000 whites in this decade; it has gained 65,000 Negroes.)

This has resulted not only in the most violent problems of neighborhood adjustment in each Northern city. It has posed a political problem of the first magnitude.

Negroes vote in the North. And they vote predominantly in the big-city states, which carry the largest blocs of electoral votes in the nation. Among them, Illinois, Pennsylvania, New York and Michigan measure out to 132 electoral votes—or almost exactly half the number needed to elect the President. In these states, the queen city of each state harbors a Negro vote that may mean the difference between success or failure in a close national election.

Time was, forty years ago, when Negroes voted solidly Republican out of gratitude to Abraham Lincoln and emancipation. ("I remember," once said Roy Wilkins, Executive Secretary of the National Association for the Advancement of Colored People, "when I was young in Kansas City, the kids threw rocks at Negroes on our street who dared to vote Democratic.") But Franklin D. Roosevelt changed that. Under Roosevelt, government came to mean social security, relief, strong unions, unemployment compensation. ("Let Jesus lead me, and welfare feed me" was a Negro depression chant.) And, like a heaving-off of ancient habit, as the Negro moved north he moved on to the Democratic voting rolls.

Many of the most eminent Negro leaders in America today have personally lived through this political transition. "I was born in Dougherty County, Georgia," said Congressman William Dawson of Chicago, senior Negro in the American Congress, several years ago, "just one step this side of Hell. I stood guard with my father all one night to stop a lynching when I was fifteen. I hated the word Democrat when I came north. I saw them bring Negroes up from the South in World War I and stuff them in here, into four and a half miles of the Black Belt, until it was the most populated spot on the face of the globe. I saw them ripping basements out of stores and pushing people to live in rat-infested filth, until the Black Belt was the damnedest pesthole ever conceived by the mind of man."

But Roosevelt made Dawson switch from the Republican to the Democratic side. Roosevelt brought assistance and relief in the depression. "Negroes would have died like flies if he hadn't kept his hand on the money until it got to them," said Dawson. And so Dawson became, as he still is, a Democratic political boss in Chicago, at first only of the Negro wards, then in the senior council of Cook County.

Just how much the Democratic Party owed to men like Dawson and the Negro vote did not become apparent until 1948. But when in 1948 Harry Truman squeezed ahead of Thomas E. Dewey by 33,612 votes in Illinois, by 17,865 votes in California, by 7,107 votes in Ohio, no practicing politician could remain ignorant of how critical was the Negro vote in the Northern big city in a close election.

Since then, as the Negro migration from the South has quickened in pace and size, the importance of the Negro vote has grown to be almost obsessive with Northern political leaders. Running proportionately in some places (like New York) at 3 to 1 Democratic and in others (like Detroit) at 8 to 1 Democratic, the Negro industrial vote is one of the most solid political properties in Democratic custody. It represents power.

Nor can this huge power, this ability to swing half the electoral votes necessary to make a President in a close election, be hidden from Negro leaders themselves.

For as the great migration has moved north, other things have been happening to Negroes besides industrialization—most noteworthy among them, education. No measurable group in American life, one can learn from a special census report of 1959, has made so remarkable a stride in education and development over the past decade as the Negro. Today, only 7 per cent of Negroes are still illiterate. Between 1940 and 1959, the proportion of college graduates among young adult Negroes tripled. And the result has been the development among Negroes of a leadership across the nation of such brilliance, devotion and zeal as to be among the most significant triumphs of faith in democracy.

Except that it is a leadership still locked in its subcommunity, still parochially devoted, and energized almost entirely and exclusively by Negro purposes, not yet willing (even if permitted) to lend its leadership to national purposes as a whole.

This Negro leadership now, in 1960, stood full of confidence and vigor after a six-year march from one triumph to another. Beginning in 1954, with the decision of the Supreme Court that all public schools in America must desegregate, this leadership had finally sensed itself backed by the might of the law. And with the law on its side, it moved year by year, issue by issue, state by state, battle by battle—from Autherine Lucy and the Montgomery bus strike of 1955 to the sit-ins of 1960—to use its leverage on the political system to win its demands of society. Never in any election before 1960 had any group, under leadership of such talent, presented its specific community demands in such blunt and forceful terms.

It would be so good and happy a thing if a political reporter could leave the Negro problem in the United States at the level of its superb political leadership; or at its bare political statistics; or at the net balance of justice, which certainly supports Negro leadership, as it did in 1960 with righteousness and justification.

But no political writer in the United States can adequately report the problem of white-Negro relations without presenting the full balance of the ledgers, or what disturbs the whites of the South and, increasingly, the whites of the big Northern cities.

For what has happened over the past twenty years, as Negro progress has come so swiftly, is that the gap between its own advanced leadership and the troops of its rear echelon has widened almost as fast as progress. If Negro education, Negro culture, Negro responsibilities have soared, so, sickeningly, has the heritage of a past now sampling life with an abandon once choked by Southern white cruelties. Perhaps the most dramatic and alarming of the figures attendant on the release of the Negro from his previous Southern punishments has been the rise in the proportion of illegitimate Negro births as the Negro has moved North. In 1940 (so records the census) 16.8 per cent of Negro children in the United States were born out of wedlock. (In that same year, the proportion of illegitimacy among American whites was 2.0 per cent.) By 1958 (the last year for which comparative figures are available) the figure for white illegitimacy was substantially the same: 2.1 per cent. The proportion of Negro illegitimacy had, however, swollen to 21.2 per cent. One fifth of the Negro children in the United States are born fatherless— and in some of the larger Northern cities, the proportion is estimated at one fourth or more.

Differing heritage and social customs produce these grim figures; in

1950, 21 per cent of the homes of nonwhite families with children under eighteen were broken homes; for white families the comparable figure was around 8 per cent. But attendant on those figures are all the figures of delinquency and street violence; and the political implications thereof.

Whether or not the present trend of violence and crime is a transitional crest in adjustment to city living among Negroes or whether it is more morbid, no one at the moment knows. Some years ago this reporter tried to investigate the dimensions of what was happening in the four Northern Cities with the largest Negro populations. At that time the latest figures available for public inspection were those of 1955, a year of high prosperity, and they read thus: In Chicago (where Negroes were then estimated at 17 per cent of the total) Negroes accounted for 65 per cent of the jail population, 70 per cent of the occupants in public housing, 75 per cent of those on relief. In New York (Negroes at that time: 12 per cent) Negroes accounted for 38 per cent in public housing, 38 per cent on relief, and the jail figures were not publicly revealed. In Philadelphia (then 21 per cent Negro) Negroes made up 80 per cent of the jail population, 43 per cent of those in public housing, 50 per cent of those on relief. In Detroit (then 19 per cent Negro) Negroes made up 58 per cent of the jail population, 50 per cent of those in public housing, 69 per cent of those on relief.

Although these figures alarm, there appear also to be two counterweights to such figures.

The first was one I heard from a distinguished and heartful Negro member of the Philadelphia City Council with whom I discussed the situation. He said, "Do you remember reading Richard Wright's book about the colored boy in the slum, looking up at the airplane in the sky and muttering, 'Fly that plane white boy, fly that plane'? He just knew it was a white boy flying that plane and it could never be him, no matter how much he wanted. The Negro feels trapped. He feels he has to fight everybody. The police kick him around, social workers treat him not like people but like a 'case,' and a 'Negro case' at that. School authorities try to restrict him, teachers as soon as they get a little experience want to be transferred elsewhere. A white boy raises hell—the police bat him around and send him home. When a Negro boy raises hell, he's fingerprinted, arrested, mugged; from then on he's got a record, he's a target. Twenty-five years ago, only one in ten arrests in Philadelphia for dope involved a Negro; now it's the other way around. Dope lets him rise above the world, above discrimination, it's another form of escape. He lives in the slums and hates it, and nobody will let him live anywhere else."

The second counterweight comes from figures alone. Los Angeles is

that city of the United States where the Negro probably receives the
most decent treatment and has the best opportunity for decent housing.
In Los Angeles, in 1955, Negroes constituted 11.3 per cent of the population—yet only 14 per cent of the jail population, 18 per cent of those
in public housing, 18 per cent of those on relief. It is possible, if the Los
Angeles figures are valid, that when Americans of any color are given
full equality in jobs and in housing, they behave with full and equal
responsibility too. It has not yet proved so in the big Northeastern
cities. Other groups from Europe, adjusting in times past to American
urban life, have done so with equal violence. Faith and history urge
today's observer to hope that Negro violence will also slowly diminish.

Such statistics as these are generally of more interest to sociologists
than to politicians. Yet politics are only sociology in action; and the
abrasions and frictions of urban life in the Northern big cities have
begun to rub off in politics. No Northern political boss has yet begun
to make political capital of these frictions as race-blind Southern politicians have done for decades; yet more than one Northern big-city
boss has privately considered the matter.

It is the ominous growth of friction in the streets that places so ex-
quisite a problem of real leadership and responsibility on both white
and Negro political leaders. In the past, white bosses have tried to find
low-grade "Uncle Tom" leadership for their Negro wards, dull puppets
who could be manipulated at white will. But the Negro community
all across the nation is now in the process of repudiating such leadership and seeking new, positive men of its own stock. Yet the new positive
men win votes in their wards only by the most unqualified denunciation
of the white "power structure," and the poverty, desolation and over-
crowding it imposes in Negro slums. It is as if all their energies and
drives were directed outward against the white enemy, with none left
for responsible guidance and attention to those patterns of Negro living
and manners that so worry the white community. In the long reach for
a social harmony in American life, responsibility for common standards
must rest upon both leaderships—white leadership and Negro leadership alike. For, if it is politically impossible that Negro leaders ignore
the demand of their community for better schooling, better housing,
better job opportunities for its youth, so is it politically impossible for
many white political leaders to ignore the demands of *their* communities
for an orderly tranquility and urban peacefulness in the process of
adjustment.

It is this growing political problem that creates the artificial and
untrusting quality of dialogue between Negro leaders and white politicians in the North. White politicians in the North know the Negro
vote to be vital. Negro leaders press publicly for equal rights, and white

leaders verbally agree. But Negroes know that white leadership always, privately, holds back on the basis of concern that both refuse to discuss.

However these matters may add up in the long run of American history, the election of 1960 was indeed to prove a bench mark. Even more than the election of 1948, the outcome of 1960 was to be dependent on Negro votes. And the leadership of the Negroes, like the leadership of so many minorities in the great cities of the United States, was to exert its electoral strength. For the Northern cities of the United States, commanding the electoral votes necessary to make an American President, have for generations provided a leverage on American power to shape and alter the world itself. During the years of World War I, the Irish of the great Northern cities had provided the leverage to free Ireland from Britain; the Czechs of Pennsylvania had actually written the first Constitution of the Free Czechoslovak Republic in Pittsburgh in 1919. During and after World War II, the Jews of the great Northern cities had exercised their political leverage to win and guarantee the independence of Israel.

And so, in 1960, the Negroes of the Northern cities meant to exercise their leverage on the Presidential election, to compel equality for their kinfolk in the South. Deeply motivated, Negro leaders watched the electoral campaign begin in the summer of 1960; and, deeply concerned, both candidates wondered how in conscience and in tactic they could honorably harness these motivations to the conquest of the American Presidency.

There remains one last division of the past to be considered as the Americans moved to consider their candidates—the largest and most important division in American society, that between Protestants and Catholics.

America as a civilization began with religion. The first and earliest migrants from Europe, those who shaped America's culture, law, tradition and ethics, were those who came from England—and they came when English civilization was in torment over the manner in which Englishmen might worship Christ. All through the seventeenth century, as the settlers arrived from the downs, the moors, and the villages of England, they came scarred with the bitterness and intensity of the religious wars of that era, wars no less bloody and ferocious for the fact that they were fought between Protestant sects, Protestant against Protestant. The harshness of Cromwell, that somber figure, was a reflection of the harshness with which Protestants assailed each other, as well as Catholics, over sect and dogma.

It was with this remembered bitterness that the English migrants began the building of a new society in a new world; and out of this

bitterness they distilled, though not without a struggle, that first great
landmark in America's unique civilization, that first of the creative
American compromises that was to set America apart from the old
world: freedom of worship, the decision that government should have
no right to make inquiry into the faith of its citizens and that the state
should remain forever divorced from any religious establishment. Never
in civilization, since the earliest ziggurats and temples went up in the
mud-walled villages of prehistoric Mesopotamia, had there been any
state that left each individual to find his way to God without the guidance of the state. In retrospect, this is probably the greatest historic
decision enshrined in the American Constitution.

The Americans of the age were not an irreligious people; and the
fact that they were Christian was very important, for the marks of
Christianity lay all across the Constitution. Although Christianity has
never been the *guarantee* of a democratic state anywhere in the world,
no democracy has ever thrived successfully for any period of time outside of Christian influence; without the quality of mercy and forgiveness, there is only logic and reason to guide a state, and these guarantee
no freedom to any man. What the American Constitution did was to
accept and code a working compromise that had been reached by men
and women of English descent escaped from the fratricidal wars of
religion in Europe and unwilling to transfer such wars to the new land.
Each man would worship in his own manner; and the state would limit
itself to the affairs of Caesar. For the Protestants who created the
American state, the very antithesis of these ideas was the code of the
Church of Rome, which their forefathers had repudiated in England
over two hundred years before.

Not until the 1850s did the Protestant civilization of America begin
to include a serious proportion of Catholics, and then (apart from the
historic New Orleans community) it was a Catholicism confined to the
few large cities of the Eastern seaboard, where the great Irish migration
was beginning to arrive. And not until 1891 did the United States census
historically begin to estimate, from Catholic sources, the number of
Catholics in the American population. In that year, estimates the census,
there were in America 8,277,000 Catholics out of a total population of
64,361,000 in America—or 13 per cent. By 1928, the year an American
Catholic, Alfred E. Smith, first ran for President, the proportion had
grown to 16 per cent (or 19,689,000 out of 120,501,000). In 1957 the
United States conducted a special census of religion in America, and in
that year one has the choice of two divergent sets of figures. Following
the old tables and accepting Catholic estimates of Catholic communicants, America held 34,564,000 Catholics out of an estimated total population of 171,229,000 citizens, or 20 per cent. Accepting instead the

special census figure of 43,037,000 Catholics at that time, the Catholic proportion of Americans amounted to 26 per cent.

The huge difference between the official Catholic claim and the higher estimate of the Bureau of the Census—a difference of 8,600,000 in the year 1957—illustrates the trickiness of all figures on religion in the United States. Some groups—such as the Christian Scientists—refuse to offer any estimate of their numbers at all. Some Protestant groups, such as the Lutherans, count all members as communicants from the moment of baptism, as do the Catholics. Other (and most Protestant) groups count their communicants only from the age of thirteen or fourteen. For some years Jewish groups numbered only the male heads of household; now Jewish groups estimate their numbers on the basis of established congregation (it is estimated that there are 5,400,000 Jews in the United States today, the largest Jewish community since the Destruction of the Temple). All figures on religious breakdowns in the United States, either by state or nation, are thus guesses, subject to error of up to 20 per cent.

It is obvious, however, from the spread of the census figures since 1890 that the increasing percentage of Catholics has come first from the great south and central European migrations of the early 1900s (Italian, Polish, some Czech, some German Catholic) ; and has thereafter been amplified by the Catholic birth rate. Dr. Donald N. Barrett of the University of Notre Dame has estimated that in the years 1950–1959 the Catholic population of the United States increased by 35.8 per cent while the general population increased by 16.6 per cent. Or in other words, as he has said, "Forty-one per cent of the total United States growth in 1950–1959 was derived from the Catholic sector of the population."

Such a statistical development reflects, of course, a change in the composition of American life, of which American politics has been aware for generations. From the Eastern Seaboard all the way through to St. Paul, Minnesota (or Omaha, Nebraska) this change has for a full generation been the working problem of practicing politicians of both parties.

In general, and for reasons quite apart from faith, most Catholics have voted Democratic. They have voted Democratic because when they arrived as immigrants in the large industrial cities they found the national political machinery at the time of their arrival in the hands of Republicans who distrusted big cities; Catholic immigrants entered, naturally, into the party that sought and cultivated their votes, the Democratic. Not only did they enter—within a period of fifty years they had come to lead and possess the Democratic Party in a bloc of states that stretched from New England to Illinois. In New York State, for

example, in a recent year, of sixty-two counties in the state, the Democratic County Committeemen in fifty-seven were Catholic. (Two of the
other five were Jewish, three were Protestant.) In Massachusetts, Connecticut and Rhode Island so sharp is the cleavage between religions
that the Democratic Party might almost be defined as the party of
Catholics, the Republican Party as the party of Protestants. In Pennsylvania, Illinois, Ohio, Democratic leadership is largely Catholic, too. For
thirty years, by tradition, the chairman of the Democratic National
Committee has been a Catholic.

Yet in American politics no figures are ever certain or stable. Groups
slowly move from party to party from generation to generation; as the
Negroes over the past thirty years have passed from being predominantly Republican to being predominantly Democratic, so have millions of Catholics over the past thirty years, as they have prospered and
moved forward in life, been slowly drifting away from the Democratic
Party to the Republican. "Ah," said a mournful political leader to me
once, "These guys whose grandfathers used to want to be captain of the
ward now all want to be president of the country club.")

This drift of Catholics away from Democratic leadership was all
through the 1950s the chief concern of Democratic Party leadership.
Roosevelt, in his later elections, had begun to lose some of that 65–70
per cent margin of the Catholic vote that the Democrats had normally
thought of as their own. Harry Truman in his 1948 election brought
them back. But Adlai Stevenson, according to the findings of the major
opinion analysts, lost Catholics to Republican Dwight D. Eisenhower in
decisive proportions. In 1952, so estimates George Gallup, Stevenson retained only 56 per cent of the Catholic vote; in 1956 he barely managed
to win a shadow margin of 51 per cent.

How to bring the Catholics back into the Democratic Party, how to
repossess the base vote of an enormous group of Americans who were no
longer immigrants, no longer dependent on political favor for progress,
no longer clients of any one party, who now exercised freely their choice
between the candidates of both parties—this had haunted Democrats
ever since 1952. For, despite some Protestant judgments of Catholics, the
Church committed itself to no narrow political loyalties; Church leadership in America has entered that stage of sophistication where it feels
as much at home with Republicans as with Democrats. In many of the
most important dioceses of the nation it was known in 1960 that if the
Catholic Church had any silent inclination, it leaned to Richard M.
Nixon rather than to John F. Kennedy.

Yet, though every man knew that the Church would remain scrupu-
lously neutral in the coming campaign; and that millions of upper
class Catholics had permanently passed into the Republican Party; and

that, further, it was impossible for either major party to make an outright bid for Catholic votes *as* Catholic votes—it was still certain that Catholics, by and large, as well as every other group in the country, Jewish and Protestant, would have a natural gravitation to a candidate of its own faith. Between two Protestants, Catholics would vote impartially by personality, economics, instinct, aspiration or tradition; but if the choice lay between Protestant and Catholic candidates, the kinship issue would certainly be raised and thus cut both ways. That was the question: would a Catholic candidate gain more from his kinsmen's inclination to vote *their* past, or would he lose more from the Protestants' inclination to vote *their* past?

This question had been debated by Democratic Party leaders ever since 1924, usually in terms of Electoral College votes. In 1924 the Party had first seriously considered a Catholic, Alfred E. Smith, for its nomination; in 1928 it had given him the nomination; ever since, with the memory of his overwhelming defeat in mind, the Party leadership (even though substantially Catholic) had believed that a Catholic candidate, in any election, would lose far more than he might gain by his faith.

This was the hazard that John F. Kennedy faced in the summer of 1956 when he sought the Vice-Presidency and that, for four years thereafter, until 1960, was his greatest political handicap. His Party's Eastern leaders were incapable of discussing the matter in terms of doctrine, of American civilization, of tolerance. They would discuss the matter only in terms of practical election arithmetic, and so only in these terms could Kennedy hope to persuade a Democratic Convention to let him offer himself against the hazard.

The arithmetic used by the Kennedys is probably as reliable as anybody else's in the vague and tentative estimates one must make of religious affiliation in the United States. According to this arithmetic, there were at least fourteen vitally important states, states which normally swing back and forth in national elections, and in which the proportion of Catholics to total citizenry was large enough to count *for* Kennedy rather than *against* him. These states were:

New York (Catholics, 40 per cent)
Pennsylvania (Catholics, 29 per cent)
Illinois (Catholics, 30 per cent)
New Jersey (Catholics, 39 per cent)
Massachusetts (Catholics, 50 per cent)
Connecticut (Catholics, 49 per cent)
Rhode Island (Catholics, 60 per cent)
California (Catholics, 22 per cent)
Michigan (Catholics, 24 per cent)

Minnesota (Catholics, 24 per cent)
Ohio (Catholics, 20 per cent)
Wisconsin (Catholics, 31 per cent)
Maryland (Catholics, 21 per cent)
Montana (Catholics, 22 per cent)

These states amounted to 261 electoral votes—only eight short of the votes necessary to carry the national election. Not even this 1956 table (prepared by Ted Sorensen and John Bailey) could convince the big-city bosses of the East (mostly Catholic) that their kinsman-in-faith could master the profound religious division in American origins and go on to win. Not until Kennedy's spring exertions of 1960 in the cross-country primaries could he convince them and the leaders of other Democratic minorities that he might win.

Thus, when finally in the summer of 1960 John F. Kennedy turned to face the nation, he turned with a campaign split as few other campaigns by the contradiction of American voting. In word, speech and idea it reflected the candidate's innermost personal spirit, which was entirely addressed to the highest purposes of the American future. Yet it could not ignore its spectacular gamble about the American past: whether, for Catholic and Protestant, the past would outweigh the future.

So much depended on how this, the transcendent issue of religion, could be shaped—whether in practice the differing qualities of fear and bigotry could be separated. For bigotry, which is unreasoning, can be cured only by death. Yet fear, if honest, can be erased by truth.

In the folk memory of the dominant Protestant American community the Roman Catholic Church was known to have used the instruments of state in the past to impose its faith on countless communities by fear, force and pressure. But this was 1960, and the place was America. The institutional policy of any Church, including the Roman Catholic Church, could be a legitimate, open and unbigoted subject of public discussion if it intruded itself in legislative matters (as later, indeed, it was to intrude violently in 1960 in the politics of an American Commonwealth, Puerto Rico). So could the attitude of any individual American seeking public office, if he sought thereby to carry into effect the policy of any church. The problem was not one of separation of church and state, a doctrine settled by the Constitution, but the attitude of an individual American to this founding doctrine—and that individual had to be judged as an individual, by the slow estimate of reasonable fellow Americans.

Yet there was no immediate American background for this kind of judgment. Few Americans had lived abroad long enough or widely enough to recognize how diverse are the attitudes and institutions of the

Roman Catholic Church in the twentieth century—how vast, for example, is the gap between the benign and tolerant humanitarianism of the French Catholic Church and the narrow intolerance of the Spanish Catholic Church. Few Protestants realized how various are the attitudes of American Catholics (however loyal they may be in faith to their sacraments) to the role of their Church in public affairs. To persuade the dominant community of Protestant Americans that he was bound by no doctrine espoused by some obscure Pope at some other time in some other country but, rather, that he sought his authority only from their will and their free choice as citizens—this, then, became the first imperative of John F. Kennedy, who believed no other. In such a delicate exercise Richard M. Nixon (as Hubert Humphrey before him) could be only a witness and a bystander.

This was the past from which both candidates departed in August to stir the emotions of America—the immediate past of growth and change, of decaying cities and swelling suburbs, of technological change and work patterns changing with them, coupled with the remote past of mothers' songs and fathers' stories, of Negro humiliation and white fears, of hymns in church and martyrs forgotten—all to be weighed against the future the two candidates might describe for all, a future of war or peace, of outer space and ocean depth, of schools and medical care, of bounty or disaster.

And no logic anywhere to guide the two candidates except the stark figure of 269—the number of electoral votes needed to win the Presidency.

William Brammer
from *The Flea Circus*

They climbed the great stone steps and headed down the main corridor of the Capitol building, taking a back elevator that let them off at a third-floor passageway near the Executive Offices. They sat waiting for a few minutes, watching the nice-legged secretaries moving back and forth. Occasionally, the Governor's voice could be heard through the thick walls, a little like Grand Opera from a great distance. Jay McGown passed through the reception room looking gloomy and efficient. He stopped and talked with them.

"He ought to be ready for you," Jay said, looking back toward the Governor's conference room. His attitude was not so much one of anxiety; Jay had more the quality, characteristic of those constantly exposed to Arthur Fenstemaker, of having peered steadily at the scene of an accident, experienced a revelation, seen death and redemption, God and Lucifer staring back, and somehow, incredibly, survived.

Jay started off toward the pressrooms down the hall. Almost immediately the Governor came banging out of his office, one arm draped round the shoulder of a state senator. The senator grinned at everyone, eyes glazed, the Governor leading him as a blind man toward the door. Then Fenstemaker turned, a great happy smile on his face. "Come on in, you two," he said.

They got to their feet to follow him inside. Fenstemaker had already collapsed in his chair, stretching out, neck and spine resting against the leather cushions. They sat across from him and stared. Fenstemaker pinched his nose, moved a big hand over his face as if probing for minute flaws in a piece of pottery. He rubbed his eyes, sucked his teeth, punched holes in a sheet of bond paper with a gold toothpick. He stood and paced about the room and stared out the windows and scratched himself. "Well goddam and hell . . ." he said. It was like a high mass, a benediction.

"Let me do you a favor, Willie," he said.

"What kind of favor?"

"I don't know. Anything you ask. I just want to get you obligated," the Governor said, grinning and winking at Roy.

"Don't know of anything I want offhand," Willie said.

"Think of something."

"How 'bout some more of that Scotch whiskey then—the smoky twenty-five-year-old stuff you served me last month."

Fenstemaker smiled, showing his shark's teeth. "Hell and damn," he said. "That's no favor." He swung round in the big chair and opened a side panel of the desk. There was the sound of ice clacking in metal tumblers, and he pushed drinks across to them. "Look at this," the Governor said, setting a seltzer bottle on the desk top "Damndest thing . . . Used to see 'em in the movies when I was growin' up. When I could afford a movin' picture show." He held the bottle in one hand and pressed the lever, sending a spray of water across the room. For a moment there was a fine mist suspended in the air between Roy and Willie and the sunlit windows. A lovely rainbow appeared.

"You're a mean sonofabitch," the Governor said, staring at the seltzer bottle. Roy wondered if he was talking about the bottle or his guests, until he repeated himself. "You're a mean sonofabitch, Willie," he said, still smiling.

"I'm lazy and no-account," Willie said. "But not mean, especially."

"You ever think about old Phillips?" He referred to a minor state official now serving a term in the penitentiary who was convicted on several counts of theft and conspiracy from evidence developed in Willie's news columns.

"I think of him," Willie said. "I keep thinking how I wish he'd come back and do it all over again. I'm running out of people to expose."

The Governor spun round in his swivel chair, grinning. "Well you keep tryin', Willie," he said. "You keep tryin'. What's your circulation now?"

"About the same as it was. About ten thousand. But only about six of it paid. We give away a hell of a lot of copies."

"That's not much," the Governor said. "Ten thousand's not much."

"No."

"How much money you losin'?"

"Lots."

"I imagine so," the Governor said.

"I try not to think about it," Willie said. He looked unhappy for a moment, thinking about it.

"Where's the money come from?"

"I'm not supposed to say."

"You got to say now," Fenstemaker said. "I give you that Scotch whiskey."

"Various sources," Willie said, raising his glass as in a toast. "I don't know who-all. Rinemiller helped raise the original amount. Got it from people like Earle Fielding . . . Some others . . . Hell! You probably know who they all are."

The Governor laughed and leaned toward them. "But it's not your circulation, Willie—it's the *quality* of your goddam readership."

"Suppose they can all read," Willie said.

"Now goddam I mean it," Fenstemaker said. "Anybody who really cares about politics subscribes to your little paper, even if they don't necessarily subscribe to your point of view. People who shape thinkin'— policy makers, lobbyists, lawyers, judges, small-time politicians."

"There's been no one else printing a lot of this stuff," Willie said. "I suppose something's better than nothin'."

Fenstemaker looked delighted. "Exactly!" he said. "Whole basis my philosophy!"

"What's that?"

"Somethin's better than nothin'."

"Half a loaf?"

"Slice of goddam bread, even," Fenstemaker said. He changed moods suddenly. "Now about these hospitals . . ."

"*What* . . . ?" Roy and Willie leaned forward, trying to follow the course of Fenstemaker's conversation.

"Hospitals," the Governor said. "You care about the hospitals?"

"Sure."

"They're a God-awful mess."

"Worse than that," Willie said.

"I got this little bill . . ."

"I know," Willie said.

"I got the votes," Fenstemaker said. "At least I *think* I got them. It's not much of a bill—not half enough of an appropriation—but it'll close up some of the worst places and build some new ones and bring in a few head doctors. And this little bill can *pass* is the main thing. I'll put it through next week if I don't get everyone all stirred up and worried about taxes and socialism and creepin' statesmanship. You gonna help me, Willie?"

"How can I help?"

Fenstemaker slapped his desk and showed his teeth. "Oppose the goddam bill!" His face beamed. "But just a little bit, understand?" he said. "Don't get real ugly about it."

"I don't understand," Willie said.

"Those fellows in the Senate—they think this is all I want, they'll give it to me. But if somebody's runnin' round whoopin' about how good this is, settin' precedents and havin' a foot in the door and braggin' on how much more we'll get next year, then all my support'll get skittish and vanish overnight."

"I see."

"Only don't oppose it too much, either. You raise hell and *your* bunch won't go along. They'll introduce their own bill askin' for the goddam aurora borealis. I need their votes, too. Just oppose it a little bit—oppose it on *principle!*"

The governor paused a moment and considered the problem. "I want," he said, beginning to laugh quietly, his sad eyes blinking, "I want unanimous consent and dead silence!" He roared his laughter at them.

Willie stirred and looked at Roy. Then he looked at Fenstemaker and said: "That all you wanted? We taking up too much of your time?"

"Oh, *no!*" Fenstemaker said. "Hell no. I got you two here for somethin' else altogether. Just a minute." He leaned across his desk and punched a button. A girl's voice came on the speaker.

"Yes, sir?"

"Hah yew, honey?"

"Just fine . . ."

"Jay in there?"

"Yes, sir."

"Tell him to get that machine of his and bring it in. Tell him I'm ready for a little transcribed soap opera."

He leaned back in the chair, resting on his spine, looking as if he were in great pain. "How you get to be one of those goddam elder statesmen?" he said.

It was such an improbable story it had to be true. If it were simply some hoked up yarn designed to discredit an enemy, old Fenstemaker's inventiveness would have served him better; there would have been some style, some magic, a sense of possibilities. Fenstemaker didn't insult a man's intelligence—you could nearly always count on that—and this story here was so coarse and bumptious there *had* to be something to it. Otherwise, the Governor would have devised a folktale with source material for his own amusement. Fenstemaker would have invented a better story.

Willie sat listening, trying to set bits and pieces to memory, wondering if he should take notes. The Governor was sprawled in his big chair, looking out the window, beyond the granite ledge where two bizarrely plumed pigeons clucked and strutted, flapping their wings for balance in the careless wind. Roy sat like a bronze figure, cigarette ash spilled down the front of his dark jacket, and Jay McGown stood next to the machine with his hands on the switches. They played the recording all the way through, listening in silence, and then once again, stopping and backing up the tape and commenting on the undecipherable sections before proceeding.

"Once again, Jay," the Governor said, and Jay McGown spun the reels like a scientist at the controls. There was scarcely any doubt—the voice, one of the voices, was Alfred Rinemiller's; the other identified by Fenstemaker as a lobbyist for a group of loan companies. They sat and listened all the way through one more time . . .

—Who'd you say?
—Huggins. He's chairman of the committee and a good friend.
—And you think you could change his mind . . . ?
—I think so. I could work on him. I've done him favors and he knows it.
—Well listen . . . We got to be damn sure. There's a lot ridin' on this. We got to be absolutely certain about it—that's why I'm down here. Our future's at stake—there's a whole pot of money we could lose with just a change of a few percentage points on the usury limitation . . .
—Then you understand it's going to cost you money to save money.
—We know that. We've done business down here before. It's just we want to be dead sure. We can't afford to go throwin' it around. We can't afford it. We've been burned before.
—I'm just telling you you've got my word. Ask anybody. You can depend on it. I can keep the bill in committee, but—hell—you understand—you got considerations.
—How many?
—There's a lot of sentiment this year for some kind of legislation in the field.
—How many considerations?
—I don't know. There's Huggins . . .
—He's a rich boy. What the hell's he need——
—Rich family. He only gets a limited amount from them, and he spends most all of it. And he likes women . . .
—We've all got our weaknesses . . .
—That's his. Women. And he's known only the inexpensive ones. I can get a couple who . . .
—Hell! You do, hah? Whyn't you get 'em up here, then. We'll have a little party.
—You pay?
—Only kidding. Listen—how much now? You got yours. I thought that would be enough. You realize how much you got there?
—Yes.
—How much? Count it.
—I believe you.
—Go ahead . . . count it . . .
—It's all here.

—How much.

—Seven-fifty. Just like you said.

—Now you goin' to deliver the goods just like you said?

—You've got my vote. I have a good deal of influence on the committee. Enough to stop the thing from being reported out. But it's going to take some work. I expect more for that work. And it'll cost *me* some hard cash to bring it off.

—How much, goddamit?

—Five thousand.

—You're crazy.

—Take it or leave it.

—You're out of your mind.

—You want your money back? Here . . .

—No, dammit. I want your *vote*. But you bring up this subject yourself of what you can do for us in workin' on the others. And then you say five thousand for chrissake. I could buy up control of the Senate for that much.

—Fat chance . . . All right then. What's your offer?

—Half.

—Half? Half of what?

—Half of five . . . That's twenty-five hundred. And I tell you, mister, we've never thrown money around like that in the history of this organization.

—It's not enough.

—The hell it isn't!

—All right.

—And we want to be damn sure.

—You can count on it.

—I mean damn sure. You're gettin' only a thousand of it now.

—*What?*

—And the balance when we're certain the bill's dead for this session.

—Well now how can I be sure I'll get the rest of it?

—You can count on it, my friend.

—There's no assurance.

—What assurance you give us? And besides—I haven't got that kind of money. Not that much. I'll have to go tap our directors, and that'll be a touchy business. They'll think I'm gettin' to *them*. Puttin' the money in my own pocket.

—All right. But they'd better come across. Otherwise, they're liable to find this legislation looking right at 'em again next session. And I'm the boy who can make sure it passes. Think that one over . . .

—Well now it seems you have a very good point there.

—Yes.

—So we're all protected.

—That's right.

—How 'bout a drink?

—Fine.

—Bourbon?

—Anything else?

—No. Just bourbon. Like I said, we're a small outfit. *Five thousand!* Why godalmighty, man, that's half my salary for a year.

—Bourbon's fine.

—Seven-Up?

—No . . . Soda.

—We don't have any . . .

—Jesus . . .

—There's a cold-water tap in the bathroom . . .

The tape came to the end of the reel and continued to spin noiselessly in the big padded room. "That's enough, Jay," the Governor said. Jay McGown packed the recorder and left the room. For a few moments they were silent. The Governor stared at his spotted pigeons on the window ledge.

Willie said, "Why'd this fellow bring it to you?"

"I don't know. He's a kind of screwball—doesn't really have much idea what's going on down here. He said he didn't know what to do with the evidence, as he called it, so he brought it to me."

"Just like that?"

"Yes. And I wish to God he hadn't."

"Sounds like something for the grand jury," Roy said. "What the hell's wrong with people? Rinemiller gone out of his mind?"

"Well now this fellow's put it on my back. Listening to what he said in that conversation, he wouldn't look so good in the courts himself. Even if he was just stringin' Rinemiller along . . ."

"He did a pretty convincing job of it," Willie said.

"Yes. So he brings this tape in—just this morning—and puts it all on me. I almost suspect *he's* trying to make a deal. Seemed to think Rinemiller was one of my boys and maybe if I'd just take care of that bill for him personally he wouldn't be out any money and would be willing to forget everything."

"He say all this?" Willie said.

"No. Just a feeling I had. He's supposed to come back to discuss it after I've had time to think it over."

"He mention calling in the law?" Roy said.

"No. He just kept saying it was a very serious matter. Very serious."

"He has a gift for understatement," Willie said.

"Well," the Governor said. "What do you think?"

"For God's sakes don't get me in on it. You know Rinemiller's an officer in the corporation of the newspaper?"

"I knew he was connected," the Governor said. "Otherwise, I wouldn't have let you know about it."

"How do you know I still won't print it?" Willie said.

"I'd be pleased if you would, as a matter of fact. Make the decision for me."

"I just might," Willie said. "It would probably ruin me, but I might if I could get that lobbyist to talk. Who's to say definitely beyond doubt it's Rinemiller?"

"It would bitch up a great many things," Fenstemaker said. "It would put you out of business, and probably take away all those great gains you people made this year in the elections. You know Rinemiller campaigned strictly on the issue of being a liberal? He kept calling himself that. Capital L."

"Why'd you want me in here?" Roy said.

"Well, you're a friend of Rinemiller's . . ."

"Rinemiller's a sewer."

"All right, then. I called you because you're about the only one of the bunch I'd put any faith in. You've got good sense. You're always honest with me. I respect you. I want your advice."

"On what?"

"I dunno. How to deal with this thing, I suppose. Tell me what you think? I don't know whether to lay it all out in the open or call Rinemiller in and let him squirm a little or let that fellow have it back and see what he's planning. If he's got a plan."

"What's that?"

"He mentioned the possibility of paying off Rinemiller in marked bills and having some state police there to grab him when he takes it."

"That would be interesting."

"I really don't think he wants any of that, though."

"You think he's bluffing?"

"He might be. Just to see what *I'll* offer *him*. Goddam. He would have me opposin' that legislation for the next four years. And I happen to believe it's needed. Had it in my campaign platform."

"Why you letting him pull you in?" Roy said.

Fenstemaker poured a glass of water, used it to wash down a pill. He got to his feet and paced around the room, pausing in front of a mirror to look at himself. He smiled, baring teeth and pink gums, tapping the enamel with his blunt finger. He turned round and said: "We haven't heard Rinemiller's side of it, you know. That recording might be faked."

"I hope so," Willie said.

"And whether anybody believes it or not, I care about those people downstairs. I care about your bunch, Roy. We got the same objectives— we just disagree on methods. Something like this here, it'll set us all back, disgrace the whole bunch of us, and blow the session all to hell. I got a program to worry about."

"Well," Willie said, "most of our people got elected on the corruption issue, and I suppose it would be only fair to go right back out again for the same reasons . . ."

They were silent for a time. Finally, the Governor suggested they think about it for a few days. They all agreed to think about it. Arthur Fenstemaker's collapsed features came together; he smiled and put an arm around each of the two young men.

In the reception room they stood and talked about seeing each other again in several days. Jay McGown was bending over one of the secretary's desks, making corrections in a television script. The Governor suddenly reached across, took several of the sheets of paper, and began to read aloud. Then he looked up at the ceiling for a moment.

"This is too prissy, Jay," he said. "Can't you brag on me some without it soundin' like I'm diggin' my toe in the ground?"

"It's a problem," Jay said, "bragging on you when you're making the speech yourself . . ."

The Governor looked resigned to another defeat. "Well forget it then—take that stuff out about receiving honorary degrees. I never even got the B.A., anyhow . . ." He turned to Roy and Willie and said: "Everybody's tryin' to blur my public image."

Then he stalked back inside the office.

William L. Riordon
To Hold Your District . . .

There's only one way to hold a district; you must study human nature and act accordin'. You can't study human nature in books. Books is a hindrance more than anything else. If you have been to college, so much the worse for you. You'll have to unlearn all you learned before you can get right down to human nature, and unlearnin' takes a lot of time. Some men can never forget what they learned at college. Such men may get to be district leaders by a fluke, but they never last.

To learn real human nature you have to go among the people, see them and be seen. I know every man, woman, and child in the Fifteenth District, except them that's been born this summer—and I know some of them, too. I know what they like and what they don't like, what they are strong at and what they are weak in, and I reach them by approachin' at the right side.

For instance, here's how I gather in the young men. I hear of a young feller that's proud of his voice, thinks that he can sing fine. I ask him to come around to Washington Hall and join our Glee Club. He comes and sings, and he's a follower of Plunkitt for life. Another young feller gains a reputation as a baseball player in a vacant lot. I bring him into our baseball club. That fixes him. You'll find him workin' for my ticket at the polls next election day. Then there's the feller that likes rowin' on the river, the young feller that makes a name as a waltzer on his block, the young feller that's handy with his dukes—I rope them all in by givin' them opportunities to show themselves off. I don't trouble them with political arguments. I just study human nature and act accordin'.

But you may say this game won't work with the high-toned fellers, the fellers that go through college and then join the Citizens' Union. Of course it wouldn't work. I have a special treatment for them. I ain't like the patent medicine man that gives the same medicine for all diseases. The Citizens' Union kind of a young man! I love him! He's the daintiest morsel of the lot, and he don't often escape me.

Before telling you how I catch him, let me mention that before the

From *Plunkitt of Tammany Hall,* by William L. Riordon, published 1948 by Alfred A. Knopf, Inc. Reprinted courtesy of the publisher.

election last year, the Citizens' Union said they had four hundred or five hundred enrolled voters in my district. They had a lovely head-quarters, too, beautiful roll-top desks and the cutest rugs in the world. If I was accused of havin' contributed to fix up the nest for them, I wouldn't deny it under oath. What do I mean by that? Never mind. You can guess from the sequel, if you're sharp.

Well, election day came. The Citizens' Union's candidate for Senator, who ran against me, just polled five votes in the district, while I polled something more than 14,000 votes. What became of the 400 or 500 Citizens' Union enrolled voters in my district? Some people guessed that many of them were good Plunkitt men all along and worked with the Cits just to bring them into the Plunkitt camp by election day. You can guess that way, too, if you want to. I never contradict stories about me, especially in hot weather. I just call your attention to the fact that on last election day 395 Citizens' Union enrolled voters in my district were missin' and unaccounted for.

I tell you frankly, though, how I have captured some of the Citizens' Union's young men. I have a plan that never fails. I watch the City Record to see when there's civil service examinations for good things. Then I take my young Cit in hand, tell him all about the good thing and get him worked up till he goes and takes an examination. I don't bother about him any more. It's a cinch that he comes back to me in a few days and asks to join Tammany Hall. Come over to Washington Hall some night and I'll show you a list of names on our rolls marked "C.S." which means, "bucked up against civil service."

As to the older voters, I reach them, too. No, I don't send them campaign literature. That's rot. People can get all the political stuff they want to read—and a good deal more, too—in the papers. Who reads speeches, nowadays, anyhow? It's bad enough to listen to them. You ain't goin' to gain any votes by stuffin' the letter-boxes with cam-paign documents. Like as not you'll lose votes, for there's nothin' a man hates more than to hear the letter-carrier ring his bell and go to the letter-box expectin' to find a letter he was lookin' for, and find only a lot of printed politics. I met a man this very mornin' who told me he voted the Democratic State ticket last year just because the Republicans kept crammin' his letter-box with campaign documents.

What tells in holdin' your grip on your district is to go right down among the poor families and help them in the different ways they need help. I've got a regular system for this. If there's a fire in Ninth, Tenth, or Eleventh Avenue, for example, any hour of the day or night, I'm usually there with some of my election district captains as soon as the fire-engines. If a family is burned out I don't ask whether they are Republicans or Democrats, and I don't refer them to the Charity Organization Society, which would investigate their case in a month or two and decide they were worthy of help about the time they are dead from starvation. I just get quarters for them, buy clothes for them if their clothes were burned up, and fix them up till they get things runnin' again. It's philanthropy, but it's politics, too—mighty good politics. Who can tell how many votes one of these fires bring me? The poor are the most grateful people in the world, and, let me tell you, they have more friends in their neighborhoods than the rich have in theirs.

If there's a family in my district in want I know it before the charitable societies do, and me and my men are first on the ground. I have a special corps to look up such cases. The consequence is that the poor look up to George W. Plunkitt as a father, come to him in trouble—and don't forget him on election day.

Another thing, I can always get a job for a deservin' man. I make it a point to keep on the track of jobs, and it seldom happens that I don't have a few up my sleeve ready for use. I know every big employer in the district and in the whole city, for that matter, and they ain't in the habit of sayin' no to me when I ask them for a job.

And the children—the little roses of the district! Do I forget them? Oh, no! They know me, every one of them, and they know that a sight of Uncle George and candy means the same thing. Some of them are the best kind of vote-getters. I'll tell you a case. Last year a little Eleventh Avenue rosebud whose father is a Republican, caught hold of his whiskers on election day and said she wouldn't let go till he'd promised to vote for me. And she didn't.

The Integrative and Disruptive Effects of Politics

The connection between politics and community is close, as many of the selections and comments in this book have suggested. The exact nature of the relationship is a matter of continuing debate in political theory and philosophy, and community has therefore persistently been a central concept for these fields of thought.

Politics is an activity having to do with the "allocation of values" in society. On the basis of authority founded on a sense of legitimacy, politics is expected to resolve the conflicts within a society, protect it against threats from without, and redistribute its resources. Such terms as legitimacy and authority suggest that the political process is presumed to be related to a sense of commitment and some degree of common purpose among the citizenry. Deeply involved in the processes of politics, therefore, is the problem of creating community, the problem of developing a consensual base on which the political structure can rest.

As a political system depends, in some sense and some degree, on the integration of the community, it also creates integration. Some theoretical perspectives maintain that the existence of community depends, first and last, on the establishment of a set of political relationships; and some hold that politics is essentially destructive of the ties of sympathy and common purpose that can bind men together. Aristotle and Rousseau, for example, held the former view, Marx and some of the anarchist theorists the latter. We are inclined to look at this as an empirical question whose answer varies from one social situation to another—political activity may promote or impede the coherence of the community depending on the type of activity, the circumstances, and the nature of social base.

In any case, however, the immediate activity of politics is often integrative in intent, consequences, or both. Perhaps it is useful to think of this integrative activity as being of two kinds, instrumental and symbolic. By instrumental we mean the activity of the political system as it discharges its "ordinary" functions: it keeps the peace, regulates economic activity, promotes the welfare of citizens. These actions seem to be directed primarily at specific goals: peace, welfare, and so on. They may also create integrative responses as side effects, though the latter need not be unintended and may even overshadow the main purpose of the activity. In other words, as government goes about doing what it does, it may generate feelings of satisfaction, dependency, and loyalty among those it serves. These feelings in turn bind that population together. One sometimes hears this sense expressed by people who take pride in their community because it maintains a high level of services.

Politics also often means symbolic activity, activity expressly intended to foster confidence in the community and attachment to it. We are most familiar with this kind of phenomenon in the nation state of the modern Western world, for in these we have seen the flags, emblems, anthems, and the like that embody symbolic politics at its most intense. As our selections from the writings of the ancient Greeks have shown, however, patriotism and loyalty have also been valued in other times and places.

These integrative effects of politics have often been much in evidence in the modern American city. The political organization played an important part, for example, in bringing the immigrant of the late nineteenth and early twentieth century into the mainstream of American life. Politics provided him with a variety of services, with career opportunities, with social contacts, and with an array of identification symbols, all of which helped him think of himself as an American and a part of his city and neighborhood.

Edward Shils discusses the effects of political ritual in a highly developed and urbanized society. His article is an analysis of the coronation of the Queen of England, one of the most elaborate ceremonials observed in contemporary statecraft. The English have harvested, from a remote past, residual symbols that help create a belief in commonality. These "meaningless" activities reintegrate a differentiated and often schismatic population in terms of national solidarity.

POLITICS AND THE DISRUPTION OF COMMUNITY

The expansion of networks of control to include more population over time and space increases the scale of the society. In the process it often destroys existing social groups and with them the local community. We had a gigantic example of this in the period of expanding European imperialism; we see it also in the expansion of the economic enterprise and the market place in peacetime, without guns or threats.

Whatever the nature of the coercive organization, it has the effect of destroying the autonomy of the small community, forcing it to depend upon the larger one. In the United States, with our bias against the recognition of violence (though not against violence itself) we have tended to moot the notion that scale increases through physical domination. To be sure, we know that we destroyed many cultures in creating our present society, even as we are just finishing off the survivals of Hispaniola culture in the Southwest and Appalachian culture in the mountains. But our picture of our history emphasizes the growing urban complex as a result of trade and manufactures; it is a vision based on *laisser faire* liberalism, not the older conflict theory.

A corrective for this tendency, and a piercing analysis of what really produces urbanization in many backward countries, is present in Van Hoey's study of organizational transformation in the region now known as the Republique de Niger. In his view violence, coercion, and dominance have been the key to urban settlements, from the slave-raiding armies of the Sultan of Zinder to the iron rule of French colonial officialdom in the twentieth century. But in looking at this example of the iron pot among the clay pots, Van Hoey makes it clear that the destruction of the original static culture, the folk society of the peasant villages, is a response to new growth. This growth, moving toward the creation of a nation state, produced cities where there had never been cities before. To be sure, it may be that the price was great; who shall say what *too* great would be?

While Niger is a case of organizational transformation brought about by politics, a move that disrupts community but also recreates order, Durrell's picture of the eruption of EOKAS in Cyprus is another matter. His narrative of the days of violence and guerilla warfare underlines the fragility of community when politics fails, for the failure of politics is the birth of warfare. His dramatic juxtaposition of the orderly relations between himself (a Briton) and the Greek and Turkish Cypriots—his friendship for the island and love of the people—as against the bombings and murders that destroyed trust and the very grounds of social order, is not only moving as a personal document; it is also a shrewd analysis of the intertwining of the political and the communal in general.

As we know, the erosion of trust between Greek and Briton, Greek and Greek, which he details, continued. It reopened the ancient bitterness between Greek and Turk and it destroyed a comity that had been centuries in the making, replacing it with an uneasy truce. Some of the major problems of our politics today are conflicts within the nation state among different ethnic populations. Racial antagonism at home is the equivalent of nationalistic struggles abroad. Both require that the family of man find some formula by which it may respect, if not love, itself in all its varieties. For it is a curious fact that ethnic groups almost never disappear; the American assumption that all moves toward assimilation is peculiarly parochial, some would say psychologically imperialistic, but certainly not true to the empirical data.

Thus politics may cripple or destroy community; politics may also create community. In this extract from *Bitter Lemons* Lawrence Durrell shows clearly, however, the everlasting task of politics. Old differences last, history will not stop, the ingenuity and actions of public men are necessary for the unending task of weaving together the various breeds in a public order that may be dignified with the name "community."

Edward Shils and Michael Young
from *The Meaning of the Coronation*

In all societies, most of the adult members possess some moral standards and beliefs about which their is agreement. There is an ordering and assessment of actions and qualities according to a definite, though usually unspoken, conception of virtue. The general acceptance of this scale of values, even though vague and inarticulate, constitutes the general moral consensus of society. Only philosophical intellectuals and prophets demand that conduct be guided by explicit moral standards. In the normal way, the general moral standards are manifested only in concrete judgments, and are seldom abstractly formulated. Persons who conduct themselves in accordance with rigorous and abstract schemes of moral value, who derive and justify every action by referring it to a general principle, impress most others as intolerable doctrinaires. To the doctrinaires, of course, the ordinary man is even more shocking; they would shake the *homme moyen sensuel* from his spiritual slothfulness and elevate him to a higher plane on which he would act knowingly only in the service of the highest good. To the doctrinaire, to the ideological intellectual, the ordinary sociable man is a poor thing—narrow, unprincipled, unmoral. The ordinary man, is, of course, by no means as poor a thing as his educated detractors pretend. He too is a moral being, and even when he evades standards and dishonours obligations, he almost always concedes their validity. The revivalist reassertion of moral standards in highly individualistic frontier groups, or among detribalized primitive societies in the process of yielding before the pressure of a modern economy, are instances of the respect vice pays to virtue. The recourse to the priestly confessor and the psychoanalyst testify to the power of moral standards even in situations where they are powerless to prevent actual wrongdoing.

We do not claim that men always act in conformity with their sense of values, nor do we claim that the measure of agreement in any society, even the most consensual, is anywhere near complete. Just as no society can exist without moral consensus, without fairly far-reaching agreement on fundamental standards and beliefs, so is every society bound

From "The Meaning of the Coronation" by Edward Shils and Michael Young, *Sociological Review*, Vol. 1 (December 1953), pp. 64–67. Reprinted by permission.

to be the scene of conflict. Not only is there a clash of interests, but moral and intellectual beliefs too are in collision. Yet intertwined with all these conflicts are agreements strong enough to keep society generally peaceful and coherent.

What are these moral values which restrain men's egotism and which enable society to hold itself together? A few can be listed illustratively: generosity, charity, loyalty, justice in the distribution of opportunities and rewards, reasonable respect for authority, the dignity of the individual and his right to freedom. Most people take these values so much for granted that argument about them seems neither necessary nor possible. Their very commonplaceness may seem to place them at the very opposite pole from the sacred. Yet these values are part of the substance of the sacred, and values like them have sacred attributes in every society.

Life in a community is not only necessary to man for the *genetic* development of his human qualities. Society is necessary to man as an object of his higher evaluations and attachments, and without it man's human qualities could not find expression. The *polis* or community is not just a group of concrete and particular persons; it is, more fundamentally, a group of persons acquiring their significance by their embodiment of values which transcend them and by their conformity with standards and rules from which they derive their dignity. The sacredness of society is at bottom the sacredness of its moral rules, which itself derives from the presumed relationship between these rules in their deepest significance and the forces and agents which men regard as having the power to influence their destiny for better or for worse.

Man, as a moral creature with the capacity to discriminate among degrees of rightness and wrongness, feels not only safe but also terribly unsafe in the presence of the abstract symbols of these moral rules. *This is one reason why there is a recurrent need in men to reaffirm the rightness of the moral rules by which they live or feel they ought to live.* The reaffirmation of the moral rules of society serves to quell their own hostility towards these rules and also reinstates them in the appropriate relations with the greater values and powers behind the moral rules.

The need to reaffirm the moral rules comes then, not only from their sacred character, which require that they and their sources be respected in the most serious manner, but also from the struggle against morality being continuously enacted in the human mind. Dr. Ernest Jones, in a perceptive essay, has pointed to the fundamental ambivalence in the attitude to authority—first towards the parents, then towards the wider authorities of State and Church, and finally towards the rules which emanate from these authorities. This ambivalence can be overcome in a number of ways of which reaction-formation and displacement are the most prominent. In order to curb an impulse to contravene a moral law, men will sometimes put all their energy into the fulfillment of the contrary impulse. Connection with the symbols of morality or proximity to them helps in this exertion and reinforces the strength which the individual can muster from his own resources to keep the moral law uppermost. It re-establishes the preponderance of positive devotion to the moral rules to enter into contact with them in their purest form. Contact with them in their most sacred form—as principles, or when symbolized in ritual activities, or when preached in moving sermons or speeches—renews their potency and makes the individual feel that he is in "good relations" with the sacred, as well as safe from his own sacrilegious tendencies.

If this argument be accepted, it is barely necessary to state the interpretation of the Coronation which follows from it: that the Coronation was the ceremonial occasion for the affirmation of the moral values by which the society lives. It was an act of national communion. In this we are merely restating the interpretation, in a particular context, of a more general view (which can apply to Christmas, Independence Day, Thanksgiving Day, May Day, or any other great communal ritual) expressed by a great sociologist. "There can be no society," said Durkheim, "which does not feel the need of upholding and reaffirming at regular intervals the collective sentiments and the collective ideas which make its unity and its personality. Now this moral remaking cannot be achieved except by the means of reunions, assemblies and meetings where the individuals, being closely united to one another, reaffirm in common their common sentiments; hence come ceremonies which do not differ from regular religious ceremonies, either in their object, the results which they produce, or the processes employed to attain these results. What essential difference is there between an assembly of Christians celebrating the principal dates of the life of Christ, or of Jews remembering the exodus from Egypt or the promulgation of the decalogue, and a reunion of citizens commemorating the promulgation of a new moral or legal system or some great event in the national life?"

The Coronation is exactly this kind of ceremonial in which the society reaffirms the moral values which constitute it as a society and renews its devotion to those values by an act of communion.

Leo Van Hoey
The Coercion of Community

Machine technology is not a necessary condition for urban development, even though it is a factor of acceleration and probably instrumental in propelling a society to high levels of urbanization. Many forms of societies structure themselves around cities, and it is necessary to study variation among and changes in different types in order to isolate the specific causal processes of urbanization.

Urbanization in the Republic of Niger occurred under apparently adverse conditions: extreme economic underdevelopment, persistent poverty of natural and technical resources, and low population pressure.

Precolonial social space in Niger had a remarkable pattern. Nomads controlled the northern area from the highland of Asbir and Tibesti. Herdsmen followed their longhorn cattle across the savannah steppe. The agricultural peoples occupied the cultivable south and southwest, and developed three types of social structure: the village, the Hausa chiefdom, and the sultanate of Zinder. The basic economic structure of most of Niger, however, was the agricultural village.

THE TRADITIONAL COMMUNITY

The basic unit of organization was the village, a cluster of compounds inside a field on the open savannah. The inhabitants extract from the earth a frugal sustenance, by means of unaided human energy and simple instruments. The target of production is local subsistence, which includes some surplus for seed, emergency exchanges, and occasional celebrations. Farming is done during the three months of rain; the sun dries up the earth the rest of the year.

The village was composed of a lineage group of agnatic kinsmen (descendants by the male line). The key principles of organization derived from rights in the cultivated field and the use of slave labor. Slaves, included as permanent members in the household, were in charge of domestic labor. The slave complex made all labor except millet growing menial; crafts were a second line of slave occupation during the nine dry months of the year.

The central function of this agriculturalist society was to insure the indefinite perpetuation of limited field resources. The ancient structural answer was kinship: the perpetuation of the resources was entrusted to the living representatives of a descent line. The structural principle allowed for a variety of kinship systems.

In Niger, the vital question of land tenure was decided by referring to the claim of an ancestor, made sacred by a sacrificial act, the bond between the ancestor's blood and the forces of the soil. The act could not be undone by anyone as long as the ancestral blood remained alive and active on the soil, and the blood continued naturally in the male line. The living agnates were entrusted with the continuation of the ancestor's claim: they owned only the fruit of their labor in the field.

The village was the place of residence of a set of agnatic kinsmen and their dependents. The kinsmen were collectively responsible for the protection of the ancestor's claim on the field, hence on the perpetuation of the resources. They kept alive by ritual the memory of the original act from which all proper relations followed. They were the decisive members in charge of the affairs of the community. The group was divided into sublineages. The oldest of a sublineage was the master of a compound, the head of the agnatically extended, polygynous household in the compound, and a member of the village council where all issues came up for decision. The oldest member of the council was elected for life by his peers for the role of village head; he was the first representative of the lineage, the final arbiter of dispute, and the chief guardian of custom.

The function of perpetuating the local field resources, ensured by the agnatic descent rule, was entrusted to the senior kinsmen. The entire organization of the community can be understood as a system protecting the decisive, central role of the senior trustees. The strict demarcation lines between youths and adults within the lineage group, between the males and the females of the community, and between the communal and extra-communal members, are the protective devices.

A radical distinction was made between youths and adults. The young male passed the critical line with his first marriage. Before it nobody had ever "heard his voice in the circle of men"; he was entitled to all the frivolous connotations of the epithet "unsettled." After marriage he took his rightful place in the senior hierarchy as a community-minded member. The young male's prolonged youth is significant; he enters his first marriage only when he is about thirty years old. Since the life expectancy of those surviving the hazards of childhood must be around sixty, the age of thirty for adulthood should lead to the turnover of community leadership every thirty years.

The procedures of marriage were elaborate. The proposal was initiated by the head of the male sublineage; approval was expressed by means of prescribed gifts. Hence the young male's marriage required the cumulative contribution of all the senior members of his sublineage. In other words, the access of the males to married status was materially controlled by the senior kinsmen in every community.

Polygyny strengthened this control. While the males married late, the women married at puberty. Consequently, the women of child-bearing age were reserved for the kinsmen above thirty and no women were available for the younger set. This particular way of linking marriages, coupled with the practice of polygyny, was a means of securing firm gerontocratic control over the fate of the community.

The males of one community must take their wives from a limited set of surrounding communities. The principle of household formation was patrilocality: i.e., the wife comes to live with her husband. For this reason, women had no rights in local land, although small gardens were given to them around the main culture field, "little plots where they can amuse themselves." The women of the community had their own organization, hierarchically structured on the seniority line of their husbands and on their own lines of seniority within each polygynous household. The most rigorous form of separation between the sexes, protected by strict deference rules of all sorts, made of the world of the women a small universe apart.

THE LOCAL GROUP CHANGES

After military conquest by the French the structure of the traditional village was radically altered by four coercive actions: (1) the change in the role of the village chief to an official in an orderly bureaucratic process, (2) the abolition of slavery, (3) the reordering of political jurisdictions with the canton chief as the main authority in local matters, and (4) the exaction of head tax.

The scope of French political control can be deduced from the role of the *commandant*. He generally combined the duties of police chief, judge, tax assessor, road engineer and constructor, inspector of sanitation, head clerk and accountant, director of census, and in leisure time writer of ethnographic reports. He was *le patron,* the law and the employer of chiefs.

For all these jobs, the village group was the work team and the village chief its foreman. He was responsible for conscript labor, military enlistment quota, public works, and the payment of taxes. He was blamed for all omission, refusal, and delay in execution. Imprisonment and demotion became normal addenda to the chief's role description. The turnover in local leadership was considerable. This changed role of the chief and the dire consequences for its incumbents elicited a locally generalized change, from the normal election process to a tactic of *hiding* the chief.

The French administration, faced with unreliable local leadership, found the solution in nominating its own. They were recruited among ex-soldiers, policemen, interpreters, and janitors, on the criteria of compatibility as servants and capacity as foremen. Thus were negated the traditional criteria of descent, seniority, and election; the result was a rapid weakening of the traditional local authority structure.

The outlawing of slavery, if literally enforced, would have ruined the local labor structure for agriculture, crafts, and domestic industry. The dilemma was solved by giving the slave a role as responsible producer on a separate corner of land. This practice resulted in the development of segregated slave villages around the master village. It did not change the essential bond of reciprocal obligation between freemen and their slaves, but it introduced the principle of residential independence for the latter, which allowed much greater spatial mobility.

The creation of local jurisdictions based solely on spatial continuity clashed with the African map of inalienable ancestral rights. The new "cantons" caused many conflicts over rights to the land and its product, while the confiscation of vacant land as government property and the authority given the canton chief to settle land disputes created acute problems. The chief, under tribal obligation, was necessarily in favor of his kinsmen.

A series of unprecedented organizational changes followed. The shaken legitimation of traditional authority, coupled with uncertainty about rights to the land, resulted in the desacralization of the social structure. Its bonds to the soil, once inalienable, became problematic while the eclipse of the core criterion of descent weakened the definition of the village as a self-contained group with collective obligations toward the land. The old land-use right turned into a claim to ownership, and the obligations of defense and perpetuation were reduced to individual households. Thus even if residence patterns were not modified, the social village became merely the sum of its component households.

The imposition of head tax not only precipitated other changes, it also enforced those discussed. Head tax had an inescapable rigor that tithe and tribute never had; it was collected in cash. The responsibility for collecting and paying it rested with the head of the conjugal household since in the French view this person was the head of the family. Thus the distinction of the conjugal family from the extended family was reinforced.

Money thus became a pressing concern of the conjugal households.

Domestic production and crafts left the household, along with the departing slaves and a substitution was needed if the use of cloth, shoeware, tools, implements, and the like was to continue. Poor soil and scarce labor precluded the extension of agriculture as a solution. Served by the older tradition of their original city states, the Hausa saw a solution in ambulant commerce. Many appeared in the administrative centers and market places as vendors and small traders.

In the Zerma zone, however, neither the use of female labor in farming, nor such menial occupations as trade, were even considered. The need for money then led the young men to explore their chances in the labor market, although the stigma on labor caused them to seek work away from home. Thus seasonal migration, after the four-month agricultural season, soon took on considerable proportions. Today it involves an estimated 160,000 migrants annually.

The young migrant remained a member of the village household, which was now simply a residence group with some members temporarily dispersed. Single, or in the early years of a first marriage, his role at home was expendable. He set out with specific objectives: first to earn head tax money and then later, when the villagers consented to sell millet and livestock, bride money. As migration became more regularized, however, it took on the character of an autonomous function rather than an expedient to achieve old values. Young men set out on the voyage regardless of whether they had the older reasons; it became an undertaking which "separates the men from the boys," and a successful venture earned prestige.

The woman's position was also radically altered. Marriage-wealth, a tangible bond linking two local groups at the level of the senior members, became a bride price, an emphatically financial transaction rationalized as due compensation for the loss of the girl. As such, it increased steadily. Traditionally in case of a separation, the wife had the right to return to her mother's household, and if the separation were permanent, a symbolic object had to be returned. Now with the establishment of the junior conjugal household as a discrete unit, the senior household became much smaller and the return of married daughters represented a heavy burden. Furthermore, justification of the bride price as compensation for the loss of a daughter raised the problem of its destination when she returned; it became an object of dispute between many kinship groups. Pressure was exerted on married daughters to stay with their husbands.

In the meantime, however, women had generally made the most of opportunities offered by their gardens and the market place. They began to accumulate a private income over which the husband had no control. Their economic independence made them less willing to comply with such pressures, and it became easier to avoid them. Where women were admitted to production roles and, under Islam, were less restricted to begin with, marital separation was frequently followed by the woman's emigration from her local kinship groups. The "free women" (*karuwa*) became a distinctive social category, with locally organized and strongly influential groups in many centers. Since prostitution, like divorce, carried little or no stigma, the status of "free woman" was normally a stage as part-time prostitute between one marriage and the next.

The dissemination of Islam was another important aspect of change at the local level. The spatial mobility of the Moslem Hausa traders, in regions where the old sacral relations between man, society, and nature were on the wane, contributed to this. Niger turned to Islam at a rate which soon alarmed the French government.

These changes in village life can be summarized as *a differentiation and release of subgroups* (slave households, conjugal households) *and membership categories* (slaves, youths, married women, and junior heads of households) *from formerly integral structures* (local groups, village groups, agnatically extended households) *for participation in expanded ː etworks of interdependence, some directly related to the expanding enterprise* (nominees in the colonial structure) *some indirectly related through the by-products* (peace allowed spatial mobility, head tax created financial pressures).

Indirectly related sub-enterprises included the Hausa trade networks which expanded to include more products for more local groups; Islamic proselytizing in the wake of traders, affecting more members of more local groups; intensified market activity of adult women; intensified craft industry of self-employed slaves; the movement of formerly non-negotiable products (land and millet) into the market, and finally, the increasing scope of seasonal migration among males seeking new resource bases for rural households under stress.

Each of these changes examined in isolation might spell disruption and disorganization. But in a larger perspective the same events can be described more clearly as a kaleidoscopic repatterning of elements, a reorganization. In isolated perspective, groups may fall apart; from a contextual point of view, however, their elements are released and the pertinent question becomes: what are they released for? The focus shifts naturally to the cities.

ADMINISTRATION AND COMMERCE

Cities appeared first of all as strategic locations of central subgroups in expanding frameworks of action. The location of Zinder, crucial for military enterprises, lost its importance for the purposes of civil administration. In 1925 the colonial governor decided to abandon Zinder in favor of Niamey as the capital of Niger.

All administrative centers were locations of authority subgroups, varying in size with the rank of the civil servants in charge. They were also loci of salaried employment. The types of occupations demanded by the offices were the same everywhere. Army and police formed one set. There were clerical tasks of lower and middle rank; interpreter and liaison jobs; and unskilled or semiskilled manual and technical tasks. The tests of eligibility for employment were certified literacy in French for clerical posts and clean military service records for police tasks. Almost nobody in Niger had either of these qualifications.

Since the colonial government was part of the entire bureaucratic establishment of A.O.F., the accessible base was enormous and the problem of personnel was solved by importing foreign populations. Dahomey supplied the clerks from primary- and secondary-school literates produced by the missions. Senegal and Mali provided the guards, policemen, and soldiers.

These decisions had far-reaching consequences. The lower and middle cadres of colonial government were occupied by Dahomeans (later also Togolese) for more than three decades. Dahomeans were Christians in Moslem country, visibly distinct by physique, costume, and life style. They enjoyed a certain ambiguous prestige from working with the French, and were for years the only salaried Africans. Their integration with other groups would never be without constraints.

Koranic literacy, formerly an avenue to higher domains of authority connected with the ruling class, was now ignored by the government. Islam, a widespread system of locally organized formal education and ritual law enforcement, was relegated to a residual institution. Yet it persisted and expanded from there as an autonomous framework of organization, which pervasively obligated all groups except the French and the Christian Dahomeans.

Western schooling was predicated as the *sine qua non* of government employment. Through its visible interests, such as income, prestige, and positional advantage for self and kinsmen, the French school was indeed the single answer to the concerns of many. Yet of the first two primary schools started in Niamey in 1931 one was a mission school for Dahomean children. Few other schools appeared before 1946.

Niamey's African settlement along the river was originally a strawhut village. In 1929 the governor ordered its relocation and, master plan in hand, initiated the construction of Niamey from the ground up. The same kind of relocation and construction took place in Maradi, also by an act of authority, in 1948. These planned cities called for labor from outside the locale, increased the charm of the sites for potential migrants, and gave more grounds and room for established residents to receive their kinsmen. More people from a wider environment came to market. Because of its large population on government payroll, Niamey became the one daily market in the colony.

More important in scope and effect was the second phase of construction, which began in 1946. A number of public works, part of long-range public investment plans, reflected the changing government policy of France in its overseas territories. The development programs included roads, airports, agricultural stations and, above all, educational, medical and electric power installations in the principal centers.

French policy required that French corporations engineer the programs. The big French West African companies, attracted by the funds and pushed by the growing African control of commerce on the coast, expanded in the interior and established their stores and warehouses in Niamey. With other smaller firms, they organized shipping and surface transportation, and brought part of the supply of equipment and materials from France to Niger. French nationals were in charge of management, supervisory and specialized technical jobs, but local labor was in demand for the lower clerical, semiskilled and unskilled manual, mechanical, and service occupations.

Once established, the larger companies reached for the African consumer. They were successful in Niamey (whereas branch houses in other centers had to rely on European consumers), for the wholesale trade of imported finished products was geared to the African market organization. Five French companies competed with Arab and Syrian family stores to supply the eight or ten principal Hausa merchants controlling most of the local market.

Under these Hausa merchants, specific ethnic groups monopolized different types of goods, which they redistributed to the neighborhood shops and the vendor's table top, rug, or tray. Besides this trunkline of trade, the Hausa merchants developed their own circuits, exchanging cattle and millet from Niger for valued consumer goods (such as colanuts, dyestuffs, caftans, sugarcane) from the coast via Kano and Maradi, and soon began to use their own motor vehicles to expand and diversify their controls. Aside from these trading patterns were the women's monopoly over spices, garden produce, and cooked food, and the products of artisans.

The intricate framework of commerce was lubricated by a ubiquitous and hierarchically ordered institution of middlemen, whose specific task was to examine, propose, and codify the terms of interdependence between groups at every juncture. Even the lesser aspects of commerce, the carrying and sale of water, the Dahomean monopoly of alcoholic beverages, the Zerma organization of taxicabs, or the Mauri monopoly of rental bicycles, operated through acknowledged mediators.

All activities worthy of a name were attributes of groups. Furthermore every group in the action of the market was in its internal organization a link with the village, no matter how distant, part of the mutual support among kinsmen and natal village members. Since agnatic lineage groups also form regionally dispersed kinship systems, the rule of preferential group formation among kinsmen gave rise in the city to groups of unprecedented ethnic and regional inclusiveness. The seniority rule, which largely determined the group's role scheme, permitted the accumulation of many members under synoptic control. However, the development of specialized teams, again on the basis of kinship and natal locality, prevented the growth of large single units. But the overall rule of kinship obtained, so that differentiation created more diversified composite frameworks.

In varying proportions all centers had some combination of Hausa, Zerma, Fulani, Dahomean, Yoruba, Bambara, Mossi, and other populations organized as social groups. Each was internally differentiated by genealogy and local origin and bound by role interdependence based on kinship and seniority. Membership was assured by the subgroup organization of chain migration linked to the natal village groups. New members were incorporated as dependents in the households of nearest kinfolk. Seniors, if salaried employees, made efforts to place them; if they were involved in the market activity, the newcomers joined their team or a kinsman's.

All male income was in some manner pooled by the head of household. Part of the income was in most cases collected in the form of regular contributions to group funds. These funds were solicited by households in emergency (birth, marriage, death) or by able male immigrants awaiting gainful employment: They were used to cover emergent expenses on behalf of the group as a whole (as, for example, ceremonial representation). They were held by a neutral senior and administered by a council of elders whose responsibility it was to discriminate between aid and charity, proper and excessive allocation. Charity (on behalf of women, children and incapable dependents) was an optional concern of the households. A way was thus found to reinforce selective recruitment in favor of able participants in the urban group.

Each group's internal organization was an amplified, regionally extended kinship system. It was wedged into the city, which was its action field and resource base; it was anchored in the village, its recruitment base. Social isolation among the villages could and in many ways did continue; in town the isolation served to create subgroup differentia-

tions and autonomous action teams, but was attenuated by their subordination to more inclusive criteria of kinship.

The groups were further integrated with one another in the total
role scheme centralized in the city. Thus in Niamey the role scheme
derived its structure from the particular coercive dependence of all
profitable activity on government employment and government labor
practices. The government payroll in its final distribution nurtured all.
In Maradi, however, the "nurturing" enterprise was more autono-
mously commercial and agricultural, based on the local production and
illegal sale of government-controlled cash crops. In Zinder it was commercial and religious, based on agriculture and crafts industry.

Ultimately these patterns of cities were determined by the evolving
integration of entire ethnic structures in composite and interactively
related networks of organization. The colonial administration was the
instrument by which Western and African social structures were connected. It was also an agency of coercion which instigated other expansive processes and, to a considerable degree, defined their limits.

The "rural exodus" will continue for some time. Regional literacy
campaigns are creating an increasing number of local education centers
in the villages and nomadic camp areas, while radio clubs and discussion groups intensify the effect of broadcasting from the capital (selected information is propagated in six languages). Party houses are
being built as local centers of information and community initiative.
They are all "branch plants" of the city; through these devices of
nation-building, through adult re-education and the stimulation of effort,
the city is confined as the symbol and center of new values, new ways, and
new relationships. It is the scene of "relevant" and lucrative activity.
Indeed, so powerful is the magnet that the principal costodians of the
traditional structure, the chiefs, have made Niamey their center of residence and authority.

THE PROCESS OF REORGANIZATION

The changing structure of the traditional village group, then, appears in a wider context as one component of a total process of re-
organization. Structurally, the process involved a redistribution of the
components in response to expanding social scale. The chief mechanisms of the process were: (1) differentiation and numerical increase
of socially distinct subgroups and categories; (2) release of these units
from formerly integral and coercive structure, allowing participation
in spatially expanded and socially more inclusive frameworks of organization in diverse (though necessarily interdependent) domains of
activity; (3) formation of cities as strategic locations for central sub-

groups which assumed responsibility for coordinating the role-systems of the spatially expanded and socially inclusive enterprises.

The process of increasing scale is begun by the formation of such enterprises. Their development defines the particular coercions exerted on the pre-existing social structures, as the Sultans dominated the villages and the French succeeded them—each having drastic effects on the old order. For the structures that lie in the operational space of the expanding enterprises become recruitment bases for the human potential with which the promoters of enterprises must work.

This integration of old parts in the new systems, however, provokes counter constraints. These derive from the actions and reactions of the pre-existing groups in terms of precedent and constituted structure. The outcome of the whole process is a newly evolving social structure, a new form of society.

The process is characteristically an expansion of recruitment bases in search of specified roles and skills. The limits of the process and the composition of the evolving society are determined by the relevant roles defined by expanding organizations. The limits of spatial expansion and social inclusiveness of these organizations, in turn, circumscribe the limits of urban concentration in the society. The particular role systems of developing enterprises produce the demographic content of cities. Differences in size and growth rates among cities depend on their differential participation as centers of activity in the general process of increasing *societal* scale.

This, in bare outline, is one way of formulating what may be called the specific coercive process of urbanization. Empirical determinants, such as industrialism (or any type of technology), mercantilism, feudalism, or nationalism, reflecting particular types of enterprise, produce urbanization only by their effects upon the spatial expansion and social inclusiveness of organization—that is, the increasing scale of the society which they promote.

Lawrence Durrell
The Feast of Unreason

Was the choice of the 1st of April fortuitous? I do not know. It was not inappropriate. We had spent the long tranquil evening walking upon the battlements of old Nicosia, watching the palms flicker in the twilight wind which the dusk brings across the bony Mesaoria. The ravens creaked home on weary wings to the tall trees by the Turkish Athletic Association, where nobody ever smiled.

My brother was due to leave, and as a tribute to him and the noisome menagerie he was taking back with him, we had friends in to drink his health, and to stare (holding their noses) into the crates and cardboard boxes which housed his catch, and which temporarily occupied my spare bedroom. Afterwards we dined by candlelight and talked, and were on the point of going to bed when the silence of the little town began to ripple and bulge all round us. Parcels of steel plates began dropping from heaven on to pavingstones, while pieces of solid air compressed themselves against the window frames making them jingle. Something appeared to walk up the garden path and lean against the front door, something of immense weight—a mammoth perhaps. The door burst open to reveal the dark garden and the heads of flowers tossing in the idle night wind. Then something appeared to go off between our teeth. "I take it you are trying to say goodbye to me appropriately," said my brother. "Believe me, I am honored."

A string of dull bumps now, from many different quarters at once—as of small geological faults opening in the earth somewhere along the battlements of the fortress. We ran down the steps and along the unlit gravel road to where the main road joined it. A few bewildered-looking civilians stood dazed in the shadows of the trees. "Over there," said a man. He pointed in the direction of the Secretariat building which was about two hundred yards down the road. The street lamps were so few that we ran in and out of pools of darkness on the fringes of the unpavemented highway. We came round the last corner abreast and walked into a wall of solid yellow fog smelling strongly of something—cordite? In the vagueness figures walked about, aimlessly, with detached curiosity, uncertain whether to go or stay. They did not seem to have any more business there than we did. There was a tidy rent in the wall of the Secretariat out of which smoke poured as if from a steam engine. "Dust," said my brother grimly, "from under the administrators' chairs." But there was no time for jests; somewhere a siren began to wail in the direction of Wren's headquarters. A lorry load of police materialized vaguely out of the yellow coils of fog. And then another series of isolated bangs and, after an interval, a deeper growl which was followed by a sudden small contortion of the still night air. "The whole bloody issue is going up," said my brother fretfully; he had been peevish all evening about the failure of his film which had run into difficulties, he said, due to a sudden wave of non-cooperation which followed hard upon a visit by the parish priest to his actors. "Wherever I go there's a bloody revolution." He had just come back from Paraguay where they had revolted under him, so to speak. A bang nearer at hand lent wings to our purpose. "I must get back to my animals," he said. "The owls have to be fed."

But I felt the tug of other duties. I took the car, ignoring the fretful pealing of the telephone in that silent, book-lumbered hall with its dripping candles, and raced down to the Police Headquarters at Paphos Gate. It had a forlorn deserted air, and was, apart from one sleepy unarmed duty sergeant, unguarded as far as I could judge. In the operations room on the top floor the Colonial Secretary sat at a desk tapping a pencil against his teeth; he was wearing a college blazer and trousers over his pyjamas, and a silk scarf. Behind him the two clerks crouched in an alcove beside the receiving set which scratched out a string of crackling messages in Doric English. "Famagusta . . . a bomb in the garden of . . . Larnaca an attack on . . . a bomb thrown at a house in Limassol . . ." He glanced at the signal pads as they were hurriedly brought in and placed before him. He was composing a message to the Secretary of State. He looked up quietly and said: "I suppose this is the sort of thing you meant?" "Yes, sir." "The worst thing so far is the radio station. Five masked men tied up the watchman and blew it up."

By now the press had begun to block the meagre lines and I diverted them to an officer where I dealt with them as faithfully as I could, but police reports were very slow in coming in and in many cases the Agencies were hours ahead of us. (They were to remain so for many a long month to come.)

The radio station was indeed badly blitzed, but it was lucky in the possession of an engineering staff which had been eating its heart out for a chance like this; by two o'clock the engineers had crawled into the wreckage and produced a fairly detailed report on the damage and the welcome information that one of the transmitters had escaped, which would allow of some sort of programme going out next day, on reduced power.

By the time I got home again to the importunities of the telephone—which thenceforward was to ring on an average every six minutes, night and day—the picture was clearing and becoming coherent. The attacks had been island-wide and synchronized. Leaflets, scattered in the street of the capital, spoke of an organization calling itself EOKA (*Ethniki Organosis Kyprion Agoniston*), which had decided to begin the "struggle for liberty." They were signed *Dighenis*, an ominous enough name which, to the Greek mind, rings the same sort of bell as Robin Hood does to our schoolboys. He is a hero who belongs to a cycle of medieval folk songs; his battles are famous and he fears no one, not even old Charon, Death. Did he not, in the course of one of them, leap across from Asia Minor and leave his fingerprints on Pentadactylos, in Cyprus, before recovering his balance and leaping back?

Next morning the swollen-eyed headlines covered the front pages of the world press and in fits and starts the power-lines grew heavy with questions and answers, with telegrams and messages, the idle-flickerings of the world's frontal brain; and the press corps began to swell.

Yet the morning, like some perfect deception, dawned fine, and nobody walking about the calm streets of the town, watching the shopkeepers taking down their shutters and sipping their morning coffee, could have told that some decisive and irrevocable action had taken place in the night; a piece of the land had broken away, had slid noiselessly into the sea. In a sense now there was no more thinking to be done. We had reached a frontier. From now it would be a question of hanging on. Such solutions as those we had dreamed about were all thrown into relief by the ugly shadow of impending insurrection. And yet everywhere there were doubts. The ordinary people of Cyprus went about their work with the same friendly good-manners, many of them genuinely shocked by the work of "hot-heads" and genuinely grateful when the Governor described them as "law-abiding." I concluded that EOKA must consist of a small body of revolutionaries, unknown to the general public. Wren did not share this view. "What would you say," he said dryly, "if every sixth-form boy in every public school in England had signed this oath?" His agents had brought in a new document.

YOUTH ORGANIZATIONS OF EOKA

Oath

I swear in the name of the Holy Trinity that:

(1) I shall work with all my power for the liberation of Cyprus from the British yoke, sacrificing for this even my life.

(2) I shall perform without question all the instructions of the organization which may be entrusted to me and I shall not bring any objection, however difficult and dangerous these may be.

(3) I shall not abandon the struggle unless I receive instructions from the leader of the organization and after our aim has been accomplished.

(4) I shall never reveal to anyone any secret of our organization neither the names of my chiefs nor those of the other members of the organization even if I am caught and tortured.

(5) I shall not reveal any of the instructions which may be given me even to my fellow combatants.

If I disobey my oath I shall be worthy of every punishment as a traitor and may eternal contempt cover me.

Signed

EOKA

"Moreover," he went on, "there appeared to be plenty of bombs to go round—we're scooping the stuff up all over the island. They seem mostly home-made; the village smithies appear to have been working overtime. It rather makes nonsense of your theory about innocent old rustics with straw in their hair toasting the queen. You can't organize these things overnight, you know." He was right, of course, and events bore him out. As the nights shook and rumbled to the crash of grenades it became clear that, despite the amateurishness of execution (there was more broken glass than anything at first), the whole thing was part of a design. Situated as we were at the frail centre of the cobweb, we held our breaths and praised heaven for the inefficiency of these mosquito raids. They succeeded overwhelmingly in one thing, however, and that was the undermining of public morale. Here and there, too, among a hundred incidents of juvenile futility there was one which bore the pug-marks of something uglier—the trained hand. Evidence began to come in of Cypriots having received paramilitary instruction somewhere outside the island—in Greece. Rumour spoke of "phased" operations which would be directed against the police to begin with, and added under its breath the words "like Palestine."

To the disorder and alarm of the night-hours were added further demonstrations and riots organized by the schools which were dealt with crisply enough—but it was obvious that the police could not work right round the clock, chasing bombardiers all night and louts all day. The field of operations, too, lent itself to these harrowing tactics, for the labyrinth of warrens in the old town could hide a veritable army of bomb-throwers—even military estimates indicated that it would take practically a Brigade to search it thoroughly in one operation. When it was cordoned off, piece by piece, malefactors could easily slip over from the Famagusta Gate to the Turkish Konak in a matter of minutes.

The public, too, always timorous and in this case deliberately sympathetic to the trouble-makers, became deaf and blind, prejudicing the course of justice by its silence—which in the end could only lead to sterner measures by which the public itself would suffer. The perversion of justice was perhaps the most serious factor from the point of view of administration; Wren found it impossible to secure convictions against people unless caught *in flagrante delicto*. And then, the age groups to which these youthful terrorists belonged struck us as alarming. Moreover the moral pressure exercised by Athens radio, which went into raptures at every evidence of what it described as an open insurrection, was backed up by the local clergy whose public utterances reached new heights of bloodcurdling ferocity. The legal apparatus found itself grappling with new and disturbing formulations. Repressive measures would have to be taken; in what light would they be regarded by a world press already critical of our attitude to the question?

And then the police—always the police; Wren's calm and measured assessments had been committed to paper and sent on their way; but how could they be "implemented"—with the best will in the world? And if things got worse would they not fall short of the requirements he now thought necessary?

The nights became stretched and tense, punctuated by the sullen crack of grenades and the roar of police traffic as Wren's forces raced to the incident in the vain hope of a capture. To the customary home-made grenades and Molotov cocktails was now added a new unpleasantness—a bomb fitted with a time-pencil: a soul-destroying weapon in its effects on the morale of peaceful civilians. These at least were not home-made.

"Freedom is acquired only by blood," shrilled Athens radio. But whose blood? A bomb placed in a letter-box at the entrance to Nicosia Central Police Station went off while the street was still crowded with market-visitors and killed a Greek outright; sprawling among the wreckage on the sidewalk were thirteen injured Turks and Armenians. The shadow of communal reprisals grew bigger as the leader of the Turkish National Party warned the Greek community against any further outrage in the Turkish quarter. Bars, private houses, restaurants, graveyards—a bewildering succession of pointless targets came up. The military sent in supporting patrols by night now to help Wren; road-blocks and searches began to mark off familiar thoroughfares. The patient taciturn soldiery now began to stop cars and lorries on the main roads to hunt for arms. . . .

And as if to echo the disorders of the towns the sleeping countryside now began to wake sporadically with intimations of more serious, more considered, operations conducted by bands which were both more informed and more resolute than the juveniles. It became clear that there were two sorts of enemy, a vast amorphous mass of secondary school-boys whose task was bombing and pamphleteering and supporting public disorder—and a group of mountain bandits whose task was to raid police stations, organize ambushes, and operate against the net of roads and telegraph wires which constituted the nervous system of the administration. They were dryly classified by Wren as the "Junior and Senior Leagues." To these he was later to add a third and final category —"The Killers," which could not have numbered above twenty or thirty, to judge by the later ballistics evidence which could point to one gun, say, as having been responsible for upwards of ten street killings. But all this was buried in futurity, still covered by the deceptive mask of a perfect spring, smothered in wild flowers and rejoicing in those long hours of perfect calm which persuaded all but the satraps that the nightmare had faded. The shopping centres would be deserted for half a day after an incident; and then people would slowly creep out again, wistfully breathing in the silent air, like animals snuffing the wind; and reassured, they would start to go about the hundred trivial tasks of the day which the automatism of ordinary life had made endearing, comprehensible—containing no element of prediction. So they would open shutters, set out chairs, dust, combine and recombine their wares in familiar patterns, or simply sighing, bend vulpine features to the loved and familiar Turkish coffee which came swinging towards them on the little pendulum-trays of the waiters. And in these same daylight hours blond and brown soldiers walked the streets, chaffing their acquaintances among the townsmen and being chaffed in return—and their wives rolled perambulators full of rosy children, about the market greeted everywhere by smiles and customary attentions. It was unreal. One has seen rabbits scatter like this at the report of a gun, only to re-emerge after half an hour and timidly come out to grass again—unaware that the hunter is still there, still watching. Civilians have no memory. Each new event comes to them on a fresh wave of time, pristine and newly delivered, with all its wonder and horror brimming with novelty. Only in dull offices with electric light burning by day the seekers sat, doggedly listing events in order to study their pattern, to relate past and present, so that like stargazers they might peer a little way into the darkening future.

The village was no less deceptive in its complete smiling calm—the flowering cyclamen and the rows of glorious roses which Kollis tended so carefully; once more, as the engine died and the silence swelled up round me, my friends detached themselves one by one from the knots of coffee-drinkers under the great tree, to bring me messages whose familiarity restored in a moment the pattern in things which already Nicosia was slowly breaking down and dispersing; talk of carob-wood, lemon-trees, silk-worms, a new wine. Of the crisis hardly a word was said, save by the *muktar* whose responsibilities weighed so heavily upon him that he felt permitted to ignore the laws of tact. "Aren't you afraid to come up here?" he said. "Why should I be?" "Are you armed?" "No." He sighed. "I will lend you a gun." "Against who—Andreas or Mr. Honey?" He laughed heartily at this. "No. None of us would harm you. But people come here sometimes from outside, at night, in cars. Look!" On the wall under the Tree of Idleness was written in blue paint: SLAVES BREAK YOUR CHAINS: LIBERTY OR DEATH. It seemed a poor place to choose for a recruiting centre, to judge by the statuesque devotees of indolence who sat there quietly enjoying a professional idleness. "They came up in a car and painted it under the headlights. I heard them. Michaelis' son saw them and said they were masked."

Up at the house everything was quiet save for the puffing and blowing of Xenu who was clearing up after my family's departure. At the spring, filling his water-bottle, stood old Morais, who catching sight of me, took a step down and shook my hand with warm agitation. "Before God," he said hoarsely, "I do not want all these things to happen." "Nor I." He stood for a long moment in deep perplexity, at a loss for words—but he had said everything; nobody wanted these things to happen, but they were happening. They prejudiced everything that could have been built out of the firm rough clasp of the old man's hand. He turned abruptly, almost angrily and stamped up the hill to his little house, muttering under his breath.

As week followed week I returned to the village less frequently, though I would have been glad to live out there if I had been able to persuade the authorities to install a telephone in Dmitri's wine-shop— but I am forgetting. To the normal hours of a standard office routine I was now forced to add hours of alertness at night, dealing with the routine questions of the press which poured in from every side. But though the corps had swollen and multiplied the work there were compensations in the form of friends whom I had not seen for some time; and my dinner-table such as it was always had a face or two I was glad to remember: Ralph Izzard, with his gentle and civilized air, Stephen Barber, boisterous and serious at once, Richard Williams whose companionable laughter and sly wit made time pass delightfully. And young Richard Lumley, who came for a week-end and stayed nearly six months, sharing the house and everything that went with it—sudden invasions of friends or visitors: telephone calls: alarms in the night: and blessed laughter (Shan Sedgwick borne through the door on gales of his own laughter with a live turkey under his arm). The crisis brought me people I might never have met again for many years.

The worlds I lived in now were like three separate ice floes gradually drifting apart on the Gulf Stream; the world of Government House or the Colonial Secretary's lodge—a world of fairy lights gleaming on well-tended flower-beds under the great stone lion and unicorn; a world where groups of well-groomed men and women tasted the rational enjoyments life had to offer to slow music, pacing upon freshly laundered grass as green as any England can show, outside time. Then the world of the office with its stereotyped routines and worries. Lastly the village, composed around the Abbey as around the echo of a quotation from Virgil, in which an amputated present was enough and the future nobody's direct concern. Once or twice I thought I remarked a trifling frigidity among the villagers which might have indicated a change of tone; but I was wrong. If anything they had become less rather than more critical of foreigners. There was something else underneath it, too, like the pressure of a wound, a pain which they carried about with them like a load. If the situation met with any response here it met only with a sad reproach from the dark eyes of the old men. They had stopped saying, "Hey, Englishman," in the old jaunty cocky way, but they had not yet abandoned the world "neighbour"—only it was beginning to feel weighty, impregnated with sadness. These things are hard to analyse.

In the midst of this deepening sense of crisis there came a welcome relief in the form of a policy statement from London, convoking a Three-Power Conference to study the "political and defence questions affecting the Eastern Mediterranean," a means of offering the issues of Cyprus at least a safety-valve if not a solution. In my usual optimistic way I thought I saw in it a possible solution to things which might halt the deathward drift of affairs in the island. Alas! it was to prove only a brief respite. By now, of course, we had become inured to the nightly gauntlet of grenades and the running fire of telephone calls; nevertheless the news was welcome, and events seemed to be smiling upon us after so long a time of waiting.

The mosquito raids went on unremittingly of course; you cannot turn Greeks on and off like a tap. The Governor had narrowly escaped

being killed by an exploding time-bomb in May—literally by moments
—for the bomb, placed in a cinema and fused to go off during a charity
performance, exploded as the hall had emptied but while the foyer was
still full of people. The raids on the police stations too went on, while
almost daily the police uncovered some new hoard of arms or ammuni-
tion.

Wren's deceptive composure covered many things—not least the realization that the task he was setting himself was an impossible one: for a
police force is not merely a collection of arms and legs, and cannot be
numbered by heads like a trayful of cabbages. Its animating force is
intelligence, and here was the gap which could not be filled by the
multiplication-table. It was fantastic in an island where everyone was
related to everyone else, in an area so circumscribed, how little general
intelligence was coming in. Usually in Cyprus gossip penetrated everywhere; if you blew your nose loudly in Larnaca before driving at speed
to Limassol you would certainly meet someone on arrival who had already heard of the fact. Partly the silence was due to fear of reprisals;
but mostly because the sympathies of the general public were engaged,
and even the noncombatant's door was always open to shelter a bomb-
thrower. Paddy Leigh Fermor had once remarked how completely sabo-
tage operations depended upon the sympathies of the general public,
adding: "After all, in Crete there were only about five of us, each with
a very small band of chaps, and we kept a number of German divisions
sprawling and pinned down for years." Were we to risk a repetition of
the same thing in Cyprus? It was hard to decide, but on balance it did
not seem that the Cypriots themselves would have the stamina to last
out a long siege. I myself might have agreed with this proposition had
I not felt that Greece was able to supply what was lacking in men,
materials or moral support; and I knew that the island could not be
effectively sealed off by sea and air.

Mine was not a widely shared view, at least among the foreign community. General opinion here suggested that tough tactics and economic
reprisals could be effective against the middle classes who would not
long withstand a direct assault upon their pockets, and indeed would if
pressed hard surrender from their midst the few active terrorists among
them. This showed a frightening political ignorance, both about the
nature of revolutions in general and about the animating spirit of the
present discontents. It was clear even at this time that the intellectuals
regarded EOKA as having behind it the irresistible momentum of
modern Greek history; Cyprus was simply a repetition of Macedonia.
Crete had, after all, been cleared in this way; and the only tragedy of
the whole affair was that the war was directed against a traditional and

much-beloved friend whose lack of historical understanding was incomprehensible. . . .

It was easy to talk in bars about tough tactics ("One touch of the stockwhip, old boy, I've seen it before" and "We must squeeze the Cyps till they squeak") but these were lines of thought which were politically unfruitful; for the stockwhip might fall upon innocent shoulders, and unwittingly cause a resentment which would provide recruits for EOKA rather than informers for the Government. There was a village proverb which said: "He couldn't catch the mule so he gave the saddle a good thrashing." This was what we were gradually being compelled to do by the pressure of events, though at this early time, with a Conference coming up at which our problems might all be rationalized, there seemed no undue cause for despondency. Indeed as far as could be judged the general public enjoyed a widespread feeling of relief that at last Cyprus was going to be submitted to the arbitration of the mind, and not allowed to rot slowly like a gangrened limb.

My own luck, too, was in; for I was offered a three days' visit to Athens and London for duty consultations, an opportunity I grasped eagerly. I also snatched a night alone at the Bellapaix house during this slight lull among the tensions of politics, glad to recreate with deliberation the routine of last year—which already seemed remote and unrecapturable; rising at four, I mean, and cooking my breakfast by rosy candlelight and writing a letter or two, to far-away Marie or my daughter, before clambering down the dark street with Frangos and his cattle, to watch the dawn breaking behind the gaunt spars of the Abbey. Clusters of gold and citron stretched taut as a violin string, upon bass Gregorian blues and greys. Then to climb the range with the light, spoke by spoke, to where the dawn spilled and spread on the bare cardboard plain with its two spikes of minaret rising out of the indistinctness, the car falling like a swallow towards the tableland of the Mesaoria. . . . I had come to love Cyprus very much by now, I realized, even its ugliness, its untidy sprawling vistas of dust and damp cloud, its hideous incongruities.

Then up over the Cyclades, into a different weightless world inhabited by the music of gulls and surf breaking upon deserted beaches, covered now in a green fleecy mist which allowed an island to become visible from time to time, tenuous as a promise. The edges of the sea limegreen, cobalt, emerald. . . .

Athens was recognizably beautiful still, as a woman who has had her face lifted may still be beautiful; but she had become a capital now, full of vast avenues and towering buildings. She had lost her grubby and endearing provinciality—had moved a step nearer towards the featureless modern problem town. It was hot, and everyone was away

in the islands. The few friends I could find writhed over the Cyprus
question like worms halved by the ploughshare—hardly able to believe
their own eyes and minds. I was able to spend one memorable afternoon
forgetting Cyprus however, with old George Katsimbalis in a favorite
taverna under the Acropolis; and a whole day recalling Belgrade with
Sir Charles Peake, who had been my Ambassador there, and who was
now grappling with the thankless task of representing us in Greece: a
Greece changed out of all recognition by the Enosis problem.

On the quiet terrace at his summer villa, near Kavouri, I recaptured
some of the old illusion of timeless peace as I watched the sky darken
at his shoulder, and the smooth black polish of that magnificent bay
become slowly encrusted with lights, sweeping and slithering upwards
into the sky, the hot black sky of Attica. Here and there a green eye or a
red glowed and smouldered, marking a ship. But sea and land had
become indistinguishable.

He spoke with gentle affection of Greece and of his hopes for the
coming Conference which might find a resolution for things and bring
us all a more breathable air; and I echoed them. It was hard to say
good-bye, though, and leave that delightful villa, to drive back through
the dry scented starlight to Athens; harder still to watch the Acropolis
from a thousand feet fade and diminish in the dawn-light, all its na-
creous marbles glowing at the sky.

London with its drooping grey mist and unemphatic tones awaited
me. Coming out of the Colonial Office I knew at once that the Empire
was all right by the animation of the three African dignitaries who
shared the lift with me, and who walked to the bus stop talking like a
trio of 'cellos. They gave off overpowering waves of Chanel Number 5—
as if they had hosed themselves down with it after breakfast like genial
elephants, before starting out on a round of official calls. I pitied the
occupants of the bus they hailed with yells and waved umbrellas.

I attended as best I could to the wants of my office, but was completely
unprepared for the honour of a personal interview with the Secretary
of State, to whose office I was summoned on my third day. His intimi-
dating height and good looks would have marked him out as extraordinary in any company; but to these were added the charm and liberal
disposition of an eighteenth-century gentleman—great style completely
untouched by affectation, and a broad cutting mind which was sophisticated in the true sense. And humour. There was no room for timidities
and attitudes in his presence—his simplicity and directness would have
riddled them. I told him what was in my mind; how great were the hopes
to be reposed in the coming Conference. I added that while sharp
Turkish reactions were to be expected, and the Turkish support of our
case might seem on the face of it politically expedient, it would be un-

wise to shelter behind it. We should face the self-determination issue squarely if we wished to achieve a lasting settlement which would mobilize the general goodwill of the people without which even a heavily defended base would be simply an enclave in a bitterly hostile area. Cyprus seemed to me one case where sovereignty and security were not necessarily compatible; and within a planned time-limit of twenty years (which I believed might be acceptable) we might achieve a great deal. The present situation was containable indefinitely by force, of course, even if it grew worse; the one dangerous aspect was the police picture in the islands. . . . I can put these points down since I made a note of them immediately after this talk.

He listened to me gravely and sympathetically, and I knew why. He himself knew the island well, had lived in Pearce's lovely house and walked the lemon-glades of Lapithos, or taken coffee with the villagers. He knew every inch of the sinuous Gothic range with its tiny hospitable villages. For him too the present situation was painful, crowded with associations, and full of thorns. He could tell me little, however, as the Cabinet was still debating the affairs of the island.

From the vantage-point of Whitehall, too, the angle of vision changed, for here in London Cyprus was not only Cyprus; it was part of a fragile chain of telecommunication centres and ports, the skeletal backbone of an Empire striving to resist the encroachments of time. If Cyprus were to be frivolously wished away then what of Hong Kong, Malta, Gibraltar, the Falklands, Aden—all troubled but stable islands in the great pattern? Palestine and Suez had been questions of foreign sovereignty; they had never been Crown possessions. Cyprus belonged, from the point of view of geography and politics, to the Empire's very backbone. Must it not, then, be held at all costs?

I could not find my way forward among all these mutually contradictory propositions; it seemed to me that everybody was right and everybody wrong. Yet a peaceful solution must be there to be won if only we could provide a formula. But the Conference would perhaps do that for us.

While I was busy with these brain-wrenching considerations I was told that the Secretary of State had decided to visit Cyprus the next day, and that I must return to my post forthwith. Arrangements had been made for me to travel back in his private plane.

The take-off was scheduled for five the next day, but frequent telephone calls were necessary to check this; we would fly all night, touching down only at Naples for refuelling.

At four that afternoon I found the sleek old-fashioned C.O.I. cars drawn up outside the private office, together with the Secretary of State's own gleaming Rolls. There still remained hurried last-minute dispositions to be made and my car was told off to pick up the personal bodyguard and Sir John Martin who was to travel out with us.

In the shady portals of New Scotland Yard we picked up a ruddy-faced, white-whiskered man in well-cut clothes, who combined the air of being a regular colonel with something else, an indefinable sense of having seen the seamy side of life; he joked slyly as his luggage was loaded. No, he did not carry machine-guns about him on assignments like these, he said. "I manage with a good eye and a very small Colt." One had the impression that anything larger would show a bulge in that well-cut suit. He had a novel and a set of pocket-chess with him, and proposed to spend the night working on a problem.

Now we swept across London, halting only to pick up Sir John and his suitcase. He was armed, more appropriately, with a copy of the *Iliad* which sorted well with his gentle and scholarly manner.

Rain was falling over London but by the time we reached Northolt the sky was clear and full of larks spiralling up from the grass of the airfield. I was impressed by the V.I.P. Lounge, which I was not likely to see, I thought, again in this life, and enjoyed the passport and customs formalities which were so cursory as to make me feel rather like the Aga Khan. Such are the pleasures of travelling in a great man's entourage. The old Valetta, however, had rather a second-hand air, and the Secretary of State inspected the guard of honour briefly. His wife and children were there to see him off, and he embraced them warmly and naturally in a way that would have touched old Frangos. The red dispatch cases were loaded and we climbed aboard and seated ourselves, while the pilot gave us a sharp talk about life-jackets, adding with a twinkle, "This is a well-victualled ship, and there won't be any closing time once we are airborne."

This however did not seem as easy as it sounded; twice we were recalled from the tarmac just as we were about to make our run, by telephone calls from the Prime Minister, and twice the Secretary of State made a good-humoured journey back to the telephone in the lounge.

Then at last we were up, in slow swerves and gyres, into a soft magical sunset over England. There was a general settling down and taking off of coats. "Whisky and soda?" Sir John posed his *Iliad* strategically on the port-hole as he accepted the offering. Our ears began to tune themselves to the hum and whistle of the machine; smiles and gestures to replace words. The pilot came forward, stood to attention, and saluted smartly as he handed the Secretary of State a piece of paper. "It's just come through, sir," he shouted. "I thought you might like to see it." I thought this must be some thrilling communication from the P.M. and was quite alarmed when the Secretary of State groaned in anguish and clutched his head. What did this portend? War, perhaps, had broken out. "England all out for 155," he cried passing the paper to Sir John who pursed his lips and looked vaguely at it, unable to respond to the news with quite the same wholeheartedness. "What a rotten show."

After an hour of acclimatization and rest the food and drink disappeared and the red dispatch cases were brought forward and their contents spread out upon the table. The party fell to work with a will and carried on through the darkness until I began to doze myself.

We refuelled at Naples on a deserted field full of hollow darkened buildings with here and there a flare picking up the rounded flanks of some great charter aircraft. Cyprus with its problems did not swim up at us until about nine the next morning, brown and misty and framed by the singing sea. Regretfully the *Iliad* was put aside, the dream surrendered for the reality; my own paper-backed P. G. Wodehouse had lain untouched in my coat pocket. (I had been too ashamed to bring it out in such distinguished company. We highbrow poets have our pride.)

For the next two days there were conferences and meetings, indecisive in themselves perhaps, but valuable in giving the Secretary of State a chance to meet the personalities whose different attitudes made up the jig-saw of the Cyprus problem. I was amused too by the consternation in the Secretariat when the great man disappeared at dawn one morning. It appeared that he had gone to Lapithos for an early bathe, and to drink a coffee with some peasant cronies at the little tavern; a typical and delightful touch in the middle of so much boring work. He was back by 9.30.

That morning a time-bomb blew up the Income Tax Office harming no one; there was great dismay when it was learned that all the Income Tax returns for the year had not been blown up with the office. Another and later bomb at the Land Registry office was discovered in time and rendered harmless. In this atmosphere of tiresome hazard the consultations continued, and more and more the question of self-determination emerged as the key factor to the political aspect of things—though of course this was now only another way of saying Enosis, since the Greeks were in a majority of five to one.

The Tripartite Conference was everywhere rumoured to be a trap, baited by an unacceptable constitution with no safeguards for a future freedom of suffrage on the Union issue; the Archbishop flew the short leg to Athens to keep the uneasy Papayos on the white line. Athens now seemed to have become quite uncertain of itself, for the question had begun to threaten the internal stability of Greece, and the stability of the very faction we had assisted into power and helped to fight the Communists. We were in danger now of letting the Right wing founder in Greece—and this process was being blissfully helped by the Cypriot Greeks who had never had any experience of foreign relations and who pressed for firmer international action. By now, of course, public opinion in Greece was in a very excitable state and anything smelling of moderation sounded "unpatriotic." Greek cabinets depend on the state of public opinion for their stability in a way that no other government does. Tail was wagging dog, Nicosia was wagging Athens. And behind it all a thundercloud was gathering over Greek-Turkish relations. There were urgent, indeed pre-eminent considerations; against them, it seemed to me, a bomb or two in Cyprus was a mere secondary feature. It was a relief to know that the Greek Government had accepted the invitation to London without asking for the conditions demanded by both the Archbishop and the Communists. It was a measure of the urgency with which the situation was viewed from Athens. They were in a nasty jam; but then so were we in Cyprus.

Meanwhile things were hardening up domestically; if terrorists could not be brought to justice they could at least be penned out of harm's way. In early July the Detention Laws were promulgated, making Wren's task a bit easier, and indirectly I suppose saving a number of lives among the apprentices and schoolboys who were locked up summarily when they could not, for lack of witnesses, be charged. This touched off a series of attacks by Athens radio, which accused us of "Fascism" and even "Genocide." The living conditions of the detainees became a staple for commentaries and hysterical knife-twisting, and the conditions of life within Kyrenia castle were hotly debated. "We again challenge the Public Information Officer to answer the following question on behalf of the Cypriot people: are there or are there not latrines at the castle? And if there are no latrines, what is the substitute? And one more question: Is it or is it not true that the contents of the metal buckets, used as horrible substitutes for latrines, are emptied at a very short distance from the castle, thereby endangering the health of the detainees? It must be true, Mr. Durrell, unless our sense of sight and smell, as well as the swarms of flies and other filthy insects, deceive us." This seemed to be going a bit far; I was tempted to ask the Greek Ministry of Information a few choice questions about the general state of sanitation in Greece—which has to be experienced to be believed—but I spared him; Philhellenism dies hard. "Nevertheless," said the Colonial Secretary, "you'd better go up yourself and have a look, and arrange to have the press taken round to show that though we may be Fascist beasts our sanitation is still sound." I reluctantly agreed to do so.

The camp had now been moved from the castle to Kokkinotrimithia, and here on the harsh bare unlovely table-land the sappers had run up a few huts and a great wire pen. It looked from far off like an abandoned turkey farm. I rode up with Foster who spoke despairingly of the lack of reason the prisoners showed, of their absolute contempt of law, of civic morality. "About two-thirds of them could be indicted on serious offences," he repeated with fussy solicitude, "the little bastards! And they throw clods at visitors and shout 'Fascist' at us. Us, Fascists, I ask you!"

It was a sad place; like one of those soulless transit camps near the western desert. The inmates looked a somewhat chastened and bedraggled lot—and a number were by no means infants. I kept an eye cocked for my students. On past form I was convinced I should find the whole of Epsilon Alpha behind bars, but I was relieved to recognize only two, the fat ruffian Joanides and Paul. Joanides was a grocer's son, and a natural comedian of such talent that I had been forced to expel him at the beginning of almost every lesson, much to my regret as his sallies (which were all in *patois*) were very funny indeed. He had spent his English hour walking up and down the corridors whistling tunelessly and pretending, when the headmaster was on the prowl, that he was going to the lavatory. He set up a great whoop when he saw me and said: "So they got you at last, Mr. Durrell? I told you you were too friendly with the Greeks. Now they've nobbled you." For a moment I think he really believed it. We entered the pen and he fairly romped up to me. "What are you doing here?" I said with severity, "fool that you are. This is where your folly has brought you, Imbecile." I asked Foster what he had been doing, and the boy shifted uneasily from one fat calf to the other. His round face fell. "He had a bomb on him," said Foster sighing with grandmotherly despair. "I ask you, a grenade." Joanides looked from Foster to me and then back again. He was sad to find us so severe. "Ach! Mr. Durrell," he said, "it was just a *little* bomb," extending his index fingers and holding them three inches apart. I passed him by in silence.

Living conditions were cramped but not bad. Probably less hard than they are for many a National Service youth. We toured the huts, examined the food and hot-water facilities. To judge by the books on most of the window-sills and beds a number of the terrorists must have been intellectuals. I saw Myrivilis' *Life Entombed* and the rare Athens edition of Cavafy; Seferis' poems and *Aeolia* by Venezis with my own preface which had been lovingly translated from the English edition. These things hurt me, as I realized for the first time that the appeal of EOKA was not to wrongdoers, congenital felons, but precisely to the most spirited and idealistic element among the youth. They would be the ones to suffer at the dictates of the ringmasters.

Paul was standing in a window, looking pointedly away across that cruel and barren no man's land of red sandstone. He gave no sign and I

did not wish to intrude upon him. I hesitated, and then joined Foster
to make a slow circuit of the room, picking up here and there an exercise book or a newspaper. At last I went up to him and put my hand on
his shoulder. "Why are you here?" I said.

He was not far from tears, but the face that he turned to me tried to
be composed, impassive. He did not speak but stared at me with a look
of furious anguish—as if indeed a wolf were gnawing at his vitals. "He
had a bomb too," said Foster wearily. "Bloody little fools! What do they
think they gain by it? He threw it in the churchyard by the cross-roads.
I suppose he thought he'd scare us all out of our wits."

"Are you in EOKA?" I asked.

"We are all EOKA. All Cyprus," he said in a low controlled voice. "If
he wants to know why I threw it in the churchyard tell him because I
was a coward. I am unworthy. But the others are not like me. They are
not afraid." I saw suddenly that what I had mistaken for hatred of my
presence, my person, was really something else—shame. "Why are you a
coward?" He moved a whole step nearer to tears and swallowed quickly.
"I was supposed to throw it in a house but there were small children
playing in the garden. I could not. I threw it in the churchyard."

Superb egotism of youth! He had been worried about his own inability to obey orders. It is, of course, not easy for youths raised in a Christian
society, to turn themselves into terrorists overnight—and in a sense his
problem was the problem of all the Cypriots Greeks. If Frangos had
been given a pistol to shoot me I am convinced that he would not have
been able to pull the trigger. "So you are sorry because you didn't kill
two children?" I said. "What a twisted brain, what a twisted stick you
must be as well as a fool!" He winced and his eyes flashed. "War is war,"
he said. I left him without another word.

I interviewed two committees, each consisting of a group of three
elected youths, whose duty it was to be responsible for the opinions of
their pen. They had little to complain of, though they complained hotly
and manfully about everything. I heard them out, wore them down, and
at last listed their grounds for complaint—the most serious of which
was that the crowded conditions prevented them from studying for their
examinations! Most of them were due to take G.C.E. this year. When I
told Foster this he took both hands off the steering wheel and put them
over his ears. "Don't," he pleaded in anguish. "Don't tell me any more.
They are *mad*. I can't take it. First they throw a bomb, then they want
to pass their School Cert., and I'm a Fascist because they can't!" He
moaned and rocked from side to side. "It's like being a male nurse in an
institution. Are all the Greeks as mad as this lot?"

The answer, of course, was yes. "Well, I'm out of my depth," said

Foster, "and the sooner I get back to U.K. the better." I must say I sympathized with him.

The days passed in purposeless riots and the screaming of demagogues and commentators; and the nights were busy with the crash of broken glass and the spiteful detonation of small grenades. The Turks began to get restive. Sabri's eyes darkened and flashed as he spoke of the situation. I had driven over on Sunday to collect some wood for the house. "How much longer are they going to tolerate these Greeks?" he demanded. The day before there had been a serious riot and he himself had turned back a mob of Turks bent upon setting fire to the Bishopric. (Sabri was a very gallant man: I once saw him dive fully clothed into Kyrenia harbour to rescue a Greek fisherman's child in difficulties.) "We Turks would not tolerate it," he said as he sat, unmoving among his perambulators. "You must take sterner measures. Fines. Severe sentences. I know these people. I was born here. They will come to heel. We Turks know the way." But of course the methods of 1821 were hardly possible to contemplate today, and the Greeks knew it. If we had been Russians or Germans the Enosis problem would have been solved in half an hour—by a series of mass murders and deportations. No democracy could think along these lines.

And then, how recognizable were the Cypriots of today from those of yesterday? That evening a Dutch journalist repeated to me a conversation he had had with a Greek consular official in which the latter said: "To be honest *we* never thought the bastards would show fight. We never dreamed all this trouble would come about. We backed them up morally because we think their claim was just; but never materially. It's entirely a Cypriot show, and it has astonished us. Cyprus is like a man who has been told he is impotent for generations; suddenly he finds himself in bed with a lovely girl and discovers that he isn't—he can actually make love! We thought it would be all over in a month, but now we think it will really go on." He had forgotten, he said, that the quality of obstinacy was something which the Cypriots did not share with metropolitan Greeks. . . . And so on. True or false?

From all these fragmented pieces of the original life of Cyprus—the quietness and certainty of ordered ways and familiar rhythms—it was impossible now to assemble a coherent picture, even up at the Abbey where the coffee drinkers still sat, drenched in the Gothic silence and coolness of those idle afternoons, against a wall with its livid cartoons which urged them to throw off their imprisoning web of sleep and act.

But the shots which rang out on the afternoon before the London Conference opened should have dispelled any hopes I entertained of a dramatic and satisfactory solution to our troubles. The death of P. C.

Poullis in the open street after a Communist rally, not only virtually put Wren's Special Branch out of commission, but later provided the Greeks with the first of the Enosis martyrs in the person of Karaolis, a mild well-mannered youth in the Income Tax department of the Government. The grotesque, the unreal, was rapidly becoming the normal. The hush of Cyprus, which had, for so many generations, been the calm unemphatic hush of an island living outside time but within the boundaries of a cherished order, had changed: the hush of a new fear had gripped it, and the air was darkened with the vague shapes and phantoms of a terror which the Government could no longer dispel or hold at bay. The political liberty of the subject was a secondary consideration where one could not offer bare security of person in the open street. We were penetrated at every point; Security in the professional police sense had become as vague a term as the personal security of the subject. The six thousand civil servants themselves now began to feel the squeeze of the terror; an invisible pistol dogged them. There was no question of loyalties—for everyone was loyal. But no informer could pass the barrier without being discovered and that meant death; conversely not to obey a terrorist command might also mean death. What was the position of a secondary schoolboy who had signed the EOKA oath and who one day found himself in a small room with three masked men who ordered him to place a time-bomb or commit a murder—*or else pay the price?* The police depended upon Cypriots for intelligence; they were penetrated. In the administration it was the same. The Colonial Secretary himself had a Cypriot secretary—devoted and loyal as he was. Secure confidence was everywhere prejudiced, and everywhere there grew the sensation of the walls closing in upon us.

But the key was finally turned upon Cyprus by the London Conference, where the Turkish attitude, which had now become as hard as a rock, could not be shifted by a degree; nor was anyone disposed to imitate Hannibal and try a little vinegar. My worst fears were realized, though here again I was guilty of misjudgement, for the Turkish case was not merely politically expedient to follow; it linked itself in other ways to pacts and agreements outside Cyprus, affecting the Arab world. Could one afford to cross Turkey? Either way we were confronted by a hedge of thorns. We had undermined the stability of Athens and indeed our whole Balkan position by an earlier refusal to take the Greek case on Cyprus seriously; we might, in any late attempt to unwind the spools of policy back to that point, unsettle the Turkish alliance, and prejudice the whole complex of Middle Eastern affairs in which this great Moslem power played such an important part. We had allowed too much time to pass, and Turkish public opinion was now in the grip of a hysteria which, though less justified, was as strong as that which was gripping

Athens. The Turkish case, as such, did not of course carry as much weight as the Greek though one could sympathize with the Turks of Cyprus. Nevertheless it was difficult to understand how a hypothetically Greek Cyprus could constitute a graver military threat to Turkey than did Rhodes or Thasos; and the two hundred thousand Turks in Thrace do not seem to find life harder than the corresponding number of Greeks living in Turkey . . . But national hysteria makes a poor counsellor, and the shocking riots which followed in September in Turkey made the argument seem hollower than ever, and revived in a flash the ancient barbaric animosities which lie buried in the hearts of Turks and Greeks, and which both until now believed dead for ever.

But the fruitless Conference had cut the frail cord which held us still attached, however tenuously, to reason and measure. So long an orphan administratively, Cyrpus was now cut adrift, a political orphan, to float slowly down the melancholy *couloirs* of Middle Eastern history, blown hither and thither by the chance winds of prejudice and passion.

I still visited Panos whenever I could, to sit and drink his heavy sweet Commanderia on the terrace under the Church of the Archangel Michael. He had changed, had aged. Did all our faces reflect, as his did, the helpless forebodings we all felt for the future? I wondered. He spoke gently and temperately still of the situation, but obviously the failure of the Conference had been a blow to him. "There is no way forward now," he said. "It is too late to go back to the point where you missed the catch. Things are going to get worse." He was not deceived by my false assurance and empty optimisms. "No," he said. "This marks a definite point. The Government will have to drop palliatives and act; that will be unpleasant for us. Then we shall have to react as firmly." He mourned, as so many Greeks did, the lost opportunity when the Foreign office refused to substitute the word "postponed" for "closed" upon the Cyprus file. Everything, he thought, had followed from that. His view of the future was not reassuring, but then neither was mine. Only the village with its calm and quiet airs lulled my fears. But here, too, the invisible thread was shortening. "I feel uneasy about you coming up here," said the *muktar* quietly. "Have you any reason to?" "None. But we hardly know what's going on inside ourselves any more." Old Michaelis was in good form still, and still told stories with his old flair over the red wine. He hardly ever spoke of politics, and then in a low apologetic voice, as if he feared to be overheard. Once he said with a regretful sigh: "Ach, neighbour, we were happy enough before these things happened." And raising his glass added: "That we pass beyond them." We drank to the idea of a peaceful Cyprus—an idea which day by day receded like a mirage before a thirsty man. "You know," he said, "I was told of a telegram which Napoleon Zervas sent to Churchill

saying 'Old man, be wise: Cyprus promised to Greece is thrice British.' "
He grinned and put a finger to his temple. "Note carefully he said
'promised' not 'given.' *There* is the matter! Yesterday the promise would
have been enough. Today . . ." He made a monkey-face to suggest a
lot of people all talking simultaneously. It was an admirable illustration
of the situation.

It was some time during that month that I myself nearly fell a victim
to gunmen, though whether by design or at a hazard I do not know. It
was my own fault. The nights were worn threadbare by telephone calls
or bomb alerts, and sleep was impossible until the small hours. Happily
there was a small bar called the Cosmopolitan almost opposite the house
on the main road, and here one could have a drink and meet journalists after filing time. I used to go along there every night at eleven or
thereabouts, where I was usually joined by one or other of my friends or
accompanied by Richard Lumley. I usually sat, too, in the same place,
to be near enough to gossip to Cyril the barkeeper and his delightful
French wife. One night the dog started barking, and Lazarus the waiter
went out of the back door to see why. The whole place was surrounded
by dense and gloomy vegetation, thick untrimmed bushes and trees
which gave it a desolate air. The waiter came back white as a sheet and
almost fainting, stammering: "Get away from the window." He had
seen three masked men levelling something from a bush outside. I had
a heavy torch, and Cyril and I, impressed by the man's very real fear but
not really believing him, went out to have a look. Reluctantly Lazarus
came to the balcony and pointed out the place. It was in a thick bush.
The grass did look a bit trampled. But not ten paces away, between
two trees, was a lighted window which I recognized as the window of
the bar. "Lazarus," said Cyril, and he too now sounded scared, "go and
sit in the seat of the Kurios." The waiter obeyed, to appear a moment
later, lit and framed ("like a photograph" said Cyril grimly), in the
window. We returned thoughtfully to the bar where the shaking Lazarus
was pouring himself a brandy, and interrogated him further. He had
come out on the balcony, he said, and found the dog barking at a bush
behind which there were three men in masks. They had some sort of
weapon—from his description it sounded like a Sten; they stared at him
for a moment and then "sank into the ground." The whole of the little
knoll was densely wooded and offered an easy escape. The episode was
most alarming.

It was an eerie feeling too to walk back to the house alone that night
down that corridor of darkness with only here and there a frail puddle
of light from the street-lamps. The whole quarter was deserted, and my
usual companions had not appeared. Doubtless the press corps had
hurried off to the scene of some new incident. As I turned off the

tarmac on to the gravel I was even more alarmed to hear footsteps behind me, following me at a leisurely pace. Now the whole front of my little house was lighted, and offered an even better firing position than the barwindow might have done, surrounded as it was with scrub and orange-trees. I felt it wiser to face a possible attacker in the darkness of the lane, consoling myself with the reflection that even if I was unarmed he would not know it and would assume I was. And I had the powerful torch. I stopped now, and the footsteps stopped too in the darkness. Frightened as I was, I felt absurdly glad that my heart was not beating faster than normal—thanks to the excellent double brandy Cyril had given me. I held my right arm as far away from me as possible and started running back the way I had come, towards the invisible man; after five paces I switched on and picked him up, shouting: "Hands up." He had nothing in his hands and was smiling good-naturedly. "Mr. Durrell," he said reproachfully. As I came up and searched him I recognized him, though by now I had forgotten his name; he was the taxi driver who had driven me across the island when first I arrived, the cousin of Basil the priest. He seemed surprised and delighted. Apparently he did not know me by my name either. "I am guarding you, sir," he said.

"Guarding me?"

"My taxi is behind the Cosmopolitan at the taxi rank. Cyril told me that you were leaving, and that some men had been after you. He told me to be answerable for your safety, so I was following you to see you came to no harm."

It was a great relief. I took him back to the house and we drank a whisky by the fire before saying good night.

The next day I borrowed a pistol from a kindly Scots major in the police. It was both a consolation and an obscenity but it symbolized the trend of events perfectly, for Cyprus was now no longer a political problem so much as an operational one—and its cares were soon to be confided to someone who was a match for the hazards it presented.

September was another milestone on the road. "Since UNO has excluded any other means to regain our liberty," read an EOKA pamphlet, distributed in Larnaca, "we have nothing else to do but to shed blood, and this will be the blood of English and Americans."

The attacks on police stations sharpened. Rioting and the hoisting of Greek flags everywhere kept the police busy. The first terrorist murderer (Karaolis) was arrested and charged. The Executive Council sustained an irreplaceable loss in the resignation of Sir Paul Pavlides, whose good offices and un-self-seeking counsel had been invaluable up to now. He too could see no way forward. Achilles was nearly murdered by two armed men one morning as he drove to work; they opened up on him from either side of the car at a range of three feet, while he was stuck in the driving-seat unable to draw his Browning. It was a lucky escape. Renos Wideson's father, a magnificent and uncompromising old man who alone dared to say publicly what so many people thought —that Enosis was all very well but could wait—was nearly murdered by a gunman. (In all, three attacks were made on him to which he responded with great spirit. The fourth time he was shot dead at point-blank range.)

To the alarms of the night were added the daylight terrors of the open street, where small groups of students patrolled on bicycles, suddenly opening fire with pistols. And yet between these incidents the calm, the good nature, of everyday life was restored as if from some fathomless source of goodwill, banishing the fear these incidents had created. The sun still shone; and in perfect September sunshine the yachts fluttered across the harbour-bar at Kyrenia, the groups of drinkers sat around the cafes in idle conversation. The whole thing had the air of some breathtaking deception. There was no way of matching the newspaper pictures of bodies lying in their own blood upon pavements crowded with shattered chairs and glass, with the serene blue of the Levant sky, the friendly sea rubbing its head upon the beaches like a sheep-dog. The casual visitor was always surprised to see men bathing now under the protection of rifles. *Autres temps autres moeurs.* I could not help reflecting wryly that had we been honest enough to admit the Greek nature of Cyprus at the beginning, it might never have been necessary to abandon the island or to fight for it. Now, it was too late!

PART IV

Community and Social Change in Today's World

Urbanization, Technology, and Increasing Scale

As the scale of the society increases, the small community, tribe or village or neighborhood, comes to depend more on the larger system of order. The loss of autonomy for the local group is often compensated by increasing wealth, power, and security. But there are real costs, and among the most important is the erosion of the existing culture—the belief system and the normative structure that have given life meaning.

Daniel Lerner, in this passage from *The Passing of Traditional Society*, describes the way of thought among the Bedouin of Jordan, a primitive nomadic society whose days are numbered. Their intense localism, their ethnocentrism, and their pride in hewing to the old ways, mark them as denizens of a small-scale world. That world, however, was originally predicated upon their maintaining military might equal or superior to that of the surrounding society upon which they preyed. As the material and social technology of that society increased in power, it was able to preëmpt the grounds for Bedouin economy—settling their grazing lands and halting their depradations.

Thus the Bedouin are driven into smaller places physically and mentally: they reaffirm their rigid, conservative style of life. Their intense moral pride in continuity of culture, the scorn with which they reject the morality of the urban society, and their almost total ignorance of the larger world are virtues to them. Literacy is evil to these desert fundamentalists, for it is either corrupting or irrelevant to the symbolic world they inhabit. Their beliefs and values have a familiar tone, for there is a similar strain in the mix of cultures existing today in the United States: perhaps the Hebraic rejection of Babylon is still with us, even though Babylon is everywhere. Or perhaps "know nothingism" is a typical response of the preliterate society to the encroachments of the outside world.

W.F. Cottrell in "Death by Dieselization" presents another case of a stable conventional community disrupted, indeed destroyed, by changes in the larger system. As a result of certain key changes in the technology of rail transportation, entire communities lacked a task to perform that would gain them a livelihood. The Caliente he speaks of may stand for hundreds of other towns, from Jerome, Arizona, which died as its copper deposits reached unprofitable levels for extraction, to Baird, Texas, which died as the improvements in roads and automobiles brought it into competition with the much larger city of Abilene.

The slogan "Progress Requires Sacrifice" conceals the question: Who will benefit and who will lose? Accepting the *laisser faire* philosophy of social change, one must say that those who control and execute change will win, those who represent the old order lose. Such an outcome, as Cottrell points out, punishes the virtuous and rewards the wicked. A similar phenomenon can be discerned in the case of the Bedouins: those who accept ungodly learning will survive and prosper, while the pious die out.

In such a dilemma, where older moralities are either irrelevant or handicaps-to solving the problems at hand, individuals and communities seek new means to old ends. But the means *is* the morality, for the means determines, if it does not corrupt, the end. Thus the railroaders turned from belief in the free market to belief in politics when it became clear that they would receive no justice from the forces of the market place. They moved toward faith in the welfare *state*. If justice is simply a situation in which one receives the response he has learned to expect as a moral right, the railroader can receive justice only through the control of economic investment by political power.

Thus we may say that out of the increasing interdependence of many men in wide networks of control, out of the change endemic to rationalized society, there will emerge conflicts between morality (based on the past) and social organization (created in the present for the future). The solution of such conflicts will result in either a change in means or a change in ends. In either case, we can expect the growth of the political at the expense of uncontrolled efforts to maximize private profit.

Daniel Lerner
The Constrictive World
of the Beduin

As Jordan is the most impoverished land in the Fertile Crescent, so the Beduin are its most depressed element. The trend of recent decades has worsened the nomadic way of life in Jordan.[1] The British extended the area of settlement and the fellahin's land was protected from Beduin herds. Newer trade and communications undermined the market for animal products, basis of the nomadic economy. Increasing control by the central government all but eliminated the raiding that had provided the tribes with excitement, pride and sustenance.

The continuous deterioration of Beduin society forced many into agriculture or into semi-nomadism, based on goat and sheep-raising in limited districts rather than camel-breeding over large areas. The true Beduin—camel-raisers belonging to one of the noble tribes—numbered only 40,000 in the 1940's compared to 120,000 semi-nomads (out of a total population of 340,000). As few interviews were made in the southern and eastern desert areas, most of the Beduin sample are semi-nomadic. But they differ enough from villagers and townfolk to be called Beduin—since the sample ranges from a nomad woman, attached to a wandering tribe which subsists only on camel products, to a dweller in a permanent camp near a village "so he is supposed to know more and therefore he wears trousers under his garments."

The condition of the Beduin elicited the pity of more than one interviewer. Their poverty was softened only by their unquestioning acceptance of it. Beduin responses revealed a fatalistic resignation to their lot: "I am satisfied with what God gives me, and that is enough." "I am living thanks to God, and everything I want is here so I am happy." Also characteristic of the Beduin was the total unawareness of the world outside their immediate environment. Geographic isolation,

Reprinted with permission of The Macmillan Company from *The Passing of Traditional Society* by Daniel Lerner. © by The Free Press of Glencoe, Inc. 1958.

[1] J. B. Glubb, The Story of the Arab Legion (1948), p. 195; Eliahu Epstein, "The Nomad Problem in Tansjordan," Palestine and Middle East Economic Magazine (February 2, 1937), p. 87 f.; Konikoff, op. cit., pp. 18, 47–48.

poverty, illiteracy have circumscribed interest in affairs beyond "our tents and our camels" and excluded them from the network of modern communication. The media have wanton ways, however, and intrude where they have not been invited. Even among the Beduin, as will appear, they have insinuated some of that restlessness which augurs change on the social horizon. But meanwhile, the dominant tonality of Beduin life still resounds, in the interviews, through classic themes.

The Tribal Focus: The mark of the Beduin is his complete absorption into tribal life. The tribe and its parts—sub-tribe, section, family— are the primary objects of personal loyalty. Tribal affiliation is the source of safety and, conversely, expulsion from the tribe for some grievous offense is the gravest sentence. Law and morality are also defined in tribal terms, for only a rare central government could effectively mete out social sanctions among the nomads. Personal allegiance to any larger social unit has been historically an expedient mode of material gain for the tribe. Beduin shaykhs were adept at playing off one ruler against another. But within the tribe, the shaykh was in principle only the first among peers. This has stimulated the theory of "Beduin democracy," though "fraternal anarchism" may more accurately describe their attitude toward public authority. This feeling shows in their responses:

> We Beduins don't have prime ministers and we don't like them.
> (Why?) We are free and have no ruler but God.
> Nobody is head here and we don't want prime ministers. (Why?)
> We are all brothers and have no need for foreign heads.

Attachment to the tribe is evident in the consistent Beduin refusal to imagine living in a different land. Imagination was constricted by primary identification not with place—for the Beduin lacks the peasant's devotion to his particular piece of land—but with *tribe.* Said one: "I will never leave this country because I will not think of becoming a foreigner to my tribe and their camp." And the interviewer pointed out:

> Beduins believe that having to travel far from one's country and relatives and friends is a curse that descends from the forefathers to the child.

The conditions under which travel becomes plausible for Beduin is movement of the intact tribe en masse to another grazing area—a far cry from personal mobility:

> I will go to any land where there is enough food for our tribe and the cattle provided they accept all of us. (Which country would you think of?) I don't care.

Disdain for Civilization: "Beduin" is a word of contempt among educated Arabs. But the Beduin regard themselves as the elite of the
human race and commonly refer to themselves as "thorough-breds."
Camel and sword are the marks of valor and virility; the aristocrat is
by definition a fighter. The corollary is Beduin disdain for the "civilized" world, which connotes soft living and femininity.[2] Attitudes toward the mass media are intertwined with these feelings, for the media
are symbols of the city:

> We Beduin don't need the cinema. . . . Those who go are not real
> men. They are useless and have lost all value of morals. Movies spoil
> men. . . . Those who go get a very bad character and are no more men. But
> if you don't go you are a man in all senses of the word.
>
> By God our hair tents to us are better than a kingly castle. What care we for
> your movies?
>
> Those who go (to the cinema) are town people and all of them are bad.

The Beduin, with a diffuse but sure sense of his own lifestyle, associates
literacy and the participant society. Reading connotes politics and the
evils of urban government:

> Those who read are politicians and trouble seekers. If you don't read you
> are far away from trouble and the government.
>
> We don't have prime ministers and nobody rules us like these girlish city
> folk. We rule ourselves. . . . The effendis who read are all hypocrites. They all
> want to be politicians. We want to live peacefully and away from politics.
>
> City people in 'Amman are liars and cheats.

Ignorance of the Modern World: Aversion to the modern world is
paralleled by a large ignorance regarding it. "God knows" was a frequent response to questions about the West, Russia, and the mass media.
After his interview, one middle-aged Beduin complained: "All the
questions were bad. (Why?) Because I couldn't answer them. You
should have asked me about hyenas and I will tell you." Another said:
"I can tell you about camels and the wild beasts of the wilderness, but
your interview was uninteresting and talking about strange things."

Many Beduin became irritated by the interview because their specialized knowledge of desert and camel lore (there are about 600 words
in the Beduin lexicon for the beast), and their fantastic memory for
genealogies and tribal exploits, remained untapped. Instead, only their
ignorance (appalling to the city-bred Jordanians who interviewed
them) was revealed. Of 26 Beduin, 15 had never heard of the United
States, and the others had only the most innocent notions:

[2] C. S. Coon, *Caravan: The Story of the Middle East* (1951), p. 201.

The U.S.? What is it? Where is it?

Where is their country exactly, and do they live like us or like 'Amman? The U.S. is a land, always dark and cold and behind the sea. It is full of beasts.

The U.S. is a very far and cold country and they sleep all winter and have lots of ice. How many days walking distance is it from here?

Concerning Russia there was almost equal ignorance: 12 had never heard of it, and the others were vague. The one literate Beduin, a desert patrol guard, told the interviewer that he had been instructed by his superior to hate all Russians and to jail anyone who praised them, but he had no idea why. A few did not like Russia because it had a different religion—Communism.

Knowledge of mass media was restricted: nine had never heard of movies, three of radio, and three of newspapers:

A radio? What is this thing you are asking me about? Is it an important place or man?

Radio? Walahee! (My God!) I have never heard such things before. How do you know about all these things . . . I am listening to riddles from your mouth.

(Do you know what a movie is?) No by the Great God, what is that . . . (Respondent showed great amazement and listened attentively while I explained shortly what a movie is.)

Ignorance of the outside world is socially acceptable in the Beduin community. A man is not expected to have opinions on large matters which, according to his neighbors, do not concern him. To mind one's own business is estimable and the Beduin contents himself with a narrow range of opinion and experience.

(Are there any sort of news that you don't care to hear about at all?) Yes. We don't like to hear about war in far away countries. When Beduins start a fight among themselves, they never bother other people about it. So why should we bother about what other countries have to go through whether in war or peace?

I am interested in news about my household and my camel because these are my life and my link with this world. I don't care for anything else because what is outside my concern I am not supposed to care for.

All I need to know is here in this tribe and that is enough. . . My business is only what happens in the tribe. Do you expect me to worry my head over what is going on outside our camp? We have enough news and activity here and we don't like to mingle it with the outside.

At the most, external "news" concerns what happens in other Beduin camps. Beyond the Beduin world lies the obscure domain of irrelevance and iniquity. A person too curious about this domain would be suspected of unBeduin activities.

The Oral Network: Constricted range is shown in Beduin recall of the last piece of news they received. The concrete local event predominates in all cases, viz:

> My neighbor slaughtered his wife . . . I felt she deserved it because she was scandalizing him by looking at other men, and sometimes smiling at them.

Other mentioned camels not producing milk, relatives getting married, locusts ravaging the pastures. For such news, traditionally the staple of oral systems, relatives and friends continue to be the only satisfactory purveyors of information: "From my friends, my brother and my cousin I get to know everything in my tribe from A to Z."

For outside news, the Beduin also depends mainly on known persons who can be "faced and placed," such as tribesmen returning from trips with gossip. The media reach him only through the "two-step flow"—occasional visitors, such as travellers and merchants, serving as oral relays of information that originated in the media.[3] One shepherd, relatively more settled than the true nomads, gets his news with some regularity "from friends or relatives who take frequent visits to 'Amman, perhaps once a month. They are usually merchants from the nearby village or on a passing drive." A Beduin woman gets her news rather more sporadically: "From people like yourself. We see someone with a paper in his hand. We ask him to tell us what is going on in the world and they do."

News is usually exchanged for tribal hospitality. Travelers are welcomed to the tent of the shaykh—social center of the encampment. While the shaykh "pounds coffee" the visitor brings tales of the outer world. Here Beduin form their images of the outside—e.g., one who "learned" that England is cold and poor from a passing Amman merchant. But even such contact is rare:

> You must be a missionary because nobody talks to us except an old English woman who tells me of a shepherd boy long ago called David and how he became a king because he believed in Jesus.

Another source of ideas about the world is the oral literature. As medieval troubadors carried information around a largely illiterate world, so itinerant poets and storytellers are news-bringers at the Beduin

---

[3] On the "two-step flow" see E. Katz and P. F. Lazarsfeld, *Personal Influence* (1955), chap. II.

campfire. Their subjects are war, camels, horses, and women, in that order of importance. Beduin, whose love for language and passion for heroic legend enliven their otherwise barren culture, prefer current events cast in this traditional mold.[4] One Beduin woman derived her opinions of British policy in Jordan and her choice of country for emigration wholly from such sources:

> Our men say that our kind loves the English people. In weddings and evenings of joy, most of our men sing for the victory of the English . . .
> (Where would you like to live if for some reason you had to move from Jordan?) By God I don't know. The Arabs say al-Yemen is a good place. They think it is the rich and fertile country. Old poetry says that al-Yemen is the Garden of Eden where every living thing lives comfortably and happily.

Opinion, as well as information, is locally derived. The shaykh is considered the authoritative source of correct ideas. Although the shaykh must respect the views of tribal elders, he occupies the seat of judgment. He is expected to have opinions, as others are not, since he is responsible for the tribe's external relations. It is his duty to be the repository of correct views, which the rank-and-file of the tribe may use if they feel the need. Note how these views converge in one response:

> (In your community who is the one whose thoughts are most highly respected?) My uncle the Sheikh. He is tall, old and respectable. He sits on his pillow all day long in his own tent and people of the tribe come around for advice. (Why is he a leader?) He is the eldest in the family and the people of the tribe go for the advice of the eldest. (Why?) Don't you know the common saying, "who is one day older in age is one year older in knowledge." Our respect is according to age, for experience counts a lot with us.
> We like to rest our heads from such responsibilities (as government). We eat our daily bread, thank our God and are satisfied and happy. Our Sheikh alone may worry about that because that is his business.

The shaykh and elders "speak for" the tribe. An interviewer noted that a venerable member of a tribal council was "quite proud because I chose him, thinking that as he answers he represents his tribe." These elders, who display surprising knowledge of even their distant desert brethren are regarded as "the true bearers of desert tradition and history."[5] The respect due them constrained one interviewer, who was too embarrassed to pose some of the scheduled questions. He could not ask

[4] A. Hourani, Syria and Lebanon (1946), p. 64; Glubb, "The Beduins of Northern Iraq," Royal Central Asian Journal, XXII, Part I (1935), pp. 18–19.
[5] "Beduin of the Negeb: Sons and Fathers of the Desert," Palestine and Middle East Economic Magazine, II (November 1937), p. 526.

one elder "To whom do you go for advice?" because it would be an affront to suggest that such a leader should have to go to anyone else for advice. Another interviewer found it difficult to ask a Beduin leader what he would like to know about Saudi Arabia, because "asking this question to a person with the mentality of the respondent and his age and he living next to that country would be quite insulting."

Since tribal leaders control the dissemination of news and views in the Beduin community, *their* attitudes are important. One such leader, with pretensions to chieftainship, is described by the interviewer as follows:

> Thirty-three years old, he is of noble descent and is greatly honored and admired in his tribe. He wears rich, clean clothes and has very sharp eyes and features with a little beard. He owns many tents and cattle. He has a shrewd and fearful personality and is very strict and hard to his servants, yet they like him.

This impressive person turns out to be little different in outlook from his tribesmen, and distinctive mainly by the resonant confidence with which he articulates traditional convictions. With regard to communications, he feels that newspapers are "uninteresting and unnecessary for life" because "the papers have nothing to offer me . . . our news are in our camp and needn't be written in a paper . . . I am only interested in news about my people." Toward radio his attitude is the same. He would not even like to listen to one "because it is unimportant in my life." Where, then, does he get his news? Not only does he fail to mention sources outside his own tribe, but he cites intratribal sources stemming only from *his own clan:* "I get to know it from my people. From my brothers and cousins and all the other members of my family."

When asked about his last two pieces of news, the response illustrated both his parochial range and his high aspirations: "Our chieftain is dying" and "He wants me to marry his daughter . . . I don't like his daughter but she is rich and, therefore, I might marry her." Regarding foreign powers, however, he showed two interesting differences from Beduin of lower status. When asked what country he would choose if he could not live in Jordan, he soared beyond the habitual self-constriction of most Beduin: "America. Because they are rich. If I go there I can open a ranch and keep thousands of sheep and horses and there is lots of fertility and pasture for them there." His final comment foreshadows the Beduin future. He asked the interviewer: "Is this information going to a school?" The interviewer replied "Yes, why?" The future chieftain said "I want to send my children to a school." *Sic Transit!*

Rejection of the Media: To people who have barely heard of the mass media, the notion that these modern contrivances might be introduced into the tribe is regarded with horror. Such innovations are beyond their understanding and many hastened to dissociate themselves from the diabolical strangeness of radio and movies:

> There must be something bad about this that (allows you to) listen to voices in the air.
> Radio? By God if I see one I will destroy it. This is from the devil. (What do you miss by not listening?) You are mocking me. Why did you ask me that? You know I hate a radio and it is evil.
> That, the cinema? Oh God forbid! It is the working of the devil. . . . To go to such things that are the inspiration of demons are terrible. Oh no, then one would be tormented by the fire of hell.

Superstition finds "evidence" quickly, since the Traditionalist logic forbids no *post hoc propter hoc.* Just as Beduin attribute rain to their incantations to the Rainmaker, so they connect media exposure and subsequent evil:

> Those who go to the movies beat their wives. The devil gets into them. I know of one who has gone to the city and then he was seduced to go to the cinema and when he came back he started being on bad terms and beating his wife.
> Those who listen are full of evil and God's curse comes upon them. *Look at the Palestinians. They listened to the radio and God destroyed them.* We don't want this trouble here.

Newspapers are rejected, not because they terrify the imagination, but because they have unpleasant connotations of government and urbanism, and because they lack utility for the Beduin. For example:

> It writes nothing for us; only for the townspeople . . . papers don't write what we want. (What do we want?) We want God's mercy and good crop this year.
> I will not lose if I don't read a paper, because papers don't write for us.
> I can't read or write, yet I don't regret it, because I don't like to read papers. They are uninteresting to me. . . . Papers don't put things about our life here in the camp. (How do you know that?) The last time my cousin, who is in the army and knows how to read, read me one and it had no news about us. . . . Those who read papers do so because it writes about their affairs and they have to read in order to know.

W. F. Cottrell
Death by Dieselization: A Case Study in the Reaction to Technological Change

In the following instance it is proposed that we examine a community confronted with radical change in its basic economic institution and to trace the effects of this change throughout the social structure. From these facts it may be possible in some degree to anticipate the resultant changing attitudes and values of the people in the community, particularly as they reveal whether or not there is a demand for modification of the social structure or a shift in function from one institution to another. Some of the implications of the facts discovered may be valuable in anticipating future social change.

The community chosen for examination has been disrupted by the dieselization of the railroads. Since the railroad is among the oldest of those industries organized around steam, and since therefore the social structure of railroad communities is a product of long-continued processes of adaptation to the technology of steam, the sharp contrast between the technological requirements of the steam engine and those of the diesel should clearly reveal the changes in social structure required. Any one of a great many railroad towns might have been chosen for examination. However, many railroad towns are only partly dependent upon the railroad for their existence. In them many of the effects which take place are blurred and not easily distinguishable by the observer. Thus, the "normal" railroad town may not be the best place to see the consequences of dieselization. For this reason a one-industry town was chosen for examination.

In a sense it is an "ideal type" railroad town, and hence not complicated by other extraneous economic factors. It lies in the desert and is here given the name "Caliente" which is the Spanish adjective for "hot." Caliente was built in a break in an eighty-mile canyon traversing the desert. Its reason for existence was to service the steam locomotive. There are few resources in the area to support it on any other basis, and such as they are they would contribute more to the growth and maintenance of other little settlements in the vicinity than to that of Caliente.

Reprinted from *American Sociological Review*, Vol. 16 (June 1951), pp. 358–365, by permission of the American Sociological Association and the author.

So long as the steam locomotive was in use, Caliente was a necessity. With the adoption of the diesel it became obsolescent.

This stark fact was not, however, part of the expectations of the residents of Caliente. Based upon the "certainty" of the railroad's need for Caliente, men built their homes there, frequently of concrete and brick, at the cost, in many cases, of their life savings. The water system was laid in cast iron which will last for centuries. Business men erected substantial buildings which could be paid for only by profits gained through many years of business. Four churches evidence the faith of Caliente people in the future of their community. A twenty-seven bed hospital serves the town. Those who built it thought that their investment was as well warranted as the fact of birth, sickness, accident and death. They believed in education. Their school buildings represent the investment of savings guaranteed by bonds and future taxes. There is a combined park and play field which, together with a recently modernized theatre, has been serving recreational needs. All these physical structures are material evidence of the expectations, morally and legally sanctioned and financially funded, of the people of Caliente. This is a normal and rational aspect of the culture of all "solid" and "sound" communities.

Similarly normal are the social organizations. These include Rotary, Chamber of Commerce, Masons, Odd Fellows, American Legion and the Veterans of Foreign Wars. There are the usual unions, churches, and myriad little clubs to which the women belong. In short, here is the average American community with normal social life, subscribing to normal American codes. Nothing its members had been taught would indicate that the whole pattern of this normal existence depended completely upon a few elements of technology which were themselves in flux. For them the continued use of the steam engine was as "natural" a phenomenon as any other element in their physical environment. Yet suddenly their life pattern was destroyed by the announcement that the railroad was moving its division point, and with it destroying the economic basis of Caliente's existence.

Turning from this specific community for a moment, let us examine the technical changes which took place and the reasons for the change. Division points on a railroad are established by the frequency with which the rolling stock must be serviced and the operating crews changed. At the turn of the century when this particular road was built, the engines produced wet steam at low temperatures. The steel in the boilers was of comparatively low tensile strength and could not withstand the high temperatures and pressures required for the efficient use of coal and water. At intervals of roughly a hundred miles the engine had to be disconnected from the train for service. At these points the cars also were inspected and if they were found to be defective they were either removed from the train or repaired while it was standing and the new engine being coupled on. Thus the location of Caliente, as far as the railroad was concerned, was a function of boiler temperature and pressure and the resultant service requirements of the locomotive.

Following World War II, the high tensile steels developed to create superior artillery and armor were used for locomotives. As a consequence it was possible to utilize steam at higher temperatures and pressure. Speed, power, and efficiency were increased and the distance between service intervals was increased.

The "ideal distance" between freight divisions became approximately 150 to 200 miles whereas it had formerly been 100 to 150. Wherever possible, freight divisions were increased in length to that formerly used by passenger trains, and passenger divisions were lengthened from two old freight divisions to three. Thus towns located at 100 miles from a terminal became obsolescent, those at 200 became freight points only, and those at three hundred miles became passenger division points.

The increase in speed permitted the train crews to make the greater distance in the time previously required for the lesser trip, and roughly a third of the train and engine crews, car inspectors, boilermakers and machinists and other service men were dropped. The towns thus abandoned were crossed off the social record of the nation in the adjustment to these technological changes in the use of the steam locomotive. Caliente, located midway between terminals about six hundred miles apart, survived. In fact it gained, since the less frequent stops caused an increase in the service required of the maintenance crews at those points where it took place. However, the introduction of the change to diesel engines projected a very different future.

In its demands for service the diesel engine differs almost completely from a steam locomotive. It requires infrequent, highly skilled service, carried on within very close limits, in contrast to the frequent, crude adjustments required by the steam locomotive. Diesels operate at about 35 per cent efficiency, in contrast to the approximately 4 per cent efficiency of the steam locomotives in use after World War II in the United States. Hence diesels require much less frequent stops for fuel and water. These facts reduce their operating costs sufficiently to compensate for their much higher initial cost.

In spite of these reductions in operating costs the introduction of diesels ordinarily would have taken a good deal of time. The changeover would have been slowed by the high capital costs of retooling the locomotive works, the long period required to recapture the costs of existing steam locomotives, and the effective resistance of the workers. World War II altered each of these factors. The locomotive works were required to make the change in order to provide marine engines, and the costs of the change were assumed by the government. Steam engines were used up by the tremendous demand placed upon the railroads by war traffic. The costs were recaptured by shipping charges. Labor shortages were such that labor resistance was less formidable and much less acceptable to the public than it would have been in peace time. Hence the shift to diesels was greatly facilitated by the war. In consequence, every third and sometimes every second division point suddenly became technologically obsolescent.

Caliente, like all other towns in similar plight, is supposed to accept its fate in the name of "progress." The general public, as shippers and consumers of shipped goods, reaps the harvest in better, faster service and eventually perhaps in lower charges. A few of the workers in Caliente will also share the gains, as they move to other division points, through higher wages. They will share in the higher pay, though whether this will be adequate to compensate for the costs of moving no one can say. Certain it is that their pay will not be adjusted to compensate for their specific losses. They will gain only as their seniority gives them the opportunity to work. These are those who gain. What are the losses, and who bears them?

The railroad company can figure its losses at Caliente fairly accurately. It owns 39 private dwellings, a modern clubhouse with 116 single rooms, and a twelve-room hotel with dining-room and lunch-counter facilities. These now become useless, as does much of the fixed physical equipment used for servicing trains. Some of the machinery can be used elsewhere. Some part of the round-house can be used to store unused locomotives and standby equipment. The rest will be torn down to save taxes. All of these costs can be entered as capital losses on the statement which the company draws up for its stockholders and for the government. Presumably they will be recovered by the use of the more efficient engines.

What are the losses that may not be entered on the company books? The total tax assessment in Caliente was $9,946.80 for the year 1948, of which $6,103.39 represented taxes assessed on the railroad. Thus the railroad valuation was about three-fifths that of the town. This does not take into account tax-free property belonging to the churches, the schools, the hospital, or the municipality itself which included all the public utilities. Some ideas of the losses sustained by the railroad in comparison with the losses of others can be surmised by reflecting on these figures for real estate alone. The story is an old one and often repeated in the economic history of America. It represents the "loss" side of a profit and loss system of adjusting to technological change.

Perhaps for sociological purposes we need an answer to the question "just who pays?"

Probably the greatest losses are suffered by the older "non-operating" employees. Seniority among these men extends only within the local shop and craft. A man with twenty-five years' seniority at Caliente has no claim on the job of a similar craftsman at another point who has only twenty-five days' seniority. Moreover, some of the skills formerly valuable are no longer needed. The boilermaker, for example, knows that jobs for his kind are disappearing and he must enter the ranks of the unskilled. The protection and status offered by the union while he was employed have become meaningless now that he is no longer needed. The cost of this is high both in loss of income and in personal demoralization.

Operating employees also pay. Their seniority extends over a division, which in this case includes three division points. The older members can move from Caliente and claim another job at another point, but in many cases they move leaving a good portion of their life savings behind. The younger men must abandon their stake in railroad employment. The loss may mean a new apprenticeship in another occupation, at a time in life when apprenticeship wages are not adequate to meet the obligations of mature men with families. A steam engine hauled 2,000 tons up the hill out of Caliente with the aid of two helpers. The four-unit diesel in command of one crew handles a train of 3,000 tons alone. Thus, to handle the same amount of tonnage required only about a fourth the man-power it formerly took. Three out of four men must start out anew at something else.

The local merchants pay. The boarded windows, half-empty shelves, and abandoned store buildings bear mute evidence of these costs. The older merchants stay, and pay; the younger ones, and those with no stake in the community will move; but the value of their property will in both cases largely be gone.

The bondholders will pay. They can't foreclose on a dead town. If the town were wiped out altogether, that which would remain for salvage would be too little to satisfy their claims. Should the town continue there is little hope that taxes adequate to carry the overhead of bonds and day-to-day expenses could be secured by taxing the diminished number of property owners or employed persons.

The church will pay. The smaller congregations cannot support services as in the past. As the church men leave, the buildings will be abandoned.

Homeowners will pay. A hundred and thirty-five men owned homes in Caliente. They must accept the available means of support or rent to

those who do. In either case the income available will be far less than
that on which the houses were built. The least desirable homes will
stand unoccupied, their value completely lost. The others must be re-
valued at a figure far below that at which they were formerly held.

In a word, those pay who are, by traditional American standards,
most moral. Those who have raised children see friendships broken
and neighborhoods disintegrated. The childless more freely shake the
dust of Caliente from their feet. Those who built their personalities into
the structure of the community watch their work destroyed. Those too
wise or too selfish to have entangled themselves in community affairs
suffer no such qualms. The chain store can pull down its sign, move its
equipment and charge the costs off against more profitable and better
located units, and against taxes. The local owner has no such alterna-
tives. In short, "good citizens" who assumed family and community
responsibility are the greatest losers. Nomads suffer least.

The people of Caliente are asked to accept as "normal" this strange
inversion of their expectations. It is assumed that they will, without
protest or change in sentiment, accept the dictum of the "law of supply
and demand." Certainly they must comply in part with this dictum.
While their behavior in part reflects this compliance, there are also other
changes perhaps equally important in their attitudes and values.

The first reaction took the form of an effort at community self-
preservation. Caliente became visible to its inhabitants as a real entity,
as meaningful as the individual personalities which they had hitherto
been taught to see as atomistic or nomadic elements. Community survival was seen as prerequisite to many of the individual values that had
been given precedence in the past. The organized community made a
search for new industry, citing elements of community organization
themselves as reasons why industry should move to Caliente. But the
conditions that led the railroad to abandon the point made the place
even less attractive to new industry than it had hitherto been. Yet the
effort to keep the community a going concern persisted.

There was also a change in sentiment. In the past the glib assertion
that progress spelled sacrifice could be offered when some distant group
was a victim of technological change. There was no such reaction when
the event struck home. The change can probably be as well revealed as
in any other way by quoting from the Caliente *Herald:*

    . . . [over the] years . . . [this] . . . railroad and its affiliates . . . became to this
writer his ideal of a railroad empire. The [company] . . . appeared to take much
more than the ordinary interest of big railroads in the development of areas
adjacent to its lines, all the while doing a great deal for the communities large
and small through which the lines passed.

Those were the days creative of [its] enviable reputation as one of the finest, most progressive—and most human—of American railroads, enjoying the confidence and respect of employees, investors, and communities alike!

One of the factors bringing about this confidence and respect was the consideration shown communities which otherwise would have suffered serious blows when division and other changes were effected. A notable example was . . . [a town] . . . where the shock of division change was made almost unnoticed by installation of a rolling stock reclamation point, which gave [that town] an opportunity to hold its community intact until tourist traffic and other industries could get better established—with the result that . . . [it] . . . is now on a firm foundation. And through this display of consideration for a community, the railroad gained friends—not only among the people of . . . [that town] . . . who were perhaps more vocal than others, but also among thousands of others throughout the country on whom this action made an indelible impression.

But things seem to have changed materially during the last few years, the . . . [company] . . . seems to this writer to have gone all out for glamor and the dollars which glamorous people have to spend, sadly neglecting one of the principal factors which helped to make . . . [it] . . . great: that fine consideration of communities and individuals, as well as employees, who have been happy in cooperating steadfastly with the railroad in times of stress as well as prosperity. The loyalty of these people and communities seems to count for little with the . . . [company] . . . of this day, though other "Big Business" corporations do not hesitate to expend huge sums to encourage the loyalty of community and people which old friends of . . . [the company] . . . have been happy to give voluntarily.

Ever since the . . . railroad was constructed . . . Caliente has been a key town on the railroad. It is true, the town owed its inception to the railroad, but it has paid this back in becoming one of the most attractive communities on the system. With nice homes, streets and parks, good school . . . good city government . . . Caliente offers advantages that most big corporations would be gratified to have for their employees—a homey spot where they could live their lives of contentment, happiness and security.

Caliente's strategic location, midway of some of the toughest road on the entire system has been a lifesaver for the road several times when floods have wrecked havoc on the roadbed in the canyon above and below Caliente. This has been possible through storage in Caliente of large stocks of repair material and equipment—and not overlooking manpower—which has thus become available on short notice.

. . . But [the railroad] or at least one of its big officials appearing to be almost completely divorced from policies which made this railroad great, has ordered changes which are about as inconsiderate as anything of which "Big Business" has ever been accused! Employees who have given the best years of their lives to this railroad are cut off without anything to which they can turn, many of them with homes in which they have taken much pride; while others similarly with nice homes, are told to move elsewhere and are given runs that only a few will be able to endure from a physical standpoint, according to common opinion.

Smart big corporations the country over encourage their employees to own their own homes—and loud are their boasts when the percentage of such employees is favorable! But in contrast, a high (company) official is reported to have said only recently that "a railroad man has no business owning a home!" Quite a departure from what has appeared to be [company] condition.

It is difficult for the Herald to believe that this official however "big" he is, speaks for the . . . [company] . . . when he enunciates a policy that, carried to the letter, would make tramps of [company] employees and their families!

No thinking person wants to stand in the way of progress, but true progress is not made when it is overshadowed by cold-blooded disregard for the loyalty of employees, their families, and the communities which have developed in the good American way through the decades of loyal service and good citizenship.

This editorial, written by a member of all the service clubs, approved by Caliente business men, and quoted with approbation by the most conservative members of the community, is significant of changing sentiment.

The people of Caliente continually profess their belief in "The American Way," but like the editor of the *Herald* they criticize decisions made solely in pursuit of profit, even though those decisions grow out of a clearcut case of technological "progress." They feel that the company should have based its decision upon consideration for loyalty, citizenship, and community morale. They assume that the company should regard the seniority rights of workers as important considerations, and that it should consider significant the effect of permanent unemployment upon old and faithful employees. They look upon community integrity as an important community asset. Caught between the support of a "rational" system of "economic" forces and laws, and sentiments which they accept as significant values, they work a solution to their dilemma which will at once permit them to retain their expected rewards for continued adherence to past forms and to defend the social system which they have been taught to revere but which now offers them a stone instead of bread.

IMPLICATIONS

We have shown that those in Caliente whose behavior most nearly approached the ideal taught are hardest hit by change. On the other hand, those seemingly farthest removed in conduct from that idea are either rewarded or pay less of the costs of change than do those who follow the ideal more closely. Absentee owners, completely anonymous, and consumers who are not expected to co-operate to make the gains possible are rewarded most highly, while the local people who must cooperate to raise productivity pay dearly for having contributed.

In a society run through sacred mysteries whose rationale it is not man's privilege to criticize, such incongruities may be explained away. Such a society may even provide some "explanation" which makes them seem rational. In a secular society, supposedly defended rationally upon scientific facts, in which the pragmatic test "Does it work?" is continually applied, such discrepancy between expectation and realization is difficult to reconcile.

Defense of our traditional system of assessing the costs of technological change is made on the theory that the costs of such change are more than offset by the benefits to "society as a whole." However, it is difficult to show the people of Caliente just why *they* should pay for advances made to benefit others whom they have never known and who, in their judgment, have done nothing to justify such rewards. Any action that will permit the people of Caliente to levy the costs of change upon those who will benefit from them will be morally justifiable to the people of Caliente. Appeals to the general welfare leave them cold and the compulsions of the price system are not felt to be self-justifying "natural laws" but are regarded as being the specific consequence of specific bookkeeping decisions as to what should be included in the costs of change. They seek to change these decisions through social action. They do not consider that the "American Way" consists primarily of acceptance of the market as the final arbiter of their destiny. Rather they conceive that the system as a whole exists to render "justice," and if the consequences of the price system are such as to produce what they consider to be "injustice" they proceed to use some other institution as a means to reverse or offset the effects of the price system. Like other groups faced with the same situation, those in Caliente seize upon the means available to them. The operating employees had in their unions a device to secure what they consider to be their rights. Union practices developed over the years make it possible for the organized workers to avoid some of the costs of change which they would otherwise have had to bear. Feather-bed rules, make-work practices, restricted work weeks, train length legislation and other similar devices were designed to permit union members to continue work even when "efficiency" dictated that they be disemployed. Members of the "Big Four" in Caliente joined with their fellows in demanding not only the retention of previously existing rules, but the imposition of new ones such as that requiring the presence of a third man in the diesel cab. For other groups there was available only the appeal to the company that it establish some other facility at Caliente, or alternatively a demand that "government" do something. One such demand took the form of a request to the Interstate Commerce Commission that it require inspection of rolling stock at Caliente. This request was denied.

It rapidly became apparent to the people of Caliente that they could not gain their objectives by organized community action nor individual endeavor but there was hope that by adding their voices to those of others similarly injured there might be hope of solution. They began to look to the activities of the whole labor movement for succor. Union strategy which forced the transfer of control from the market to goverment mediation or to legislation and operation was widely approved on all sides. This was not confined to those only who were currently seeking rule changes but was equally approved by the great bulk of those in the community who had been hit by the change. Cries of public outrage at their demands for make-work rules were looked upon as coming from those at best ignorant, illinformed or stupid, and at worst as being the hypocritical efforts of others to gain at the workers' expense. When the union threat of a national strike for rule changes was met by government seizure, Caliente workers like most of their compatriots across the country welcomed this shift in control, secure in their belief that if "justice" were done they could only be gainers by government intervention. These attitudes are not "class" phenomena purely nor are they merely occupational sentiments. They result from the fact that modern life, with the interdependence that it creates, particularly in one-industry communities, imposes penalties far beyond the membership of the groups presumably involved in industry. When make-work rules contributed to the livelihood of the community, the support of the churches, and the taxes which maintain the schools; when feather-bed practices determine the standard of living, the profits of the business man and the circulation of the press; when they contribute to the salary of the teacher and the preacher; they can no longer be treated as accidental, immoral, deviant or temporary. Rather they are elevated into the position of emergent morality and law. Such practices generate a morality which serves them just as the practices in turn nourish those who participate in and preserve them. They are as firmly a part of what one "has a right to expect" from industry as are parity payments to the farmer, bonuses and pensions to the veterans, assistance to the aged, tariffs to the industrialist, or the sanctity of property to those who inherit. On the other hand, all these practices conceivably help create a structure that is particularly vulnerable to changes such as that described here.

Practices which force the company to spend in Caliente part of what has been saved through technological change, or failing that, to reward those who are forced to move by increased income for the same service, are not, by the people of Caliente, considered to be unjustifiable. Confronted by a choice between the old means and resultant "injustice" which their use entails, and the acceptance of new means which they believe will secure them the "justice" they hold to be their right, they are willing to abandon (in so far as this particular area is concerned) the liberal state and the omnicompetent market in favor of something that works to provide "justice."

The study of the politics of pressure groups will show how widely the reactions of Caliente people are paralleled by those of other groups. Amongst them it is in politics that the decisions as to whom will pay and who will profit are made. Through organized political force railroaders maintain the continuance of rules which operate to their benefit rather than for "the public good" or "the general welfare." Their defense of these practices is found in the argument that only so can their rights be protected against the power of other groups who hope to gain at their expense by functioning through the corporation and the market.

We should expect that where there are other groups similarly affected by technological change, there will be similar efforts to change the operation of our institutions. The case cited is not unique. Not only is it duplicated in hundreds of railroad division points but also in other towns abandoned by management for similar reasons. Changes in the location of markets or in the method of calculating transportation costs, changes in technology making necessary the use of new materials, changes due to the exhaustion of old sources of materials, changes to avoid labor costs such as the shift of the textile industry from New England to the South, changes to expedite decentralization to avoid the consequences of bombing, or those of congested living, all give rise to the question, "Who benefits, and at whose expense?"

The accounting practices of the corporation permit the entry only of those costs which have become "legitimate" claims upon the company. But the tremendous risks borne by the workers and frequently all the members of the community in an era of technological change are real phenomena. Rapid shifts in technology which destroy the "legitimate" expectations derived from past experience force the recognition of new obligations. Such recognition may be made voluntarily as management foresees the necessity, or it may be thrust upon it by political or other action. Rigidity of property concepts, the legal structure controlling directors in what they may admit to be costs, and the stereotyped nature of the "economics" used by management make rapid change within the corporation itself difficult even in a "free democratic society." Hence while management is likely to be permitted or required to initiate technological change in the interest of profits, it may and probably will be barred from compensating for the social consequences certain to arise from those changes. Management thus shuts out the rising flood of demands in its cost-accounting only to have them reappear in its tax accounts, in legal regulations or in new insistent union demands. If economics fails to provide an answer to social demands then politics will be tried.

It is clear that while traditional morality provides a means of protecting some groups from the consequences of technological change, or some method of meliorating the effects of change upon them, other large segments of the population are left unprotected. It should be equally clear that rather than a quiet acquiescence in the finality and justice of such arrangements, there is an active effort to force new devices into being which will extend protection to those hitherto expected to bear the brunt of these costs. A good proportion of these inventions increasingly call for the intervention of the state. To call such arrangements immoral, unpatriotic, socialistic or to hurl other epithets at them is not to deal effectively with them. They are as "natural" as are the "normal" reactions for which we have "rational" explanations based upon some pre-scientific generalization about human nature such as "the law of supply and demand" or "the inevitability of progress." To be dealt with effectively they will have to be understood and treated as such.

CHAPTER 12

Social and Personal Consequences of Change

The social and personal consequences of change are vast, various, and many of them are dimly seen and poorly understood by social scientists. The entire matter of sorting out the effects of technology, increase in scale, industrialization, urbanization, modernization, and so on, constitutes an agenda for scholarship that stretches far into the future, and all the while, of course, the change process continues. This problem has indeed been a principal concern of social science over the past century, and interest in it continues to grow as the development of the "new nations" occupies so much of the world's attention.

Some of the consequences that can be ascribed to social change are definitional, that is, implied in the way we describe the basic processes of change themselves. Urbanization, for example, is used to mean the development of heterogeneity, specialization, and interdependence among the men in a spatially identified social group. Specialization and interdependence are in turn inextricably related to the social characteristics of the organizations in which men live and work.

The problem reaches much further than that, however, for it is commonly supposed that specialization, division of labor, and dense living have effects on the whole texture of human life. In the nineteenth century scholars were talking about the replacement of *Gemeinschaft* (community) by *Gesellschaft* (society), or using other similar terms to describe the contrast between nonmodern and modern modes of social organization. Essentially, this sort of analysis supposes that in earlier Western societies, and in "underdeveloped" contemporary ones, the individual occupies an ascribed place in a static structure. The relationships within this structure are relatively firmly fixed, and the whole has the "feel" of being natural. On the other hand, in the modern setting there is much mobility (social as well as geographic) and fluidity. Men invent social relationships that are artificial in character, based in effect on contract. They relate to other men not through fixed and established devices but through changing, "negotiated" ones. Thus the secondary group replaces the primary group as the site of social engagement, the family declines in importance, the relationship of man to his work is depersonalized.

Three questions grow out of such an approach to the social structure of the changing society. Do these generalizations truly describe the effects of change, and if so to what extent and in what circumstances? If true, what are the consequences for individual life? Are these good or bad? We cannot pretend to offer answers here, but can suggest some ways to think about the subject.

In the first place, most scholars would probably agree that terms like those cited above generally describe but do not accurately depict the social change process, that neither the old nor the new society was as simply understood as they suggest. Change is probably more uneven and has more dimensions, and it is more usefully seen as movement on a continuum than as progression from one categoric box to another. Still, it is probably generally true that urbanization throws man upon secondary relationships, that it leads him toward specialization, makes social organization more complex, and brings about its bureaucratization.

As to the consequences for individuals, many have argued that in the urban circumstance men, being cut adrift from their "natural" and comfortable social attachments, develop the ills identified as "alienation" or "anomie." These arise, purportedly, out of a sense of detachment and powerlessness. In turn, this condition gives rise to the phenomena of mass society, in which people are subject to irrationality, manipulation, and the appeals of demagoguery. Hence in reaction to his situation, urban man is thought to become an automaton at the mercy of the accidents and exploitation of an impersonal world.

On the other hand, critics of this thesis argue that while urbanites are often subject to such threats, social change also brings about other results, some of them counteracting the ones described above. Thus the "old" society was (or is) not secure but instead repressive, and it may be the ties of slavery that urbanization can break. The "artificial" society is one in which man has freedom, the freedom to establish his own network of activities and contacts. Modern man, with his enhanced capacity to deal with his physical environment and with the opportunity to create his own social world, is freed for a potential life of creativity. Given the heterogeneity of the urban society, it is also a life of greater variety and richness, for to the urban man is presented a much broader range of social choices.

The question of "good or bad" we will leave aside, for the application of individual evaluation to the consequences described. It should be plain, however, why the literature of the subject often turns out to be judgmental of urban society either explicitly, or implicitly.

Our selections for this section include two, the one by Gerth and Mills and the one by Shils, that explicate and discuss the "mass society" theme from slightly different points of view. The third, a passage from Anthony Burgess' fiction *Beds in the East* contrasts the old, in this case colonial, with the developing, newly independent life. The story is set in Malaysia at the time of its passage from British rule and suggests some of the processes, political, social, and personal, that accompany the development of a new world.

Hans Gerth and C. Wright Mills
Master Trends

It is in this world context of total integrations and bureaucratization that we must understand the decline of liberalism as a style of thinking and the rise and spread of totalitarian slogan manipulation and opinion management. For the problems of mass insecurity and of anxiety levels, of mental imbalances and unclear definitions of unstructured situations now form the sociological context of political and economic psychology.

As one of the great thought systems of the Western world, liberalism is rooted in the "enlightenment movement" of the Occidental middle classes and their intellectual vanguards; it incorporates the legacy of Greece and of Rome—a legacy which has been reassimilated by various renaissances since the waning of the Middle Ages.[1]

Liberalism has made its greatest and least questioned headway in the United States. In Europe it has met with older and more entrenched patterns having elaborate defensives of their own. Among these have been Catholic and Protestant orthodoxies, often linked with modern conservative thinking, and anticapitalist intellectuals and parties. From the "right" and from the "left" anticapitalist thinking has emerged: European liberalism has been identified with "the middle." But no such position and no such identification occurred in the United States, where liberalism has become, at least as rhetoric, a common denominator.

This difference between liberalism in Europe and America is due to many factors, but the most important of them is the fact that in Europe capitalist societies developed from older feudal structures, which were never entirely displaced but which, in a number of ways, were transformed and adapted to new societies. The nobility moved from the military camp to the court, becoming an "office nobility"; and to this day nobles play a significant part in the high ranks of ecclesiastic dignitaries in the Roman Catholic Church, of royalty in Lutheran Scandinavian countries, and in the established church of England. Landlordism in Italy and Spain, in France, Great Britain, and Germany,

From *Character and Social Structure* by Hans Gerth and C. Wright Mills, copyright 1953 by Harcourt, Brace & World, Inc. and reprinted with their permission.
[1] See L. T. Hobhouse, *Liberalism* (New York: Holt, 1911); and G. DeRuggiero, *The History of European Liberalism* (Collingwood, Tr., London, 1927).

although affected by the complex history of capitalism, has allowed strong feudal elements to adapt themselves and so survive in complicated forms.

The rise of capitalist society in Central Europe and in large areas of Eastern Europe did not involve the transfer of political and military power to the economically most powerful group—the urban capitalist middle class. Because of the failure of the 1848 revolutions, and the complexities of national formations in Italy, Germany, and Japan during the second half of the nineteenth century, princely power, although reduced in prerogative, maintained itself in the status structure and retained its prestigeful influence among intellectuals. The cultural patronage of petty courts and nobles continues to exist in some European societies right into the present.

To all this the United States is the great exception, for here there was no feudal age, and from their beginnings the middle classes combined economic ascendancy and expansion over a continent-wide territory with unhampered dominance of economic wealth and monopoly of status structures. Their monopoly of status was facilitated by their financing of numerous prestigeful institutions: art collections and museums bound intellectual and cultural elites to the "donors" and "philanthropists." Educational institutions, libraries, colleges, universities, and research institutions were impressively endowed, sponsored, and controlled by wealthy "private" citizens, and the dependent personnel became indebted to them; if they were not sycophantic, they were at least grateful.

Wealth in the United States also asserted itself through politics as the ascending middle class became the upper class without having to compromise with ecclesiastic or monarchal elements or with wealthy elites of older standing. Nor did they need to compromise in military, diplomatic, and cultural areas with the standards or traditions of feudal or semifeudal groups clustering around the courts of landed princes and nobles or state university chairs. One has of course to make allowance for the "slavocracy" of the southern plantation society as quasi-feudal, but the Civil War and the reconstruction period eliminated it as a setup not having clear-cut capitalist aspect.

Political and economic power, religious and educational institutions, military and judicial elements as well as status dominance—all these could be vested in the hands of a ruling class of bourgeois extraction and composition. Accordingly, the United States became the great scene for an unadulterated capitalist society and a business civilization built in its image.

The unique situation of a geographical area which allowed continental expansion until the turn of the twentieth century, and the growth of a nation of 5 million into one of 150 million in the short span of 150 years—this made liberalism uniquely fit the reality of American society. For liberalism is "generous": it requires and assumes a friendly universe of equal and open opportunities, and it assumes that men are born "free and equal." Here, the coming of the immigrant coincided with "unlimited opportunities" and a "consciousness of abundance." Liberalism thus found its affirmation in the daily experience of millions of people living in an expanding society.

Instrumental and efficiency values could be and were readily seen as one with moral values. Characteristically, the obvious problem of the double-edged nature of technology—capable of working for good or for evil—was profoundly and insistently impressed upon the American public mind only after the dropping of the atom bomb.

In America the marriage of science and technology, and the joyful reliance upon the values of efficiency, did not entail the destruction or the displacement of cultural legacies, which in Europe aroused the esthetic and nostalgic reactions of men in "romantic agony." Here there was no sense of tragic loss, for on virgin territory such romantic sentiments could at best be attached to the lure of distant horizons and the image of the "noble savage," who, at any rate, upon closer view seemed more savage than noble. The superiority of the white man's advancing efficiency over the primitive ways of the Indian never led to doubts about God-willed stewardship. Besides, "these illiterate savages" could neither work steadily in the fields nor read the Bible or the catechism; hence all the easier the slogan, "the only good Indian is a dead Indian." Their displacement led to no more travail than that of other preliterate societies on the widening colonial frontiers of the "expansion of Europe."

The widening of economic opportunities and the extension of the territorial setting of United States society went hand in hand and reinforced each other, as did technical progress and the rising levels of skill and education. Entrepreneurial, propertied groups, in urban as well as rural sectors of the society, pulled in the same direction: both have been money-minded groups which took the competitive market for granted.

In this setting, the social costs and liabilities of capitalism could be overlooked, in fact, many of them could be socially defined as ethnic peculiarities of immigrant minorities, and hence not truly American. The anticapitalist sentiments of protesting intellectuals such as John Ruskin or Thomas Carlyle could not perturb the onrushing multitude in its "pursuit of happiness."

The dominance of Puritanism, with its conception of property as "stewardship," cast a religious halo about the successful, and the secu-

larization of Puritanism could easily make for the self-righteous identification of "success" in this world with the complacent sense of being
"blessed by God." This was all the more possible as property was for a
long time work-property, and the linkage between such personal virtues
as diligence and initiative, persistence and hard work, with property
was highly and widely visible. Mass literature, from juveniles to human
interest stories and novels, succeeded in publicizing the lore of success
and the romance of those who had made it: the titans, the tycoons, the
robber barons, the founding fathers, the pioneers, the technological
heroes. Such men, standing at the center of popular attention, have
provided popular models of aspiration. In American society nothing
has been able to rival such affirmations of the efficient, successful heroes
of liberalism.

In other countries, Germany for example,[2] the middle-class industri-
alists who had economic power did not thereby have status and power in
political, educational, or religious orders. For princely power continued,
entrenched in Bismarck's constitution of 1870–1918, that underpinned
the position of nobles in diplomatic and officer corps, in Protestant
church, and student association. Access to such positions was denied
the bourgeoisie, which accordingly was forced to adapt feudal and
bureaucratic prestige models, to seek intermarriage with nobles, to
purchase titles: in short, to renounce liberalism.

The course of Japan is comparable, except in its case, the lower
nobility absorbed capitalist business and, in the absence of a productive
middle class in the Western style, assimilated the corporate phase of
capitalism to the feudal ways of noble and military clan.[3]

In Britain,[4] repeated compromises between landed gentry and court
society, on the one hand, and the political and economic ascendancy of
the new entrepreneurial class on the other, led to an integrative process
in which *rentier* strata of feudal aristocrats and urban patricians could
fuse in exclusive clubs and hold their own in navy and army, in "society"
and diplomacy. In this they were aided by the "public school" pattern
and a widespread system of scholarships which implemented educational opportunities and made for the staying power of feudal elements
as well as for the ascending bourgeois elements. The liberal heritage was
thus assimilated to the reconstructed conservative thinking of Edmund
Burke and his successors.

[2] See Paul Kosok, *Modern Germany* (Chicago: University of Chicago Press, 1933);
Max Weber, *From Max Weber . . . op. cit.*, pp. 363–85.

[3] See the excellent monograph, E. Herbert Norman, *Japan's Emergence as a
Modern State* (New York: Institute of Pacific Relations, 1946).

[4] See Wilhelm Dibelius, *England: Its Character and Genius*, M. A. Hamilton, tr.
(New York: Harper, 1930).

In Russia, capitalism was tied in with foreign (largely French) political and strategic loans.[5] In the short period from the emancipation of the serfs in 1861 to the revolution 1917, this capitalism did not allow an economically independent and politically self-reliant middle class to emerge. Moreover, the agrarian problems of Tsarist Russia coincided with the oppressive social evils of early industrialization. The peculiarities of the Russian agrarian commune, and the quasi-religious fervor of the intelligentsia provided a barren soil for the ideas of Western liberalism. In addition to the illiterate peasant masses, there was the Eastern Orthodox Church, and the oppressive weight of the Tsarist office and court nobility. There was the anti-Western turn of writers such as Tolstoi and Dostoevski, of the Slavophiles and populists, whether repentant noblemen, or proletarian writers such as Maxim Gorki; and there was the anticapitalist turn of the nihilist, anarchist, and socialist intellectuals, acting as the conscience of their time and people. Accordingly, liberalism as a temper of mind or as a political system had little ground in which to take root.

Since World War I, the international scene, as it bears on the fate of liberalism, has been greatly changed: Nationalist restrictionism and economic protectionism has led to increasing stress and strain.[6] The United States, as well as the dominions and colonies of the British Empire, closed their doors to immigration, and so the great nineteenth-century mobility of population ceased. Currency policies and protective tariffs fenced off economic areas against unwanted competitors and deadlocked the market system. The rise of large corporations and monopolistic practices made for a new scene, which no longer lent itself to liberal models of social reflection. There was a "scarcity consciousness" in regard to educational and to job opportunities, in regard to migratory opportunities, and even the marriage opportunities for women in the war-decimated nations after the two world wars. "Free and open competition," instead of rationing and planful administration of market processes, now becomes—as in postwar Germany—a mechanism for distributing what is to be had, in which the physically weak, the morally scrupulous, the politically unorganized are pushed to the side. Those who in the eastern areas of Europe have lost everything they once had—their farms, houses, businesses, and skilled jobs—were the last to find jobs for themselves and opportunities for their children in the west. As "new citizens" they are unwanted competitors, walled out

---

[5] See Leon Trotsky, *The History of the Russian Revolution*, Max Eastman, tr. (New York: Simon & Schuster, 1936).

[6] See E. H. Carr, *The Twenty Years' Crisis* (London: Macmillan, 1949) and *The New Society* (London: Macmillan, 1951).

by the competitive endeavor of the older residents to build fences wherever possible around preferred opportunities.

Liberalism under such conditions means free competition for all vested groups—from trade unions to businessmen's associations, from villages to metropolitan communities and new states—to build fences. The highminded endeavors of welfare bureaucracies might soften and mitigate and channel the pressures, but they have not prevented the emergence of irate, embittered mass movements among the "disinherited." Mass unemployment and impoverishment remains a lasting threat, despite the phoenixlike upswing of the Western German economy with American aid.

Such facts can no longer be viewed as temporary or exceptional; in present-day contexts the incongruity of liberal ideologies with modern social facts are glaringly evident. The sense of an open horizon of unlimited opportunities is gone; competition as a fair and equitable way for mating merit and compensation is no longer believed in. The competitive group pressures of society appear to many as "rackets," and freedom takes on the attributes not of rational and moral self-determination among neighbors but of a Hobbesian jungle where the "elastic man," the man without conscience, fends for himself with tooth and claw, a lone wolf in an unfriendly universe.

Such sentiments and feelings of bitter frustration are greatest where "competition among unequals" prevails—in the commodity market, where little and big units, with quite different capital assets and capacities for risk, meet in "free and open competition"; where the little man risks his all and the big corporation risks practically nothing; where economic heavyweights are free to knock out flyweight competitors.

In international relations, the economically strong country transfers the burden of unemployment to weaker countries by maintaining an active balance of trade in its favor, and by attracting whatever capital takes to "flight" from the pressured nation. Thus, in the "family of nations" economic nationalism disintegrates. International trade dwindles, a common currency standard does not exist, weaker nations are indebted to strong creditors, who refuse to accept imports which alone can serve as payment. Hence debtor countries mortgage or sell their land and other capital assets to creditor nations, and are virtually reduced to colonial status.

As in trade, so in war and diplomacy: a weak state may be peacefully carved up—as was Czechoslovakia at Munich by Hitler and Mussolini with the assistance of Chamberlain and Daladier. Strong powers do not deem it honorable to live up to treaty commitments unless it is expedient to do so. In 1914 the Kaiser's chancellor still expressed guilt feelings about the invasion of Belgium and the breaking of neutrality treaties, but great powers now project alleged acts of "aggression" upon the prospective victim, however helpless and weak, of their attack. In the world of nations today might makes right and all is fair in war. And when the shooting pauses, not moral and legal norms but the *de facto* principles of action and power in a world at war is the order of the age.

Industrialized peoples adjust to these changes by building up huge "pressure groups" which emerge out of the upward and downward shifts in economic opportunities for the aggregates of people in common class situations. These pressure groups seek, on various levels, to translate their organized power into policy decisions. The price of bread thus becomes as much a political price as are the rents of tenement houses. "Bloc competition" and "bloc bargaining" replace the competitive scatter of small units; strivings for security replace the sense of joyful individual initiative; feelings of solidarity become more important than self-reliance. Self-help becomes a joke, and "breaking out of line," that is, lack of loyalty to one's organized comrades or colleagues or the "business community" becomes just short of a crime. The term "self-made man" becomes slightly embarrassing; inherited wealth is believed a prerequisite for high status; and the glamour of "the heiress" becomes equivalent if not superior to the majesty of an old-world princess.

In the face of all these changes, Liberalism as an ideology becomes "formalized"; it becomes a political rhetoric which is increasingly meaningless and banal to large masses. The prerequisites for the classic "freedoms" espoused in its name are often simply not available, and hence its classic tenets are easily perverted.[7]

Social and psychological changes of a wide and deep sort thus undermine the moorings of liberalism. In the face of such changes, cynical upper classes may be ready to discard the democratic legacy and allow or support policies that end in a totalitarian society of Fascist or Nazi type. In industrial societies, such movements have arisen at times when the power of labor was declining, as in Italy after the revolutionary upsurge of the post-World War I, and in Germany, as labor's strength was enervated by depression, and unemployment led to mass agony. On both occasions, terrorist organizations were subsidized and turned loose on labor, and the labor press suppressed, as chauvinist frenzy replaced rational public debate. Hero worship drowned the competition in rational ideas and arguments in public. The policy of the street, the assassination of leaders, the orgiastic howling and pogroms against

7 See John Hallowell, *The Decline of Liberalism as an Ideology* (Berkeley and Los Angeles: University of California Press, 1943). For counter-tendencies, however, see Morton G. White, "The Revolt against Formalism in American Social Thought of the Twentieth Century," *Journal of the History of Ideas,* Vol. VIII, No. 2, April 1947, pp. 131–52.

scapegoated minority groups implemented the transitions. A political landslide occurred among the masses, and after some bargaining and compromising, the old elites fused with the ascending political movement, which established its own brand of dictatorship. Society was put on a war footing.

Totalitarianism is an imperialist response to the impasse of corporate capitalism. It is a twentieth-century response, occurring in a time when scarcity consciousness prevails and when to many liberal ideologies seem hollow. Despite its destruction in Central Europe by the last war, neo-Fascist and neo-Nazi tendencies have appeared in Western Germany and Italy. Nobody could call Péron's or Tito's or De Gaulle's program liberal democracy; and nobody can call Franco Spain anything but a fascist dictatorship. In France and Italy close to one-third of the electorate demonstratively and persistently votes Communist. Only the complacent and the uninformed can feel assured of liberal and democratic developments in the world today.

Edward Shils
The Theory of Mass Society

A specter is haunting sociologists. It is the specter of "mass society."
This phantasm is not of the sociologist's own making. The conception
of mass society, that had its origin in the Roman historians' idea
of the tumultuous populace and its greatest literary expression in
Coriolanus, is largely a product of the nineteenth century. In this
epoch, it is a product of the reaction against the French Revolutions
which ran from 1789, through 1830 and 1848, to 1871. Jakob Burckhardt
and Friedrich Nietzsche, fearful of the inflammability of the mob in the
presence of a heated demagogue—that demagogue was Louis Napoléon
—came to envisage modern society, particularly modern democratic
society, as tending toward an inert and formless mass, lying in brutish
torpor most of the time and occasionally aroused to plebiscitary accla-
mation by a "great simplifier." Tocqueville's critique of the absolutist
ancien régime, centered on a vision of a society which has lost its framework of feudal liberty through the destruction of the autonomous corporations and estates on which it rested, is a cornerstone of that construction. The no-man's land between the absolute prince and the mass
of the population became a field open to passion and manipulation.

This notion of the mob received a certain amount of subsequent
embroidery through the work of Le Bon and Sighele. A deeper extension, which was not realized at the time, lay in the work of the German
sociologists. They distinguished between *Gemeinschaft* and *Gesellschaft;*
the latter, characterized by the evaporation of moral bonds, the shrivel-
ling of kinship and traditional institutions and beliefs, and the isolation
of the individual from his fellows, was alleged to be representative of
modern Western society.

The synthesis of these elements took place in the quasi-Marxist assessments of the regime of National Socialist Germany: the disintegrative
influence of capitalism and urban life had left man alone and helpless.
To protect himself, he fled into the arms of the all-absorbing totalitarian party. Thus the *coup d'état* of Louis Napoléon of December,
1851, and the *Machtergreifung* of March, 1933, became the prototypical

Reprinted from *Diogenes,* Fall 1962, No. 39, by permission of the author and
publisher.

events of modern society, and the society of the Weimar Republic was declared to be the characteristic pattern of modern society in preparation for its natural culmination.

This is the intellectual background from which the conception of mass society has grown. It has gained new strength from the developments in the technology of communication, which were called "mass communications," before their association with mass society occurred. Yet the accident of similar designation has facilitated the fusion of the criticism of the intellectual and cultural content of press, wireless, and television with the apprehension about the dangers inherent in standardless and defenseless condition of the "masses."

The result is the following image of "mass society:" a territorially extensive society, with a large population, highly urbanized and industrialized. Power is concentrated in this society and much of the power takes the form of manipulation of the mass through the media of mass communication. Civic spirit is poor, local loyalties are few, primordial solidarity is virtually nonexistent. There is no individuality, only a restless and frustrated egoism. It is like the state of nature described by Thomas Hobbes, except that public disorder is restrained through the manipulation of the elite and the apathetic idiocy of the mass. The latter is broken only when, in a state of crisis, the masses rally round some demagogue.

I think that this is an untruthful picture of Western society of recent decades. It is a gross distortion of certain features of the large-scale liberal-democratic societies of the West. It is taken from a standpoint which postulates, as the right ordering of life, an entirely consensual, perfectly integrated, small-scale society, permeated by a set of common theological beliefs which give meaning to every aspect of life. Empirically, this view is blind to the whole range of phenomena indicated in this paper; theoretically, it fails to see that no society could go on reproducing itself and maintaining even a coerced order if it corresponded to the description given by the critics of "mass society." Yet the conception of mass society has the merit of having responded, however erroneously, to a characteristic feature of this recent phase of modern society; namely, the entry of the mass of the population into greater proximity to the center of society. Although I think that most of the analysis contained in the prevailing conception of this form of twentieth-century Western society is incorrect, it has the virtue of having perceived a certain historical uniqueness and of having given it a name.

The name does not appeal to me. I use it with much misgiving because it has cognitive and ethical overtones which are repugnant to me. Yet, since it has the merit of having focused attention on a historically and sociologically very significant phase of modern society, and since it is the resultant analysis which I wish to correct, I shall go on using the term, while trying not to be a captive of the problems and categories which it carries with it in its overtones. Furthermore, there is no other term which has a comparable evocative power.

I

The term "mass society" points generally and unsteadily at something genuinely novel in the history of human society. It refers to a new order of society which acquired visibility between the two World Wars, and actually came noisily and ponderously into our presence after the end of the Second. In the United States above all, but also in Great Britain, France, Germany, Northern Italy, the Low and Northern European Countries, Australia and Japan, this new society has become tangibly established. Less evenly and more partially, some of its features have begun to appear in Eastern and Central Europe and they have here and there begun to show incipient and premonitory signs of existence in Asian and African countries.

The novelty of the "mass society" lies in the relationship of the mass of the population to the center of the society. The relationship is a closer integration into the central institutional and value systems of the society.

An aggregate of individual human beings living over a territory constitutes a society by virtue of their integration into a system in which the parts are interdependent. The types of societies with which we are concerned here are those in which the integration occurs, not through kinship, but through the exercise and acceptance of authority in the major subsystems of the society, in the polity, the economy, and the status and cultural orders, i.e., in educational and religious institutions and their associated norms and beliefs. Integration occurs in two directions—vertically and horizontally. A society is vertically integrated in a hierarchy of power and authority and a status order; it is horizontally integrated by the unity of the elites of the various sectors or subsystems of the society and through the moral consensus of the whole.

The absolutist societies of the European *ancien régime,* and indeed the great monarchies of the Orient and of Western antiquity, were characterized from time to time by a fairly high degree of horizontal integration of the elites at each level of the society, although as one descended in the hierarchy, the territorial radius within which elites were horizontally integrated diminished. There was a close affinity and cooperation between the governmental, political, religious, military, and intellectual elites, although there were often severe struggles within the political elite which spread to the elites of the other spheres. Vertically, however, these societies were very seldom highly integrated. Villages, estates, regions lived their own lives, connected with the center through the payment of taxes, the provision of obligatory labor services, the performance of religious rites in which the central authority had an acknowledged place and the occasional recourse to a more or less unitary judiciary. These connections were, on the whole, highly intermittent. The major continuous integration from the center was through the church, where such existed, as in Europe, or through common religious beliefs where there was no formal ecclesiastical body, country-wide in the comprehensiveness of its coverage. The central institutions of government, education, and religion did not reach very far into the life of the mass. The cultural, economic, and administrative autonomy of territorially restricted areas was great, and the center intruded into local life only occasionally. The symbols of the center to which there was a wide-spread, fairly continuous, and common attachment were practically nonexistent. The very meagre coverage of the educational system meant that the culture possessed by the educated classes was scarcely shared at all by the vast majority of the population; and, correspondingly, the conception of the world, and the standards of judgment of the various strata of society, must have had little in common. To a limited extent, this feebleness, of the vertical integration from the center was probably offset by the closer contacts between the "big house" and the tenants and laborers on the large estates. Even within this small local radius, however, the amount of vertical integration, although strong through the exercise of authority, must have been consensually slight because of the very steep hierarchy of status and the profound differences in culture among the various strata.

At the lower levels, the regimes of the great states were hardly integrated at all horizontally. Villages and estates, over the country as a whole, were scarcely in contact with each other either directly through exchange or sympathy or even through their links with the center.

Indeed, it might be said that, except at the level of the highest political, ecclesiastical, administrative, military, and cultural elites, there really was scarcely a society covering a large territory. The mass was a part of this society largely in the ecological sense; it was only faintly part of its moral order, or even, for that matter, of its system of authority except on narrow occasions.

When we turn our attention to advanced modern societies, the situation is quite otherwise. Government is more continuously and effectively in contact with much of the population through the variety and comprehensiveness of its legislation, through the continuity and intensity of administration, through nearly universal public education until well into adolescence. The capital of a country and its major urban centers are no longer centers only to the notabilities of the society, but for the ordinary people as well. The economy of a mass society is much more integrated both horizontally and vertically than has ever been the case in past epochs of history and outside the advanced industrial societies. Whether by a nation-wide market economy, dominated by large nation-wide corporations and by central governmental regulation, or by a socialistically planned economy, scarcely any part of the economic order of the society lives in isolation from its rulers or competitors.

The higher level of educational attainment, the higher degree of literacy, and the greater availability of cultural products like books, periodicals, gramophone records, television, and wireless programs, spread the culture which was once confined to a narrow circle at the center over a far greater radius. These, and the much greater "politicization" of the population, bring about an historically unique measure of community of culture.

The intensity of vertical integration differs among societies. Federations are less intensely integrated vertically than unitary regimes; regimes with strong local government are less integrated vertically than regimes like France, where local government is largely in the hands of centrally appointed officials; regimes which allow private and parochial schools are less integrated than those which require that everyone receive his education at a state educational institution. The fundamental distinction among societies with a fairly high degree of integration is that between pluralistic and totalitarian regimes. The totalitarian regimes are much more completely integrated vertically.

Their intense vertical integration is reinforced, furthermore, by an almost equally intense horizontal integration. Their horizontal integration is expressed in the unitary structure of their elites. Their elites are, in their functions, as differentiated, as the elites of a pluralistic regime. Only a very small and very simple society could have an elite in which the same persons performed practically all elite tasks. Differentiation of roles and specialization to the roles of the persons who fill them are an unavoidable and monumental fact of any advanced civilization, however much overlap there is among roles and however much passage there might be among them. The elites of a pluralistic regime are much less integrated horizontally and vertically, authoritatively and consensually, than the totalitarian elites.

II

The mass society is a new phenomenon, but the elements from which it has arisen are not new. The *polis* was its seed; it was nurtured and developed in the Roman idea of a common citizenship extending over a vast territory. The growth of the sense of nationality, from an occasional expression prior to the French Revolution to an expanding reality in the social life of the nineteenth century and the early twentieth century, was the course taken by this deepening sense of affinity among the members of diverse strata and regions of modern countries. When the proponents and agents of the modern idea of the nation put forward the view that life on a bounded, continuous, and common territory, beyond the confines of kinship, caste, and religious belief, united the human beings living within that territory into a single collectivity, and made language the evidence of that membership, they committed themselves, not often wittingly, to the mass society. The primordial root of territorial location persists—like other primordial things, it can only become attenuated, but never disappear. Language, and all that is contained in language and transmitted by it, becomes the link through which the members of the mass society are bound to each other and to the center. The sharing of a language is the sharing of the essential quality which confers membership in society.

The sense of the primordial and attachment to it has been transformed and dispersed in mass society. Common existence on a contiguous territory has passed ahead of biological kinship, which obviously has insuperable limitations as a basis for union over a large territory. At the most, it is capable of extension into ethnicity and in this transmutation, it still has very great vitality. Common territoriality is capable of greater extension as a basis of union. It is the rise to prominence of the symbol of territoriality which is one of the main features of the modern sense of nationality, which is, in its turn, a precondition for the emergence of mass society. The fact that a man lives in one's own territory however extensive, now confers on him rights to one's consideration which earlier societies did not know on this scale. In modern society, the territory which possesses this capacity to establish communion has become greatly extended.

This shift in the balance within the category of primordiality has been part of a wider sublimation of the sacred from the primordial to the dispositional. In early modern times, it was a disposition of belief—even of specific theological belief—which those most involved in authority thought was necessary for the formation of union over a bounded territory. The dominion of this category of assessment of one's fellow man has been lightened to the advantage of a more tolerant inclination to view another human being in accordance with a conception of him as a bearer of less specific dispositions—either entirely personal or more or less civil. The civil disposition is nothing more than the acknowledgment of the legitimacy of the authority—definitely located in persons or offices or diffuse in the form of the legitimacy of the social order—which prevails over a bounded and extensive territory.

This change has made possible a consensus, fundamental and broad, which includes as fellow men, all those living on a bounded territory responsible by their presence to the legitimacy of the order and the authorities who prevail there. The inclusion of the entire population in the society, or a pronounced tendency towards that inclusion, is what makes the mass society.

III

When we say that this new order of mass society is a consensual society, this does not mean, however, that it is completely consensual, a fabric of seamless harmony. The competition and conflict of corporate bodies resting on diverse class, ethnic, professional, and regional identifications and attachments are vigorous and outspoken in this new order of society. So are the unorganized antagonisms of individuals and families of these diverse classes, ethnic, professional, and regional sectors. Inequalities exist in mass society and they call forth at least as much resentment, if not more, than they ever did. Indeed, there is perhaps more awareness of the diversity of situation and the conflict of sectional aspirations in this society than in most societies of the past.

What is specific to this modern "mass society," with all its conflicts, is the establishment of consensually legitimate institutions within which much of this conflict takes place and which impose limits on this conflict. Parliaments, the system of representation of interests through pressure groups, systems of negotiation between employers and employees, are the novel ways of permitting and confining the conflict of interests and ideals characteristic of modern mass societies. These institutions, the very constitution of the mass society, can exist because a widespread consensus, particularly a consensus of the most active members of the society, legitimates them, and, more fundamentally, because a more general and more amorphous consensus of the less active imposes restraint on the more active when they might otherwise infringe on the constitution. This consensus grows in part from an attachment to the center, to the central institutional system and value order of the society. It is also a product of a newly emergent—at least on such a vast scale—feeling of unity with one's fellow men, particularly within the territorial boundaries of the modern societies.

Hence, despite all internal conflicts, bridging and confining them, there are, within the mass society, more of a sense of attachment to the society as a whole, more sense of affinity with one's fellows, more openness to understanding, and more reaching out of understanding among men, than in any earlier society of our Western history or in any of the great Oriental societies of the past. The mass society is not the most peaceful or "orderly" society that has ever existed; but it is the most consensual.

The maintenance of public peace through apathy and coercion in a structure of extremely discontinuous interaction is a rather different thing from its maintenance through consensus in a structure of a more continuous interaction between center and periphery and among various peripheral sectors. The greater activity of the periphery of the society, both in conflict and in consensus—especially in the latter—is what makes this a mass society. The historical uniqueness of the modern society, notably in its latterday phases, is the incorporation of the mass into the moral order of its society. The mass of the population is no longer merely an object which the elite takes into account as a reservoir of military and labor power or as a possible or actual source of public disorder. Nor does it any longer consist of a set of relatively discreet local societies occasionally in contact with the center under the impulsion of coercion and interest.

The center of society—the central institutions governed by the elites and the central value orders which guide and legitimate these institutions—has extended its boundaries. A center still exists and must always exist; and this entails an inevitable unevenness of the participation in the consensus formed around the center. It is, however, now an unevenness which slopes less steeply, so that most of the population—the "mass"—stand in a closer moral affinity and in a more frequent, even though mediated, interaction with the center than has been the case in either pre-modern societies or the earlier phases of modern society. The greater proximity to the center of society consists in a greater attachment to that center—to the institutions which constitute it and the values which are embodied in it. There is, accordingly, a greater feeling within the mass of being continuous with the center, of being part of it, and of its being a part of the same substance of which one is oneself formed.

This consensus has not, however, been unilaterally formed, and it is not sustained merely by the affirmation at the periphery of what emanates from the center, in which the mass has come to share the standards and beliefs of the elites. It consists also in the greater attachment of the center to the peripheral sectors of the society. The elites have changed as well as the masses. One feature of the mass society is that, at least to some extent and in various ways, the elites have come to share many of the objects of attention and fundamental standards which originate, or at least have their main support, in the mass. Of course, elite and mass are not indentical in their outlooks or tastes, but the mass means more to elites now than it did in other great societies. It has come to life in the minds of its rulers more vividly than ever before. This change has been brought about in part by the increased political, and then by the increased purchasing power of the mass; but, ultimately and profoundly, by the change in moral attitudes which has underlain the enhancement of the dignity of ordinary people. The enhanced dignity of the mass, the belief that, in one way or another, *vox populi, vox dei,* is the source of the mass society. Both elites and the masses have received this into their judgment of themselves and the world; and, although they believe in much else, and believe in this quite unequally, this maxim which locates the sacred in the mass of the population is the shaping force of the most recent development in society.

The sacredness of authority diminished with the dispersal of the sacred into the mass of the population. It is still an object of awe. Charisma is still attributed to it. The awe-inspiring, charismatic quality of authority can never be completely eradicated. Even in mass society, the charisma of the elite is alive, and not solely as a survival from an earlier epoch. It is simply given in the nature of power. The unique feature of the mass society is, however, the dispersion of charismatic quality more widely throughout the society, so that everyone who is a member of the society, because he is a member, comes to possess some of it.

This diminution in the status of authority is part of the same process which loosens the hold of traditional beliefs, especially those promulgated and espoused by hierarchical institutions. A society entirely without tradition is inconceivable. Traditions continue to exert their influence; but they are less overtly acknowledged, somewhat more ambiguous, and more open to divergent interpretations.

The diminished weight of primordiality, the greater concentration on the disposition of those residing at the moment on the bounded territory, means that the mass society is the society of the living, contemporaneous mass. It is almost as if society possessed a quantum of charisma, which, if it be attributed to the living, leaves little over for attribution to the ancestors. Since, however, no society can ever cut itself off from its past as a source of its own legitimacy, any more than its sensitivity to the primordial can ever evaporate completely, the traditional inheritance is adapted to the necessities of mass society by the diverse interpretations of rights which correspond to the vital heterogeneity of interests within the mass society itself.

The attenuation of traditional belief and of attachment to the past is accentuated by the less authoritative relationship of adults to children—which in itself is an outcome of the same moral shift which has enabled modern society to become a mass society. The dispersal of the charisma which confers dignity may be observed in the attitudes towards the working classes, women, youth, and ethnic groups that have hitherto been in a disadvantageous position. It is noticeable within families, in the rights of children, and within corporate bodies like factories, universities, and churches, in the rights of subordinates.

IV

This dispersion of charisma from the center outward has manifested itself in a greater stress on individual dignity and individual rights in all generations, in all strata, in both sexes, and in the whole variety of ethnic groups and peoples. This extension does not always reach equally into all spheres of life; and it does not equally embrace all sectors of the population. Inequalities remain, partly from tradition, partly from functional necessity, and partly from the fact that the movement toward equality is not the only fundamental impulse that moves men and women. Sadism, pride, interest, awe before the creative, still persist and limit the spread of equality.

Nonetheless, this consensus, which leans toward the interpretation of every living human being as a participant in the uniting essence which defines the society, has produced a wide distribution of civility. Civility is the virtue of the citizen, not the virtue of the hero or of the private man. It is the acceptance of the tasks of the management of public affairs in collaboration with others and with a regard to the interests, individual, sectional, and collective, of the entire society. The sense of responsibility for and to the whole, and a general acceptance of the rules which are valid within it, are integral to civility. Civil politics are the politics of effective compromise within an institutional system accepted as of inherent legitimacy. The idea of civility is not a modern creation; but it is in the mass society that it has found a more widely diffused, if still a deeply imperfect, realization. The very idea of a citizenry practically conterminous with the adult population living within far-flung territorial boundaries is a product of this extension of the "center," i.e., of the belief that charisma belongs in the mass as well as in the elite.

The moral equalitarianism which is such a unique trait of the West, in real practice, and not just as the dream of philosophers, is another manifestation of this expansion of the "center."[1]

1 In a society touched by moral equalitarianism, the possibility of a populistic inequalitarianism in which some become "more equal than others" is by no means remote. In American society, and possibly in Australia, which have gone farther in this direction than any other countries, and where populism is not merely a doctrine of the intellectuals but a belief and practice of the populace and its politicians, there is always some danger that a strong gust of populistic sentiment

The moral equality which has a tangible reality in mass societies is the equality which is a function of the sharing in membership in a community, by the sharing of the language in which the essence of the society is expressed. Those who share in this membership, as it is evinced by their share in the language, come to be regarded as sharing in the charismatic essence of the society and therewith may legitimately claim an irreducible dignity.

V

The mass society lifted the lid on impulse, hitherto held down by the hierarchy of authority, tradition and ancestry. The relocation of the charisma of the social order into one's ordinary, individual fellow man marches hand in hand with a redirection of sensitivity to disposition, to qualities lying within the individual. The civil disposition is only one such disposition. There is also the personal disposition which has been increasingly discovered in mass society. It is discovered in oneself and in others.

The personal dispositions, those qualities of rationality and impulsiveness, amiability and surliness, kindliness and harshness, lovingness and hatefulness are the constitution of the individual. Felt by himself, acknowledged by himself, coped with by himself, they are formed into his individuality. The perception and appreciation of individuality in others moves in unison with its development in the self.

Personal individuality and the sacredness of the individual in the civil order are not identical. Indeed, they are almost polar opposites; the latter is in a certain sense a denial of the former. It transcends personal individuality and suspends it. Nonetheless they both have grown from the lightening of pressure of the primordial and from the loosening of the rigor of a sacred order based on common belief, on a shared communion with divinity.

Individuality, personal relationships and love have not been discovered by mass society. They have been known in practically all cultures. It is, however, only in mass society that they have come to be regarded as part of the right order of life, and have come to be striven for and occasionally, however unstably, attained.

The mass society has gone further in the creation of a common culture than any previous society. Regional cultural variations have di-

---

can disrupt the civil order. Such was the situation during the years from 1947 to 1954, when the late Senator McCarthy stirred and was carried by the whirlpool of an extreme populism. But it never spread into the entire society; and, in the end, it broke on the rocks of Republican respectability. It remains a latent possibility, inherent in the ethos of mass society.

minished as well as those of class and profession and even those of generation. Yet this more widely extended uniformity, which for sheer repressive force might be no smaller or greater than the repression of the more local sectional cultures of the past, has been dialectically connected with the emergence of a greater individuality. The high evaluation of contemporaneity in mass society, the heavier stress on present enjoyment rather than on the obligation of respect towards tradition, involves necessarily an opening to experience. The diminished respect for the sacredness of authority has been accompanied by the shift of the center of gravity into the individual. Of course, as the critics of mass society often point out, this can result in a dull acceptance of what is readily available in the most visible models in the culture, and in fact it frequently does so, with the result that individuality in many instances is no better situated in mass society than it was in more hierarchical and traditional societies. Nonetheless, there has been a great change, not too different from that which Burckhardt perceived in the Renaissance. The individual organism has become a seeker after experience, a repository of experience, an imaginative elaborator of experience. To a greater extent than in the past, the experience of the ordinary person, at least in youth, is admitted to consciousness and comes to form part of the core of the individual's outlook. There has come about a greater openness to experience, an efflorescence and intensification of sensibility. There has been a transcendence of the primordially and authoritatively given, a movement outward towards experience, not only towards organic sensation, but towards the experience of other minds and personalities. It gives rise to and lives in *personal* attachment, it grows from the expansion of the empathic capacities of the human being.

In a crude, often grotesque way, the mass society has seen the growth, over wide areas of society, of an appreciation of the value of the experience of personal relationships, of the intrinsic value of a personal attachment, nowhere more than in the vicissitudes of love and marriage in modern society, with all its conflict and dissolution. Perhaps too much is demanded of the frail and unstable capacities of the organism for personal attachment, but the sensitivity and the striving are there. The talk about "human relations" in private and public administration might be largely cant and unthinking cliché, but not entirely. This is the age in which man has begun to live, to breathe with less congestion and to open his pores. The pleasures of eye and ear and taste and touch and conviviality have become values in larger sections of the population.

People make many choices in many spheres of life and do not have choices made for them simply by tradition, authority and scarcity. They enjoy some degree of freedom of choice, and they exercise that freedom in more spheres than in societies which are not mass societies. The choices are often unwise, and manifest an unrefined taste. They are often ill considered. But they are choices and not the dumb acceptance of what is given.

Prior to the emergence of modern mass society, the mass of the population lived in a primordial, traditional, hierarchical condition. All of these three properties of a society hamper the formation of individuality and restrict its movement once it is generated. The twin processes of civilization and industrialization have reduced some of these hindrances, and set loose the cognitive, appreciative and moral potential of the mass of the population.

I would not wish to have the foregoing observations interpreted to imply that the individuality which has flowered in mass society has been an unqualified moral and aesthetic success or that it is universally attained within the boundaries of mass society, or that there are not persons to whom it is not a value, nor am I unaware that in Germany the elite of the society went to the opposite extreme and that many of its members enthusiastically and brutally denied the value of individual human existence. A significant proportion of the population in every society lives in a nearly vegetative routine, withdrawn and unresponsive except for occasional patches of harsh aggressive expansiveness. In the mass society of the present century, the proportion seems smaller, the period of sensitivity in the individual's course of life longer.

Personal relations, friendship and love, are beset by vicissitudes and frequently culminate in painful disruption; sensibility and curiosity are often perverse and injurious. Privacy is frequently affronted and transgressed and frequently indiscriminately renounced. In certain sections of the population, the discovery of the possibility and pleasures of sensation have been carried to the far reaches of a negative withdrawal from society and of an often active rejection. In others, it releases an egoistic hedonism, an individual expansiveness which leaves nothing available to the civil sphere, and the consensus which it requires.

Some of these are as much the products of man's nature amidst the possibilities of mass society as are the heightened individuality, curiosity and sensibility, the enhanced capacity for experience, conviviality and affection which are its novel contributions. They are the price which is paid for entering into the opening of human potentialities on a massive scale.

VI

The mass society is a welfare society. As a function of a greater attachment to the whole society and the strengthening of the sense of affinity which cuts across class, ethnic and kinship boundaries, there has grown the concern for the well-being of others. Christianity as a body of specific beliefs might have faded from men's minds—although probably not as much as the *laudator temporis acti* insists—but the sentiment embodied in the ideas of Christian charity and Christian love has expanded and spread. These are now a part of the constitution of mass society—in the allegedly "secular state." Material help and emotional sympathy may be claimed without specific payment or counter-performance. Regardless of whether the economic regime is nominally socialistic or capitalistic, and whether the ruling political party regards itself as socialist or "bourgeois," it is commonly acknowledged that at least at the lower levels of the social and economic scale, there need not be any commensurate relationship between specific performance and reward. In the corporate bodies which conduct the main industrial and commercial activities of the mass society, trade union principles and the practices of personnel management have eroded the standard that rewards must be precisely correlated to specific performances in a role. This process, like the other processes which characterize mass society, has its limitations. It comes into conflict with the exigencies of operation of any large scale undertaking which require impersonal administration in accordance with reasonably explicit and differentiated rules. The requirement of a modicum of efficiency and of justice too require a measure of specificity in the standards which govern the allocation of opportunity for access to many occupational roles. It requires also a fixation of the rules governing rights and obligations in the society at large and within particular corporate bodies.

VII

Mass society is an industrial society. Without industry, i.e., without the replacement of simple tools by complicated machines, mass society would be intellectually inconceivable and actually impossible. Modern industrial technique through its creation of an elaborate network of transportation and communication has rendered it possible for the various parts of mass society to have a frequency of contact with each other that is unknown to earlier, non-industrial societies. The different social classes and regional sectors of a society can become more aware of each other's modes of life. This heightened mutual awareness, impossible without the modern technology of communication and transportation, has enlarged the internal population which dwells in the minds of men.

Modern industrial technique makes possible and requires the proliferation of the intellectual professions. It has produced the education which, numerous though its deficiencies might be, has, through reading and instruction, opened the mind to the varieties of experience of other human beings. It has liberated men from the burden of physically exhausting labor; it has given him a part of each day and week free from the discipline and strain of labor and it has given him resources through which new experiences of sensation, expansion into conviviality and interior elaboration have become realities.

Mass society has witnessed a reinterpretation of the value of a human being. Simply by virtue of his quality of membership in the society he acquires a minimal dignity.

The elevation of the *qualities* of humanity and of membership in a wider, territorially circumscribed community to a position in which they markedly determine the status and rights of individuals, groups and classes, has led to a diminution of the importance of individual *achievement* as a standard for the direction of ones' actions and as a criterion of status. The increased value of experience, of pleasurable experience, most easily obtainable in mass society through the cultivation of a style of life, has had a parallel effect. The *quality* of life has tended—the nature of man would never allow it wholly to succeed—to replace occupational role and proficiency as a source of self-esteem and as a criterion for esteeming others.

This produces a grandiose historical paradox. Mass society, which has been made possible by technological and economic progress, which in turn has been impelled by the desire for achievement, for the proficient performance of a role, contributes towards a situation in which occupational role and achievement have become less important in the guidance of action and in the claiming and acknowledgment of status.

A large-scale society requires large-scale bureaucratic administration. Its well-being depends on technological progress. Both of these depend on the wide distribution in the population of individuals capable of acting in the light of impersonal, universalistic standards, capable of performing specific and specialized tasks, capable of discipline. All of these are alien to the characteristic ethos of mass society. The disjunction can only make for an incessant tension of the mass of the population, and in many personalities, towards the value-orientations required by the type of society to which contemporary men are commited by the circumstances of their birth and their own desires.

VIII

The mass society is a large-scale society. It involves populations running into the millions and hundreds of millions and it covers large territories. It is therefore inevitably a differentiated society, differentiated in function, outlook and attachments. The complete homogeneity which the critics of mass society perceive is an impossibility. There is, of course, perhaps a greater homogeneity than in the much less loosely integrated societies of the past—this is given in the fact of the greater consensuality, the greater sense of unity, the speaking of a common language. There are, however, real although probably undeterminable, limits to the homogeneity which any large-scale society can sustain. Similar limits are imposed on the consensuality of the society, even if it had not inherited such a variety of cultural traditions, of class-orientations and religious beliefs.

IX

The picture which I have given here will immediately strike any moderately informed person as widely at variance with the image of the mass society which has been set going by the creators and the patrons of that term. They have stressed alienation, belieflessness, atomization, amorality, conformity, rootless homogeneity, moral emptiness, facelessness, egotism, the utter evaporation of any kind of loyalty (except occasionally the passionately zealous attachment to an ideological movement). They point to the indiscipline of youth and the neglect of the aged; they allege a frivolous hedonism and a joyless vulgarity. There is a little truth in these assertions but not very much. All of the phenomena referred to do exist in modern mass societies but a great deal more exists. Some of the features to which the critics of "mass society" point are closely connected with these others which I have emphasized. The alienation so often mentioned is an extreme form of the denial of the sacredness (*Entzauberung*) of authority. The unchecked egotism and frivolous hedonism are associated with the growth of individual sensibility, the indiscipline of youth is a product of the lightening of the force of the primordial and the diminished pressure of hierarchy. The narrowing of the scope of local autonomy is connected with the formation of a more integral society. The apathy, which so many notice, is brought to the forefront of attention as a result of the greatly extended opportunity for judgment and sharing in the exercise of decision which mass society offers. The vulgarity is one of the manifestations of the expansion of sensibility which replaces the long prevailing torpor of much of the race.

The consensuality of mass society, the closer approximation of center and periphery, the greater moral equality of the various strata and sectors, the growth of sensibility and individuality are all, as I have said, imperfect. Their imperfection comes from the inherent impossibility for any large-scale society to attain perfection in those caegories, or of any society to attain perfection in any category. The imperfections of mass society are in part a result of the distribution of moral qualities in human beings. In part they come from the nature of mass society as such and its inheritance from the past of mankind.

Mass society has arisen from an inegalitarian, pluralistic society— pluralistic out of the separateness of the classes, the isolation of localities from each other and in modern times, the very principle of organization of society. It has arisen against a background of puritanical authority which, whatever its own practices, viewed with disapproval the pleasures of the mass of the population and of all that seemed to distract them from their twin obligations of labour and obedience. The proletariat of these past societies, except for a few skilled occupations, with elaborate traditions of their own, were a poor besotted lot: the peasantry were clods, sometimes woodenly pious, sometimes simply woodenly dull. In so far as they had loyalties, they were strictly local. There is practically no history of civility in the lower classes of premodern societies and it appears only fitfully, albeit impressively, among the highest level of the artisan stratum in the 19th century.

The emancipation of the hitherto disadvantaged classes from the burdensome moral traditions and the sheer poverty and heavy labor which confined the development of their emotional and moral poten-tialities let loose, together with the more positive striving for experience and pleasure, a hitherto suppressed antiauthoritarian aggressiveness. The transfer of a certain amount of libido from kinship, class and ethnic groups to the larger community has not been a readily encom-passable task. In many cases, the old loyalties have fallen away and the larger loyalty has not replaced them. It is quite possible that many human beings lack the capacity to sustain a loyalty to such remote symbols and they are, in consequence, left suspended in apathy and dissatisfaction between narrower loyalties no longer effective—and they probably were never very effective for most—and broader loyalties not yet effective—and perhaps never to become effective for all.

None of these conditions has been very conducive to the realization of a fully civil, cultivated, consensual, more egalitarian society—quite apart from ineluctable functional constraints.

X

Can it ever be fully realized? Can mass society move forward to the fulfilment of the possibilities which have been opened by technological progress and the moral transmutation arising from the shift in the locus of charisma?

There are very stringent limitations. There are limitations which the trend towards moral equality must encounter because the propensities which impel men to seek and acknowledge some measure of fundamental moral equality are neither deeper nor more enduring than those which demand and produce moral inequality. A large-scale society will necessarily be regionally differentiated and this will entail differences in interests and loyalties. The natural differences in intellectual capacities and in temperament will inevitably make for differences in assimilation of the central value system. Occupational differences will sustain different streams of cultural tradition, different orientations to the principle of achievement and different relationships to the authorities at the heart of the central institutional system. And naturally, the differences of age and the culture of the various generations will also be a source of fissure. These differences are all anchored in "objective" differences, inevitably associated with the human lot in general or with the unavoidable conditions of any large-scale industrial society. They are objective differences on which the dispositions towards evaluative discrimination will always seize. Then, too, there is not only the need for communion. There is the need for separation and distance—collective as well as individual—which will create, in any society, lines of fissure in the surface of union and in the sense of moral equality which attends it.

For the same reasons, the full realization of a common culture is an impossibility. The growth of individuality is another obstacle which stands in the way of an all-comprehending growth of a common culture. The growth of individuality too has its limits imposed in part by the other features of mass society and, in part by the wide range of dispersion among human beings of the intensity of need and capacity for individuality.

Finally, the propensities which have been released and cultivated by the mass society are not harmonious with the concurrent necessity of a complex division of labor, with many occupational and professional roles, some of which are highly creative and others quite routine, some of which will be highly remunerated, others less so. Equality of status will not grow from these occupational and income differences. Some of these occupations will call for and nurture dispositions which are contrary to the diffusely equalitarian, consensual, hedonistic, effective, humanitarian tendencies inherent in mass society. The dispositions to primordial attachment will also persist—kinship, and its ethnic sublimation, locality, sexuality—might be further transmuted in mass society but they can never be eradicated. They will continue to be at war with the elements which constitute mass society and with those required for a large-scale society. Thus there is likely always to be tension among these diverse sets of elements, which are so dependent on each other. Each will limit the expansion of the others and contend against them and will prevent the society from ever becoming wholly a mass society. But the tension will never be able to prevent these properties of the mass society from finding a grandiose expression.

The potentiality for the mass society has always lain within the human soul. It could only find its opportunity for realization in the peculiar conjunction of spiritual, political and technological events which are at the basis of modern society. It comes into realization in an age when the human race is for the first time in its history in considerable prospect of extinction at its own hands, and that, as the result of skills which were essential to the ideals of the Enlightenment and to the genesis of mass society. Yet, even if the race were to end, the philosophers of the Enlightenment, if they could pass judgment, or their heirs who might be born in a new beginning, would have to admit that their ideals had not been vainly espoused and that the human race, on behalf of which their thought, had not ended before many of their deepest ideals had come close to attainment.

Anthony Burgess
Beds in the East

The river was broad and silver, and the sunlight was merry on it. But to port and starboard jungle exerted an influence more powerful than the sun, its smell as strong as the smell of warmed wood in the boat or of the sun-warmed river. And it was finally to the jungle-gods that the Malays would be most faithful. The sun of Islam, disguising itself cunningly as a sickle moon, was appropriate only to the clearings, which meant the towns with their refrigerators and mosques, where the muezzin's call mingled well with the music of the bars. Now the towns were beginning to entertain their vain dream of realized independence—the bright fresh paint for the visitors, the new stadium and the luxury hotel. Some Arab theologian-philosopher had said that Islam decayed in the towns. Only when the decay of Islam brought the decay of the cities, when the desert, with its frail tented communities, reasserted itself, only then could the faith be renewed. But there was no desert here, no dominion of sun and oasis. There was nothing to believe in except the jungle. That was home, that was reality. Crabbe gazed in a kind of horror mixed with peace at the endless vista of soaring trunks, lianas, garish flowers. They were chugging towards the *hulu*, the head or fount of everything, where there was no pretence or deception.

Settled to the river life, the transiently permanent, a fragile community was possible. The Chinese assistant manager spoke, with a wide smile of insincere teeth, to Crabbe, asking: "Did you have the bad luck to fall down when you were drunk, Mr. Crabbe?" It was not an insolent question, it was Chinese and clinical. The Tamil hospital dresser bubbled away, showing teeth as good: "The monsoon drains are very treacherous. It is possible to break a leg when one is not walking straight." They smiled and smiled, waiting for confirmation.

"I was struck by a scorpion," said Crabbe, "when I was perfectly sober." There was polite laughter of sixty-four teeth. "I am now

Clubfoot the Tyrant." The teeth disappeared in sympathy. "But I didn't kill my father and I didn't marry my mother."

"Marry your mother," laughed the Chinese. "That is very good."

"Marry my mother," suddenly said Vythilingam. Those were his first words of the voyage, and they were spoken with unstuttered labials. He provoked a fresh silence. "Kill my father," he added, for good measure.

"The Japanese killed my father," smiled the Chinese. "They poured petrol on him and then threw a lighted match." He laughed modestly. "They made me watch. They were not very good people."

"History," said Crabbe, battering his pain with words at random. "The best thing to do is to put all that in books and forget about it. A book is a kind of lavatory. We've got to throw up the past, otherwise we can't live in the present. The past has got to be killed." But, in saying that, off his guard with the pain in his foot, he reverted to his own past, and pronounced the very word in the Northern style, the style of his childhood.

"Excuse me," said the Tamil dresser. "To which pest do you refer? Surely all pests have to be killed? I do not quite understand the drift of your statement."

"It was only talk," said Crabbe. "It didn't mean anything."

And now the colour changed to brown, the soft brown of Malay, for one of the Malays of undefined occupation spoke, sitting on a bench by the gunwale, his brown arm stretched out, gripping the boat's side. "Allah," he said, "disposes all things. The tea-cup I broke as a child, and the lottery my father failed to win by only one number. That was only two years after I broke the tea-cup. I blamed the breaking of the tea-cup on my younger brother, and this, as it turned out, was not unjust, for four years later, two years after my father failed to win the lottery, he broke a tea-cup on his own account. Then we had more tea-cups than formerly, and my mother was never very clever at counting. So he escaped punishment, which in a sense was just, for he had already been wrongly punished." He now gave an exhibition of Malay teeth, bits of gold glinting in the sun and river, teeth not so good as the others' teeth.

"But the lottery ticket," said the Tamil in Malay. "I am not able to see the drift."

"Allah disposes all things," repeated the Malay, his teeth hidden in solemnity. "If my father had been predestined to win he would have won. It was of no use for him to prate about injustice." He smiled around and then closed up his mouth for the rest of the voyage, leaving his boat-mates with much to think about. The broken tea-cup tinkled in their brains and the number by which this man's father had failed to win glowed dimly and faded. Meanwhile the river narrowed somewhat, and the green bodies and arms and legs of the twin jungles shambled nearer.

"But, despite your father's failure to become rich," said the Chinese assistant manager, "you still had more tea-cups than you could count."

The Malay nodded, smiling, saying nothing. Ahead, on the starboard side, the jungle began to thin out to scrub, and then came a regular forest of rubber trees. Crabbe remembered an English politician of a mystical frame of mind who, having spent two days in Malaya, wrote in a Sunday paper that the very jungles were symmetrical, neat as the trim garden of British rule. Crabbe thought of many other palm-beach-suited visitors who, through pink mists of hospitable whisky, had mistaken Malays for Chinese, mosques for Anglican churches, plantations for jungles, neat dishes of canapés for calm and happy order. But at the *hulu* or head of the river the two halves of the jungle joined up and became one, and there there was no mistaking one thing for another. The jungle called "OM," like the Malay showman of the shadow-play, one and indivisible, ultimate numen.

The launch moved into the landing-stage of Rambutan Estate, and here the Chinese and the Tamil disembarked, with smiles and waves. Beyond was a pleasance of lawn, a company bungalow magnificent in shining glass, beyond again the rubber and the coolie lines. The launch moved out to mid-river, Crabbe and Vythilingam silent, the Malays silent with cigarettes, the boatmen chattering. Next stop was Durian Estate.

After a mile of further narrowing river Crabbe celebrated the slight easing of his pain by saying a few polite words to Vythilingam, asking him why he was going to the up-river plantation. Vythilingam jerked out, with throbbing larnyx, the one word: "Beasts."

"To examine the cattle?" Vythilingam did not nod; Crabbe said: "I'm going to see the family of this Tamil schoolmaster who was murdered. Perhaps you know him. He ran the estate school."

Vythilingam turned to look at Crabbe, nodding that he thought he knew the man. He uttered the name "Yogam." He added: "Not a good man. A drunkard."

"He'll never drink again."

Vythilingam said nothing more. It was not long before they arrived at the final river outpost of industry and civilization. Here were even wider lawns than at Rambutan Estate, with Tamil gardeners at work with hoses on flowerbeds. The planter's house was no mere bungalow. It stood on high pillars, shading under its belly an armoured car for running round the many square miles of rubber, and soaring up in two storeys to a roof garden with striped umbrellas. Here the lonely manager had to drink desperately of whatever solace boat could bring and private power-station could drive. For few now would risk the holiday trip to huge curry tiffins, gin parties with dancing, moonlight swimming in the pool that stood, its water changed daily, surrounded by banyan and rain tree, bougainvillea and hibiscus, before the proud manor house. It was a nail-biting life for the exile, soothed inadequately by the hum of his refrigerators, the roar of his many fans, the high fidelity tone of his record-player. He drank much before dinner, and the dinner with its many courses appeared in the early hours of the morning, the fish and the mutton dried up, the tired cook forgetting about the coffee. Coombes, thought Crabbe, poor Coombes, despite his many thousands in the bank, the welcome of plush chairs and cigars on his rare trips to the London office.

The Malays smilingly helped Crabbe ashore, leaving him with his stick and his bag while they strolled off, waving, to their lines. Vythilingam stood hesitant, his black bag of medicine and instruments swinging in his right hand, smiling nervously, saying at length: "The cattle. Cancerous growths on the cattle."

"You'd better come and see Coombes first," said Crabbe, "and have a drink or something." Vythilingam shook his head. "My duty," he said without stuttering. Then he went off in the direction of the labourers' houses, the self-contained world of village shop, cows and chickens, school and first-aid post. Alone, Crabbe walked painfully towards the house, a long stretch from the riverside, hearing the boat throbbing finally, then the click-off of the engine as it was moored against the later afternoon's return journey.

As Crabbe approached the outer stairs of the house a man appeared in the doorway. He called: "Hello, hello, hello" in heavy welcome and then athletically began to run down the wooden steps. He was a stranger to Crabbe, and Crabbe said: "I was looking for Mr. Coombes."

"Just a day too late, old boy," said the man. "Here you *are* in a bad way, aren't you? Let me give you a helping hand." He was a big chubby man, in his middle thirties, the muscle of his rugger days now settling placidly to reminiscent fat. He was not unhandsome. He had dark polished hair, a moustache, a plummy patrician voice, fine fat brown dimpled knees between blue shorts and football stockings. His shirt was of checked cotton, and within it a loose stomach and fleshy breasts bounced gently.

"You're the education chap," he said, as he steered Crabbe strongly up the steps. He laughed, the loud laugh of rugger dinners. "There's a telegram about you inside. Coombes left it for me. Something about this chap getting murdered. But I don't see what you can do."

"It's quite usual," said Crabbe, as they reached the top of the steps and stood before the large open doorway among potted plants. "Condolences for the widow, find out what really happened for the records, assure her that she'll get a widow's and orphans' pension. We don't know how many orphans there are." He panted, standing there, waiting to be asked in.

"This telegram," said the man. He picked it up from the hall table. The hall was wide, magnificent with inlays of imported oak, heads of African beasts on the walls, flowers, a suite of rattan furniture. "It says: 'Murder regretted. Am sending my assistant as I must stay in the office.' And it's signed Something bin Somebody. Never could read these Malay names. Tamil's my language." He laughed again, plummily. "Sounds as though he'd committed the murder himself. Well, come inside, Mr. Assistant. Damn cheek of that bloke calling you his assistant. You give him hell when you get back."

"It's true in a way, you know," said Crabbe. They went slowly, Crabbe limping, into the vast drawing-room. "I *am* an assistant. I'm assisting this chap to take over my job." The drawing-room seemed an acre of polished floorboards, with complete units for sitting or lounging— drink-table, settee, arm-chairs—placed at intervals along the walls, by the windows that looked down at river and jungle beyond, in the body of the echoing room. It was monstrous and pathetic, this lavishness, a child's tongue put out at the great green giant. On the walls were square patches unfaded by sun, where pictures had been and would be again. On the floor were treasures of this new man—gramophone records, books, papers, group photographs of rugger clubs—half unpacked. A radio-gramophone stood in the middle of the floor, a voice in the wilderness at present silent, though it was already plugged into a light socket high above. "Where," asked Crabbe, "is Coombes?"

"He's been moved. Apparently this place has been getting on his nerves." The man made a swigging motion and winked. "He's gone to a place in Johore. Demotion really. And this is promotion for me." He looked round with satisfaction at the vast anonymous room. "I was in Negri Duabelas," he said. "I ran the Union Jack Society in Timbang. And a music club. I wasn't so isolated there as I'm going to be here. But I don't mind isolation. I've got my records and my books. I read a lot of poetry. My name's George Costard. I don't think I quite caught yours."

Crabbe thought for an instant and then said: "Victor." If this man read poetry it was just possible he might have read some of Fenella's. After all, Crabbe was his name before it was hers; why should she usurp it and make it well known on her own behalf? "Victor," he said.

"So you're Mr. Victor," said Costard, "assistant to Whoisit bin Whatshisname. Sit down, Victor, and take a load off that foot. You been playing soccer in your bare feet or something? I never did care for soccer. I'll get some beer from the fridge." He went off, briskly walking the half-mile or so to the kitchen, and then called a Tamil name and Tamil orders. He walked the half-mile back again, saying: "I've asked Tambi to bring a large bottle every twenty minutes. Is that all right with you? It saves the trouble of going to the kitchen and shouting. This is a hell of a big place." He sat down, one big bare knee over the other, and looked at Crabbe complacently. "Music," he said. "Do you care for music?" Crabbe said he did. The Tamil boy came with beer. "Watch this," said Costard with pride. "This lad can do anything." He gave Tamil orders and the Tamil boy, lean, black, sly-looking, took a random pile of thick smeared records (old style: seventy-eight revolutions per minute) and carried them over to the radio-gramophone. With practised skill he set the machine working: the first of the skewered pile submitted to the needle and, through loud scratch noises, the opening theme of Beethoven's Ninth Symphony began to emerge. "I like it that way," said Costard. "I never know what I'm going to get. After this you'll probably get a bit of Schubert or Brahms or a Hebridean folksong. I just leave it to him. I've got catholic tastes. Catholic with a small "c," of course. The family's always been Church of England. There was an Archbishop George Costard in the eighteenth century. You may have heard of him."

Crabbe settled as comfortably as he could with his beer. "Here we go again," he thought. "Drink and reminiscence. Another day of wasted time. They're right when they say we drink too much out here. And we slobber too much over ourselves. 'Did you ever hear how I came out here? It's rather an interesting story, really. Have another drink and I'll tell you about it.' We're all sorry for ourselves because we're not big executives or artists or happily married men in a civilized temperate climate." Crabbe noted that the pain in his foot was going, to be followed by a numbness as though the foot were not really there.

"Some people make fun of the name," said Costard. "Ignorant people. Although at school I didn't suffer too much because most of the kids had heard of Custer's last stand. I don't think he'd anything to do with our family, though. I think the two names are different in origin. Costard means an apple, you know."

Over in a flash, Beethoven's first theme having been just about stated, the record was replaced mechanically by part of the music for King George VI's Coronation, Parry's "I was glad when they said unto me." Costard said happily: "You just never know what you're going to get." Crabbe was glad Costard said that to him, changing the subject, for, off his guard, he had very nearly begun to say that his own name meant a kind of apple. "Have a cigarette, Victor," said Costard. The table was full of half-empty Capstan tins, and Crabbe helped himself. Again off his guard, warmed by the sound of his Christian name, he said automatically: "Thank you, George." Then he blushed.

"Funny," said Costard. "You're a Christian name man. I shouldn't have thought that. I've never found it easy to call a man by his Christian name, except my brothers, of course. It's public school training, I suppose." He looked at Crabbe suspiciously. "What was your school, if I may ask?"

"You wouldn't know it," said Crabbe. "It was a rather obscure grammar school in the north of England."

"You a 'Varsity man?"

"Oh yes," and he named his red-brick university.

"Oxford, me," said Costard. "The House. I took a first in Greats. You wouldn't think that to look at me, would you? Perhaps you wonder why I came out here at all. It's rather an interesting story, really. Look," he said urgently, "twenty minutes is nearly up, and you haven't finished your beer. That boy of mine's a walking clock." He examined his watch narrowly. "One minute to go. Time." Sure enough, the Tamil boy smugly reappeared, bearing another large bottle. And then Parry's anthem finished triumphantly. There was the muffled fall of a new record, a click, and the sound of Schubert's "Trout" Quintet, half-buried under surface noise, swam sweetly forth. "We ought to have bets on it," suggested Costard. "I bet you five dollars the next record will be more Beethoven."

"I can't bet," said Crabbe. "I just don't know what records you've got."

"No more do I," said Costard cheerfully. "That's the fun of it. Some of these records down there on the floor—why, I haven't seen them for years. When we were packing up to leave Negri Duabelas my boy discovered stacks of them in the place under the stairs where I kept the Christmas decorations. What time would you like lunch?"

"Any time that suits you," said Crabbe.

"I thought you'd say that. I normally have lunch about four. Dinner at any time after midnight. Except when I have lady guests. You must stay for dinner."

"I really ought to go and see this woman," said Crabbe. "And then get back."

"Nonsense," said Costard warmly. "It's a real stroke of luck, you dropping in like this. You can tell me the set-up in this state, and who the important people are, and what the local Cold Storage is like. And I can tell you my story, which is pretty interesting, really."

"But I really came down to see this woman," said Crabbe.

"You can't speak Tamil, can you? No. Well, I can. I'll get the dope from her and send it on in an official letter. And I don't suppose you can walk very far with that foot of yours."

"It's not painful now. It's just a bit numb."

"Ah. Well, when I left Oxford, I wondered for a long time what to do. The family has money, of course, so there was no immediate urgency. Yes, I know what you're thinking. You want to know why I didn't go straight into the army. But, you see, I joined up in my first year at Oxford, and finished my degree after the war. Were you in the Forces, by any chance?"

"Army."

"What rank?" Crabbe told him. "I," said Costard, "didn't do too badly, all things considered. Captain at twenty-one isn't too bad, is it? No. I wasn't all that heroic, though they were good enough to mention me in dispatches. Anyway, after the war, I went back to Oxford and did pretty well, on the whole. A first in Greats and a Rugger Blue. Soccer's your game, I take it?"

"No."

"Ah," beamed Costard, as the record changed. "What did I tell you? Beethoven. That's the Hammerklavier. I knew a girl who played that marvellously. A fragile little thing, to look at, but the strength in those wrists." His face grew dark. "Poor, poor girl. Poor, poor, poor little thing. But I'll come to her in due course. She's part of the story."

"Not if it makes you sad," said Crabbe.

"Oh, it's life. We all get over these things. We've got to, else life just couldn't go on. But she meant a lot, a hell of a lot. Perhaps, really, I'd better not speak about her. I mean, to a stranger. And I'm used to keeping it bottled up. There was never really anybody I could tell. I just couldn't. My mother was always strait-laced. Don't get me wrong; I abore her, but there were some things she could never understand." He sighed. "Adultery." He sighed again. "That's a hard word. And yet it never seemed as though we were doing wrong. I don't know why I'm telling you these things. It seemed rather as though her marriage was all wrong. He was to blame, not us."

"On the whole," said Crabbe in swift embarrassment, "this isn't too bad a state to be in. The Sultan's go-ahead, modern in some of his views. There aren't so many British left now, of course, and the British Adviser's gone. But if you're a club man you'll find plenty of Asians to drink with, and there's even a sort of Rugger Club."

"What do you mean—'sort of'?"

"They don't find it easy to get anybody to play with. They just meet and drink beer and sing songs. But they talk about rugger: most of them were educated in England."

"Asians, you say?" Costard looked darkly. "No," he said. "That's not really my line. The Asians are all right in their place, I suppose, but I don't think they ought to do that sort of thing. After all, it is an English game. And you mean to say that they sing, 'If I were a marrying maid which thank the Lord I'm not, sir'? That's a kind of desecration. Oh, I know you'll probably think me stupidly conservative, and all that sort of rot, but that's the way I was brought up. I can't help it." The record changed. They were now treated to Clara Butt singing "Land of Hope and Glory." She sang through a thick mist of scratches. Costard began to swing his beer-mug gently in time. Then he looked at his watch. "I say," he said, "you *are* slow. Tambi will be here in . . ." He computed carefully. ". . . in exactly twenty seconds." And, lo, Tambi appeared at that very moment. "He's a bit too early," said Costard. "Still, it's a fault on the right side. I'm always punctual to a fault, personally. It's a family tradition. The old man used to knock hell out of me if I was ever late for anything. He was right, I see that now. I've always insisted on punctuality in my own underlings. It's no good their saying they haven't got watches or their watches stopped or something. Where there's a will there's a way." Beer was poured for Costard and his guest. His feet flapping gently on the parquet, Tambi returned to his kitchen. There was a silent space, during which Dame Clara Butt, with brass behind her, was able to boom her climax to two conventionally grave, lonely, moved, head-drooping exiles. The Edwardian expansionist prayer came to an end. "I suppose I am a bit old-fashioned, really," admitted Costard. "But I'm enough of a realist to know that those days are over. The Empire's cracking up, they say. Well, some of us must keep the traditions alive. That's the meaning of Conservatism, as I see it. Some of us have got to conserve."

"But you're not an Empire-builder," said Crabbe. "You're a rubber-planter. You're a commercial man." A new record started—a dance of clean dainty shepherdesses by Edward German. Costard looked at Crabbe with beetled brows and a pout of distaste.

"That's where you're wrong," he said. "Do you think the money matters to me? I'm in this game to keep something alive that's very, very beautiful. The feudal tradition, the enlightened patriarchal principle. You people have been throwing it all away, educating them to revolt against us. They won't be happy, any of them. It's only on the estates now that the old ideas can be preserved. I'm the father of these people. They can look up to me, bring me their troubles and let me participate in their joys. Don't you think that's good and beautiful? They're my children, all of them. I correct them, I cherish them, I show them the way that they should go. Of course, you could say that it's more than just an ideological matter with me. I suppose I'm really the paternal type." He looked it, big and dark and comely, his large knees comfortable stools for climbing brats lisping "Daddy."

"And yet you've never married," said Crabbe. "You've no children of your own."

"How about you?"

"Oh yes, married. No children, though. But I've been a school-master for a long time. That's satisfied and finally cured any paternal instinct in me." The Tamil boy had entered again, without a tray. Crabbe said: "Something's gone wrong with your human clock."

Costard smiled with infinite complacency. "That boy's marvellous. He's counted the number of records. Now he's going to change them." And indeed the boy lifted the pile of worn discs tenderly from the turn table and, at random, picked up a new pile—dusty twelve inchers. And now for some reason Crabbe felt a strange uneasiness in his stomach.

"Good," said Costard, settling himself anew, listening to a boy soprano of the nineteen-thirties singing "Oh, for the wings of a dove." Crabbe's uneasiness passed: it was pure breakfastlessness, he decided, hearing a comforting rumble from the pit. Costard insisted on silence for the creamy Mendelssohn. And then, as the march from *Aida* struck up— Sunday school outing trumpets and a smell of orange-peel—he big-drummed the air with his fist, lalling the square tune vigorously. "Come on," he paused to invite, "join in. Grand stuff, this." Crabbe smiled with the corners of his lips, and then sought an alibi in his tankard. "Good man," said Costard. "You couldn't have timed that better." For there again was Tambi with beer. . . .

. . . .

Independence achieved and celebrated, everybody went back to work. "Many people," said the Chinese leader-writer in the *Singapore Bugle,* "many people seem to consider independence is licensed irresponsibility. Nothing could be further from the truth. We must all, the Malays especially, put our shoulders to the wheel and prove ourselves worthy of the great gift of freedom and self-determination. The clerks in the offices, the coolies on the rubber estates, tin-miners, fisher-folk and paddy-planters, have had their brief hour of rejoicing and now must buckle down to the hard tasks ahead. There have been too many false promises made by politicians to ignorant members of the *ra'ayat,* promises about there being no further need to work once the British disgorged the wealth they had stolen from the sons of the soil. Now perhaps those promises are being seen for what they are—mere straws and bubbles in the wind of self-advancement." And so on. But few people read the leaders. Nobody worked any harder, though few worked (which a cynic might allege to be impossible) less hard.

But the Communists in the jungle buckled to and put their shoulders to the wheel. Independence meant little: the capitalists had been at their tricks again. In at least one state the Communists redoubled their attacks on villages, their ambushings of motorists, their decapitations and guttings of the jackals of the rubber-sucking white parasites, and sometimes of the parasites themselves. It was grossly unfair to suggest, however, as Syed Omar once suggested, that this was because Vythilingam had gone over to the rebels. But the independent Government of the Federation of Malaya acted promptly. "Il faut en finir," said a Malay minister. So into at least one state troops poured, a battalion of decent National Service lads, to continue to carry, posthumously as it must be supposed, the White Man's Burden. The more subtle warfare of ideas was carried on by the Information Department and by certain American organizations which did heroic—and voluntary—work. There was more to it than just ideas, of course. The library of the United States Information Service contained plenty of good clean non-ideological books, in Chinese, English, and Malay, and—better still—provided an air-conditioned refuge from the day's heat, much appreciated by workless illiterates.

. . . .

One evening Syed Hassan and Idris and Azman and Hamzah were sitting in Loo's shop. All wore a costume suggestive of a more tranquil and prosperous age than this—Dame Clara Butt singing, in a voice not quite so deep as Arumugam's, "Land of Hope and Glory," the gold squeezed from tropical helots enhancing the upper-class comforts of a cold climate. Their costumes were not suitable for Malayan heat, but they were stoics prepared to suffer for smartness and conformity. To their interest and joy three soldiers of the Royal Barsets came in, and they were wearing this idential uniform of drainpipe trousers and serge waisted jacket and bootlace tie.

They strutted to the bar, bringing their plentiful back-hair behind them. "Here, John," said one of the newcomers to Robert Loo. "Give us three beers." Robert Loo looked up distractedly from his music. "And stand to attention when a corporal's talkin' to yer," added the man jocularly. This disguised corporal then turned lordly to survey the other customers and caught sight of Syed Hassan and his friends. "Cor," he said. "Teds 'ere too. Oo'd 'ave thought we'd meet nigger Teds?" He greeted the four Malay boys cordially and, without invitation, brought his fresh-faced party of two to their table. "More chairs, John," he called to one of Robert Loo's brothers. "We're goin'ter sit 'ere."

"What is a Ted?" asked Hamzah shyly.

"Speak English, do yer? A Ted's what you are. Teds is what we are. Teddy boys. Edwardian strutters was what they used to call 'em in the old days. Cor, flamin' 'ot in 'ere. Turn up that fan, John, will yer?"

"Why do they call you that?" asked Hassan. He found difficulty in following much of the corporal's English, but, not doubting that this was *echt* English, began to feel resentment towards those English masters of his who had taught him English. It was colonial English they had taught him, that was it. But he would soon learn this new, free, democratic English.

"Why? Because we go back to the good old days, see, when there was none of the bleedin' nonsense. No wars and what not. Beer a penny a gallon and all that. Bleedin' sight more than that 'ere. 'Ere, gizza bit er music, John. What you lads goin' to 'ave?"

The Malay boys now drank beer for the first time in their lives. It was itself, as Crabbe had once said, a language. Robert Loo, at his father's behest, gave the new customers a free gift of juke-box music. He himself listened to the brave harmonics of saxophones and brass, the sedative drum-beat, not without a minimal physical tingling. Syed Hassan winked at him; he winked back—stiffly, however, not being used to such social gestures.

But there now started a sodality that was to prove more fruitful in promoting inter-racial harmony than any of Crabbe's vague dreams. Wandering down the street one night, the seven of them, they came across a Tamil youth in Edwardian costume. "Wotcher, Sambo," said the corporal. "You doin' anything?" And later there were two Chinese boys who joined the gang, and one of these, whose name was Philip Aloysius Tan, swiftly became the gang-leader. The corporal was good-humored about it, glad to see it: after all, the days of British rule were over.

For Rosemary the days of glorious expectation had returned. There was a lieutenant-colonel in the town, majors, captains, raw conscript lieutenants. Jalil? "The unspeakable Turk should be immediately struck out of the question." (Letter from Carlyle to Howard, 24th, 1876, as Crabbe might have verified from his books had Crabbe still been alive and his books not on their way home to his widow.) Jalil was not a gentleman. Colonel Richman was, so was Major Anstruther, so were Captains Tickell and Forsyth. Lieutenants Creek, Looker, Jones, Dwyer? Callow, guffawish, no longer her meat. Major Anstruther was unmarried, a good dancer, skilled in the arts of love. He had a neat square face, hair greying neatly, a neat broad body, a voice and accent like Lim Cheng Po's. To Rosemary he was England—fog, primroses, Shaftesbury Avenue, South Kensington Tube Station, the Antelope and the Captain's Cabin, the downstairs bar of the Café Royal, Kew in lilac-time; only occasionally Crew at 3 am, Stoke-on-Trent on a Sunday, the smells of Warrington. She was, you might say, in love again.

There was something for everybody in the new dispensation. Syed Omar was given a van with a left-hand drive and a salary of two hundred dollars a month. (Malayan dollars, not American dollars, though at the end of his first month he had sworn to his employers that he had thought it would be American dollars, else he would not have taken the job on. He was promised an increase in the near future.) On this van was painted a picture of an eagle shaking claws with a tiger, symbolic of new friendship between two free peoples. In this van were stacked, weekly, copies of a newspaper printed in the most beautiful Arabic script, called *Suara Amerika* (The Voice of America). This newspaper had to be delivered to humble *kampong* folk who else would know nothing of events in the great world outside. Few of them could read, however. Still, they welcomed Syed Omar's appearances and treated him to fresh toddy and simple curries, and they never tired of laughing at the picture of the eagle shaking claws with the tiger.

Syed Omar did quite a profitable side-line selling *Suara Amerika* to various shops in the towns as wrapping-paper. But, to do justice to his loyalty, he always took a copy of the paper home with him and read extracts to his wives about the private affairs of film stars. They liked this. In the evenings too, when he was in, Syed Hassan gave his father English lessons. The two got on quite well together now, especially as Syed Hassan had a job with prospects: he was fifth driver to the Sultan and occasionally had the thrill of running the new Cadillac round town.

Robert Loo was one day summoned to the United States Information Service building. This had formerly been the British Residency: the Americans paid a generous rent to the Sultan for its use. Robert Loo was cordially greeted by two youngish American gentlemen who expressed interest in his music. He was taken to a music-room whose air-conditioning made him shiver, and he was asked to sit down at the tropicalized Bechstein and play some of his works. Robert Loo smiled.

"I'm not a pianist," he said. "I'm a composer."

"You can't play the piano at all?"

"No."

"Well, how do you know what your music sounds like?"

"I hear it in my head."

"Well, then, perhaps you'd be good enough to leave some of your manuscripts with us."

"I've not very much," said Robert Loo. "I destroyed a lot of my early work. There was a symphony and a string quartet. They were immature, so I destroyed them."

"What have you, then?"

"This." Robert Loo took from his case the score of a brief work.

"This," he said, "is a Legend for Piano and Orchestra."

"Legend, eh?"

"I call it that. I don't know why." Robert Loo smiled nervously.

"Well, leave it with us, and we'll call you back in a couple of days."

Robert Loo was duly called back and treated kindly. "You know all the tricks," they said. "It's very competent. You've obviously heard a lot of the better class of film music."

"I never go to the films," said Robert Loo.

"Well, it's a very neat pastiche of the sort of Rachmaninoff film-piano-concerto stuff you used to hear a lot of just after the war."

"Pastiche?" Robert Loo did not know the word.

"Yes. It's funny that you haven't absorbed much of the local musical idioms. Very rich possibilities there. Look what Bartok did, for instance."

"I want to write music from the heart," said Robert Loo.

"Yes? Well, very commendable, I suppose, in its way. Thank you, Mr. Loo. It was very kind of you to give us the opportunity to look at your music." And Robert Loo was kindly dismissed.

Mr. Roget, one of these two gentlemen, wrote a friendly note to Temple Haynes, who was at the time running a course in the Phonetics of Anglo-American in Kuala Hantu.

Dear Temple,

Joe and I had a look at the music of this Chinese boy that the Englishman told you about before he died. Frankly, I don't think there's much we can do. He's got past the stage of elementary harmony and counterpoint and so on: in fact, he's technically very competent. But it's not technique we're after. We can soon give them the technique. What we want is the indigenous stuff—folk-song and dance, six-tone scales and the rest of it. Our assignment is to study indigenous music and find out some of the real native artists. This Chinese boy has sort of rejected the native stuff (for instance, there's not a trace of the Chinese pentatonic in his work) and turns out very competent imitations of imitations—second-rate cinematic romantic stuff, complete with big Rachmaninoff tunes on the violins and chords banging out on the solo piano. We've heard it all before. We can do it far better ourselves. In fact, we didn't come out these thousands of miles to see a distorted image of ourselves in a mirror. So there it is. Hope the course is going well. Joe and I hope soon to do a bit of travelling round the remoter villages, complete with recording apparatus, of course. A Malay here is proving helpful—Syed Omar, who says he's descended from Mohammed—and he's going to take us around. For a consideration, of course, but what the hell!

Be seeing you,

Harry.

CHAPTER 13

New Hopes
for an Old Concept

The importance of the concept of community lies in its very ambiguity. Like the concept of the human, it embodies both the descriptive and the ideal; it recalls to us our power to make as well as to accept, to act as well as to behave. Community refers to whatever groups exist; it also refers to our aspirations for the groups. Social science began with the efforts of the Greeks to make what existed into something nearer to their hearts' desires. Since no effort succeeds perfectly, since all achievement entails unanticipated side effects, since we must pay for any achievement by yielding alternative opportunities, it is probably best to think of community as a variable, existing to some degree in many collectives, to an extreme degree in a few.

Community is then an aspect of the way men relate to one another, the primary dimension of human interaction, that aspect which goes far and away beyond the coerced and the necessary, the "functional requisites." Beginning in the experiences of children in the family, it moves outward to include neighborhood and peer group, congregation and collegium, the nation, and in some cases the human race. But it attenuates as we move further from the immediate; feeling and conception are replaced by principle and abstraction. There are limits to the possible inclusiveness of community.

John Dewey in *The Public and Its Problems* struggles with the question: Can we have a democratic community in this nation? He then notes some prerequistes for such a community—education, social inquiry, and particularly the development of a competent citizenry. The failures of American society are the result of the failure of the American educational experience to produce the kind of person who could and would govern himself.

One cost of this failure has been the long and difficult struggle imposed upon black Americans who would participate in the greater society. Robert Penn Warren's *Who Speaks For the Negro?* presents interviews with some important and representative spokesmen. In his interview with Ralph Ellison he and Ellison examine at length the historical role and the present-day character of black America. But they do more; Warren, as a white ex-Southerner, Ellison as a black ex-Southerner, probe shrewdly at the complex of region and race, mores and models, that make up the great barrier between colors.

Ellison's discussion of black America's character and culture evokes many dimensions of community. Commonality of experience is at the root of much of it—common enemies, dangers, opportunities, heros, games. It is a community forged out of coercive, rural, working-class life, and perpetuated by the same kinds of conditions. Yet in Ellison's view, it is a creative response to the coercion, it is an entity of importance, an achievement that protects and nurtures human dignity. The ethnic community is usually based upon the need for solidarity, protection, and comfort against the surrounding strangers. It is not spatially defined, but it is a strong community for all of that.

Finally Paul Goodman's work from *Growing Up Absurd* closes this volume. Goodman is at once a clever analyst of what the American community is, a harsh critic of much in that state of affairs, and a continually hopeful, pragmatic utopian. The curse of our times, in his view, is not the increase in choice resulting from increasing societal scale, but the lag and unevenness in that trend. We must increase freedom further, faster: we cannot free the young from work and poverty and keep them in submission at school; we cannot free adults from energy-absorbing work and leave them captive to their miseducation and the mass media. In short, half-revolutions are the source of our discontent, more dangerous to the society than would be the follow-through.

The new age of men requires new definitions of community. We have noted some that exist—the professions, the ethnic enclave, the religious congregation—and others will come about. Such communities will probably never completely lose their old, localized, suspicious approach to those excluded. Perhaps, however, the lines between excluded and included will change as all men are included in some communities and some men in many.

John Dewey
The Search for the Great Community

What are the conditions under which it is possible for the Great Society to approach more closely and vitally the status of a Great Community, and thus take form in genuinely democratic societies and state? What are the conditions under which we may reasonably picture the Public emerging from its eclipse?

The study will be an intellectual or hypothetical one. There will be no attempt to state how the required conditions might come into existence, nor to prophesy that they will occur. The object of the analysis will be to show that *unless* ascertained specifications are realized, the Community cannot be organized as a democratically effective Public. It is not claimed that the conditions which will be noted will suffice, but only that at least they are indispensable. In other words, we shall endeavor to frame a hypothesis regarding the democratic state to stand in contrast with the earlier doctrine which has been nullified by the course of events.

Two essential constituents in that older theory, as will be recalled, were the notions that each individual is of himself equipped with the intelligence needed, under the operation of self-interest, to engage in political affairs; and that general suffrage, frequent elections of officials and majority rule are sufficient to ensure the responsibility of elected rulers to the desires and interests of the public. As we shall see, the second conception is logically bound up with the first and stands or falls with it. At the basis of the scheme lies what Lippmann has well called the idea of the "omnicompetent" individual: competent to frame policies, to judge their results; competent to know in all situations demanding political action what is for his own good, and competent to enforce his idea of good and the will to effect it against contrary forces. Subsequent history has proved that the assumption involved illusion. Had it not been for the misleading influence of a false psychology, the illusion might have been detected in advance. But current philosophy held that ideas and knowledge were functions of a mind or consciousness which originated in individuals by means of isolated con-

Reprinted by permission. Copyright 1927 Henry Holt; renewed 1954 Mrs. John Dewey.

tact with objects. But in fact, knowledge is a function of association and communication; it depends upon tradition, upon tools and methods socially transmitted, developed and sanctioned. Faculties of effectual observation, reflection and desire are habits acquired under the influence of the culture and institutions of society, not ready-made inherent powers. The fact that man acts from crudely intelligized emotion and from habit rather than from rational consideration, is now so familiar that it is not easy to appreciate that the other idea was taken seriously as the basis of economic and political philosophy. The measure of truth which it contains was derived from observation of a relatively small group of shrewd business men who regulated their enterprises by calculation and accounting, and of citizens of small and stable local communities who were so intimately acquainted with the persons and affairs of their locality that they could pass competent judgment upon the bearing of proposed measures upon their own concerns.

Habit is the mainspring of human action, and habits are formed for the most part under the influence of the customs of a group. The organic structure of man entails the formation of habit, for, whether we wish it or not, whether we are aware of it or not, every act effects a modification of attitude and set which directs future behavior. The dependence of habit-forming upon those habits of a group which constitute customs and institutions is a natural consequence of the helplessness of infancy. The social consequences of habit have been stated once for all by James: "Habit is the enormous fly-wheel of society, its most precious conservative influence. It alone is what keeps us within the bounds of ordinance, and saves the children of fortune from the uprisings of the poor. It alone prevents the hardest and most repulsive walks of life from being deserted by those brought up to tread therein. It keeps the fisherman and the deck-hand at sea through the winter; it holds the miner in his darkness, and nails the country-man to his log cabin and his lonely farm through all the months of snow; it protects us from invasion by the natives of the desert and the frozen zone. It dooms us all to fight out the battle of life upon the lines of our nurture or our early choice, and to make the best of a pursuit that disagrees, because there is no other for which we are fitted and it is too late to begin again. It keeps different social strata from mixing."

The influence of habit is decisive because all distinctively human action has to be learned, and the very heart, blood and sinews of learning is creation of habitudes. Habits bind us to orderly and established ways of action because they generate ease, skill and interest in things to which we have grown used and because they instigate fear to walk in different ways, and because they leave us incapacitated for the trial of them. Habit does not preclude the use of thought, but it determines the

channels within which it operates. Thinking is secreted in the inter-
stices of habits. The sailor, miner, fisherman and farmer think, but
their thoughts fall within the framework of accustomed occupations
and relationships. We dream beyond the limits of use and wont, but
only rarely does revery become a source of acts which break bounds; so
rarely that we name those in whom it happens demonic geniuses and
marvel at the spectacle. Thinking itself becomes habitual along certain
lines; a specialized occupation. Scientific men, philosophers, literary
persons, are not men and women who have so broken the bonds of
habits that pure reason and emotion undefiled by use and wont speak
through them. They are persons of a specialized infrequent habit. Hence
the idea that men are moved by an intelligent and calculated regard
for their own good is pure mythology. Even if the principle of self-love
actuated behavior, it would still be true that the *objects* in which men
find their love manifested, the objects which they take as constituting
their peculiar interests, are set by habits reflecting social customs.

These facts explain why the social doctrinaires of the new industrial
movement had so little prescience of what was to follow in consequence
of it. These facts explain why the more things changed, the more they
were the same; they account, that is, for the fact that instead of the
sweeping revolution which was expected to result from democratic political machinery, there was in the main but a transfer of vested power
from one class to another. A few men, whether or not they were good
judges of their own true interest and good, were competent judges of the
conduct of business for pecuniary profit, and of how the new governmental machinery could be made to serve their ends. It would have
taken a new race of human beings to escape, in the use made of political forms, from the influence of deeply engrained habits, of old
institutions and customary social status, with their inwrought limitations
of expectation, desire and demand. And such a race, unless of disem-
bodied angelic constitution, would simply have taken up the task where
human beings assumed it upon emergence from the condition of anthro-
poid apes. In spite of sudden and catastrophic revolutions, the essential
continuity of history is doubly guaranteed. Not only are personal desire
and belief functions of habit and custom, but the objective conditions
which provide the resources and tools of action, together with its limitations, obstructions and traps, are precipitates of the past, perpetuating,
willy-nilly, its hold and power. The creation of a *tabula rasa* in order to
permit the creation of a new order is so impossible as to set at naught
both the hope of buoyant revolutionaries and the timidity of scared
conservatives.

Nevertheless, changes take place and are cumulative in character.
Observation of them in the light of their recognized consequences

arouses reflection, discovery, invention, experimentation. When a certain state of accumulated knowledge, of techniques and instrumentalities is attained, the process of change is so accelerated, that, as to-day, it appears externally to be the dominant trait. But there is a marked lag in any corresponding change of ideas and desires. Habits of opinion are the toughest of all habits; when they have become second nature, and are supposedly thrown out of the door, they creep in again as stealthily and surely as does first nature. And as they are modified, the alteration first shows itself negatively, in the disintegration of old beliefs, to be replaced by floating, volatile and accidentally snatched up opinions. Of course, there has been an enormous increase in the amount of knowledge possessed by mankind, but it does not equal, probably, the increase in the amount of errors and half-truths which have got into circulation. In social and human matters, especially, the development of a critical sense and methods of discriminating judgment has not kept pace with the growth of careless reports and of motives for positive misrepresentation.

What is more important, however, is that so much of knowledge is not knowledge in the ordinary sense of the word, but is "science." The quotation marks are not used disrespectfully, but to suggest the technical character of scientific material. The layman takes certain conclusions which get into circulation to be science. But the scientific inquirer knows that they constitute science only in connection with the methods by which they are reached. Even when true, they are not science in virtue of their correctness, but by reason of the apparatus which is employed in reaching them. This apparatus is so highly specialized that it requires more labor to acquire ability to use and understand it than to get skill in any other instrumentalities possessed by man. Science, in other words, is a highly specialized language, more difficult to learn than any natural language. It is an artificial language, not in the sense of being factitious, but in that of being a work of intricate art, devoted to a particular purpose and not capable of being acquired nor understood in the way in which the mother tongue is learned. It is, indeed, conceivable that sometime methods of instruction will be devised which will enable laymen to read and hear scientific material with comprehension, even when they do not themselves use the apparatus which is science. The latter may then become for large numbers what students of language call a passive, if not an active, vocabulary. But that time is in the future.

For most men, save the scientific workers, science is a mystery in the hands of initiates, who have become adepts in virtue of following ritualistic ceremonies from which the profane herd is excluded. They are fortunate who get as far as a sympathetic appreciation of the methods which give pattern to the complicated apparatus: methods of analytic, experimental observation, mathematical formulation and deduction, constant and elaborate check and test. For most persons, the reality of the apparatus is found only in its embodiments in practical affairs, in mechanical devices and in techniques which touch life as it is lived. For them, electricity is *known* by means of the telephones, bells and lights they use, by the generators and magnetos in the automobiles they drive, by the trolley cars in which they ride. The physiology and biology they are acquainted with is that they have learned in taking precautions against germs and from the physicians they depend upon for health. The science of what might be supposed to be closest to them, of human nature, was for them an esoteric mystery until it was applied in advertising, salesmanship and personnel selection and management, and until, through psychiatry, it spilled over into life and popular consciousness, through its bearings upon "nerves," the morbidities and common forms of crankiness which make it difficult for persons to get along with one another and with themselves. Even now, popular psychology is a mass of cant, of slush and of superstition worthy of the most flourishing days of the medicine man.

Meanwhile the technological application of the complex apparatus which is science has revolutionized the conditions under which associated life goes on. This may be known as a fact which is stated in a proposition and assented to. But it is not known in the sense that men understand it. They do not know it as they know some machine which they operate, or as they know electric light and steam locomotives. They do not understand *how* the change has gone on nor *how* it affects their conduct. Not understanding its "how," they cannot use and control its manifestations. They undergo the consequences, they are affected by them. They cannot manage them, though some are fortunate enough— what is commonly called good fortune—to be able to exploit some phase of the process for their own personal profit. But even the most shrewd and successful man does not in any analytic and systematic way—in a way worthy to compare with the knowledge which he has won in lesser affairs by means of the stress of experience—know the system within which he operates. Skill and ability work within a framework which we have not created and do not comprehend. Some occupy strategic positions which give them advance information of forces that affect the market; and by training and an innate turn that way they have acquired a special technique which enables them to use the vast impersonal tide to turn their own wheels. They can dam the current here and release it there. The current itself is as much beyond them as was ever the river by the side of which some ingenious mechanic, employing a knowledge which was transmitted to him, erected his saw-mill to make boards of trees which he had not grown. That within limits those successful in affairs have knowledge and skill is not to be doubted. But such knowledge goes relatively but little further than that of the competent skilled operator who manages a machine. It suffices to employ the conditions which are before him. Skill enables him to turn the flux of events this way or that in his own neighborhood. It gives him no control of the flux.

Why should the public and its officers, even if the latter are termed statesman, be wiser and more effective? The prime condition of a democratically organized public is a kind of knowledge and insight which does not yet exist. In its absence, it would be the height of absurdity to try to tell what it would be like if it existed. But some of the conditions which must be fulfilled if it is to exist can be indicated. We can borrow that much from the spirit and method of science even if we are ignorant of it as a specialized apparatus. An obvious requirement is freedom of social inquiry and of distribution of its conclusions. The notion that men may be free in their thought even when they are not in its expression and dissemination has been sedulously propagated. It had its origin in the idea of a mind complete in itself, apart from action and from objects. Such a consciousness presents in fact the spectacle of mind deprived of its normal functioning, because it is baffled by the actualities in connection with which alone it is truly mind, and is driven back into secluded and impotent revery.

There can be no public without full publicity in respect to all consequences which concern it. Whatever obstructs and restricts publicity, limits and distorts public opinion and checks and distorts thinking on social affairs. Without freedom of expression, not even methods of social inquiry can be developed. For tools can be evolved and perfected only in operation; in application to observing, reporting and organizing actual subject-matter; and this application cannot occur save through free and systematic communication. The early history of physical knowledge, of Greek conceptions of natural phenomena, proves how inept become the conceptions of the best endowed minds when those ideas are elaborated apart from the closest contact with the events which they purport to state and explain. The ruling ideas and methods of the human sciences are in much the same condition to-day. They are also evolved on the basis of past gross observations, remote from constant use in regulation of the material of new observations.

Robert Penn Warren
Leadership from the Periphery

In 1952, *Invisible Man* was published. It is now a classic of our time. It has been translated into seven languages. The title has become a key phrase: the Negro is the invisible man.

Ralph Ellison is not invisible and had done some thirty-eight years of living before the novel appeared, and the complex and rich experience of those years underlies the novel, or is absorbed into the novel, as it undergirds, or is absorbed into, his casual conversation.

Ralph Ellison was born in 1914, in Oklahoma City, of Southern parents. His father, who had been a soldier in China, the Philippines, and in the Spanish American War, was a man of energy and ambition, and an avid reader; he named his son for Emerson. He died when Ralph was three years old, but Ralph's mother managed to support the children and encouraged them in their ambitions.

As a boy, Ralph sold newspapers, shined shoes, collected bottles for bootleggers, was a lab assistant to a dentist, waited on tables, hunted, hiked, played varsity football, conducted the school band, held first chair in the trumpet section of the school orchestra. "Was constantly fighting," he says, "until I reached the age when I realized that I was strong enough and violent enough to kill someone in a fit of anger."

With some help from his mother, whom he describes as an "idealist and a Christian," he worked his way through Tuskegee, as a music major. But there he read Eliot, and that fact, though for some years he was to keep his ambition as a composer, was the beginning of his literary career. In 1937, during a winter in Dayton, Ohio, where he had gone for the funeral of his mother (who had died, he says, "at the hands of an ignorant and negligent Negro physician"), and where he was living in poverty and making what money he could by hunting birds to sell to General Motors officials, he took up writing seriously: "This occuring at a time when I was agitating for intervention in the Spanish Civil War, my personal loss was tied to events taking place far from these shores. Thus the complexity of events forced itself to my attention even before I had developed the primary skill for dealing with it. I was forced to see that both as observer and as writer, and as my mother's son, I would always have to do my homework."

Ralph Ellison has traveled widely and lived in many parts of the United States; he has known a great variety of people, including "jazz-men, veterans, ex-slaves, dope fiends, prostitutes, pimps, preachers, folk singers, farmers, teamsters, railroad men, slaughter-house and round-house workers, bell boys, headwaiters, punch-drunk fighters, barbers, gamblers, bootleggers, and the tramps and down-and-outers who often knocked on our back door for handouts." He might have added that he has known the academic world and the world of the arts, has lived for two years in Italy as a Fellow of the American Academy, and has traveled in Mexico and the Orient.

Ralph Ellison is something above medium height, of a strong, well-fleshed figure not yet showing any slackness of middle age. He is light brown. His brow slopes back, but not decidedly, and is finely vaulted, an effect accentuated by the receding hair line. The skin of his face is un-lined, and the whole effect of his smoothly modeled face is one of calmness and control; his gestures have the same control, the same bal-ance and calmness. The calmness has a history, I should imagine, a history based on self-conquest and hard lessons of sympathy learned through a burgeoning and forgiving imagination. Lurking in the calm-ness is, too, the impression of the possibility of a sudden nervous striking-out, not entirely mastered; and too, an impression of with-drawal—a withdrawal tempered by humor, and flashes of sympathy. It is a wry humor, sometimes self-directed. And a characteristic mannerism is the utterance of a little sound—"ee-ee-"—breathed out through the teeth, a humorous, ironical recognition of the little traps and blind alleys of the world, and of the self.

His voice is not deep, but is well-modulated, pleasing. He speaks slowly, not quite in a drawl, and when he speaks on a matter of some weight, he tends to move his head almost imperceptibly from side to side, or even his shoulders.

He does this as he sits on a couch in his study high above the Hudson River, where the afternoon sun strikes and a string of barges moves leadenly against the current. I have just quoted the passage to him from Du Bois on the split in the Negro psyche.

ELLISON: It's a little bit more complicated than Dr. Du Bois thought it. That is, there's no way for me not to be influenced by American values, and they're coming at me through the newspapers, through the products I buy, through all the various media—through the language. What becomes a problem, of course, is when you turn from the implicit cultural pluralism of the country to politics, social customs. But it seems to me that the real goal of the pressure now being asserted by Negroes is to achieve on the socio-political level something of the same pluralism which exists on the level of culture. The idea that the Negro psyche is split is not as viable as it seems—although it might have been true of Dr. Du Bois personally. My problem is not whether I will accept or reject American values. It is, rather, how can I get into a position where I can have the maximum influence upon those values. There is also the matter, as you have pointed out, of those American ideals which were so fatefully put down on paper which I want to see made manifest.

WARREN: One sometimes encounters the Negro who says he regrets the possible long-range absorption of the Negro blood, the possibility of the loss of Negro identity.

ELLISON: That's like wishing your father's father wasn't your grandfather. I don't fear Negro blood being absorbed, but I am afraid that the Negro American cultural expression might be absorbed and obliterated through lack of appreciation and through commercialization and banalization. But as for the question of diffusing of blood—it isn't blood which makes a Negro American: Adam Clayton Powell's reply to a white TV interviewer's query, "I hear that you have a lot of white blood," was "Yes, probably more than you, Mike."[1] If it should suddenly become true that being a Negro rested on the possession of African blood alone, without reference to culture, social experience, and political circumstance, quite a number of people who are white and who enjoy the privileges of white status would find themselves beyond the pale.

Anyway, I don't think the problem of blood absorption works so simply. There are principles of selection which have little to do with the status accorded to whiteness, and these assert themselves despite the absence of outside pressure. On the aesthetic level alone there are certain types you like, certain sensibilities, certain voices—a number of other qualities. Another factor is that Negroes, despite what some of our spokesmen say, do not dislike being Negro—no matter how inconvenient it frequently is. *I* like being a Negro.

WARREN: Then it's not merely suffering and deprivation, it's a challenge and enrichment?

ELLISON: Yes, indeed—these complete the circle and make it human. And as I was telling the kids this morning at Rutgers, I have no desire to escape the struggle, because I'm just too interested in how it's going to work out, and I want to impose my will upon the outcome to the extent that I can. I want to help shape events and our general culture, not merely as a semi-outsider but as one who is in a position to have a responsible impact upon the American value system.

[1] Mike Wallace.

WARREN: Some Negroes—some leaders—say that there is no challenge or en-
            richment in the situation of Negroes. Of course, it may be a matter
            of strategy to insist on the total agony.

ELLISON: Perhaps I can talk this way because I'm not a leader. But I under-
            stand that this has become part of the strategy of exerting pressure.
            There is a danger in this, nevertheless. The danger lies in over-
            emphasizing the extent to which Negroes are alienated, and in
            overstressing the extent to which the racial predicament imposes an
            agony upon the individual. For the Negro youth this emphasis
            can become an excuse and a blinder, leading to an avoidance of
            the individual assertion. It can encourage him to ignore his per-
            sonal talent in favor of reducing himself to a generalized definition
            of alienation and agony. Thus is accomplished what the entire his-
            tory of repression and brutalization has failed to do: the individual
            reduces himself to a cipher. Ironically, some of those who yell
            loudest about alienation are doing it in some of the most con-
            servative journals and newspapers and are very well paid for so
            yelling. Yet, obviously, the agony which they display has other than
            racial sources.
                Actually, I doubt the existence of a "total" agony, for where
            personality is involved two-plus-two seldom equals four. But I
            agree that agony and alienation do form a valid source of appeal.
                However, there's another aspect of reality which applies: The
            American Negro has a dual identity, just as most Americans have,
            and it seems to me ironic that the discipline out of which this
            present action is being exerted comes from no simple agony—
            nor simple despair—but out of long years of learning how to live
            under pressure, of learning to deal with provocation and with
            violence. It issues out of the Negro's necessity of establishing his
            own value system and his own conception of Negro experience
            and Negro personality, conceptions which seldom get into the
            sociology and psychology textbooks.

WARREN: The power of character, of self-control—the qualities that are
            making this Movement now effective—did not come out of blind
            suffering?

ELLISON: Nor did they come out of self-pity or self-hate—which is a belief
            shared by many black and white sociologists, journalists, by the
            Black Muslims, and by many white liberals, But even though some
            of these elements—the Negro being human—are present within the
            Movement—the power of character, of self-control—these qualities
            are no expression of blind suffering or self-hate. For when the
            world was not looking, when the country was not looking at
            Negroes, and when we were restrained in certain of our activities
            by the interpretation of the law of the land, something was present
            in our lives to sustain us. This is evident when we go back and look
            at our cultural expression, when we look at the folklore in a truly
            questioning way, when we scrutinize and listen before passing judg-

ment. Listen to those tales which are told by Negroes among themselves. I'm so annoyed whenever I come across a perfectly well-meaning person saying of the present struggle, "Well, the Negro has suddenly discovered courage."

*   *   *

In all of Ellison's conversation and writing there is the impulse to re-inspect, to break through, some of the standard formulations of the Revolution, which are in constant danger of becoming mere stereotypes. One is that the Negro has been deprived of a sense of identity and is a "self-hater." When James Baldwin says that "for the first time in American Negro history, the American black man is not at the mercy of the American white man's image of him," he is referring to the question of identity; as he is when he goes on to say that, though it is "very romantic," the American Negro finds it "a necessary step" to think of "himself as an African." Martin Luther King says that he recognized "the psychic split" as a "real issue," and Wyatt Tee Walker says that only now the "Negro really accepts his identity." Izell Blair says that the young Negro, in facing the dominant values of white society, says: "Well, what am I?" And then: "You feel rubbed out, as if you never existed." The question arises in a number of case histories; for instance, in one of the persons studied by Kardiner and Ovesay: "I know I don't want to be identified with Negroes, but I am identified regardless of how I feel." And, as we have seen, the Black Muslims, including the defector Malcolm X, take the recognition of the problem of identity and self-hate as the beginning of redemption.

In the past, in the essay "Harlem Is Nowhere," written in 1948, Ellison accepted the notion of self-hate among Negroes in connection with what Dr. Frederick Wertham calls the "free-floating hostility" which the Negro senses, and sometimes takes "as a punishment for some racial or personal guilt." Ellison is quite specific: "Negro Americans are in a desperate search for identity . . . their whole lives have become a search for answers to the questions: Who am I?, What am I?, Why am I?, and, Where?" But later (as in the present interview), Ellison insists, over and over again, on the Negro's will, even under slavery, to develop discipline and achieve individuality. For instance, in a review of *Blue People* (1964), by Le Roi Jones, he writes:

"A slave," writes Le Roi Jones, "cannot be a man." But what, might one ask, of those moments when he feels his metabolism aroused by the rising of the sap in the spring? What of his identity among other slaves? With his wife? And isn't it closer to the truth that far from considering themselves only in terms of the abstraction, "a slave," the enslaved really thought of themselves as *men* who had been unjustly enslaved?

What are we to make of those apparent contradictions? In the first place, we have to grant that a man is the final authority about his own feelings. If Izell Blair says that, at a certain time, he felt "rubbed out," he ought to know. By the same token, Ralph Ellison ought to know what he felt, or how he feels. The trouble only starts when one generalizes, and attributes a certain feeling to that abstraction "the Negro" —that is, to all Negroes—and creates a stereotype. But, of course, we would be nearer the truth if we thought not of "the Negro" but of pressures and tendencies implicit in the situation of oppression and of an enormous variety of persons upon whom they act.

Ellison, in thinking of those Negroes who set models for resistance, puts his emphasis on the individual, on the achieving of personal identity. On this point, some psychologists, in discussing the situation of the Negro under slavery, will distinguish between the personal ego and the social ego. For instance, Kardiner and Ovesey say that there were "among the slaves powerful and resourceful leaders," that slavery was not accepted with docility, and that "individual protests were many." But they distinguish such protests from group action, organized action. The fact that rebellions were so few and so promptly failed they attribute to the destruction by slavery of "the fabric out of which social cohesion is made." Under slavery the individual might have "enormous self-confidence," but such confidence would not be available for common use; its reference would remain almost strictly individual.

The explanation for this they would take to be complex. There would be, of course, the breakup of cultural bonds, the inability to form permanent and dignified family ties, the spy system, the use of Negro "drivers" and pace-setters, the system of special privilege for house-servants and "pets". Furthermore, Kardiner and Ovesey emphasize the nature of work under slavery: "No slave can take pride in his work, except perhaps in that it may serve another form of self-interest through ingratiation"—and this would be a bid for discrimination in favor of oneself, to the implied disadvantage of everyone else. The slave—except among favored craftsmen—did not plan work and had no opportunity to cooperate in work, and this fact would also have had a deep psychological effect. And, always, there would have been the pressure to accept the master's values. Under such pressures individuals might, and clearly did, achieve "identity," but with a special struggle—and a struggle that might have emphasized the special personal nature of that identity, an identity that might be expressed in individual acts of resistance or by flight.

As we have said earlier in discussing Samboism, we must think in terms not of pressures inherent in the situation. And in this instance, common sense would dictate that the distinction between the personal self and the social self cannot be taken as absolute. Certainly, the example of resistance or flight would fire something in those who to that moment had not resisted or fled; and such examples, entering the local folklore, might have continuing effect. And on this point Ellison was continuing, telling of a man who, long after slavery, had entered folklore as the intransigent, individual discoverer of the self:

ELLISON: I remember that when I was riding freight trains through Alabama to get to Tuskegee Institute there was a well-known figure of Birmingham, called Ice Cream Charlie, whose story was also told over and over again whenever we evoked the unwritten history of the group. Ice Cream Charlie was an ice cream maker and his product must have been very good (Negro folklore has it, by the way, and erroneously, I'm afraid, that a Negro slave woman invented ice cream) because the demand for it led to his death. His white competitors ordered him to stop selling his product to white people, but the white people wanted it and, believing in free enterprise, he ignored the warning. This led to his competitors' sending the police after Charlie, and it ended with his killing twelve policemen before they burned him out and killed him. Now there are many, many such stories which Negroes keep alive among themselves, and they form part of our image of Negro experience—nonviolence notwithstanding.

Many people don't even bother to know or care about this part of Negro history. They project their own notions—or prefabricated stereotypes—upon Negroes—they make a slow and arduous development seem a dramatic event.[2]

The freedom movement, such a person assumes, exists simply because *he* is looking at it. Thus it becomes an accident or an artistic contrivance, or a conspiracy, instead of the slow development in time, in history, and in group discipline and organizational technique which it actually is.

I shouldn't be annoyed, of course, since Americans know very little of their history and we tend to act as though we believed that by refusing to look at history there'll be no necessity to confront its consequences. And we have so many facile ways of disguising the issues, of rendering them banal.

Sometime back I saw a revival of an old Al Jolson movie on television. This was about the time of the summer riots in Harlem, and in one of the big scenes Jolson appears in blackface singing a refrain which goes, "I don't want to make your laws, I just want

---

[2] In this connection we may remark that Ellison's great admiration for Faulkner stems, in part, from the impulse that made Faulkner more willing perhaps than any other artist to start with the stereotype of the Negro, accept it as true, and then seek out the human truth which it hides. See "Twentieth Century Fiction and the Black Mask of Humanity," in *Shadow and Act*.

to sing my songs and be happy!" Well, whatever the reality of the Negro attitudes or whatever the stage of the Negro freedom struggle at the time the picture was originally released—yes, and no matter how many white people were lulled into believing that Jolson's "passing for black" granted him the authority to express authentic Negro attitudes—this piece of popular culture tells us more about Jolson, about Hollywood, and about American techniques for converting serious moral issues into sentimental and banal entertainment than about Negroes. Anyone who bothers to consult history would know that not only were Negroes anxious to change the laws but were trying even then to do so. By 1954, they had helped to discover how—with Charles S. Houston's mock supreme court cases held at Howard University Law School.

Viewed from this perspective of Al Jolson, America has been terribly damaged by bad art. Perhaps those Negro writers who wish to be praised for shoddy work, and who regard serious literary criticism as a form of racial prejudice, should remember that bad art which toys with serious issues is ultimately destructive and the entertainment which it provides is poisonous, regardless of the racial background of the artist.

WARREN: What do you think of the suggestion that part of the Southern resistance is not based on the question of race as such but on the impulse to maintain identity? A white Southerner feeling that his identity is involved may defend a lot of things in one package as being Southern, and one of those things is segregation. He feels he has to have the whole package to define his identity. Does that make any sense to you?

ELLISON: It makes a lot of sense to me, because one of the areas that I feel, and which I think I see when I look at the Southerner who has these feelings, is that he has been imprisoned by them, and that he has been prevented from achieving his individuality, perhaps more than Negroes have. And very often this is a tough one for Northerners to understand—that is, Northern whites, and sometimes even for Northern Negroes.

WARREN: I think it is too—some of the people I know.

ELLISON: Yes, it is very difficult to get that across and I wish it could be spelled out. I wish that we could break this thing down so that it could be seen that desegregation isn't going to stop people from being Southern, that freedom for Negroes isn't going to destroy the main current of that way of life, which becomes, like most ways of life when we *talk* about them, more real on the level of myth, memory and dream than on the level of actuality anyway. The climate will remain the same, and that has a lot to do with it, the heroes of Southern history will remain, and so on. The economy will probably expand, and a hell of a lot of energy which has gone into keeping the Negro "in his place" will be released for more creative pursuits. And the dictionary will become more accurate.

the language a bit purified, and the singing in the schools will sound better. I suspect that what is valuable and worth preserving in the white Southern way of life is no more exclusively dependent upon the existence of segregation than what is valuable in Southern Negro life depends upon its being recognized by white people—or for that matter, by Northern Negroes. Besides, from what I've seen of the South, as a musician and as a waiter and so on, some of the people who are most afraid of Negroes' invading them will never be bothered, because their way of life is structured in a manner which isn't particularly attractive to Negroes.

WARREN: There's an interlocking structure, I sometimes think, supported by just one thing—segregation.

ELLISON: Yes, and their fear is so unreal, actually, when you can see the whole political structure being changed anyway. And when the political structure changes and desegregation is achieved, it will be easily seen where Negroes were stopped by the law and where they would have been stopped anyway, because of income and by their own preference—a matter of taste. There is, after all, a tiny bit of Negro truth in the story which Southern whites love to tell, to the effect that if a white man could be a Negro on Saturday night he'd never wish to be white again.

That bit of consolation aside, however, I don't think it sufficiently appreciated that over and over again Negroes of certain backgrounds take on aristocratic values. They are rural and Southern and not drawn to business because business was not part of the general pattern. This is one reason—over and beyond the realities of discrimination by banks, suppliers, poor training opportunities, and even individual lack of initiative—that we've developed no powerful middle class. Here again a cultural factor cuts across the racial and political appearances of things. Southern whites were also slow to take to business.

WARREN: That's been one of the things that have been commented on by observers from the eighteenth century on.

ELLISON: But over and over again, my intellectual friends—they have no conception of this. They can't understand—I mean, it appears ludicrous to them when I say that so-and-so is aristocratic in his image of himself and in the values which he has taken over from the white South. Nevertheless it's true, and some of the biggest snobs that you could run into are some of these poor Negroes—well, they might not be poor actually, they might be living very well—but there are just certain things, certain codes, certain values which they express and they will die by them. And there's quite a lot of that.

WARREN: In Washington I was talking to a Miss Lucy Thornton, in the Howard University Law School, and she's been through the demonstrations, she's been in jail and so forth. She said, "I'm optimistic about the way things are probably going to go here—or may go here—about getting a human settlement after the troubles are over." I asked, "Why?" She said, "Well, because we have been on the land together. We have a common history which is some basis for communication for living together afterwards."

ELLISON: Well, it is true that when you share a common background, you don't have to spell out so many things, even though you might be fighting over recognizing the common identity, and I think that that's part of the South's struggle. For instance, it's just very hard for Governor Wallace to recognize that he has got to share not only the background but the power of looking after the State of Alabama with Negroes who probably know as much about it as he does. Now, here in New York I know many, many people with many, many backgrounds—and I have very often found people who think that they know me as an individual reveal that they have no sense of the experience behind me, the extent of it and the complexity of it. What they have instead is good will and a passion for abstraction.

WARREN: That's a human problem, of course, all the way. It can be special in a case like this, I presume.

ELLISON: It can be special because suddenly something comes up and I realize, "Well, my gosh, all the pieces aren't here." That is, I've won my individuality in relation to those friends at the cost of that great part of me which is really representative of a group experience. I'm sometimes viewed as "different" or a "special instance"—when in fact I'm special only to the extent that I'm a fairly conscious example, and in some ways a lucky instance, of the general run of American Negroes.

WARREN: I encounter the same thing, I suppose, in a way. I've been congratulated by well meaning friends who say, "It's so nice to meet a reconstructed Southerner." I don't feel reconstructed, you see. And I don't feel liberal. I feel logical, and I resent the word—I resent the word *reconstructed*.

ELLISON: It's like this notion of the culturally deprived child—one of those phrases which I don't like—as I have taught white middle-class young people who are what I would call "culturally deprived." They are culturally deprived because they are not oriented within the society in such a way that they are prepared to deal with its problems.

WARREN: It's a different kind of cultural deprivation, isn't it? And actually a more radical one.

ELLISON: That's right, but they don't even realize it. These people can be much more troubled than the child who lives in the slum and knows how to exist in the slum.

WARREN: It's more mysterious, what's happening to him—the middle-class child?

ELLISON: Yes, it's quite mysterious, because he has everything, all of the opportunities, but he can make nothing of the society or of his obligations. And often he has no clear idea of his own goals.

WARREN: It's twice as difficult to remedy because you can't see how to remedy it.

ELLISON: He can't see how to remedy it, and he doesn't know to what extent he has given up his past. He thinks he has a history, but every time you really talk to him seriously you discover that, well, it's kind of floating out there, and the distance between the parent and the child—the parents might have had it, they might have had it in the old country, they might have had it from the farm, and so on, but something happens with the young ones.

WARREN: Do you think there's a real crisis of values in the American middle class, then?

ELLISON: I think so. Perhaps that is what I am trying to say.

WARREN: I think there is, too.

ELLISON: I think there's a terrific crisis, and one of the events by which the middle class is being tested, and one of the forms in which the crisis expresses itself is the necessity of dealing with the Negro freedom movement.

WARREN: Is this why there are some young white people who move into it—because it is their personal salvation to find a cause to identify with, something outside themselves, outside the flatness of their middle-class American spiritual ghetto? Several people, including Robert Moses in Mississippi, have remarked on the resistance of Negroes there to white well-wishers or even courageous fellow workers. One thing, some whites try to absorp arbitrarily the Negro culture, Negro speech, Negro musical terms, Negro musical tastes—move in and grab, as it were, the other man's soul.

ELLISON: Yes, and the resentment has existed for a long time now. But what is new today is that it is being stated, articulated. It is important to recognize, however, that the resentment arises not from simple jealousy over others' admiring certain aspects of our life style and expression and seeking to share them, but because all too often that idiom, that style, that expressiveness for which we've suffered and struggled and which is a product of our effort to make meaning of our experience—is taken over by those who would distort it and reduce it to banality. This happened with jazz, resulting in great reputations and millions of dollars for certain white musicians while their artistic superiors barely got along. Worse, the standards of the art were corrupted. But another aspect of Negro resentment arises because all too often whites approach us with an unconscious assumption of racial superiority. And this leads to the naive, and implicitly arrogant, assumption that a characteristic cultural expression can, because it is Negro (it's American too, but that's a very complex matter), simply be picked up, appropriated, without bothering to learn its subtleties, its inner complexity, or its human cost, its source in tradition, its idiomatic allusiveness, its rooting in the density of lived life.

WARREN: Grab an apple off the cart and run——

ELLISON: It's like Christopher Newman, in James's *The American*, going over and trying to move into French society and finding a dense complexity of values and attitudes. But to get back to the other point, I'm sure that there must have been quite a lot of resentment even among the Negroes who encountered certain Abolitionists, because they displayed a tendency to use other people for their own convenience.

WARREN: It's awful human, isn't it?

ELLISON: It is, it's awful human.

WARREN: Let's turn to something else. Here in the midst of what has been an expanding economy you have a contracting economy for the unprepared, for the Negro.

ELLISON: That's the paradox. And this particularly explains something new which has come into the picture; that is, a determination by the Negro no longer to be the scapegoat, no longer to pay, to be sacrificed to—the inadequacies of other Americans. We want to socialize the cost. A cost has been exacted in terms of character, in terms of courage, and determination, and in terms of self-knowledge and self-discovery. Worse, it has led to social, economic, political, and intellectual disadvantages and to a contempt even for our lives. And one motive for our rejection of the old traditional role of national scapegoat is an intensified awareness that not only are we being destroyed by the sacrifice, but that the nation has been rotting at its moral core. Thus we are determined to bring America's conduct into line with its professed ideals. The obligation is dual, in fact mixed, to ourselves and to the nation. Negroes are forcing the confrontation between the nation's conduct and its ideal, and they are most American in that they are doing so. Other Americans are going to have to do the same thing. Well, I say "have to"—I don't mean that we're in a position to force anything, except the exertion of——

WARREN: Well, let's say force.

ELLISON: Yes—a matter of pressuring—keeping this country stirred up. Because we have desperately to keep it stirred up.

WARREN: What has been historically proved—not just in America but elsewhere—social change doesn't happen automatically—something has to happen.

ELLISON: One can only hope about these things. We've had the luxury of evading moral necessities from the Reconstruction on. Much of the moral looseness from which we suffer can be dated back to that period. It just seems to follow that you have to learn how to be morally correct and when you have so much mobility, as Americans have, and so much natural wealth, then you come to believe that you can eternally postpone the moment of historical truth. But I think that as a result of becoming the major power in the world, we are being disciplined in the experience of frustration, and the experience of being found inadequate. We're slowly learning that the wealth does us little good, that something more is needed. We're in trouble simply because we've compromised so damned much with events and with ourselves. Something is wrong and it isn't the presence of Negroes. It isn't even the presence of the civil rights problem, although this is an aspect of it.

WARREN: I agree with you immediately that that is not the central fact. But it flows into an American national situation and aggravates it.

ELLISON: The national values have become so confused that you can't even depend upon your writers for some sense of the realism of character. There is a basic strength in this country, but so much of it is being sapped away and no one seems to be too much interested in it.

WARREN: Let me switch the topic, if you will. You know Dr. Kenneth Clark's view of Martin Luther King's philosophy—this will lead us back to the whole question of the nature of violence and nonviolence.

ELLISON: Well, Dr. Clark misses the heroic side of this thing—perhaps because he has an investment in negative propaganda as a means of raising funds with which to correct some of the injustices common to Negro slums. But he seems so intent upon describing the negative that he forgets that there is another side, and in doing so he reveals how much he doesn't know about Southern Negroes. Where Negroes are concerned, the *open sesame* to many of the money vaults in this country seems to be a description, replete with graphs, statistics, and footnotes, of Negro life as so depraved, hopeless, and semi-human that the best service that money could perform would be to stuff the mouths of the describers so that the details of horror could stop. I'm reminded of the Black Guinea disguise in which Melville's Confidence Man blackened his face and twisted his limbs and then crawled about the ship deck whimpering like a dog begging and catching coins in his mouth.

Getting back to King and Clark, I think this—and it might sound mystical, but I don't think so because it is being acted out every day: there is a great power in humility. Dostoevski has made us aware—in fact, Jesus Christ has made us aware. It can be terribly ambiguous and it can contain many, many contradictory forces, and most of all, it can be a form of courage. Martin Luther King isn't working out of yesterday nor the day before yesterday. He is working out of a long history of Negro tradition and wisdom, and he certainly knows more about the psychology of his followers than Dr. Clark. He knows that these people have been conditioned to contain not only the physical pressures involved in their struggle, but that they are capable, through this same tradition, of mastering the psychological pressures of which Clark speaks.

WARREN: Do you mean conditioned by their training or by their history?

ELLISON: I'm talking about the old necessity of having to stay alive during periods when violence was loose in the land and when many were being casually killed. Violence has been so ever-present and so often unleashed through incidents of such pettiness and capriciousness, that for us personal courage had either to take another form or be negated, become meaningless.

Often the individual's personal courage had to be held in check, since not only could his exaction of personal satisfaction from a white man lead to the destruction of other innocent Negroes, his self-evaluation could be called into question by the smallest things and the most inconsequential gesture could become imbued with power over life or death. Thus in situations in which courage appeared the normal response, he had to determine with whom he was involved and whether the issue was as important as his white opponent wished to make it. In other words, he has always to determine at what point and over which specific issue he will pay the ultimate price of his life.

This has certainly been part of my own experience. There have been situations where in facing hostile whites I had to determine not what *they* thought was at issue, because in any case they were bent on violence, but what *I* wanted it to be. "This guy wants me to fight, most likely he wants an excuse to kill me—what do I have to gain? And am I going to let *him* impose his values upon my life?"

WARREN: To let him determine your worth to you, is that it?

ELLISON: Yes. So, Dr. Clark notwithstanding, if I couldn't love my would-be provocateur as Dr. King advises, I could dismiss him as childish and, perhaps, even forgive him. This, even though at the time I ached to meet him on neutral ground and on equal terms.

One thing that Dr. Clark overlooks is that Southern Negroes learned about violence in a very tough school. They have known for a long time that they can take a lot of headwhipping and survive and go on working toward their own goals. We learned about forbearance and forgiveness in that same school, and about hope too. So today we sacrifice, as we sacrificed yesterday, the pleasure of personal retaliation in the interest of the common good. And where violence was once a casual matter, it has now become a matter of national political significance. Clark regards the necessary psychological complexity of Southern Negroes as intolerable, but I'm afraid that he would impose a psychological norm upon Negro life which is not only inadequate to deal with its complexity, but implicitly negative.

WARREN: Let's go back to what you said a moment ago— you said he lacked a conception of the basic heroism involved in the Negro struggle.

ELLISON: Yes, I'm referring to the basic, implicit heroism of people who
             must live within a society without recognition, real status, but who
             are involved in the ideals of that society and who are trying to
             make their way, trying to determine their true position and their
             rightful position within it. Such people learn more about the real
             nature of that society, more about the true character of its values
             than those who can afford to take their own place in society for
             granted. They might not be able to spell it out philosophically but
             they *act* it out. And as against the white man's indictments of the
             conduct, folkways, and values which express their sense of social
             reality, their actions say, "But you are being dishonest. You know
             that our view of things is true. We live and act out the truth
             of American reality, while to the extent that you refuse to take
             these aspects of reality, these inconsistencies, into consideration—
             you do not live the truth." Such a position raises a people above a
             simple position of social and political inferiority and it imposes
             upon them the necessity of understanding the other man and, while
             still pressing for their freedom, they have the obligation to
             themselves of giving up some of their need for revenge. Clark
             would probably reply that this is too much to ask of any people,
             and my answer would be: "There are no abstract rules. And al-
             though the human goal of a higher humanity is the same for all,
             each group must play the cards as history deals with them." This
             requires understanding.

WARREN: Understanding themselves, too?

ELLISON: Understanding themselves, too—yes—in terms of their own live
             definition of value, and of understanding themselves in relation-
             ship to other Americans. This places a big moral strain upon the
             individual, and it requires self-confidence, self-consciousness, self-
             mastery, insight, and compassion. In the broader sense it requires
             an alertness to human complexity. Men in our situation simply
             cannot afford to ignore the nuances of human relationships. And
             although action is necessary, forthright action, it must be guided—
             tempered by insight and compassion. Nevertheless, isn't this what
             civilization is all about? And isn't this what tragedy has always
             sought to teach us?

             At any rate, this too has been part of the American Negro
             experience, and I believe that one of the important clues to the
             meaning of that experience lies in the idea, the *ideal* of sacrifice.
             Hannah Arendt's failure to grasp the importance of this ideal
             among Southern Negros caused her to fly way off into left field in
             her "Reflections on Little Rock," in which she charged Negro
             parents with exploiting their children during the struggle to in-
             tegrate the schools. But she has absolutely no conception of what
             goes on in the minds of Negro parents when they send their kids
             through those lines of hostile people. Yet they are aware of the
             overtones of a rite of initiation which such events actually con-

stitute for the child, a confrontation of the terrors of social life with all the mysteries tripped away. And in the outlook of many of these parents (who wish that the problem didn't exist), the child is expected to face the terror and contain his fear and anger *precisely* because he is a Negro American. Thus he's required to master the inner tensions created by this racial situation, and if he gets hurt—then his is one more sacrifice. It is a harsh requirement, but if he fails this basic test, his life will be even harsher.

WARREN: White Southerners have been imprisoned by a loyalty to being Southern. Now, there's a remark often made about Negroes, that they are frequently imprisoned, or the genius of the Negro is imprisoned, in the race problem. I am concerned with a kind of parallelism here between these two things.

ELLISON: Well, I think that the parallel is very real. We're often so imprisoned in the problem that we don't stop to analyze our assets, and our leaders are often so preoccupied with an effort to interpret Negro life in terms which sociology has laid down that they not only fail to question the validity of such limited and limiting terms, they seem unaware that there are any others. One reason seems to be that they exclude themselves from the limitations of the definitions.

Now, we know that there is an area in Southern experience wherein Negroes and whites achieve a sort of human communication, and even social intercourse, which is not always possible in the North. I mean, that there is an implacably human side to race relationships. But at certain moments a reality which is political and social and ideological asserts itself, and the human relationship breaks up and both groups of people fall into their abstract roles. Thus a great loss of human energy goes into maintaining our stylized identities. In fact, much of the energy of the imagination—much of the *psychic* energy of the South, among both whites and blacks, has gone, I think, into this particular negative art form. If I may speak of it in such terms.

WARREN: Just from the strain of maintaining this stance?

ELLISON: I think so. Because in the end, when the barriers are down, there are human assertions to be made, whatever one's race, in terms of one's own taste and one's own affirmations of one's own self, one's own way and one's own group's sense of life. But this makes a big problem for Negroes because there's always the dominance of white standards—which we influence and partially share— imposed upon us. Nevertheless, there is much about Negro life which Negroes like, just as we like certain kinds of food. One of our problems is going to be that of affirming those things which we love about Negro life when there is no pressure upon us from outside. Then the time will come when our old ways of life will say, "Well, all right, you're no longer kept within a Jim Crow community, what are you going to do about your life now? Do you think there is going to be a way of enjoying yourself which is absolutely better, more human than what you've known?" You see it's a question of recognizing the human core, the universality of our experience. It's a matter of defining value as one has actually lived reality. And I think that this will hold true for white people It certainly shows up in the white Southerners who turn up in the North, as with the hill people who are now clinging to their own folkways in the city of Chicago.

WARREN: You are thinking simply of a pluralistic society, without—

ELLISON: Yes, without any racial judgments, negative or positive, being placed upon it. I watch other people enjoying themselves, I watch their customs, and I think it one of my greatest privileges as an American, as a human being living in this particular time in the world's history, to be able to project myself into various backgrounds, into various cultural patterns, *not* because I want to cease being a Negro or because I think that these are automatically better ways of realizing oneself, but because it is one of the great glories of being an American. You can be somebody else while still being yourself, and you don't have to take an ocean voyage to do it. In fact, one of the advantages of being a Negro is that we have always had the freedom to choose or to select and to affirm those traits, those values, those culture forms, which we have taken from any and everybody. And with our own cultural expressions we have been quite generous. It's like the story they tell about Louis Armstrong teaching Bix Beiderbecke certain things about jazz. It was a joyful exchange and that was the way in which Negro jazzmen acted when I was a kid. They were delighted when anyone liked their music—especially white Americans—and their response was, "You like this? Well, this is a celebration of something we feel about life and art. You feel it too? Well, all right, we're all here together; let the good times roll!"

I think their attitude reveals much about Negro life generally which isn't recognized by sociologists and journalists who consider Negroes powerless to make choices. We probably have more freedom than anyone; we only need to become more conscious of it and use it to protect ourselves from some of the more tawdry American values. Besides, it's always a good thing to remember why it was that Br'er Rabbit loved his brier patch, and it wasn't simply for protection.

WARREN: I know some people, Ralph, white people and Negroes, who would say that what you are saying is an apology for a segregated society. I know it's not. How would you answer such a charge?

ELLISON: There's no real answer to such a charge, but I left the South in 1936. My writing speaks for itself. I've never pretended for one minute that the injustices and limitations of Negro life do not exist. On the other hand I think it important to recognize that Negroes have achieved a very rich humanity despite these restrictive conditions. I wish to be free not to be less Negro American but so that I can make the term mean something even richer. Now, if I can't recognize this, or if recognizing this makes me an Uncle Tom, then heaven help us all.

WARREN: How do you relate this, either positively or negatively, to the notion that the Negro Movement of our time invokes a discovery of identity?

ELLISON: I don't think it's a discovery of identity. I think rather that it is an affirmation and *assertion* of identification. And it's an assertion of a pluralistic identity. The assertion, in political terms, is that of the old American tradition. In terms of group identity and the current agitation it's revealing the real identity of a people who have been here for a hell of a long time. Negroes were Americans even before there was a United States, and if we're going to talk at all about what we are, this historical and cultural fact has to be recognized. And if we're going to accept this as true, then the identity of Negroes is bound up intricately, irrevocably, with the identities of white Americans, and especially is this true in the South.

WARREN: It is, indeed.

ELLISON: There's no Southerner who hasn't been touched by the presence of Negroes. There's no Negro who hasn't been touched by the presence of white Southerners. And of course this extends beyond the region. It gets—the moment you start touching culture you touch music, you touch dance attitudes, you touch movies— touch the structure anywhere—and the Negro is right in there helping to shape it.

Paul Goodman
The Missing Community

Imagine that these modern radical positions had been more fully achieved: we should have a society where:

A premium is placed on technical improvement and on the engineering style of functional simplicity and clarity. Where the community is planned as a whole, with an organic integration of work, living, and play. Where buildings have the variety of their real functions with the uniformity of the prevailing technology. Where a lot of money is spent on public goods. Where workers are technically educated and have a say in management. Where no one drops out of society and there is an easy mobility of classes. Where production is primarily for use. Where social groups are laboratories for solving their own problems, experimentally. Where democracy begins in the town meeting, and a man seeks office only because he has a program. Where regional variety is encouraged and there is pride in the Republic. And young men are free of conscription. Where all feel themselves citizens of the universal Republic of Reason. Where it is the policy to give an adequate voice to the unusual and unpopular opinion, and to give a trial and a market to new enterprise. Where people are not afraid to make friends. Where races are factually equal. Where vocation is sought out and cultivated as God-given capacity, to be conserved and embellished, and where the church is the spirit of its congregation. Where ordinary experience is habitually scientifically assayed by the average man. Where it is felt that the suggestion of reason is practical. And speech leads to the corresponding action. Where the popular culture is a daring and passionate culture. Where children can make themselves useful and earn their own money. Where their sexuality is taken for granted. Where the community carries on its important adult business and the children fall in at their own pace. And where education is concerned with fostering human powers as they develop in the growing child.

In such an utopian society, as was aimed at by modern radicals but has not eventuated, it would be very easy to grow up. There would be plenty of objective, worth-while activities for a child to observe, fall in with, do, learn, improvise on his own. That is to say, it is not the spirit of modern times that makes our society difficult for the young; it is that that spirit has not sufficiently realized itself.

In this light, the present plight of the young is not surprising. In the rapid changes, people have not kept enough in their mind that the growing young also exist and the world must fit their needs. So instead, we have the present phenomena of excessive attention to the children as such, in psychology and suburbs, and coping with "juvenile delinquency" as if it were an entity. Adults fighting for some profoundly conceived fundamental change naturally give up, exhausted, when they have achieved some gain that makes life tolerable again and seems to be the substance of their demand. But to grow up, the young need a world of finished situations and society made whole again.

Indeed, the bother with the above little utopian sketch is that many adults would be restive in such a stable modern world if it were achieved. They would say: It is a fine place for growing boys. I agree with this criticism.

I think the case is as follows: Every profound new proposal, of culture or institution, invents and discovers a new property of "Human Nature." Henceforth it is going to be in *these* terms that a young fellow will grow up and find his identity and his task. So if we accumulate the revolutionary proposals of modern times, we have named the *goals of modern education*. We saw that it was the aim of Progressive Education to carry this program through.

But education is not life. The existing situation of a grown man is to confront an uninvented and undiscovered present. Unfortunately, *at present*, he must also try to perfect his unfinished past: this bad inheritance is part of the existing situation, and must be stoically worked through.

Let me repeat the proposition of this chapter: *It is the missed revolutions of modern times—the fallings-short and the compromises—that add up to the conditions that make it hard for the young to grow up in our society.*

The existing local community, region, and nation is the real environment of the young. Conversely, we could define community spirit and patriotism as the conviction in which it is possible to grow up. (An independent and not too defeated adult confronts a broader historical, international, and cosmic scene as his environment for action.)

Modern times have been characterized by fundamental changes occuring with unusual rapidity. These have shattered tradition but often have not succeeded in creating a new whole community. We have no recourse to going back, there is nothing to go back to. If we are to have a stable and whole community in which the young can grow to man-hood, we must painfully perfect the revolutionary modern tradition we have.

This stoical resolve, is, paradoxically, a *conservative* proposition, aiming at stability and social balance. For often it is not a question of making innovations, but of catching up and restoring the right propor-tions. But no doubt, in our runaway, one-sided way of life, the proposal to conserve human resources and develop human capacities has become a radical innovation.

Right proportion cannot be restored by adding a few new teachers formally equivalent to the growth in population. Probably we need a million new minds and more put to teaching. Even Dr. Conant says that we must nearly double our present annual expenditure on education for teaching alone, not counting plant and the central schools he wants. And this does not take into account essentially new fields such as making sense of adult leisure.

It must be understood that with the increase in population and crowding, the number and variety of human services increase dispro-portionately, and the laissez-faire areas, both geographical and social, decrease. Therefore the *units* of human service, such as school classes or the clientele of a physician (and even political districts?), ought to be made *smaller,* to avoid the creation of masses: mass teaching, mass medicine, mass psychotherapy, mass penology, mass politics. Yet our normal schools and medical schools cannot cope with even the arithme-tic increase.

Right proportion requires reversing the goal in vocational guidance, from fitting the man to the machine and chopping him down to fit, to finding the opportunity in the economy that brings out the man, and if you can't find such an opportunity, make it. This involves encourag-ing new small enterprises and unblocking and perhaps underwriting invention. Again, if at present production is inhuman and stupid, it is that too few minds are put to it: this can be remedied by giving the workman more voice in production and the kind of training to make that voice wise.

Probably, right proportion involves considerable decentralizing and increasing the rural-urban ratio. Certainly it involves transforming the scores of thousands of neglected small places, hopelessly dull and same, into interesting villages that someone could be proud of. A lot of the booming production has got to go into publicly useful goods, propor-tionate to the apparently forgotten fact that it is on public grounds, because of public investment, and the growth of population, that private wealth is produced and enjoyed. We have to learn again, what city man always used to know, that belonging to the city, to its squares, its market, its neighborhoods, and its high culture, is a public good; it is not a field for "investment to yield a long-term modest profit." A proportionate allocation of public funds, again, is not likely to devote more money to escape roads convenient for automobiles than to improving the city center. (If I may make a pleasant suggestion, we could underwrite a handsome program for serious adult leisure by a 10 per cent luxury tax on new cars; it would yield over a billion.)

Since prosperity itself has made it more difficult for the underprivileged immigrant to get started, right proportion requires devoting all the more money and ingenuity to helping him find himself and get started. (In such cases, by the way, ingenuity and friendly aid are more important than money, as some of our settlement houses in New York have beautifully demonstrated.) And some way will have to be found, again, for a man to be decently poor, to work for a subsistence without necessarily choosing to involve himself in the total high-standard economy. One way of achieving this would be directly producing subsistence goods in distinction from the total economy.

In arts and letters, there is a right balance between the customary social standard and creative novelty, and between popular entertainment and esthetic experience. Then, to offset Hollywood and Madison Avenue, we must have hundreds of new little theaters, little magazines, and journals of dissenting opinion with means of circulation; because it is only in such that new things can develop and begin to win their way in the world.

It is essential that our democratic legislatures and public spokesmen be balanced by more learned and honorable voices that, as in Britain, can thoughtfully broach fundamental issues of community plan, penal code, morality, cultural tone, with some certainty of reaching a public forum and some possibility of being effective. For there is no other way of getting the best of lead, to have some conviction and even passionate intensity, to save America from going to managers, developers, and politicians by default.

Certainly right proportion, in a society tightly organized and conformist, requires a vast increase in the jealous safeguard of civil liberties, to put the fear of God back into local police, district attorneys, and the Federal Bureau of Investigation.

Here is a program of more than a dozen essential changes, all practicable, all difficult. A wiser and more experienced author could suggest a dozen more.

Let me expand one of these: Making sense of adult leisure.

What are the present goals of the philosophers of leisure, for instance, the National Recreation Association? and now imagine those goals achieved. There would be a hundred million adults who have cultured hobbies to occupy their spare time: some expert on the flute, some with do-it-yourself kits, some good at chess and go, some square dancing, some camping out and enjoying nature, and all playing various athletic games. Leaf through the entire catalogue of the National Recreation Association, take all the items together, apply them to one hundred million adults—and there is the picture. (This costs *at present* forty billion dollars a year, according to the guess of Robert Coughlan in *Life*.) The philosophy of leadership, correspondingly, is to get people to participate—everybody must "belong."

Now even if all these people were indeed getting deep personal satisfaction from these activities, this is a dismaying picture. It doesn't add up to anything. It isn't important. There is no ethical necessity in it, no standard. *One cannot waste a hundred million people that way.*

The error is in the NRS's basic concept of recreation. Let me quote from a recent editorial in *Recreation*: Recreation is "any activity participated in . . . merely for the enjoyment it affords. . . . The rewards of recreational activities depend upon the degree to which they provide outlets for personal interests." (Outlets again, as in the Governor's prescription for the juvenile delinquents.) But enjoyment is *not* a goal, it is a feeling that accompanies important ongoing activity; pleasure, as Freud said, is always dependent on function.

From the present philosophy of leisure, no new culture can emerge. What is lacking is worth-while community necessity, as the serious leisure, the σχολή of the Athenians had communal necessity, whether in the theater, the games, the architecture and festivals, or even the talk.

That we find it hard to think in these terms is a profound sign of our social imbalance. Yet we do *not* need, as Dr. Douglass claimed in the passage we quoted above, "a new ethics, a new esthetic." For the activities of serious leisure are right there, glaring in our communities, to avoid shame and achieve grandeur.

But the question is: If there is little interest, honor, or manliness in the working part of our way of life, can we hope for much in the leisure part?

The best exposition of what I have been trying to say in this chapter is the classic of conservative thinking, Coleridge's *On the Constitution of the Church and State*. His point in that essay is simply this: *In order to have citizens, you must first be sure that you have produced men.* There must therefore be a large part of the common wealth specifically devoted to cultivating "freedom and civilization," and especially to the education of the young growing up.

Country-town estate, purpose, 92
Cultural institutions, 30
Culture, 26, 30
  American, influence of Irish on, 193
  and community, 187
  comparison of, 27
  destruction of, 224
  diversity of, 38
  history, 43
  and human society, 30
  in medieval Jewish community, 44–46
  and monetary values, 30
  as precedent to social organization, 26
Customs, 7, 8
Cyprus, and the fight for independence,
  240–262

Daladier, Edouard, 295
Dawson, William, 199
Declaration of Independence, 129
De Gaulle, Charles, 297
De Man, H., 164
Democracy, in America, 97
Democratic Party, 195, 199, 206
  and influence of the Irish, 194
Democratic public, conditions for, 338
Democratic revolution, 136, 137
De Ruggiero, G., 290 n.
Dewey, John, 331, 333–338
Dewey, Thomas E., 199
Dibelius, Wilhelm, 293 n.
Dickens, Charles, 108, 120–122
Dostoevski, Fedor, 294
Du Bois, W. E. B., 340
Durkheim, Émile, 228
Durrell, Lawrence, 224, 225, 240–262

Economics, x, 68, 134, 163
Edwards, Alba, 154 n.
Eisenhower, Dwight D., 169, 206
Eister, Allan W., 152 n.
Ellison, Ralph, 332, 339–356
EOKA (*Ethniki Organosis Kyprion Ago-
  niston*), 224, 242, 248, 249, 255,
  256, 258, 261
  Youth Organization of, 243
Epstein, Eliahu, 267 n.
Equalitarianism, moral, 307, 307 n.
Ethnic groups, 193, 195, 225

Family, 6, 7
  as structure within community, 63
  see also Farm family
Farm family, 6, 7
  American, 6, 10
  Irish, 8, 11, 12
  relationship among members of, 8–10

Faulkner, William, 345 n.
Fisher, Lloyd, 163
Flexner, Abraham, 153 n.
Friedman, Milton, 154 n.
Functional community, 140, 141
  in contemporary society, 141
Functional importance, 64
Functional interdependence, 64

Geography, 47
Gerth, Hans, 289, 290–297
Glubb, J. B., 267 n.
Golding, William, 4, 20–25
Goode, William J., 140, 152–162
Goodman, Paul, 332, 357–361
Gorki, Maxim, 294
"Great Community," 333
Greeks, x, xi, 65–76
Greer, Scott, 60, 62–64
Gresham's law, 108
Gunther, John, 166

Habits, and human action, 334
Hacker, Andrew, 175
Hall, Oswald, 155 n., 158 n.
Hallowell, John, 297 n.
Hawley, Cameron, 169 n.
Hawthorne experiment, 164
Hegel, Georg Wilhelm Friedrich, 95
Hering, Oswald, 155 n.
Hippodamas, 66
Hitler, Adolf, 295
Hobbes, Thomas, 295, 299
Hobhouse, L. T., 290 n.
Homans, George, 3, 4, 5–19
Homer, 65, 73, 190, 191
  see also Economic system
Honor; *see* Warfare
Hudnut, Joseph, 155 n.
Hughes, Everett C., 158
Human behavior, 6, 7, 8, 142
Human contact, 47
Humphrey, Hubert, 209
Hunter, Floyd, 174
Huntington, Mary Jean, 152 n., 156 n.
Huxley, Aldous, ix

Idomeneus, 65
Imperialist exploitation of West Indies,
  137
Individuals, concentration of social organizations among, ix
  see also Liberal individualism
Industrial revolution of nineteenth century, 137
Integration of groups, 62

Shils, Edward, 223, 226–228, 289, 298–316
Sighele, 298
Simmel, Georg, 152 n.
Singer, Isaac Bashevis, 27, 44–46
Slavery
  abomination, 196
  effect of abolition in Niger, 232
Smith, Alfred E., 204, 207
Snow, C. P., 140, 141
Social action, 4
  among children, 20–25
  in medieval Jewish community, 27
Social behavior, 7
  element of, 13
  see also Interaction, as element of social behavior; Sentiments, as element of social behavior
Social change, view of, 266
Social community and physical layout of city, 108
Social interaction, 3
  and time coordination, 142
Social life, 3
  historical origin, 61
Social organization, ix, 3
  conflict between morality and, 266
  description of, 287
Social relationships, 6, 7
  based on contract, 288
  controlled by time, 142
  multifunctional, 62
  through ritual in the bush, 57
Social systems, 47
  effect of agriculture on, 62
Sociometric test, 18, 19
Society
  developing of independent from colonial, 317–330
  increase of, 265
  as necessity to men, 227
Sociometry, 17
Socrates, 60, 75
Sophocles, 70
Sorokin, Pitirim, 142, 154 n.
Sovereign nations, world of, 127
Status differentiation, 62
Steffee, Donald M., 145, 146
Steffens, Lincoln, 173
Steiner, Lee R., 155 n.
Stevenson, Adlai, 206
Stigler, George, 154 n.
Suara Amerika (The Voice of America) in Malaya, 329

Tammany Hall, 195, 220
Taxes and fines, 64

Technological change, 285
  and personal consequences, 287
  cost of, 283
  and social consequences, 287
  and traditional morality, 286
  results of, 266
Technology
  and urban development, 229
  about community without profit of, 120–122
  and understanding of it, 337
Thucydides, 70, 72, 77–82
Time
  concept of, 142
  importance of, to different social groups, 142–144
  importance of, to railroader, 143–151
  and social participation, 142
Time-emphasis, for all moderns, 147
Time regulation for railroader, by Federal Government, 147
Tito, Marshal, 297
Tocqueville, Alexis de, 298
Tolstoi, Leo, 62, 294
Towns
  beginning of, 68
  new, 111
  as site of attachment, 58–59
  trade in, 112
  see also Railroad town
Tribal society of Bedouin, 268
  attachment to, 268
  law in, 268
  morality in, 268
Trotsky, Leon, 294
Truman, Harry, 199, 206
Turner, Ralph, 63 n.
"Tyranny of customs," and effect on social organization, 8

United Nations, 134, 261
University, as functional organization, 141
Urban cultures, rise of, 62
Urban society, 288, 289
  and specialization and functional interdependence, 140
Urbanization
  and change in relationship of men, 60
  consequences of characteristics, 64
  effects of, 288
  meaning, 287
  and mobility, 64
  in Republic of Niger, 229, 239
Utopian society, 357 ff.

Van Hoey, Leo, 224, 229–239